Software Optimization for High-Performance Computing

ISBN 0-13-017008-9

90000

Hewlett-Packard® Professional Books

Software Optimization for High-Performance Computing

Kevin R. Wadleigh & Isom L. Crawford

Hewlett-Packard Company

www.hp.com/go/retailbooks

Prentice Hall PTR
Upper Saddle River, New Jersey 07458
www.phptr.com

Editorial/production supervision: *Kathleen M. Caren*
Cover design director: *Jerry Votta*
Cover design: *Talar Agasyan*
Manufacturing manager: *Maura Goldstaub*
Acquisitions editor: *Jill Pisoni*
Editorial assistant: *Justin Somma*
Marketing manager: *Bryan Gambrel*

Manager, Hewlett-Packard Retail Book Publishing: *Patricia Pekary*
Editor, Hewlett-Packard Professional Books: *Susan Wright*

Published by Prentice Hall PTR
Prentice-Hall, Inc.
Upper Saddle River, New Jersey 07458

Prentice Hall books are widely used by corporations and government agencies for training, marketing, and resale.
The publisher offers discounts on this book when ordered in bulk quantities. For more information, contact Corporate Sales Department, Phone: 800-382-3419; FAX: 201-236-7141;
E-mail: corpsales@prenhall.com
Or write: Prentice Hall PTR, Corporate Sales Dept., One Lake Street, Upper Saddle River, NJ 07458.

Printed in the United States of America
10 9 8 7 6 5 4 3 2 1

ISBN 0-13-017008-9

Prentice-Hall International (UK) Limited, *London*
Prentice-Hall of Australia Pty. Limited, *Sydney*
Prentice-Hall Canada Inc., *Toronto*
Prentice-Hall Hispanoamericana, S.A., *Mexico*
Prentice-Hall of India Private Limited, *New Delhi*
Prentice-Hall of Japan, Inc., *Tokyo*
Pearson Education Asia Pte. Ltd.
Editora Prentice-Hall do Brasil, Ltda., *Rio de Janeiro*

To my wife Laurie for all the love, support and encouragement.
To our wonderful children, Leslie and John, of
whom I am very proud.
— Kevin

———————————————————

To my wife, Kathy, and son, Gavyn, for their love,
understanding, and encouragement.
In memory of my father, Isom L. Crawford, Sr.
— Isom

Trademarks

We use many trademarked terms in this book, so we'd like to recognize the following: CYDRA is a trademark of Cydrome, Inc. CoSORT is a trademark of Innovative Routines International, Inc. Cray, T3E, T3D, T90, and Y-MP are trademarks of Cray Research, Inc. Alpha AXP, DEC, VAX, are trademarks of Digital Equipment Corp. Convex, HP-UX, PA-RISC, and MLIB are trademarks of the Hewlett-Packard Company. Intel, Itanium, Pentium, and Pentium Pro are trademarks of Intel, Inc. AIX, ESSL, IBM, PowerPC are trademarks of International Business Machines Corp. Linux is a trademark of Linus Torvald. Windows, Windows NT, Visual Studio, Visual C++, and Microsoft are trademarks of Microsoft Corporation. Maspar is a trademark of Maspar Corporation. MIPS and MIPS R10000 are trademarks of MIPS Technologies, Inc. Nastran is a registered trademark of NASA. MSC and MSC.Nastran are trademarks of the MSC.Software Corporation. NAg is a trademark of the Numerical Algorithms Group, Ltd. OpenMP is a trademark of the OpenMP Architecture Review Board. Quantify is a trademark of Rational Software Corporation. IRIX, MIPS, SCSL, and SGI are trademarks of Silicon Graphics, Inc. SPECint95 and SPECfp95 are trademarks of the Standard Performance Evaluation Council. Solaris, NFS, Network File System, Performance Library, and Sun are trademarks of Sun Microsystems, Inc. Syncsort is a trademark of Syncsort, Inc. All SPARC trademarks are trademarks or registered trademarks of SPARC International, Inc. Products bearing SPARC trademarks are based on an architecture developed by Sun Microsystems, Inc. TMC is a trademark of Thinking Machines Corporation. UNIX is a trademark of X/Open Company, Ltd. Ethernet is a trademark of Xerox Corp. IMSL is a trademark of Visual Numerics, Inc. FrameMaker is a trademark of Adobe Systems, Inc.

AIX is used as a short form for AIX operating system. AIX/6000 V3 is used as a short form of AIX Version 3 for RISC System/6000. UNIX is used as a short form for UNIX operating system.

All other product names mentioned herein may be trademarks or registered trademarks of other manufacturers. We respectfully acknowledge any such that have not been included above.

Contents

List of Figures

List of Tables

Foreword

Computation. Is this truly the third scientific method? To be a peer to theory and experimentation, any method must be pervasive, productive, long-standing and important. It is the opinion of many that, in fact, computation *is* the third branch of scientific study. It is clear that large numbers of people, large sums of money (in the form of computers), large numbers of peer-reviewed papers, and large numbers of organizations are involved in computation in essentially all fields of scientific, and non-scientific, endeavor.

It is not possible to design any significant product today without prodigious amounts of computation. This covers the spectrum from aluminum beverage cans to jet aircraft. If you are convinced that computation ranks as a valid scientific method, then the follow-on question is: "Exactly what is it that constitutes computation?" It is my view that it embodies the algorithm, the code, and the computer architecture. Yes, even the computer architecture.

There was a time when a numerical analyst would write code to implement an algorithm. The code was myopic in that it was written with only the view of implementing the algorithm. There was some consideration given to performance, but generally it was more the view of saving computer memory. Memory was the precious commodity in the early days of computation. "Tuning" the code for the underlying architecture was not a first-order consideration.

As computer architectures evolved, the coding task had to be enlarged to encompass the exploitation of the architecture. This was necessary in order to get the performance that is demanded from application codes. This trend continues today.

The evolution of demands on computation has grown at least exponentially. While a one-dimensional analysis was the status quo in the 1970's, today a three-dimensional time-varying solution, with mixed physics, is the norm. More is demanded of computation in the form of accuracy, precision, dimensionality, parametric analysis, and time-scale. Even the "Moore's Law"-like growth of computing power is inadequate in the face of the growing expectation—no, *demand*—on computation. Thus the performance of scientific codes today is necessarily dependent upon and intimately tied to the computer architecture, including single-processor performance and parallelism.

The theme in the above paragraphs leads us to the point of this foreword and, more importantly, this book: The numerical analysts of today must know computer architectures. Performance gains through the knowledge and exploitation of the architecture are significant and essential. It is this knowledge that will hopefully be the "take away" for readers of this book.

There are many books on mathematical algorithms and numerical analysis. This book purposely and skillfully avoids these topics. Rather, it provides the bridge between *code* and useful modifications to the code to gain performance. To keep the size of the exposition in manageable proportions, it is not a book on architectures. It is a book on code modifications and the reason why they are successful on today's pervasive architecture type: multiprocessor RISC systems.

In this book the reader is exposed at a moderate level to the "art" of programming to gain the best performance from a computer architecture. Proficiency is gained from repeated exposure to the principles and techniques the authors provide. It can be argued that the best approach to programming is to consider performance issues as every line of code is written. This is the computer scientist's perspective. A physicist, engineer, computational chemist, or mathematician tends to write code to solve the problem at hand in order to achieve a solution. Code modifications to gain better performance come later. This book will help with either approach.

There are frequently occurring algorithms that have become pervasive throughout much of numerical analysis, in particular, the BLAS and FFTs. Both of these are covered in sufficient detail so that the reader will understand the types of optimizations that matter.

In the formative years of scientific computation the *lingua franca* was Fortran. At this time C is being used increasingly as the language of choice for scientific applications. While there are strong reasons for continuing to use Fortran as the programming language, this book is language-agnostic. The examples provided alternate between Fortran and C.

The authors are well-qualified to write this book. Each has many years of direct experience in code development. Their experience spans classic vector computers, through clusters and "MPPs" to today's scalable architectures. To this day, each of the authors is active in the area that he writes about in this book.

Readers are advised to read closely and then, in practice, to apply what is described. It is likely the result will be code that performs much better than the original.

Greg Astfalk
Chief Scientist
Technical Computing Division
Hewlett-Packard Company

Preface

Once you start asking questions, innocence is gone.

Mary Astor

This purpose of this book is to document many of the techniques used by people who implement applications on modern computers and want their programs to execute as quickly as possible.

There are four major components that determine the speed of an application: the architecture, the compiler, the source code, and the algorithm. You usually don't have control over the architecture you use, but you need to understand it so you'll know what it is capable of achieving. You do have control over your source code and how compilers are used on it. This book discusses how to perform source code modifications and use the compiler to generate better performing applications. The final and arguably the most important part is the algorithms used. By replacing the algorithms you have or were given with better performing ones, or even tweaking the existing ones, you can reap huge performance gains and perform problems that had previously been unachievable.

There are many reasons to want applications to execute quickly. Sometimes it is the only way to make sure that a program finishes execution in a reasonable amount of time. For example, the decision to bid or no-bid an oil lease is often determined by whether a seismic image can be completed before the bid deadline. A new automotive body design may or may not appear in next year's model depending on whether the structural and aerodynamic analysis can be completed in time. Since developers of applications would like an advantage over their competitors, speed can sometimes be the differentiator between two similar products. Thus, writing programs to run quickly can be a good investment.

P.1 A Tool Box

We like to think of this book as a tool box. The individual tools are the various optimization techniques discussed. As expected, some tools are more useful than others. Reducing the memory requirements of an application is a general tool that frequently results in better single processor performance. Other tools, such as the techniques used to optimize a code for parallel execution, have a more limited scope.

These tools are designed to help applications perform well on computer system components. You can apply them to existing code to improve performance or use them to design efficient code from scratch. As you become proficient with the tools, some general trends become apparent. All applications have a theoretical performance limit on any computer. The first attempts at optimization may involve choosing between basic compiler options. This doesn't take much time and can help performance considerably. The next steps may involve more complicated compiler options, modifying a few lines of source code, or reformulating an algorithm. As shown in Figure P-1, the theoretical peak performance is like the speed of light. As more and

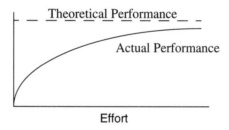

Figure P-1   Effort versus performance.

more energy, or time, is expended, the theoretical peak is approached, but never quite achieved. Before optimizing applications, it is prudent to consider how much time you can, or should, commit to optimization.

In the past, one of the problems with tuning code was that even with a large investment of time the optimizations quickly became outdated. For example, there were many applications that had been optimized for vector computers which subsequently had to be completely reoptimized for massively parallel computers. This sometimes took many person-years of effort. Since massively parallel computers never became plentiful, much of this effort had very short-term benefit.

In the 1990s, many computer companies either went bankrupt or were purchased by other companies as the cost of designing and manufacturing computers skyrocketed. As a result, there are very few computer vendors left today and most of today's processors have similar characteristics. For example, they nearly all have high-speed caches. Thus, making sure that code is structured to run well on cache-based systems ensures that the code runs well across almost all modern platforms.

The examples in this book are biased in favor of the UNIX operating system and RISC processors. This is because they are most characteristic of modern high performance computing. The recent EPIC (IA-64) processors have cache structures identical to those of RISC processors, so the examples also apply to them.

P.2 Language Issues

This book uses lots of examples. They are written in Fortran, C, or in a language-independent pseudo-code. Fortran examples use uppercase letters while the others use lowercase. For example,

```
DO I = 1,N
   Y(I) = Y(I) + A * X(I)
ENDDO
```

takes a scalar A, multiplies it by a vector X of length N and adds it to a vector Y of length N. Languages such as Fortran 90/95 and C++ are very powerful and allow vector or matrix notation. For example, if X and Y are two-dimensional arrays and A is a scalar, writing

```
Y = Y + A * X
```

means to multiple the array X by A and add the result to the matrix Y. This notation has been avoided since it can obscure the analysis performed. The notation may also make it more difficult to compilers to optimize the source code.

There is an entire chapter devoted to language specifics, but pseudo-code and Fortran examples assume that multidimensional arrays such as Y(200,100) have the data stored in memory in column-major order. Thus the elements of Y(200,100) are stored as

```
Y(1,1), Y(2,1), Y(3,1),..., Y(200,1), Y(1,2), Y(1,3),...
```

This is the opposite of C data storage where data is stored in row-major order.

P.3 Notation

When terms are defined, we'll use *italics* to set the term apart from other text. Courier font will be used for all examples. Mathematical terms and equations use *italic* font. We'll use lots of prefixes for the magnitude of measurements, so the standard ones are defined in the following table.

Table P-1 Standard Prefixes.

Prefix	Factor	Factor
tera	10^{12}	2^{40}
giga	10^9	2^{30}
mega	10^6	2^{20}
kilo	10^3	2^{10}
milli	10^{-3}	
micro	10^{-6}	
nano	10^{-9}	

Note that some prefixes are defined using both powers of 10 and powers of two. The exact arithmetic values are somewhat different. Observe that $10^6 = 1,000,000$ while $2^{10} = 1,048,576$. This can be confusing, but when quantifying memory, cache, or data in general, associate the prefixes with powers of two. Otherwise, use the more common powers of 10.

Finally, optimizing applications should be fun. It's really a contest between you and the computer. Computers sometimes give up performance grudgingly, so understand what the computer is realistically capable of and see that you get it. Enjoy the challenge!

About the Authors

Kevin Wadleigh works in the Mathematical Software Group of Hewlett-Packard Company developing and optimizing high performance algorithms for Hewlett-Packard's mathematical library MLIB. A substantial portion of his time is spent working with independent software vendors optimizing their algorithms for Hewlett-Packard high performance computers.

Kevin holds a Bachelor of Science degree in Mathematics from Oral Roberts University, a Master of Science in Applied Mathematics from the University of Tulsa and a Doctor of Education in Mathematics from Oklahoma State University. While working on his doctorate in algebraic ring theory, he developed X-ray diffraction and fluorescence algorithms for Amoco Corporation. Upon graduation, he worked for E-Systems, Inc. (now a part of Raytheon Company) optimizing algorithms for Cray vector computers. He spent several years employed by Convex Computer Corporation optimizing math algorithms for their vector computers until its acquisition by Hewlett-Packard Company. Since the early 1990s he has been immersed in optimization for Hewlett-Packard's PA-RISC processors and in 1996 began writing assembly code for IA-64 processors. He has published articles on Fast Fourier Transform algorithms and holds a patent relating to cache bank conflict avoidance.

Outside of work, Kevin enjoys his family, playing the piano, the music of Tom Lehrer, mineral collecting and genealogy.

Isom L. Crawford, Jr. is the Mathematical Software project manager at Hewlett-Packard Company's Technical Systems Lab. He works closely with multiple software development teams to improve application performance on Hewlett-Packard computer systems while leading the design and development of the MLIB product there.

Isom earned a Bachelor of Science degree in Mathematics from Henderson State University, a Master of Science degree in Applied Mathematics from Oklahoma State University. He did research in multivariate nonlinear system realization which earned him a degree of Doctor of Philosophy in Mathematical Sciences from the University of Texas at Dallas.

Previously, Dr. Crawford developed data processor models and combinatorial optimization algorithms while employed by E-Systems, Inc. Subsequently, Isom was employed by Convex Computer Corporation, optimizing parallel applications for SMP and ccNUMA machines. During this time he developed a keen interest in all aspects of parallel processing, ranging from parallel do loops to programming model development for ccNUMA architectures. After Hewlett-Packard acquired Convex, Dr. Crawford was the technical server performance program manager until 1999 when he joined the Mathematical Software group.

When not engaged in the above activities, Isom enjoys a good work of non-fiction or a mystery novel. He also collects pottery and dabbles in agriculture more than he should.

Acknowledgments

It takes a lot of people to produce a technical book, so thanks to all of the folks who made this possible. Our sincere appreciation to Susan Wright, editor at HP Press, Jill Pisoni, executive editor at Prentice-Hall PTR and Justin Somma, editorial assistant PTR, for shepherding this book from its inception. To Kathleen Caren and our copyeditor at Prentice-Hall PTR for their polishing of the manuscript.

Several people at Hewlett-Packard were instrumental in creating this book. Thanks to Paco Romero and Joe Green, our book champion and book sponsor respectively. Several of our HP colleagues were particularly helpful. Thanks to Adam Schwartz for his assistance with our initial proposal and Brent Henderson for profiling information. We're grateful to Lee Killough and Norman Lindsey for last minute proofreading. Thanks also to Raja Daoud for contributing much of the MPI performance information. We especially appreciate Camille Krug for answering our numerous FrameMaker questions.

Finally, a special thanks to our technical reviewer. He provided the initial inspiration for the book and many insightful suggestions along the way.

## CHAPTER 1

Introduction

The Devil is in the details.
Anonymous

Every day computer centers upgrade systems with faster processors, more processors, more memory, and improved I/O subsystems, only to discover application performance improves little, if at all. After some analysis by the system or software vendors, they find that their application simply wasn't designed to exploit improvements in computer architecture. Although the developers had read texts on high performance computing and had learned the meaning of the associated buzz words, acronyms, benchmarks and abstract concepts, they were never given the details on how to actually design or modify software that can benefit from computer architecture improvements. This book provides the details necessary to understand and improve the performance of your applications.

Each year, users see new models of high performance computers that are significantly faster than last year's models. The number of high performance computers has exploded over the last two decades, but the typical application achieves only a small fraction of a computer's peak performance. Reasons for this are:

- programs are written without any knowledge of the computers they will run on
- programmers don't know how to use compilers effectively
- programmers don't know how to modify code to improve performance

It's unfortunate how little the average programmer knows about his computer hardware. You don't have to be a hardware architect to write fast code, but having a basic understanding of architectures allows you to be a more proficient programmer. This also enables you to understand why certain software optimizations and compiler techniques help performance dramatically. Once armed with these tools, you can apply them to your favorite application to improve its performance. To address these issues, this book is divided into three parts: hardware overview, software techniques, and applications.

1.1 Hardware Overview — Your Work Area

In 1965, Gordon Moore, a co-founder of Intel, stated that the number of transistors on an integrated circuit doubles every 18 months. Subsequently, this observation was applied to computer performance with the conclusion that it also doubles every 18 months. This observation came to be known as Moore's law and, despite predictions of its demise, it has been remarkably accurate so far.

Computers systems consist of different components such as the processor, cache, main memory and input/output devices. In general, processors are fast, caches are small and fast, and memory is large and relatively slow. Each of these parts has its own rate of improvement over time. Some trends are:

- Faster processors
- Larger caches, but cache sizes are not scaling as fast as processor speed
- Larger memory, but memory speed improvements are not scaling as fast as processor speed
- More chip level parallelism
- More processors

Each of the major components of a computer has an effect on the overall speed of an application. To ensure that an application runs well, it is necessary to know which part, or parts, of a computer system determines its performance.

The processor (Chapter 2) is the most important part of a computer. Some processor features, such as pipelining, are found on all high performance processors, while others are characteristic of a specific processor family. Different processor families are defined and discussed. Of course, the processor is only one part of a computer. For example, if an application is completely dependent on the rate in which data can be delivered from memory, it may not matter how fast a processor is.

Data storage (Chapter 3) exists as a hierarchy on computers, with cache being "close" to the processor in terms of access time. Sometimes the cache is even part of the processor chip. This is in contrast to the large system memory, which is far away from the processor in terms of access time. The way data storage is accessed frequently determines the speed of a program.

Most high performance computers contain more than one processor. Designing computers for parallelism greatly complicates computer design. Chapter 4 discusses the various types of connections that tie processors and memory together, as well as distributed-memory and shared-memory paradigms.

1.2 Software Techniques — The Tools

Our goal is to make applications run fast. The architecture is outside the control of most programmers. Some users do get to determine which computer to purchase for their application or the processor speeds, cache size, or the amount of memory purchased, but most of us use the computers we have access to. Programmers do get to control many of the "dials" that control performance, though. The single most important piece of software used to develop applications is the compiler. Chapter 5 discusses basic compiler optimizations. These include simple optimizations that nearly all compilers perform, as well as very complex optimizations that are implemented in very few compilers. The important thing to note is that users can implement many of these optimizations independent of the sophistication of their compiler. Additional techniques to restructure code for better performance are discussed.

How do you know if your application is running efficiently? You must time or profile the code's execution (Chapter 6) to determine bottlenecks in performance to find where optimization effort should be expended. Once the most important sections of code have been located, programmers can use the architecture (Chapters 2 through 4) to predict what the theoretical performance should be and whether the current performance is acceptable. Some common mathematical kernels are analyzed in detail.

Compilers are, of course, specific to the language in which the application is written. Language choice greatly affects how much a compiler can do when optimizing source. The programming languages of C and Fortran are contrasted in Chapter 7 and inter-language ramifications are discussed. To understand compiler optimizations, it is also helpful to understand the assembly code that the compiler generates.

After a code has been optimized for single processor performance, it may then be optimized for parallel execution (Chapter 8). This is usually accomplished using shared-memory techniques such as vendor-provided compiler directives, OpenMP directives, POSIX threads, or message-passing techniques such as the Message Passing Interface (MPI).

1.3 Applications — Using the Tools

In the first two parts of the book, optimization techniques are very general. The last section uses the results of the previous sections to analyze common algorithms and kernels. Using other people's code can be an economical way to improve performance. Hardware and software vendors provide routines to perform basic through advanced mathematical algorithms (Chapter 9). There are also repositories of high-quality software for math algorithms that are available. These routines frequently have performance superior to the code most programmers write.

One way to achieve good performance is to have a set of building blocks, each of which is designed for good performance. Chapter 10 discusses some of these, including the Basic Linear Algebra Subprograms (BLAS). These routines include dot products, matrix-vector, and matrix-matrix multiplication.

The final two chapters investigate some common algorithms. Many mechanical design and analysis applications simulate structures such as automobiles using numerical linear algebra. This frequently involves solving systems of equations (Chapter 11). Some signal processing applications generate large amounts of data which are interpreted using convolutions and Fast Fourier Transforms (Chapter 12). Even if you have limited interest in these algorithms, you should at least skim the material to see how the techniques of previous chapters can be applied to improve application performance.

Hardware Overview — Your Work Area

Processors: The Core of High Performance Computing

Computers are like Old Testament gods; lots of rules and no mercy.

Joseph Campbell

2.1 Introduction

Computers are complex machines with many parts that affect application performance. Undoubtedly the most important component is the *processor*, since it is responsible for performing arithmetic and logical calculations. The processor loads data from memory, processes it, and sends the processed data back to memory. The processor performs these tasks by executing instructions. The lowest-level instructions which are visible to users are *assembly language* instructions. Each processor has an internal clock that determines the speed of operations. The amount of time to execute any instruction is an integer multiple of this *clock period*.

Over the last three decades there have been many different types of processors. Computer architects group processors into different categories according to the *instruction set architecture* (ISA) that a processor executes. This is the set of assembly language instructions defined for a given processor. Many different types of processors may use the same ISA. For example, Hewlett-Packard's PA-8000, PA-8200, PA-8500, and PA-8600 processors all execute the same assembly code and use the PA-RISC 2.0 ISA. The most common method to generate the assembly language instructions is for a user to write her programs in a high-level language such as Fortran, C or Java and use a *compiler* to translate these programs into the assembly language instructions.

Processors also belong to *processor families* that have certain high-level design features in common. High performance computing uses several different processor families, so an understanding of their design is important. The PA-8x processors mentioned above all belong to the

RISC processor family. Processor families are a reflection of the technology available when they were designed. A processor family may be appropriate for many years until advances in hardware, software, or even the cost to fabricate it make it less attractive. They evolve over time and conform to a survival-of-the-fittest policy. Most of this chapter consists of defining processor features. Different processor families are created by integrating many of these features.

2.2 Types

High performance processors of the last three decades belong to one of four families:

- Complex Instruction Set Computer (CISC)
- Reduced Instruction Set Computer (RISC)
- Vector
- Very Long Instruction Word (VLIW)

Table 2-1 shows the different processor families we'll discuss and representative architectures and processors in each family.

Table 2-1   Processor Families.

Processor Families	Instruction Set Architecture (ISA)	Processors
CISC	DEC VAX	VAX-11/780
	Intel 80x86 (IA-32)	Intel Pentium Pro
Vector	Cray	Cray T90
	Convex	Convex C-4
RISC	HP PA-RISC	PA-8600
	SGI MIPS	MIPS R10000
	DEC Alpha	Alpha21264
	Sun SPARC	Sun UltraSparc-3
	IBM PowerPC	IBM Power3
VLIW	Multiflow	Multiflow Trace
	Cydrome	Cydrome Cydra 5
	Intel IA-64	Intel Itanium

Before describing the characteristics of the processor families, certain processor features need to be defined and discussed. Some of the features exist in multiple families while others are unique to a particular family or a specific subset.

2.3 Pipelining

For an instruction to be executed, there are several steps that must be performed. For example, execution of a single instruction may contain the following stages:

1. Instruction fetch and decode (IF). Bring the instruction from memory into the processor and interpret it.
2. Read data (RD). Read the data from memory to prepare for execution.
3. Execution (EX). Execute operation.
4. Write-back (WB). Write the results back to where they came from.

Each of the four stages has to perform similar functions since they

- receive data from the previous stage,
- process data, and
- pass data to the next stage.

Note that we haven't said how long (i.e., how many clocks) it takes to perform each of the stages. However, let's assume each stage takes one cycle. Suppose there is a sequence of n instructions to perform, that all instructions are independent and we can start one instruction per cycle. In clock cycle one, an instruction fetch and decode is performed on instruction one. In clock cycle two, the data necessary for instruction one is read and instruction two is fetched and decoded. In clock cycle three, operations with instruction three begin and instructions one and two move to their next stages. This sequence of events is illustrated in Figure 2-1. At cycle four one instruction can be completed with every subsequent clock cycle. This process is know as *pipelining* instructions and is a central concept to high performance computing. Pipelining makes the processor operate more efficiently and is similar to how a factory assembly line operates.

Each instruction has a *latency* associated with it. This is the amount of time it takes before the result of the operation can be used. Obviously a small latency is desired. The instructions shown in Figure 2-1 have a four-cycle latency (each stage takes one cycle and there are four stages). If an instruction starts executing in clock cycle one, its result is available in clock cycle five.

2.4 Instruction Length

Another processor feature associated with performance is instruction length. Individual instructions can be measured by their length in binary digits or *bits*. An instruction must contain

INSTRUCTION

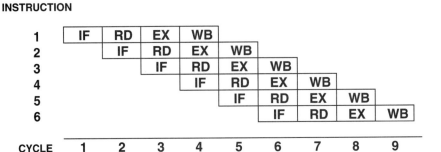

Figure 2-1   Pipelining.

the information necessary to identify it and to provide exactly what the instruction needs to accomplish. Simple instructions don't need as many bits as complicated instructions. For example, suppose an instruction tells the processor to initialize a value to zero. The only information necessary is the name or operation code of the instruction, the quantity zero, and the register or address that should be modified. Another instruction might load two values, multiply them together and store the result to a third quantity. The first instruction could be much shorter than the second instruction since it doesn't need to convey as much information.

Having a variable number of bits for instructions allows computer designers to load the minimum number of bits necessary to execute the instruction. However, this makes it difficult to predict how many instructions are in a stream of instruction bits. This lack of prediction effects how well instructions can be pipelined.

For example, assume that the processor knows where the next instruction begins in memory. The processor must load some number of bits (it doesn't know how many) to determine what the following instruction is. If the instruction is long, it may have to make multiple loads from memory to get the complete instruction. Having to make multiple loads for an instruction is especially bad. Remember that for pipelining to occur as illustrated above, the instruction fetch stage must take only one cycle. If all instructions have a constant length of n bits, the logic is much simpler since the processor can make a single load of n bits from memory and know it has a complete instruction.

So there's a trade-off in processor design. Is it better to load fewer bits and have complicated logic to find the instruction, or load more bits and know exactly how many instructions it contains? Because of the performance benefits of pipelining, computer designers today prefer instructions of constant length.

2.5 Registers

The performance of a processor is closely tied to how data is accessed. The closest (and smallest) storage areas are the *registers* that are contained in modern processors. Computers can be designed without registers, though. Some early computers had every instruction load data from memory, process it, and store the results back to memory. These are known as memory-memory architectures. Computers with registers fall into two groups: processors that allow every instruction to access memory (register-memory architectures) and processors that allow only load or store instructions to access memory (load-store architectures). All recently designed processors have load-store architectures. General trends regarding registers are:

- more registers
- wider registers
- more types of registers

2.5.1 General Registers

The first type of register was the general register. It contained integer data used in address calculations. Although the first computers to use registers contained only a few general registers, most computers today have at least 32. Accessing memory is time-consuming, and having many registers helps reduce the number of memory accesses. Hence, having a large number of registers helps performance significantly. Instruction latencies (i.e., the number of stages) have grown over time, so having more registers provides additional high speed memory for multiple, independent instruction streams. This allows the compiler to schedule instructions so that pipelining is more efficient.

Data in a computer is represented in bits. A group of eight bits is called a *byte* and can represent $2^8 = 256$ values. A typical width for general registers is 32-bits, as shown in Figure 2-2. A

Figure 2-2   Integer data representations.

common way to interpret integer data is to have the left-most bit be a sign bit and the rest of the bits determine the magnitude of the number. Let the zero's bit (the right-most bit) be a_0, the one's bit be a_1, and so on. For a positive number (sign bit equal to zero), the magnitude is

$$a_0 \, 2^0 + a_1 \, 2^1 + a_2 \, 2^2 + ...$$

There are multiple methods for representing negative numbers. In the *one's-complement* system, the negative of a number is obtained by complementing each bit (i.e., all zeros are changed to ones and all ones are changed to zeros). Most computers use the *two's-complement* method, which is found by taking the one's complement and adding one. Thus the numbers 1 and −1 are represented by

$$1 \ = 0000 \ ... \ 0001$$
$$-1 = 1111 \ ... \ 1110 \quad \text{(one's complement)}$$
$$-1 = 1111 \ ... \ 1111 \quad \text{(two's complement)}$$

Using a two's-complement format for 32-bit integer data, numbers in the range -2^{31} to $2^{31}-1$ (−2,147,483,648 to 2,147,483,647) can be represented. 32-bit integers are not large enough for many applications today, so most high performance processors have general registers that are 64 bits wide.

When discussing the computer representation of numbers, it is often necessary to discuss the binary representation of numbers instead of their more familiar decimal representation. This quickly becomes cumbersome due to the large number of digits in most binary representations. A more succinct way to represent binary numbers is by using *hexadecimal* (base 16) notation. Binary notation is converted to hexadecimal notation by combining 4 binary digits to a single hexadecimal digit. Hexadecimal digits are 0, 1,..., 9, A, B, C, D, E, F, where F represents the binary number 1111 (or the decimal number 15.) Representations of two numbers using two's-complement forms follow:

$$+1{,}610{,}612{,}738 = \ (\ 2^{30} + 2^{29} + 2^1\ ) = 0110\ 0000\ ...\ 0000\ 0010_2 = 60000002_{16}$$
$$-1{,}610{,}612{,}738 = -(\ 2^{30} + 2^{29} + 2^1\ ) = 1001\ 1111\ ...\ 1111\ 1110_2 = 9FFFFFFE_{16}$$

Hexadecimal numbers are frequently denoted by prepending them with a 0x, so the above numbers may be written as 0x60000002 and 0x9FFFFFFE.

2.5.2   Floating-Point Registers

Integer data isn't sufficient for most applications. Most users need real numbers, or at least a sufficiently large subset of them. *Floating-point* data consists of three fields:

- the fractional part (significand) that contains the number's significant digits,
- an exponent to indicate the power of two that is multiplied by the significand, and
- a sign bit to indicate whether the number is positive or negative.

Due to the widespread use of floating-point data, most processors have separate registers for integers (general registers) and floating-point data (floating-point registers). Today most vendors use 64-bit floating-point registers which can contain 32-bit or 64-bit data. There was a time when vendors used different sizes for the significand, but now virtually all conform to the ANSI/IEEE 754-1985 standards for 32-bit and 64-bit floating-point data, as shown in Figure 2-3.

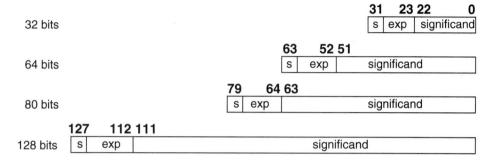

Figure 2-3 IEEE floating-point data representations.

For 32-bit floating-point data, the sign bit is zero for positive numbers and one for negative numbers. The exponent is eight bits long and the significand is 23 bits long. The exponent uses a bias of 127 and the significand contains an implied one to the left of the binary point. If s is the sign bit, e is the exponent and m is the significand, then a 32-bit floating-point number corresponds to

$$(-1)^s \, (1.m) \times 2^{(e-127)}$$

For example, to represent $3/4 = 1.5 \times 2^{(126-127)}$, set e = 126 and m = 5 for the binary representation 001111110100...0. The hexadecimal representation for 3/4 is 3F400000 and the representation of −3/4 is BF400000. Adding two floating-point values is more complicated than adding two integers. Let Y and Z be two floating-point numbers:

$$Y = (1.my) \times 2^{(ey-127)}$$
$$Z = (1.mz) \times 2^{(ez-127)}$$

If $ey \le ez$, then their sum is

$$Y + Z = [(1.mz) + ((1.my) \times 2^{(ey-ez)})] \times 2^{(ez-127)}$$

If $ez < ey$, then their sum is

$$Y + Z = [(1.my) + ((1.mz) \times 2^{(ez-ey)})] \times 2^{(ey-127)}$$

So, addition of floating-point values involves comparing exponents, shifting significands, addition, and possibly a renormalization of the results. This is a lot more complicated that integer addition! The range of magnitudes for 32-bit values using IEEE 754 is $1.1754945 \times 10^{-38}$ to 3.4028232×10^{38}. The corresponding range for 64-bit quantities is $2.225073858507202 \times 10^{-308}$ to $1.797693134862312 \times 10^{308}$. Some applications need only the accuracy obtained using 32-bit numbers. For example, if data is obtained from a sensor that provides only 10 bits for each data element, then 32-bit arithmetic probably contains more than enough accuracy to process this data. However, many applications do require the accuracy provided by 64-bit numbers. For even more precision, the IEEE 754 standard defines double-extended (80-bit) and quad-precision (128-bit) floating-point numbers. There are only a few applications that require this amount of accuracy, so most vendors provide quad-precision by treating two 64-bit registers as a 128-bit register and operating on the two components separately. Thus the performance of using 128-bit data may be significantly slower than that of 64-bit data.

2.5.3   Vector Registers

Users frequently operate on lists or *vectors* of numbers. For example, suppose x and y are vectors that each contain 50 elements. The addition of real vectors x and y creates another vector, z, as follows:

```
for (i = 0; i < 50; i++)
   z[i] = x[i] + y[i];
```

Vector operations are well-suited to pipelining since the operations on the individual elements of the vector are independent. Therefore, some processors have vector registers which contain many data elements. In the above example, a single vector register, v1, could hold all the elements of x and another vector register, v2, could contain the elements of y. Vector registers can be thought of as a collection of general or floating-point registers tightly bound together. So, in the above example, two vectors of length 50 hold an amount of data that is equivalent to using 100 floating-point registers. One advantage of vector registers is that they allow a large amount of data to be located close to the processor functional units which manipulate them. Vector registers are usually a power of two in size with 128 elements per vector register being representative. There is also a vector length register associated with vector registers that determines how many elements in the vector are to be used in each operation.

2.5.4   Data Dependence

Efficient scheduling of instructions for pipelining requires analysis of whether one instruction depends on another. Data dependencies and control dependencies are frequent inhibitors of pipelining and hence high performance. A *data dependence* occurs when an instruction is dependent on data from a previous instruction and therefore cannot be moved before the earlier instruction. So the code,

```
y = foo(x);
z = y;
```

has a data dependence since the second expression cannot be moved before the first one.

A *control dependence* is when an instruction occurs after a conditional branch and therefore it is not known whether the instruction will be executed at all. Thus

```
if (n == 0)
   x = y;
```

has a control dependence. Some dependencies can be eliminated by software techniques discussed in Chapter 5. Some processors have hardware features that lessen the effect of dependencies. This section discusses features related to data dependence while the next discusses control dependence.

2.5.4.1   Register Renaming

Register dependence is when two instructions use the same register, but neither instruction uses the result of the other. For example, consider the sequence of instructions

```
register 13 = register 12 + register 8
register 8 = register 17 * register 4
```

The second instructions does not depend on the result of the first, but it cannot begin execution until the first instruction finishes using register 8. If another register were available, then the processor could use that register in place of register 8 in the second instruction. It could then move the result of the second instruction into register 8 at its convenience. Then these instructions could be pipelined.

This use of another dummy register in place of a register specified by the instruction is generally referred to as *register renaming*. Some processors have a set of hidden registers used for just this purpose. These processors dynamically rename a register to one of these hidden registers so that register dependence is removed and better instruction scheduling is facilitated.

2.5.4.2   Rotating Registers

Result dependence occurs when one instruction produces a result that is required by another instruction. This is illustrated by the following sequence of instructions:

```
DO I = 1,N
   Y(I) = X(I)
ENDDO
```

The naive way to implement this data copy using pseudo-assembly language is

```
DO I = 1,N
   load X(i) into register 1
   store register 1 to Y(i)
ENDDO
```

If the load instruction has a four-cycle latency, then the store cannot start until four cycles after the load begins. This causes the processor to stall or sit idle for four cycles.

Rotating registers are those which rotate or are renumbered with each iteration of a loop. For example, if registers rotate, the data in register 1 in the first iteration of a loop would appear in register 2 in the second iteration.

If registers rotate, then the above loop may be implemented as

```
load X(1) into register 5
load X(2) into register 4
load X(3) into register 3
load X(4) into register 2
DO I = 1, N-4
   load X(i+4) into register 1
   store register 5 to Y(i)
ENDDO
store register 4 to Y(N-3)
store register 3 to Y(N-2)
store register 2 to Y(N-1)
store register 1 to Y(N)
```

With this implementation, the store in the loop can start immediately since it is storing data that was loaded four iterations before (and hence at least four cycles earlier). Note, however, a prologue is necessary before the loop body to load the first values of x. There is also an epilogue after the loop for the last store operations.

2.5.4.3   Data Speculation

Since memory is far away from the processor, a load of data should be initiated as far in advance as its use as possible. There are logical inhibitors to this in practice. Consider the following sequence of instructions:

```
store register 4 to x
load y to register 5
```

It would probably help performance to move the load before the store since the load would be started earlier. However, if it is known that the addresses of x and y are different, this instruction movement is legal since the store may modify the value of y.

One way to attack this problem is to define a special type of load, called an *advanced load*, and a special address table to keep track of the advanced load addresses. The above sequence could be converted to appear as follows:

```
advanced load of y to register 5 and mark the address of y in table
store register 4 to x and note whether this address is the same
   as y's address
check instruction (if any stores have updated the address
   of y repeat the load of y)
```

Thus, if the address of y had never been updated by a store, the advanced load was valid and performed earlier than would have been normally been possible. If the address of y was modified by the store, the load is repeated and the correct value of y is produced.

2.5.5 Control Dependence

Branches cause control dependencies by forcing the instruction stream (control) to jump from one region of instructions to another. This usually results in severe performance penalties by interfering with pipelining as well as stalling the processor.

2.5.5.1 Branch Delay Slots

Loop structures are great for pipelining except for one feature. There's a branch at the end of every loop. The simple loop

```
for (i = 0; i < n; i++)
   s = s + 3.0;
```

can be converted to the pseudo-assembly code

```
   i = -1
loop:
   s = s + 3.0
   i = i + 1
   if (i < n), branch to loop
```

When a branch is taken, the instruction stream jumps from one location to another. The first time in the instruction sequence where a branch can be recognized is during instruction decode. Many processors will have the next instruction being fetched before the branch can be interpreted. For a taken branch, the processor has to undo any work that has been done for that next instruction and jump to the new location. This causes a gap in the instruction pipeline that degrades performance. The *branch delay slot* is the instruction located immediately after a branch instruction. Some processors always execute the branch delay slot to improve pipelining. The loop above could then appear as

```
    i = -1
loop:
    s = s + 3.0
    i = i + 1
    if (i < n), branch to loop
    nop ! branch delay slot, always execute
```

This instruction shown after the loop is a dummy instruction called a no-operation instructions or *nop*. It doesn't do work, but acts as a place holder so that pipelining can continue until the loop is exited. Of course, the code would be smaller (and more efficient) if there was real work in the branch delay slot, so it would be better for the code to appear as

```
    i = -1
loop:
    i = i + 1
    if (i < n), branch to loop
    s = s + 3.0 ! branch delay slot, always execute
```

Ideally, the instruction stream should contain as few jumps as possible. This makes it easier for pipelining to continue. Even simple if-tests are a problem, though. For example, the code

```
IF (N > 0) then
    A = 0.3
ELSE
    A = 0.7
ENDIF
```

is interpreted as

```
    if (N <= 0) branch to label_1
    A = 0.3
    branch to label_2
label_1:
    A = 0.7
label_2:
```

This contains two branches. On architectures which always execute the branch delay slot, the pseudo-code could be written as

```
    if (N <= 0) branch to label_1
    nop ! branch delay slot, always execute
    branch to label_2
    A = 0.3 ! branch delay slot, always execute
label_1:
    A = 0.7
label_2:
```

When the instruction fetch stage takes more than one cycle, or a processor can fetch more than one instruction at a time, the multiple branches above interfere with pipelining.

2.5.5.2   Predicate Registers

Predicate registers allow some branches to execute more efficiently. These are single-bit registers associated with instructions on some architectures that allow the conditional execution of instructions. Normally, instructions appear as

```
y = 2.0
```

If predication is supported, then the instruction might appear as

```
(p1) y = 2.0
```

If the predicate register p1 is one, i.e., true, y is set to 2.0. However, if p1 is zero or false, the instruction is interpreted as a nop. Predicate registers allow some control dependencies introduced by branches to be turned into data dependencies. If p1 and p2 are predicate registers, then the original if-test in the previous section results in the sequence,

```
    if (N > 0) set p1=true, p2=false; else p1=false, p2=true;
    (p1) A = 0.3
    (p2) A = 0.7
```

This takes only three instructions since the if-else test is a single instruction. Note that one of the predicated instructions is not needed (but we don't know which one) and will not update A. However, since this instruction must be loaded from the instruction stream, it is not completely free. The cost for this instruction is the same as a nop.

Predicate registers allow architectures with rotating registers to be even more effective. Recall how rotating registers were used on the loop

```
    DO I = 1,N
        Y(I) = X(I)
    ENDDO
```

and the prologue and epilogue they generated. Predicate registers allow the prologue and epilogue to be moved into the loop body as shown below.

```
DO I = 1, N+4
   if (I <= N) set p1=true; else p1=false;
   if (I >= 4) set p2=true; else p2=false;
   (p1) load X(I) into register 1
   (p2) store register 5 to Y(I-4)
ENDDO
```

Thus, rotating registers and predicate registers used together reduce the number of instructions required.

2.5.5.3   Control Speculation

A conditional branch keeps normal loads from being placed in the instruction stream so they occur before a branch. In the following code, it is not safe to move the load before the branch since the location of z may not even be defined when the test $x > y$ is performed.

```
if x > y branch to skip_load
...
load z to register 5
skip_load:
```

Therefore, a normal load might generate exceptions if the data is loaded and the program may abort.

There is a special type of load, a *speculative load*, that allows these situations to be handled efficiently. Any exceptions are held in a special buffer area and the processor checks these at the location where the original load would have appeared in the code stream. The above code could be converted to appear as follows:

```
speculative load of z to register 5 and put exception
   information in buffer
if x > y branch to skip_load
...
check instruction (if an exception appears in buffer, reload Z
   and take normal exception and processor interrupt)
skip_load:
```

Thus, if no exceptions had appeared, the speculative load was valid and was performed earlier than would have normally been possible.

2.6 Functional Units

Memory and registers contain the data that gets processed, but the parts of the processor that actually do the work are the *functional units*. Most processors have functional units for the following:

- memory operations
- integer arithmetic
- floating-point arithmetic

In load-store architectures, the memory functional units execute instructions that contain memory addresses and registers. Other functional units execute instructions that operate exclusively on registers. The examples so far have been simplified by assuming that all instructions spend one cycle in the execution stage. The number of cycles in the execution stage is determined by the amount of time spent in the corresponding functional unit.

Memory functional units have varying degrees of sophistication. Load instructions reference an address in memory where a datum is to be loaded from and a register where the datum is put. As always, an important goal is to ensure efficient pipelining. Simple processors stall until the loaded data moves from memory into a register. This behavior is known as *stall-on-load*. Processors that *stall-on-use* allow the load and subsequent instructions to be executed until the processor actually tries to use the register that the load referenced. If the data is not in the register, then the processor stalls until it arrives from memory. Some processors support having several outstanding loads occurring simultaneously. Processors may also allow advanced and speculative loads as discussed above.

Most integer instructions have a lower latency than floating-point instructions since integer operations are easy to implement in hardware. Examples of integer operations are adding integers, shifting bits, Boolean operations, and bitwise operations such as extracting or depositing a string of bits. Since computers use a binary representation, multiplication and division by a power of two is easily accomplished by shifting bits. For example, multiplying a positive value by eight is accomplished by shifting the binary representation to the left by three bits. Multiplication and division by arbitrary integer values is much more difficult and time-consuming. These are sometimes accomplished by converting the integer data to floating-point data, performing floating-point operations and converting the result back to an integer.

Floating-point data contains an exponent and significand, so adding two floating-point numbers involves much more logic and hence more complex circuitry. Actual latencies vary among processors, but floating-point additions may take three times longer than integer additions, while floating-point divides may take several times longer than floating-point additions. Table 2-2 shows representative latencies on one modern architecture.

Table 2-2 Instruction Latencies.

Instruction Type	Latency (clocks)
Integer addition	1
Floating-point addition	3
Floating-point multiplication	3
Floating-point division (64-bit)	31

Many processors have single instructions that perform multiple operations using a single functional unit. It is usually advantageous to use these since they result in getting more work done in a unit of time. Below are multiple operation instructions implemented in some contemporary processors:

- Shift and Mask—shift an integer a specified number of bits and perform a Boolean AND operation. These instructions can be used for integer arithmetic (especially multiplication by powers of two) involved in common tasks such as address calculation and modular arithmetic.

- Floating-point Fused Multiply and Add (*fma*)—multiply two floating-point registers and add the result to another register. This instruction is also known as Floating-point Multiply and Accumulate. This instruction brings up several interesting issues. This instruction is implemented a couple of different ways. The most efficient processors have one or more functional units that can perform an `fma`. The `fma` instruction is a big advantage on these processors since two floating-point operations are produced by the functional unit. Less efficient processors have separate functional units for multiply and addition and a `fma` instruction is split into two parts that uses both functional units. There's no advantage to using an `fma` on these processors. If an `fma` instruction is executed by a single functional unit, the result may be different than if the multiply and addition are done separately. This is because the intermediate multiply result can be more accurate since it doesn't need to be stored. This has caused problems because some users believe any answer that differs from what they've obtained in the past must be a wrong answer.

- Some processors have instructions that take 64-bit integer registers and operate on the four 16-bit components contained in the register. An add of this type performs four 16-bit additions with a single instruction. These instructions are used in multimedia applications. These types of instructions are known as Single Instruction Multiple Data (*SIMD*) instructions and are a form of instruction level parallelism.

- Applications which use 32-bit floating-point numbers can use another type of SIMD instruction that operates on the two 32-bit halves of a 64-bit floating-point register. An `fma` of this type performs four 32-bit floating-point operations with a single instruction.

Now that we've defined lots of processor features, we'll put them together to build the processor families we discussed earlier.

2.7 CISC and RISC Processors

Since the 1970's, most computers are what are now called Complex Instruction Set Computers (CISC). The personal computer or laptop you use probably contains a CISC processor. This is in contrast to the more streamlined and powerful Reduced Instruction Set Computers (RISC). The names CISC and RISC indicate that the difference between the two families is that the CISC instruction set is larger or more complicated that RISC's. While this is true, the names don't touch on many other important differences. High performance processors are designed for speed. But when CISC processors were being designed in the 1970s, the technological landscape was very different than it is today. Design goals in the 1970s were focused on defining a set of assembly instructions so that high-level language constructs such as those found in Cobol or Fortran could be translated into as few assembly language instructions as possible. As a result, many of these instructions access memory and there are many instruction types. To simplify all of these instructions for the processor logic, the processor breaks them down into even lower level instructions called *microcode*. A CISC processor actually executes the microcode instead of assembly code. The advantage of microcode is that it simplifies using the same assembly code for many generations of a processor family because only the underlying microcode must change. Due to the existence of microcode, the large number of instructions, memory based instructions, and varying instruction length, it is difficult to pipeline instructions on CISC processors.

By the end of the 1970s, many researchers were studying the performance of processors trying to find ways to improve, i.e., decrease, the number of clocks per instruction *(CPI)*. An advantage that these architects had over CISC designers was that they were starting their design from scratch and didn't have the legacy of existing CISC designs to carry with them. One result of this research was the creation of RISC processors. The overriding desire of the RISC processor architects was to design computers to pipeline instructions as much as possible.

By reducing the number of assembly language instruction types, they were able to make processors more efficient. They didn't use microcode, but had the assembly instructions executed directly by the processor. This is not without cost. If there is a serious flaw in the processor design, it must be thrown away and redesigned, whereas many flaws in CISC processors can be fixed by rewriting the microcode to avoid the flaw. An extremely important result of having a small number of assembly language instruction types is that it makes it easier for all instructions to have the same instruction length.

Most RISC designs also execute one or more branch delay slots to aid pipelining. Reducing the number of memory accesses is also important, so they also contain a large number of general and floating-point registers. Therefore, some features that encourage pipelining and hence help define RISC processors are

- no microcode
- relatively few instructions
- only load and store instructions access memory
- a common instruction word length
- execution of branch delay slots
- more registers than CISC processors

The first RISC processors functioned very much as shown in Figure 2-1. In each clock cycle, after the pipeline is full, a new instruction is dispatched and an instruction completes execution. So ideally there is one CPI.

It should be noted that on RISC processors there are still some instructions that cannot be pipelined. One example is the floating-point divide instruction. As mentioned above, division is much more difficult to perform than addition or multiplication. When divide is implemented in hardware, it takes so many clocks to execute that it cannot be pipelined. Fortunately, the vast majority of instructions can be pipelined on RISC processors.

In the quest to increase performance on RISC processors, many new design features appeared. On the pipelined processor shown in Figure 2-1, several instructions are executed in parallel in each cycle. However, at any given point in time each instruction being executed is in a different stage. One way to increase performance is to have multiple instances of each stage, so that more than one instruction is at the same stage at the same time. This is known as Instruction Level Parallelism (*ILP*) and is the idea behind *superscalar* RISC processors. A superscalar RISC processor can issue or dispatch more than one instruction per clock cycle. For example, a two-way superscalar processor is one that can dispatch two instructions every clock period. Figure 2-4 shows a four-way superscalar RISC pipeline.

Another way to increase performance is *out-of-order execution*. Sometimes a processor will attempt to execute an instruction only to find out that the instruction cannot be executed due to a dependency between it and previous instructions. Out-of-order execution processors attempt to locate and dispatch only instructions that are ready for execution regardless of their order in the instruction sequence.

As one would expect, the logic to optimally perform this analysis is very complicated. Also, out-of-order execution introduces a randomness into the instruction execution ordering that is not present in simpler RISC processors. This can make it more difficult for optimization experts or compiler writers, to optimize code, because some of the determinism may vanish at

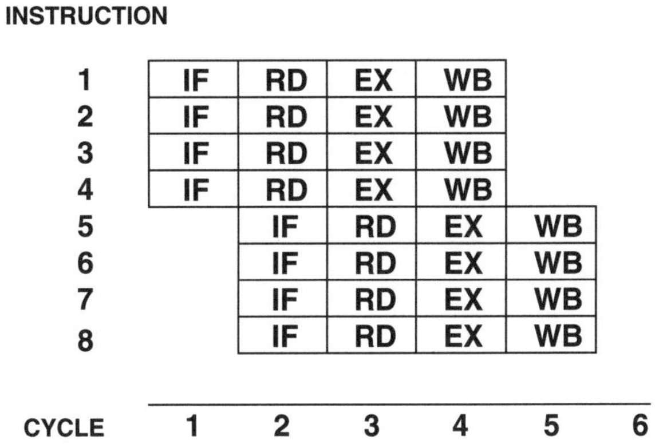

INSTRUCTION

1	IF	RD	EX	WB	
2	IF	RD	EX	WB	
3	IF	RD	EX	WB	
4	IF	RD	EX	WB	
5		IF	RD	EX	WB
6		IF	RD	EX	WB
7		IF	RD	EX	WB
8		IF	RD	EX	WB

CYCLE   1   2   3   4   5   6

Figure 2-4   Four-way superscalar RISC pipeline.

dispatch time. Another feature that improves instruction scheduling is register renaming, so many RISC processors also support this functionality.

When RISC processors first appeared, their clock periods were slower than CISC processors. By the early 1990s, RISC processor clock periods had improved so much that they were faster than their CISC counterparts and RISC superseded CISC in most high performance computers. Examples of RISC processor ISA's include:

- Hewlett-Packard Precision Architecture - RISC
- Silicon Graphics Incorporated MIPS
- Compaq (Digital Equipment Corporation) Alpha
- International Business Machines PowerPC
- Sun SPARC

What has happened to CISC processors since the RISC revolution? Intel's Pentium Pro architecture is a recent CISC processor. While it is difficult to overcome all of CISC's design constraints, the Intel processor has very good performance because the microcode has been designed to be very RISC-like. The Pentium Pro also has many more registers than previous generations of the processor family and uses register renaming. So CISC processors are copying the best attributes of RISC processors.

2.8 Vector Processors

From the 1970s to the early 1990s, high performance computing was closely tied to vector computers. As discussed earlier, a vector is an array or a list of numbers. Vector computers are efficient since they perform operations on vectors of data, instead of a single point or scalar. The premier designer of vector computers was the late Seymour Cray. Working at Cray Research Corporation and Cray Computer Corporation, Cray's goal was to build the fastest computer in existence. For many years he did just that. Cray's computers were so much faster than other computers that they were called *supercomputers*. In the 1980s, one definition of supercomputer was the latest computer Seymour Cray designed. These supercomputers were all vector computers. Like RISC computers, the high performance of vector computers is obtained by pipelining instructions. Some argue that Cray's computers were early RISC computers since the instruction set was simple, instructions were all the same size, and they did not use microcode.

Vector computers use a single instruction to repeat an operation on many pieces of data (i.e., a vector) so that they execute far fewer instructions than scalar (CISC or RISC) processors. There is always a hardware imposed maximum vector length associated with a vector processor. This is the number of data items in the longest vector register. For vector operations in excess of this length, the compiler generates a loop where each iteration of the loop executes vector instructions using the maximum vector length. This is referred to as *strip-mining* the loop. On vector processors, the branch that occurs at the end of a loop is much less important than it is on a scalar processor, since the branch is executed far fewer times.

Suppose that two vectors of data, x and y, each have 512 elements and these vectors are to be added and stored to another vector z as shown below:

```
for (i = 0; i < 512; i++)
   z[i] = x[i] + y[i];
```

For this example, assume that vector registers can hold 128 elements. Table 2-3 shows a comparison between the instructions that scalar and vector processors produce.

Table 2-3   Scalar versus Vector Instructions.

Scalar	Vector
set counter = 0	set counter = 0
loop_label:	loop_label:
load element of x	load 128 elements of x
increment address of x by 1	increment address of x by 128
load element of y	load 128 elements of y
increment address of y by 1	increment address of y by 128
add x + y = z	add 128 elements x + y = z
store element of z	store 128 elements of z
increment address of z by 1	increment address of z by 128
counter = counter + 1	counter = counter + 128
if counter is < 512 go to loop_label	if counter is < 512 go to loop_label

Processors using scalar or vector instructions may both have a goal of one operation per clock period. At a fixed clock period, the two approaches may achieve similar performance results on ideal code. Not all code can be vectorized, though. Codes that are not vectorizable are called *scalar* codes. In general, if codes are vectorizable, they are also capable of being pipelined on a RISC processor. However, there are many scalar codes that can also be pipelined on a RISC processor.

An additional level of pipelining available on most vector processors is *chaining*. This is when the result of a vector instruction is fed into, or chained with, another vector instruction without having to wait for the first instruction to complete execution. A common form of chaining is when a vector multiply instruction chains with a vector addition. This is analogous to the fma instruction discussed earlier.

Just as there are superscalar RISC processors that dispatch multiple instructions per clock period, there are also vector architectures that allow multiple independent vector instructions to be initiated and executed in parallel. Figure 2-5 shows a vector pipeline with a vector length of 128 that executes two independent vector load instructions chained to a vector addition instruction, which is chained to a vector store.

INSTRUCTION

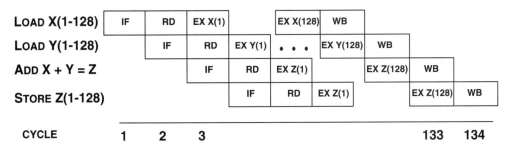

Figure 2-5 Vector pipeline.

The selling price of a processor is proportional to the volume produced. The number of vector processors has always been very small compared to the number of other types of processors, so they cost much more. However, in the 1970s and 1980s their performance was so superior to that of other processors that companies were willing to pay exorbitant prices for vector computers. This was due to their much faster clock periods, the inherent pipelining of vectorization, and advanced memory systems.

When Seymour Cray introduced the Cray 1 in 1976, its performance was over 10 times faster than the fastest CISC processor. Throughout the 1980s and 1990s, RISC processor technology matured and the performance of these relatively inexpensive processors improved more rapidly than that of vector processors.

The LINPACK benchmarks are used to measure the performance of linear algebra software (see Chapter 9). The LINPACK 1000x1000 benchmark solves a system of 1000 equations for 1000 unknowns. One of the creators of the LINPACK software and benchmark, Jack Dongarra, maintains a database of benchmark results at `http://www.netlib.org/benchmark/performance.ps`. Hardware vendors are encouraged to send results to Dongarra. The database contains entries for hundreds of computers. Figure 2-6 shows single processor LINPACK 1000x1000 performance comparing Cray vector processors and Hewlett-Packard RISC processors. The data points represent the number of million floating-point operations per second

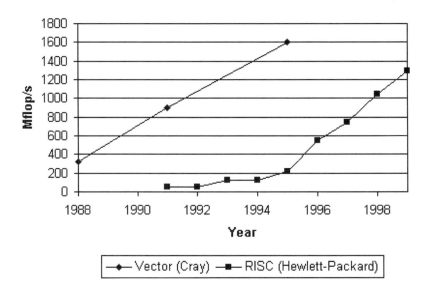

Figure 2-6   Comparison of processor performance
using LINPACK 1000x1000.

(*Mflop/s*) in the year of introduction of the respective processors and show how the processor families have improved over time.

This is a very good benchmark to show the benefits of vector processors and a poor benchmark for CISC processors. On the other hand, RISC processor performance is rapidly approaching vector processor performance. There are many other benchmarks where the speed of RISC processors exceeds the speed of vector processors. In fact, for today's general-purpose computing, RISC processors are faster than vector processors. Since the cost of RISC processors is much less than the cost of vector processors, the number of vector computers continues to shrink.

2.9 VLIW

Most RISC instructions are 32-bits in length. Using long instruction words that contain multiple tightly bound instructions is another way to increase the amount of parallelism and hence performance. This is the rationale for long instruction word (*LIW*) and very long instruction word (*VLIW*) processors. The difference between LIW and VLIW processors is somewhat arbitrary, so the two terms will be used interchangeably. The performance of processors is limited by their clock periods, which are ultimately limited by the laws of physics. That is, electricity travels at a significant fraction of the speed of light, which is a constant. If clock speed is held constant, the way to gain performance is to increase the amount of work done in a clock cycle. RISC superseded CISC in high performance computing because RISC processors could execute more instructions in a clock cycle than a CISC processor could. As RISC processors matured, they were improved and made more complicated by designing them to dispatch multiple instructions in a clock cycle. This works fine for some applications, but it is sometimes difficult for the hardware to determine which instructions can be executed in parallel. LIW processors are explicitly designed for instruction parallelism. With LIW processors, software determines which instructions can be performed in parallel, bundles this information and the instructions and passes them to the hardware. As processor clock speed increases become more difficult to obtain, LIW architectures facilitate increased performance without increasing the clock period.

Early LIW designs in the 1980s such as the Multiflow Trace computers had little commercial success. This was partly due to long compile times. A characteristic of the Multiflow computers was a variable word length. One type of Multiflow processor had seven instructions packed in a long instruction word, while another one had 14 instructions in a long instruction word. A great deal of research went into producing compilers to generate instructions that were optimal for each word length. The resulting complexity resulted in compilers that took a long time to generate even very simple executables. Another financially unsuccessful computer was Cydrome's Cydra 5. It was more sophisticated than the Trace computer and included rotating and predicate registers.

Intel and Hewlett-Packard have announced Explicit Parallel Instruction Computing (EPIC) processors. These represent an update to the LIW concept. Two features that make EPIC attractive are that processors have a common instruction word length and compiler technology and processor speed has advanced to allow quick compilation time. The EPIC instruction word or *bundle* is 128 bits long and consists of three 41-bit *instruction slots*, as shown in Figure 2-7.

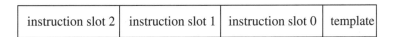

Figure 2-7 EPIC instruction format.

The five-bit template field defines the mapping of instructions contained in the bundle to functional units and whether the instructions in the bundle can be executed in parallel with the next instruction. Since the bundle length is constant, objects that are created on one processor will be compatible with future processors that have the same bundle length. Some features that help define EPIC processors are

- instruction bundle consists of three instructions
- predicate registers
- rotating registers
- more registers than CISC, RISC processors
- advanced and speculative loads

Figure 2-8 shows the execution of an a single EPIC instruction.

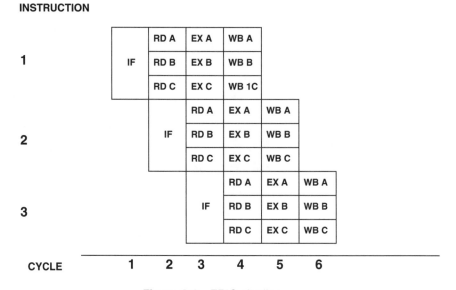

Figure 2-8 EPIC pipeline.

The first ISA in the EPIC processor family is Intel Architecture - 64 (IA-64) [2]. It contains a large number of general and floating-point registers (128 of each). Itanium is the first IA-64 processor and it can dispatch two long word instructions in a clock cycle to achieve additional parallelism. To demonstrate improvements in instruction level parallelism, Figure 2-9 compares representative number of instructions per clock cycle for some of the processors we've discussed.

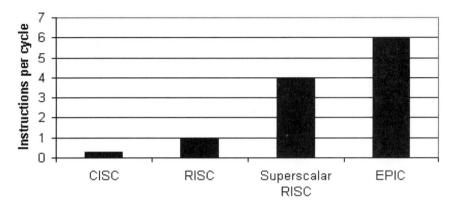

Figure 2-9 Instruction level parallelism.

2.10 Summary

Trends in processor design in the last twenty years include increased use of pipelining and increased instruction level parallelism. As a result, there is increased reliance on software to generate efficient instruction scheduling. These trends have resulted in processor evolution from CISC through vector and RISC architectures to LIW. While it's impossible to predict all the characteristics of processors ten or twenty years from now, the trends will likely continue, so processors of the near future will contain many of the features described in this chapter.

Processor design is crucial for high performance, but other components of a computer system such as memory systems can cripple even the best designed processor. The next chapters will discuss some of the other system components.

References:

1. Hwang, K. *Advanced Computer Architecture: Parallelism, Scalability, Programmability*. New York: McGraw-Hill, Inc., 1993, ISBN 0-13-182734-0.
2. *Intel IA-64 Architecture Software Developer's Manual*, Intel, http://www.intel.com/, January 2000.
3. Kane, G. *PA-RISC 2.0 Architecture*. Upper Saddle River, New Jersey: Prentice Hall PTR, 1996, ISBN 0-07-031622-8.
4. Mahlke, S. A.; Chen, W. Y.; Hwu, W. W.; Rau, B. R.; Schlansker, M. S. *Sentinel Scheduling for VLIW and Superscalar Processors*. Proceedings of the Fifth International Confer-

ence on Architectural Support for Programming Languages and Operating Systems, SIGPLAN Notices, Vol. 27, No. 9, 238-247, 1992.

5. Patterson, D. A.; Hennessy, J. L. *Computer Architecture: A Quantitative Approach*. San Francisco: Morgan Kaufmann Publishers, Inc., 1996, ISBN 1-55860-329-8.

6. Rau, B. R.; Lee, M.; Tirumalai, P. P.; Schlansker, M. S. *Register Allocation for Software Pipelined Loops*. Proceedings of the ACM SIGPLAN '92 Conference on Programming Language Design and Implementation, 283-299, 1992.

Data Storage

Some day, on the corporate balance sheet, there will be an entry which reads, "Information";
for in most cases, the information is more valuable than the hardware which processes it.

Grace Murray Hopper

Many applications perform relatively simple operations on vast amounts of data. In such cases, the performance of a computer's data storage devices impact overall application performance more than processor performance. Data storage devices include, but are not limited to, processor registers, caches, main memory, disk (hard, compact disk, etc.) and magnetic tape. In this chapter we will discuss performance aspects of memory systems and caches and how application developers can avoid common performance problems. This will be followed by a brief overview of disk file system performance issues.

3.1 Introduction

Suppose for a moment that you are a carpenter. You have a tool belt, a lightweight tool box, a tool chest permanently attached to your vehicle, and a shop that contains more tools and larger machinery. For any particular carpentry job you put a different set of tools into your tool belt, tool box, and tool chest to reduce the number of trips you have to make up and down the ladder to the tool box, walking back and forth to the tool chest and driving to and from the shop. The combination of tools in your tool belt varies with the job, simply because it isn't practical to carry everything on your belt. The same applies to the tool box, chest, and even the shop. The things you need most often are kept in closer proximity to you.

Computer architectures have adopted an analogous strategy of keeping data close to the processor. Moreover, the distance, measured in processor clocks, to storage devices increases as their capacity increases. The processor's set of registers are, of course, the closest storage devices. The next closest storage devices are referred to as caches and usually vary in size from a few hundred bytes to several megabytes (MB). Caches are usually made with static random access memory (SRAM) chips. Beyond caches lies the main memory system. Most computer main memory systems are built from dynamic random access memory (DRAM) chips. Some memory systems are built with SRAMs (e.g., the Cray T90), rendering them faster than DRAM, but expensive. At the next level of storage hierarchy is the magnetic disk. Magnetic disks are truly the workhorses of data storage, playing important roles in virtual memory and file systems. As storage devices become larger, they typically are farther away from the processor and the path to them becomes narrower and sometimes more complicated. The typical memory hierarchy and its basic components are illustrated in Figure 3-1.

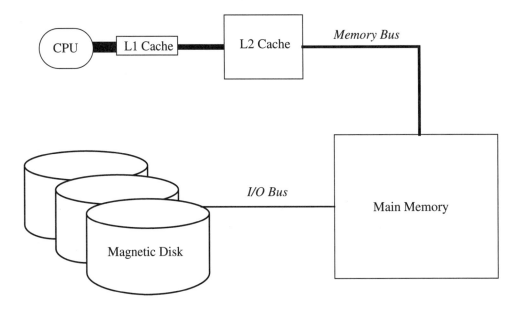

Figure 3-1   Typical memory hierarchy for modern computers.

3.2 Caches

Registers are the closest user accessible data storage areas to the functional units. Typically, CISC and RISC processors have fewer than 100 registers and hence these don't contain much data. Memory is very far from the processor in terms of processor clocks, so intermediate storage areas are desired. Cache is a type of memory located between the processor and main memory.

The largest data caches on high performance processors are usually a few megabytes in size. Cache may be on-chip (physically part of the processor chip) or off-chip.

3.2.1 Cache Line

A cache line is the smallest unit of data that can be transferred to or from memory. A cache line may contain more than one datum. These are the blocks of data that are brought into the cache from memory. Cache lines are usually between 32 and 128 bytes. Since memory is many times larger than cache, multiple addresses from memory MUST map to the same cache line. To not do this would mean that only a small portion of memory could utilize the cache.

There are advantages and disadvantages to having longer (i.e., larger) cache lines. Measured in clocks, the overhead in identifying which cache line to move is likely to be the same regardless of line size. So, if we assume that the time per byte of data is the same, then the resulting bandwidth (bytes/second) will be better. Hence, processors with longer cache lines typically have higher memory bandwidth performance. Long cache lines are good for algorithms that access memory with unit stride accesses since each element of the cache line is used. On the other hand, if an algorithm accesses memory in a random manner (e.g., indirect accesses), then computers with short cache lines may perform better, since the algorithm may access only a single datum in any given cache line.

3.2.2 Cache Organization

Generally speaking, caches are organized so that a cache line can be placed in a certain set of locations in the cache. If there are multiple sets, then the cache is referred to as being set associative. Usually the cache is organized so that any cache line from memory can map to one cache line in any of n sets. This is referred to as a n-way set associative cache. Fully associative caches are those where a cache line can be placed anywhere in the cache.

The simplest (and cheapest) type of cache is direct mapped, which is actually a one-way set associative cache. If the cache size is one MB, then any two locations in memory that are one MB apart map to the same cache line in the cache. For example, data located at hexadecimal addresses 0x0010000, 0x00200000, 0x00300000, ... , 0xFFF00000 are multiples of one MB apart and all must use the same location in a direct mapped cache. An improvement on the direct mapped cache is a two-way associative cache. When a cache line is brought into cache, it is placed in one, but not both, of the two sets. If the cache line and total cache size are held constant, a two-way set associative cache will experience less cache thrashing than a direct mapped cache. Increasing the associativity usually continues to increase performance, but the additional benefit decreases beyond a certain way of associativity.

A fully associative cache is the most advanced (and expensive) type of cache. Due to the complexities involved and resulting expense, these caches tend to be small in size.

3.2.3   Cache Mechanisms

Cache line replacement strategy and write policies are two important performance issues relating to caches. Strategies for cache line replacement are manifested in n-way set associative caches for n > 1. Users don't have to worry about this functionality with direct mapped caches because the decision is already made for you! Some processors update the cache line in the set that was Least Recently Used (LRU), while others randomly choose which one to update or use round-robin replacement. There are other replacement strategies, but these are actually the two most common and they represent both ends of the performance spectrum. LRU usually performs better than random replacement, but it is more difficult to implement.

When a processor performs a store instruction, it typically writes data into the cache-resident line containing the address. In general, there are two policies for dealing with the cache line subsequent to its having data written into it. In the first policy, the data is written to both the cache line in the cache and to main memory. This is referred to as *write through* since the write is made to main memory through the cache. The second policy, which is much more common, is referred to as *write back*. In this case, when a processor executes a store instruction, the data is written only to the cache line in the cache. This modified cache line is written to memory only when necessary (usually when it is replaced in the cache by another cache line). Note that this write back may occur much later than the actual store instruction's execution. As a result, write back caches usually make fewer memory transactions, which is a good thing as we shall see later. All caches discussed in this chapter are assumed to be write back caches.

3.2.4   Cache Thrashing

The main problem with direct mapped caches is that severe cache thrashing can occur. To illustrate what is meant by *cache thrashing*, consider the following:

```
REAL*8 X(*), Y(*)
...
DO I = 1, N
   Y(I) = X(I) + Y(I)
ENDDO
```

This requires loading X(I), loading Y(I), adding X(I) and Y(I), and storing Y(I) for each iteration (value of I).

Suppose we are executing this loop on a machine with a single, direct mapped, 1 MB cache and that a cache line is 32 bytes in length. If X and Y are arrays of eight-byte data (e.g., data declared as REAL*8 in Fortran) then X and Y could be allocated as illustrated in Figure 3-2. That is, X and Y are a multiple of the cache size apart in memory. On the first iteration elements X(1) through X(4) are loaded into cache and X(1) is loaded into a register. Note that operations in Figure 3-2 that force cache lines to be moved between the cache and memory are highlighted in bold. Then Y(1) through Y(4) are loaded into cache from memory and Y(1) is loaded into a register. Note that the cache line containing Y(1) displaces the cache line contain-

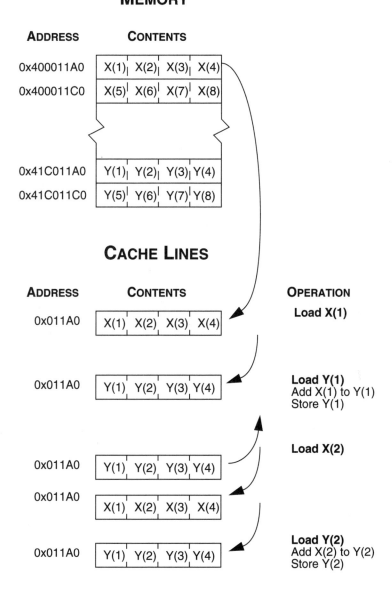

Figure 3-2   Example of cache thrashing.

ing X(1) through X(4). Completing the iteration, X(1) and Y(1) are added and Y(1) is stored. On the second iteration, X(2) must be loaded. This requires that elements X(1) through X(4) be again loaded into cache. But this displaces the cache line containing Y(1) and hence forces that line to be stored to memory (because Y(1) has been modified) before the line containing X(1) through X(4) can be loaded into the cache. Each load of X and each load of Y requires that the data be moved to and from memory. In this case, the cache is nearly useless. This process of repeatedly displacing and loading cache lines is referred to as *cache thrashing*.

If the cache happened to be a two-way set associative cache, then most, if not all, of this thrashing would be eliminated. This is because the cache line for X would likely reside in one set of the cache and the cache line for Y in the other. Both round-robin and least-recently-used replacement strategies would address this situation very well. A random replacement approach might take a few iterations before getting it right. That is, since the set number to be replaced is generated randomly, the result could easily be that the first set is replaced multiple times before selecting the second set (or vice-versa).

The previous example was derived from an example where the arrays X and Y were declared as follows:

```
REAL*8 X(7340032), Y(7340032)
```

Note that 7340032 in hexadecimal is 0x700000, which is seven MB, an integral multiple of the cache size.

If the first array had been "padded" so that it was not a multiple of the cache size apart, then this cache thrashing could have been avoided. Suppose X and Y were declared as follows:

```
REAL*8 X(7340036), Y(7340036)
```

Then many memory transactions will be eliminated. Note that the padding is for four elements. Since each element is eight bytes, this is effectively padding the array by one cache line (32 bytes = 4×8 bytes). With the arrays declared as above, we then have a sequence of operations as outlined in Figure 3-3. Not only does the second iteration not require any memory transactions, neither does iteration 3 or 4! At the beginning of iteration five, the cache line containing Y(1) through Y(4) will have to be stored to memory, so we will have roughly three memory transactions for every four iterations. Compare this to the previous example where we had three memory transactions for every single iteration.

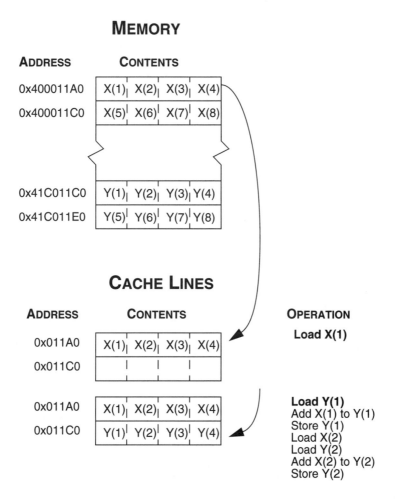

Figure 3-3 Cache thrashing eliminated by padding arrays.

To demonstrate the difference in performance, the example above was executed on an HP V-Class computer with a two MB direct-mapped cache. With N set to 7340032 in both cases, the resulting times to execute the loop are shown in Table 3-1.

Table 3-1   Performance of $Y(I) = X(I) + Y(I)$ for Loop with Fixed Length.

Array Dimension	Elapsed Time (sec.)
7340032	7.21
7340036	3.52

3.2.5   Caching Instructions Versus Data

One compelling reason for using direct mapped caches is that they are easier to implement than associative caches. One benefit of this is that processors can access direct mapped caches faster than associative caches. This can be extremely important for data as well as instructions. It may not matter how much data you have in registers if the processor continuously stalls waiting on instructions.

The area of memory reserved for the executable instructions of a program is referred to as the *text* area. Nearly all workloads require more megabytes of data than they do of text. Some architectures use a single cache for both instructions and data. Such caches are generally referred to as *unified* caches. One can easily imagine a situation where a series of instructions that are repeatedly executed (e.g., a loop) just happen to map to the same cache line(s) as the data. This sort of cache thrashing is very difficult to identify, not to mention remedy. Modern computer architectures have alleviated this problem in two different ways. One is to have associative unified caches and another is to have the instruction cache separate from the data cache. The latter solution is to literally have two, independent caches. Unified associative caches still run the risk of text displacing data (and vice versa), but having separate instruction cache and data cache eliminates this problem. So, what is becoming the most common implementation in the industry? A combination of the two, of course! Most new architectures feature separate I and D caches that are small and very close to the processor with another, larger unified cache that is a little farther away. This brings us to the next topic.

3.2.6   Multiple Levels of Caches

It's already been established that faster memory is more expensive than slower memory. In particular, cache is much faster and more expensive than main memory. There is so much truth in this that one sometimes wonders if caches should be spelled c-a-s-h! Given the advantages of cache to today's processor performance, it is easy to see how an intermediate level of cache might be beneficial and economically feasible. Consider the Compaq AlphaServer DS20 machine which has a 500 MHz Alpha 21264 processor with a 64 KB instruction cache and 64 KB data cache on chip and an intermediate (or secondary) cache that is four MB in size. The primary benefit of such caches is, of course, to reduce the average time per access to memory.

Suppose we have a workload which we have studied and we are able to produce a rough estimate of how often memory accesses occur as a function of the data storage available. Table 3-2 is a representative listing of this information.

Table 3-2   Memory Accesses Relative to Data Storage Available for a Synthetic Workload.

Size Range	Cumulative Percentage of Memory Accesses	Percentage of Accesses in This Range
0 - 4 KB	72%	72%
4 - 16 KB	83%	11%
16 - 64KB	87%	4%
64 - 256 KB	90%	3%
256 KB - 1 MB	92%	2%
1 - 4 MB	95%	3%
4 - 16 MB	99%	4%
16 - 64 MB	100%	1%

Now consider three different cache architectures with the same processor and memory system. Suppose they have cache structure and attributes as shown in Table 3-3. Note that only Architecture 3 has two caches.

Table 3-3   Data Storage Sizes and Associated Access Times for Hypothetical Architectures.

Architecture	L1 Cache Size	L1 Access Time (Cycles)	L2 Cache Size	L2 Access Time (Cycles)
1	1 MB	3	None	N/A
2	4 MB	5	None	N/A
3	16 KB	1	4 MB	6

If we assume it is 100 clocks from the processor to main memory for all three architectures, then, using the data in Table 3-2 and Table 3-3, we can produce the expected number of clock cycles for an average data access for all three architectures.

For architecture 1, 92% of the accesses are in one MB of data storage or less. So:

Expected latency for architecture 1 = 92% × 3 cycles + 8% × 100 cycles = 10.76 cycles.

Now, architecture 2 has a four MB cache and so 95% of the accesses are estimated to occur within it. Thus:

Expected latency for architecture 2 = 95% × 5 cycles + 5% × 100 cycles = 9.75 cycles.

So, all else being equal, architecture 1 is likely to be faster for this application than architecture 2 even though it has a smaller cache! The remaining cache architecture has the following:

Expected latency for architecture 3 = 83% × 1 cycle + 12% × 6 cycles + 5% × 100 cycles = 6.55 cycles

What an improvement! Even though the primary cache is very small and the secondary cache is the same size and slower than that of architecture 2, it is much faster than either of the other cache architectures.

3.3 Virtual Memory Issues

3.3.1 Overview

Most of today's computers are virtual memory machines. Such machines translate logical memory addresses in a user's program to physical memory addresses. There are several advantages that virtual memory machines have over those machines that do not have virtual memory.

They allow programs that have logical address space requirements larger than physical memory to execute, albeit slowly. Virtual memory machines are capable of executing multiple processes which, when combined, occupy several times more memory than is actually in the machine.

Even though a process' address space appears to be sequential on a virtual memory, it is likely not to be in the physical address space. This is because virtual memory systems break up a process' memory into blocks, usually referred to as *pages*. Page sizes are typically four KB or larger in size and do not always have to be uniform, i.e., a process may have several pages that are four KB in size and yet several more pages which are one MB or larger. By breaking virtual memory into pages, the operating system can place some of the pages on magnetic disk. In this way, the operating system can keep only those pages currently being accessed by the process in physical memory, with the remainder residing on disk. When memory is accessed in a page that is not currently in physical memory, the operating system copies the page in question from disk and places it in physical memory. This may cause another page to be displaced from physical memory, which forces the operating system to place it on disk. The location on magnetic disk that is used for virtual memory pages is called *swap space* since it is used to swap pages in and out of physical memory.

The operating system needs a map to translate virtual memory addresses to physical memory addresses. This is done by mapping pages in virtual memory to those in physical memory. A common way to accomplish this is with a lookup table, generally referred to as a *page table*. Processes typically have multiple page tables, including page tables for text, data areas, etc.

3.3.2   The Translation Lookaside Buffer

So, accessing a particular location in memory involves identifying which page table to use and then performing the virtual to physical translation, using that table to finally retrieve the data. Many applications access memory sequentially, so translations for the same page are often repeated many times. To take advantage of this situation, most virtual memory machines have a special cache referred to as a *Translation Lookaside Buffer* (TLB), which contains physical to virtual memory translations. Typically, the TLB translations (or lookups) and instruction execution occur simultaneously so that memory operations occur very quickly. In the event that a process accesses memory which does not have its translation in the TLB, it is said to encounter a TLB *miss*. When a TLB miss occurs, the page identification and subsequent translation need to be constructed and the result placed in the TLB.

Most TLBs are located on chip and, as a result, are small in size. This fact, in combination with inadvertent programming mistakes, can result in a high number of TLB misses. There are two primary solutions for this problem—reducing the number of pages that need to be translated or programming to avoid causing a high number of TLB misses.

Probably the most common cause of TLB misses is due to memory being accessed with large, often constant, distances between them. The distance between memory accesses is usually referred to as stride. Unit stride is used to describe memory accesses that are sequential, i.e., the next element is exactly one element away. A stride of seven refers to a memory access pattern where every seventh element in a list is accessed, skipping over six elements at a time. Multidimensional arrays have inherently long strides, depending on how they are accessed. For example, an array declared as follows,

```
REAL*8 X(1000,2000)
```

has a stride of 1000 between columns, meaning that x(N,1) and x(N,2) are 1000 elements apart, regardless of the value of N. Consider the following sequence of code:

```
REAL*8 X(1000,1000), Y(1000,1000)
...
DO I=1, M
  DO J=1, N
    X(I,J) = Y(I,J)
  END DO
END DO
```

Assume that both X and Y are declared as above. Then, regardless of the values of M or N, the execution of this sequence of code results in both X and Y being accessed with strides of 1000. Note that this means that X(I,1) and X(I,2) are 8000 bytes apart. Many computers use a page size of only four KB. If this code were executed on such a machine, then each iteration of the inner loop forces two different TLB entries (one for X() and one for Y()).

To illustrate the severity of TLB misses and the benefit of being able to use larger page sizes, the following sequence of code was executed on a HP N-4000 computer:

```
for( j = 0; j < jmax; j++ )
{
  for( i = 0; i < imax; i++ )
    x[i*stride + j] = 1.1 + x[i*stride + j];
}
```

This is clearly a deliberate attempt to cause TLB misses, because the array x is a double precision array and hence each element is eight bytes in size. The value of stride is set to 516, which translates to a byte stride of 4128; the value of jmax is fixed at 256 while imax is varied from 256 to 2048. The result is a test which accessed from 0.5 MB to 4 MB of data. The HP N-4000 has a 1 MB, four-way set associative cache which, when combined with a stride of 516, keeps the cache misses to a minimum. The results are astounding, as illustrated in Table 3-4. Note the time per access for the 0.5 MB problem size drops sharply after the page size is increased from 4 KB to 16 KB. This implies that a TLB miss takes roughly 160 ns since the data

(0.5 MB) resides entirely in cache. More importantly, it's interesting that TLB misses can cause your code to run over 30 times slower!

Table 3-4   TLB Misses in Nanoseconds as a Function of Page Size and Overall Problem Size.

Page Size	Problem Size			
	512 KB	1 MB	2 MB	4 MB
4 KB	163.4	170.3	216.1	224.5
16 KB	4.9	6.3	77.9	81.9
64 KB	4.9	6.1	22.0	23.8
256 KB	4.9	6.2	22.0	23.8
1 MB	4.9	6.1	22.4	24.1
4 MB	4.9	6.2	22.2	23.9

3.4 Memory

To the casual observer, memory systems appear to be the most elementary part of the computer. It seems to be simply a large number of identical computer chips which store data. This is, of course, far from reality.

The memory system or *main memory,* as it is typically described, is the crossroads of data movement in the computer. Data moving to and from caches moves through the memory system. Input and output devices such as magnetic disk, network devices, and magnetic tape all have the main memory system as the target of their output and the source of their input.

Computer hardware vendors have, by increasing address space capabilities, themselves caused memory capacity demands to increase. During the 70's almost all computer vendors moved from 16-bit addresses to 32-bit. As we move into the next millennium, most computers will have 64-bit address spaces. As a result, memory systems that used to be measured in kilobytes (KB) are now measured in gigabytes (GB).

With the economies of scale in processors, multiprocessor computers have evolved from simply having two processors in the 80's to configurations with literally thousands of processors. At the same time, memory systems are expected to be capable of "feeding" all these data-consuming processors.

So, while complexity in processor design has increased at a dramatic rate, memory systems have been driven to keep up with them—albeit unsuccessfully. Added to this pressure is the tremendous increase in multiprocessor systems that require not just faster memory systems, but larger capacity systems that allow overall performance to scale with the number of processors.

3.4.1   Basics of Memory Technology

Random access memory is by far the most popular memory chip technology today. It is described as random because it allows you to address any particular memory location without having to step through memory in sequential fashion until you arrive at the desired destination. Most memory systems today (including caches) consist of dynamic random access memory (DRAM) or static random access memory (SRAM).

DRAM is less expensive as it typically requires only a single transistor per bit. The downside is that, due their simplicity, the electrical charge must be periodically refreshed. Hence, DRAM can be periodically unavailable because it is being refreshed. SRAM doesn't require periodic refreshes, which allows it to be faster but more complex—generally requiring five to six transistors per bit. The result is a more expensive piece of hardware.

There are two times that are important in measuring memory performance: access time and cycle time. *Access time* is the total time from when a read or write is requested until it actually arrives at its destination. *Cycle time* is the minimum time between requests to memory. Note that since SRAM does not need to be refreshed, there is no difference between access time and cycle time.

3.4.2   Interleaving

Simple memory system organizations using DRAM (which is most likely since it is less expensive than SRAM) result in each memory transaction's requiring the sum of access time plus cycle time. One way to improve this is to construct the memory system so that it consists of multiple banks of memory organized so that sequential words of memory are located in different banks. Addresses can be sent to multiple banks simultaneously and multiple words can then be retrieved simultaneously. This will improve performance substantially. Having multiple, independent memory banks benefits single processor performance as well as multiprocessor performance because, with enough banks, different processors can be accessing different sets of banks simultaneously. This practice of having multiple memory banks with sequential words distributed across them in a round-robin fashion is referred to as *interleaving*. Interleaving reduces the effective cycle time by enabling multiple memory requests to be performed simultaneously.

The benefits of interleaving can be defeated when the memory access pattern is such that the same banks are accessed repeatedly. Let us assume that we have a memory system with 16 banks and that the computer uses cache lines which contain 4 words, with each word being 8 bytes in size. If the following loop is executed on this computer, then the same set of banks is being accessed repeatedly (since stride = 64 words = 16 * 4 words):

```
double *x;
...
stride = 64;
sum = 0.0;
for( j = 0; j < jmax; j++ )
{
   for( i = 0; i < imax; i++ )
      sum += x[i*stride + j];
}
```

As a result, each successive memory access has to wait until the previous one completes (the sum of the access time and cycle time). This causes the processor (and hence the user's program) to stall on each memory access. This predicament is referred to as a *bank stall* or *bank contention*.

Let's revisit the sequence of code used in the previous TLB discussion:

```
for( j = 0; j < jmax; j++ )
{
   for( i = 0; i < imax; i++ )
      x[i*stride + j] = 1.1 + x[i*stride + j];
}
```

First, fix `imax` at 16384 and `jmax` at 512 so that the problem size is 64 MB in size. In Figure 3-4, we show the average access time for various hardware platforms using several values of stride. Two sets of data are charted for the HP N-4000, one using 4 KB pages and another using 1 MB pages. Note the tremendous difference in performance for the N-4000 caused by TLB misses, as illustrated by the divergence in the graphs after a stride of 16. This data was generated using 8 KB pages on the SUN UE3500 and 16 KB pages on the SGI Origin 2000. Note that, even with 1 MB pages, the N-4000's performance decreases after a stride of 8, indicating that memory bank contention is hindering performance.

Page size does not just benefit applications that use a lot of data, it also benefits those that have a large text (i.e., instructions) segment. Electronic design simulations, relational database engines, and operating systems are all examples of applications whose performance is sensitive to text size.

How does one alter the page size for an executable? HP-UX provides a mechanism to change the attributes of an executable file. This can be accomplished by a system utility, `chatr`. For the tests discussed here, the executable was modified to request four KB data pages with the following command:

```
chatr +pd 4K ./a.out
```

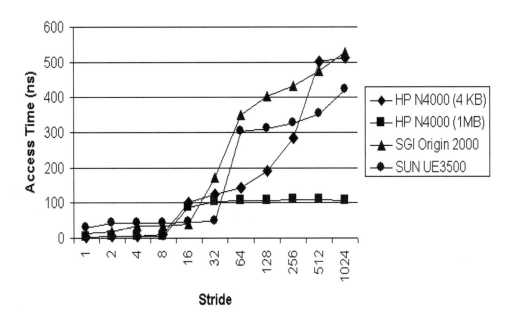

Figure 3-4   Memory access time as a function of word stride for various computers.

Similarly,

```
chatr +pd 1M ./a.out
```

modified the executable to request 1 MB data pages.

Does this imply that all applications should use huge, say, one MB, pages to improve performance? Not necessarily. Consider the processes that are executing constantly (e.g., daemons) on a computer; usually there are a dozen or more. Daemons typically occupy only about 100 to 200 KB of memory and hence with 4 KB pages a couple dozen of them would use less than 5 MB of memory. However, if each of them were to use one MB pages, then they would each occupy at least one MB of memory per daemon for a total of 24 MB. Since these applications run constantly, the computer will be using 19 MB (24 - 5) of memory unnecessarily! So, it's not always a good idea to use huge pages, but for applications that use a large amount of memory, it can give large boosts in performance.

3.4.3 Hiding Latency

With processor speeds improving at a faster rate than memory speeds, there have been multiple approaches to overcome delays due to memory accesses. One solution we've discussed is the creation of caches. Another successful approach enables processors to issue memory requests and continue execution until the data requested is used by another instruction in the program. This is referred to as *stall-on-use*. Another strategy is to enable prefetching of data either automatically (in hardware) or through the use of special prefetch instructions.

Processors implemented with stall-on-use which can issue multiple memory transactions can do a good job of hiding or reducing effective memory latency. For example, suppose such a processor is capable of issuing up to 10 memory transactions and the realizable memory latency is 200 clocks. Then the effective memory latency can be as little as 200 / 10 = 20 clocks!

Prefetching can also dramatically reduce effective memory latency. Note that if a prefetch instruction can be issued for data more than 200 clocks before the data is accessed by a regular memory instruction, then the memory latency will be reduced to that of the cache latency. This is because the delay of 200 clocks or more allows the data to be moved into the cache (i.e., prefetched).

Data prefetching can be accomplished with software or hardware. Some hardware platforms actually detect when a processor is accessing memory sequentially and will begin prefetching the data from memory into the processor's cache without any other intervention. Most computers that support prefetching do so with software prefetching. This is typically done through the use of special instructions or instruction arguments. For example, PA-RISC 2.0 processors perform software prefetching by interpreting load instructions into a special register as prefetches.

3.5 Input/Output Devices

3.5.1 Magnetic Storage Device Issues

Today's magnetic disk technology provides the consumer with a dilemma that is not likely to resolve itself in the near future. On the one hand, disk space is cheap, with single disk drives providing several GB of capacity at a fraction of a penny per MB. Performance is another story. These same disk drives are capable of only several MB/sec of bandwidth performance. A single disk drive may have a capacity of 70 GB but can only sustain eight MB/sec of I/O bandwidth.

One way to improve bandwidth is to define a logical device which consists of multiple disks. With this sort of approach a single I/O transaction can simultaneously move blocks of data to multiple disks. For example, if a logical device is created from eight disks, each of which is capable of sustaining 10 MB/sec, then this logical device is capable of delivering up to 80 MB/sec of I/O bandwidth! Such logical devices are commonplace and are critical to the delivery of high bandwidth to and from files stored on magnetic disk.

Unfortunately, the construction of such logical devices so that they are able to deliver good I/O bandwidth can be tricky. One common mistake is to assume that multiple disk drives can be chained from a single I/O slot (that is, a single card/controller). Frequently I/O cards have a peak bandwidth inherent in their design which ultimately limits realizable I/O performance. To illustrate the problem, consider an I/O card that is capable of only 40 MB/sec. Building a logical device using a single card with the 8 disks mentioned above limits performance to only half of the disks' aggregate capabilities. However, if two cards are used with the 8 disks (4 disks on each card), then the logical device is capable of up to 80 MB/sec of I/O bandwidth.

Most memory systems of server or mainframe class computers today are capable of delivering over 400 MB/sec of memory bandwidth per processor. In order to construct a logical device with magnetic disks capable of providing data at half this rate, one would need 20 of the disks discussed above. The capacity of these disks, using 10 GB disks, is a whopping 200 GB—for just one processor! Such is the dilemma of system configuration with regard to magnetic disk storage: High performance magnetic disk will go hand-in-hand with a tremendous amount of storage, perhaps far more than is necessary.

3.5.2   Buffer Cache

Most operating systems today maintain a block of memory to hold files or at least pieces of files that processes are reading or writing. This block of memory is usually referred to as the file system buffer, or simply buffer cache. Buffer cache plays a role very much like the processor cache. Whenever a process accesses a location in a file, the operating system moves a block, usually a file system block, into the buffer cache. Subsequent accesses to locations in that block will be made using the memory system rather than having to access magnetic disk (which is often an order of magnitude slower).

Not only can a buffer cache improve I/O to a block (of a file) that has already been accessed, but it also allows the operating system to predict user accesses. Probably the most common example of this is *read ahead*. Many applications will access a file sequentially, from beginning to end. Sophisticated operating systems will monitor an application's accesses to a file and, once it detects that the file is being read sequentially, it will begin reading blocks into buffer cache asynchronously to the user process. This is yet another form of prefetching.

As it turns out, many applications also read files sequentially from the end to the beginning. Yet others stride through files, skipping over a constant number of blocks between those it accesses. HP's SPP-UX was one of the very few operating systems sophisticated enough to perform read ahead with such complicated patterns.

3.6 I/O Performance Tips for Application Writers

3.6.1   The I/O Routines You Use Will Make a Difference

Let's start this section with a simple question—do you travel to the supermarket and purchase two slices of bread each time you make a sandwich? Well, we certainly hope not. You probably buy a loaf of bread at a time and take two slices of bread from it each time you make a sandwich. The time and economics involved in travelling to the supermarket for individual items are not practical.

In an effort to duplicate this efficiency of getting several things with each trip to the more remote storage devices, buffered I/O mechanisms were developed. The most common is that found in the C programming language with the `fread()` and `fwrite()` subroutines.

This mechanism, described as buffered binary I/O to a stream file, works roughly as follows. A file is opened with the `fopen()` subroutine call instead of the `open()` system call. In the process of opening this file, `fopen()` also initializes data structures to maintain a buffer, allocated in the user's address space (as opposed to the kernel's address space). This buffer varies in size and the user can actually manipulate how this buffer is allocated and what its size will be. Subsequent to the `fopen()` call, transfers to and from the file are accomplished with calls to the subroutines `fwrite()` and `fread()`, respectively. These subroutines first check to see if the data being requested is already in the buffer. If it is, then the data is simply copied from the buffer into the destination specified by the procedure call. Thus, no system call is made and no transfer of data is made to or from the kernel's address space (i.e., buffer cache). If the data is not already in the buffer, then the subroutines make the necessary system call to move blocks of data into and out of the buffer from the file.

Some implementations of these buffered binary I/O routines use relatively small buffers. As a result, these routines can be slower than system calls for large transfers. One way to improve this situation is to make use of the `setvbuf()` routine. This routine allows the user to specify another buffer that can be much larger in size. For example, to change the internal buffer used by buffered I/O, one might use the following C code:

```
work_buffer = (char *)malloc(65536);
fp = fopen( workfile, "r+" );
if( fp == NULL ) { perror("fopen"); exit(-1); }
setvbuf( fp, work_buffer, _IOFBF, (size_t)65536 );
```

This sequence assigns the 64 KB array `work_buffer` to the file pointer `fp` to be used for its buffering. The performance benefit of doing this will be shown below.

Using language-specific I/O routines such as the Fortran I/O statements (e.g., `open()`, `read()`, `write()`, etc.) can be extremely detrimental to performance. Implementations vary, but in many cases these routines are built on top of the buffered binary I/O mechanisms (`fopen()`, `fread()`, `fwrite()`, etc.) discussed above. Fortran provides for some additional functionality in these I/O routines, which leads to yet more overhead for doing the actual I/O transfers. Fortran read performance is typically worse than either using the system call interface or the buffered binary I/O mechanisms.

To illustrate this, a comparison of reading a file using the `read()` system call, `fread()`, `fread()` with a 64 KB transfer size, and Fortran I/O was made on a HP N-4000 server using HP-UX 11.0 operating system. The Fortran I/O was performed with an implied DO loop using the following calls:

```
OPEN( FILDES, FORM='UNFORMATTED', FILE='./tmp/temp.test' );
...
READ( FILDES ) ( BUFFER(J),J=1,BUFFER_SIZE );
```

Note that the default buffer size for HP-UX's buffered binary I/O is eight KB. The time to make transfers of various sizes is given in Table 3-5. The times shown are the milliseconds per transfer for using various I/O interfaces. A 100 MB file was read sequentially starting from the beginning of the file to produce these times. The file system buffer cache was configured to be roughly 500 MB in size so that the file would fit entirely in the buffer cache. So, the times reflect transfers from the buffer cache and not from magnetic disk.

Table 3-5   Average Time, in Microseconds, to Read Data From Files Using Three Common Interfaces as a Function of Transfer Size.

Transfer Size (bytes)	read system call	fread	Fortran unformatted read
8	5.76	0.27	2.87
64	6.47	0.43	3.09
1 K	9.09	3.13	5.41
8 K	20.11	23.48	30.30
64 K	115.74	198.05	244.34

From the table, one can draw many conclusions. Note that the buffered binary I/O mechanism is very efficient for small (less than four KB) transfers. For transfers of eight KB or more, the binary I/O interface (`fread`) benefits from a larger I/O buffer; in this case, 64 KB was used. However, note that using a system call to perform the I/O is substantially faster than the other methods for transfers of eight KB or more. Under no circumstances is the Fortran I/O faster than any of the other interfaces.

One word of warning with regard to the use of large (more than 64 KB) transfer sizes and system calls. Some file systems are capable of being configured so that transfers exceeding a certain size will bypass the file system buffer cache. This is referred to as *direct I/O* or *buffer cache bypass*. The intent is to keep extremely large files from occupying the entire buffer cache and/or to reduce the load on the memory system by eliminating the additional copy from buffer cache memory to user memory. The downside to this approach is that the operating system cannot perform read-ahead. Hence, the user will not benefit from memory-to-memory copy speeds.

There's actually another lesson in Table 3-5. If we divide the transfer sizes by the time, we can get bandwidth performance. Table 3-6 contains a variation of Table 3-5 modified to reflect bandwidth rather than the amount of time per transfer. Note that the read system call delivers roughly twice the performance of other common interfaces. Thus if an application can do its own buffering, that is, read in 64 KB of data at a time, then the benefits can be tremendous.

Table 3-6 Effective Bandwidth in MB/Second for Various I/O Interfaces as a Function of Transfer Size.

Transfer Size (bytes)	read system call	fread	Fortran unformatted read
8	1.33	28.30	2.66
64	9.43	142.31	19.73
1 K	107.43	312.41	180.44
8 K	388.43	332.72	257.82
64 K	539.99	315.57	244.34

The poor performance of Fortran I/O is now clear. Note that the read system call using large transfers delivers the best bandwidth. So, if your application can do its own buffering and use system calls to transfer data between your buffer and files, then that could well be the best performance option.

3.6.2   Asynchronous I/O

The Portable Operating System Interface (POSIX) standard defines a set of interfaces that enables the programmer to perform I/O asynchronous to program execution. Basically, an asynchronous read or write is accomplished by creating or using an additional flow of control to perform the actual I/O while the user's program continues to execute. This is illustrated for an asynchronous read in Figure 3-5 below. Note the use of the `aio_suspend()` routine to cause the calling program to suspend processing until the read completes.

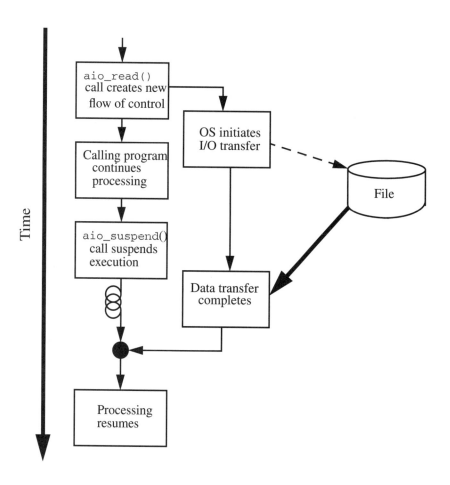

Figure 3-5 Asynchronous I/O enables processing to continue without waiting for file transfers to complete.

Asynchronous I/O provides the benefits of system call performance with parallelism. Details of the POSIX asynchronous I/O facility will be discussed in Chapter 8, and it should be considered for use in I/O intensive applications. There are some downsides to use of asynchronous I/O functions. Some implementations of asynchronous I/O actually create an additional flow of control in the operating system and then destroy it upon the function's completion. This can add a tremendous amount of time to that required to actually transfer the data. SGI's IRIX operating system provides the `aio_sgi_init()` function to alleviate this problem. The user can identify the number of asynchronous operations to be used by the program, allowing the operating system to more efficiently service those operations.

3.7 Summary

This chapter has provided many tips to the application writer on how to avoid performance problems related to storage devices ranging from caches to file systems. The important issues are:

- Avoid cache thrashing and memory bank contention by dimensioning multidimensional arrays so that the dimensions are not powers of two.

- Eliminate TLB misses and memory bank contention by accessing arrays in unit stride.

- Reduce TLB misses by using large pages on applications with large memory (data or text) usage.

- Avoid Fortran I/O interfaces.

- Do your own buffering for I/O and use system calls to transfer large blocks of data to and from files.

References:

The following publications are excellent resources for the parallel programming and other topics discussed in this section:

1. Hennessy, J. L.; Patterson, D. A. *Computer Architecture, A Quantitative Approach,* Morgan Kaufmann, 1996. ISBN 1-55860-329-8.

2. Pfister, G. F. *In Search of Clusters*, Prentice Hall PTR, 1998. ISBN 0-13-899709-8.

3. Dowd, K. *High Performance Computing*, O'Reilly, 1993. ISBN 1-56592-032-5.

4. Kane, G. *PA-RISC 2.0 Architecture*, Prentice Hall PTR, 1996. ISBN 0-13-182734-0.

5. Institute of Electrical and Electronics Engineers. *Information Technology—Portable Operating System Interface (POSIX), Part 1: System Application Program Interface (API) [C Language]*, IEEE Std 1003.1-1990. ISBN 1-55937-061-0.

An Overview of Parallel Processing

If one ox could not do the job they did not try to grow a bigger ox, but used two oxen.

Grace Murray Hopper

4.1 Introduction

In a sense, we all perform parallel processing every day. Vision is accomplished through the use of one eye, but two eyes give additional peripheral vision as well as depth perception. Washing dishes is much faster when using two hands instead of one (especially in the absence of a dishwasher!). Getting work done faster by performing multiple tasks simultaneously is the driving force behind parallel processing.

In this chapter, the basic concepts of parallel processing are highlighted from both a software and hardware perspective. Details of efficient algorithm approaches and software implementation are discussed in Chapter 8.

Many years ago, Michael Flynn proposed a simple, common model of categorizing all computers that continues to be useful and applicable. The categories are determined by the instruction stream and the data stream that the computer can process at any given instant. All computers can be placed in one of these four categories:

- Single Instruction, Single Data (SISD)—This is the most common computer in the market-place today, the single processor system with one instruction stream and one data stream. Most PCs fall into this category.
- Multiple Instruction, Single Data (MISD)—The same data point is processed by multiple processors. No system of this type has ever been made commercially available.
- Single Instruction, Multiple Data (SIMD)—Multiple data streams are processed by multiple processors, each of which is executing the same (single) stream of instructions. There

have been several commercially successful manufacturers of SIMD machines, MASPAR and TMC are two well-known examples. Such machines have a single processor which executes the single instruction stream and dispatches subsets of these instructions to all the other processors (which are usually much simpler in design). Each of these slave processors processes its own data stream. SIMD computers are not very flexible. They are good for applications which perform similar operations on a lot of data, like linear algebra computations, but don't perform well on instruction streams that have a lot of branches—a description which fits most modern applications!

• Multiple Instruction, Multiple Data (MIMD)—This applies to machines which have multiple processors which are capable of executing independent instruction streams using their own, separate data streams. Such machines are far more flexible than SIMD systems and there are hundreds of different MIMD machines that are now available.

SISD and MIMD machines are the primary focus of this book. They also happen to account for about 99% of the computers sold today.

There's another term that sounds like it is another category, but it isn't. The acronym is SPMD and it stands for Single Program Multiple Data. This is a description of one approach to parallel programming. In SPMD there is one program and multiple processors execute the same program on multiple data sets. This is discussed again in Chapter 8.

4.2 Parallel Models

From an operating system perspective, there are two important means of accomplishing parallel processing: multiple processes and multiple threads.

When one executes a program on a computer, the operating system creates an entity called a *process* which has a set of resources associated with it. These resources include, but are not limited to, data structures containing information about the process, a virtual address space which contains the program's text (instructions) and data, and at least one thread. This begs the question, "What is a thread?"

A *thread* is an independent flow of control within a process, composed of a context (which includes a register set) and a sequence of instructions to execute. By independent flow of control, we mean an execution path through the program.

There are different levels of parallelism in computer systems today. As discussed in Chapter 2, LIW and superscalar RISC processors achieve parallelism at the instruction level. However, in the context of this book, we use the term *parallel processing* to describe the use of more than one thread of execution executing in a single program. Note that this allows more than one process to accomplish parallel processing. This leads to our being able to categorize parallel processing into three general categories:

- Process parallelism—Using more than one process to perform a set of tasks
- Thread parallelism—Using multiple threads within a single process to execute a set of tasks
- Hybrid parallelism—Using multiple processes, at least one of which is a thread-parallel process, to perform a set of tasks

Since parallelism can be achieved with multiple processes, why bother with thread-parallelism? There are at least two potential reasons: conservation of system resources and faster execution.

Threads share access to process data, open files, and other process attributes. For the following discussion, define a job as a set of tasks to be executed. Sharing data and text can dramatically reduce the resource requirements for a particular job. Contrast this to a collection of processes which will often duplicate the text and data areas in memory required for the job.

4.2.1   Thread Basics

Since a thread's context does not include all of a process's attributes, it is much easier to manage threads than processes. For example, threads can be created and destroyed much faster than processes. Threads do have other important, performance-related, attributes.

An idle thread is one which has no processing to do and is waiting for its next set of tasks. A thread is usually put into a wait state by having it check the value of a special variable. This variable usually is assigned one of two values, "locked" and "unlocked", which indicates that the thread has to wait or it can continue processing, respectively.

Idle threads can be suspended or spin-waiting. Suspended threads will relinquish their control of the processor that they were executing on. Spin-waiting threads will repeatedly check the variable to see if it is unlocked yet. This inhibits other processes from executing on that processor and, as a result, can dramatically degrade system throughput. However, restarting a suspended thread can take hundreds, if not thousands, of cycles.

Another thread attribute is affinity. When a suspended thread is reactivated, the operating system may have a choice of processors on which to schedule the thread. The practice of keeping a thread executing on and returning to the same processor for as long as possible is referred to as *affinity*. This is important because affinity enables the thread to benefit from any data encached during the thread's execution before it was suspended. Otherwise, it would have to load all the data it needs to execute from memory into the new processor's cache. One word of caution with regard to affinity: many computer vendors treat affinity as a request rather than a mandate that the thread *always* execute on a particular processor.

4.2.2   POSIX Threads

Although computer vendors have implemented threads in their operating systems for decades, there was no standardization until 1995, when a standard for thread programming was established as part of the Portable Operating System Interface (POSIX) standard. In particular,

POSIX 1003.1c is the portion of the overall POSIX standard covering threads. Included are the functions and Application Programming Interfaces (APIs) that support multiple flows of control within a process. Threads created and manipulated via this standard are generally referred to as *pthreads*. Previous to the establishment of pthreads, thread APIs were hardware vendor-specific, which made portability of thread-parallel applications an oxymoron. This, combined with the complexity of rewriting applications to use (and benefit from!) explicit thread control, resulted in very few thread-parallel applications.

4.2.3   Compiler Directives and OpenMP

The use of compiler directives to achieve parallelism is one attempt to alleviate these complexity and portability hurdles. Directive-based parallelism pushes most of the parallel mechanics work onto the compiler (e.g., generating the threads, creating synchronization constructs, etc.). That is, the compiler will translate the compiler directive into the appropriate procedure calls necessary for thread management and perform any needed code restructuring as well. Parallel loop directives became very popular as they provided an easy means of achieving parallelism.

Roughly speaking, this was the method of choice for achieving thread parallelism until the mid 1990s, and some argue that it still is. One thing that has furthered the use of directives is the OpenMP "standard" for parallel compiler directives. OpenMP is an *ad hoc* standard jointly defined for Fortran by computer hardware and software vendors and other organizations in October 1997. This was followed by a specification for C and C++ in November 1998. Before this standard, compiler directives were hardware vendor-specific and this made portability difficult, but not as difficult as using vendor-specific thread APIs. See `http://www.openmp.org/` for more details.

To illustrate the convenience, first consider the following code which uses pthreads interfaces to create four threads, each of which calls the subroutine `foobar()`:

```
#include <pthread.h>
#include <stdio.h>

void foobar(int *i)
{
    printf("Hello World <%d>\n",*i);
    pthread_exit( (void *) NULL );
    return;
}

main()
{

    pthread_t        tid[4];
    int       i, n, retval;
    int       iarg[4];
```

```
   for( i = 0; i < 4; i++ )
{
   iarg[i] = i;
   retval = pthread_create( tid+i, (pthread_attr_t *) NULL,
   (void *(*)())foobar,
   (void *) (iarg+i));
   if( retval > 0 ) perror("pthread_create");
}

   for( i = 0; i < 4; i++ )
{
   retval = pthread_join( tid[i], (void **) NULL );
   if( retval > 0 ) perror("pthread_create");
}
   exit(0);
}
```

Now consider the same effective result—four threads call `foobar()`—using an OpenMP compiler directive.

```
#include <stdio.h>

void foobar(int *i)
{
    printf("Hello World <%d>\n",*i);
    return;
}

main()
{

    pthread_t        tid[4];
    int      i, n, retval;
    int      iarg[4];

#    pragma omp parallel for
    for( i = 0; i < 4; i++ )
  {
     iarg[i] = i;
     foobar( iarg+i );
  }

    exit(0);
}
```

With regard to programming complexity, the examples speak for themselves, don't they?

Both explicit thread-parallel implementations (e.g., pthreads) and directive based parallelism (e.g., OpenMP) benefit from what is loosely referred to as "shared-memory." In both models, the threads can access the same virtual memory locations allocated before the threads are created. That is, thread 0 and 1 can both access x in the example below. Moreover, if thread 0 modifies the value of x, then thread 1 can subsequently retrieve this new value of x. Computer hardware manages the complexity of keeping such shared-memory values current. This feat is generally referred to as *coherency* and will be discussed later in Section 4.3.

4.2.4   Shared-Memory Parallelism — The fork/exec Model

As it turns out, thread-parallelism depends on the existence of shared-memory for communication. Another parallel model, older yet fairly portable, also uses shared-memory, but the memory is shared between processes! This model is generally referred to as *process parallelism* and is typically achieved through use of the `fork()` and `exec()` system calls (or their analogs). For this reason, it is often referred to as the *fork/exec model*. Memory is shared between the processes by virtue of the `mmap()` (derived from Berkeley UNIX) or `shmget()` (from System V UNIX) system calls.

Note that `fork()`, `exec()`, `mmap()`, and `shmget()` have been around for quite some time and are fairly standard in most UNIX implementations. So, it is easy to see why early shared-memory parallelism was actually achieved in a fairly portable way through the fork/exec model.

4.2.5   Message-passing

The fork/exec model does not imply the existence of shared-memory. Quite the contrary! Processes can communicate through I/O interfaces such as the `read()` and `write()` system calls. This communication can occur through a typical file or via sockets.

Communication via a file is easily done between processes which share a file system. This can be achieved on multiple systems via a shared file system such as NFS. Typically, communication is accomplished by creating a file lock (commonly a separate file with the suffix `.lck`) to establish exclusive access to the communication file.

Sockets are usually a more efficient means of communication between processes since they remove a lot of the overhead inherent in performing operations on the file system.

Both of these common variations, file system and sockets, rely on the process sending the data to be communicated to the file or socket. This data can be described as a message, that is, the sending process is passing a message to a receiving process. Hence the name for this model: *message-passing*.

There have been many different implementations of message-passing libraries. PARMACS (for parallel macros) and PVM (Parallel Virtual Machine) are two early examples that were successful. In an attempt to bring about a standard message-passing API, the Message-passing Interface (MPI) Forum put together a specification which was published in May 1994. See `http://www.mpi-forum.org/` for more details. MPI soon eclipsed PVM and some of the advantages of PVM, such as dynamic process creation, are slowly being adopted by the MPI standard. While it was intended primarily for distributed memory machines, it has the advantage that it can be used for parallel applications on shared-memory machines as well! MPI is intended for process parallelism, not thread-parallelism. This actually worked to MPI's benefit in its adoption by parallel software developers.

It is worth noting that the first specification for MPI occurred in 1994, a full four years before POSIX defined a thread-parallel API standard. The combination of early definition with its more general purpose utility resulted in more highly parallel applications being implemented with MPI than any other parallel programming model at the turn of the millennium.

4.3 Hardware Infrastructures for Parallelism

Historically, parallel computer architectures have been very diverse. There are still several basic architectures commercially available today. Moving forward, it is likely that only a few parallel architectures will be successful, but it isn't obvious what those architectures will be (or whether they all exist today!). The following sections give an overview of current parallel architectures and highlight their strengths and weaknesses. Entire books have been (and will be) written on this subject. The various parallel architectures are discussed from a programmer's perspective, providing enough insight to know what to expect in terms of performance and usability.

4.3.1   Clusters

A cluster is an interconnected collection of stand-alone computers that are used as a single computing resource. One extreme, yet common, example of a cluster is simply a set of several workstations that are placed in a room and interconnected by a low bandwidth connection like Ethernet. Since the workstations are just sitting on the floor somewhere with no special cabinet or rack, such a "system" is often referred to as a *carpet cluster*.

We'll loosely define a computing *node* as a collection of processors that share the lowest memory latency. By its very definition, a cluster's node is a single stand-alone computer. One of the advantages of a cluster is that each node is usually well-balanced in terms of processor, memory system, and I/O capabilities (because each node is a computer). Another of its advantages is cost; it usually consists of individual off-the-shelf workstations. Interconnect technology can be purchased off-the-shelf as well in the form of Ethernet, FDDI, etc. There are also proprietary interconnect technologies that offer higher performance but also have the inevitably higher price tags. Clusters are also very scalable since you can continue to add nodes to your parallel system by simply adding another workstation. The principal limiting factor is, of course, the capacity and performance of the interconnect.

The capacity and performance of interconnects are two disadvantages of clusters. Access to data that resides on the same node on which the application is running will be fast (as fast as the workstation, anyway). Data that exists on other nodes is another matter. Since the other node is a whole computer by itself, the data will likely have to be transferred via an I/O system call as discussed above in message-passing. That means that the data must travel across the wire (and protocol) from the remote node to the node that needs the data. This can be very slow, anywhere from 1 to 3 orders of magnitude slower than accessing local main memory.

Note that there is the issue of address space for an application. Clusters have multiple, independent address spaces, one for each node.

There's also the problem of system management. Without special cluster management software, it is very difficult to manage the system. Software must be installed on each individual node which can be a very time-consuming and expensive process (e.g., you may need a software license for each node!).

There's also the issue of the system's giving the impression of being a single system rather than a bunch of computers. Any user would like to log onto a system and find his data (e.g., files) as he left it when he was last working on the system. Without sophisticated cluster system software, this is not the case with clusters. There are extremes in this experience. On the one hand, the user may log on to the same workstation in the cluster on every occasion. This may actually be a good thing; at least the data will look like it did last time he worked on the system. However, if every user is placed on the same workstation, they are likely to see poor performance while they all contend for that single workstation's processing resources to address their basic login requirements. The other extreme is that users may actually log on to a different workstation within the cluster every time. In this scenario, one's environment may look different every time, causing immense confusion for the cluster neophyte.

To summarize, the advantages of clusters include truly scalable systems at a relatively inexpensive cost. The disadvantages of clusters include system administration difficulties, lack of a single system image, and poor interconnect performance.

4.3.2   Symmetric MultiProcessors (SMPs)

Most computer hardware manufacturers are taking another approach to avoid the problems of clusters. Enter the multiprocessor computer in which all the processors have access to all machine resources, including memory and I/O devices. When the processors are all the same and each has equal access to the computer's resources, i.e., it's symmetric, then the system is said to be a *symmetric multiprocessor* (SMP).

Many people go a step further and require that the multiprocessor computer also have the ability where all of its processors can execute in kernel mode. *Kernel mode* occurs when a program executes some special instruction or procedure (i.e., system call) which requires the operating system to take over the program's thread of execution for some period of time. If the multiprocessor allowed only a single CPU at a time to execute in kernel mode, then we'd immediately have a bottleneck. An example of such a situation might be one in which multiple processes are searching through a huge database to determine how many pink Buicks were sold to 32-year-old single parents worldwide. So, each process is pulling records from disk and looking for such individuals, resulting in an incredible number of I/O system calls, which only one processor can perform at a time. Suddenly the multiprocessor computer has been transformed into a single processor system! We'll include the requirement that an SMP must also be capable of having all of its processors execute in kernel mode.

SMPs do provide a single address space for applications. This can make application development much easier than it would be on a system with multiple, independent address spaces such as clusters.

An SMP will have multiple processors but it doesn't really have multiple I/O systems or multiple memory systems. Since SMPs have equal or uniform access to memory, they are *Uniform Memory Access* (UMA) machines. UMA carries the implication that all processors can access all of memory with the same latency. In any computer (not just parallel computers), the various resources must have interfaces to each other. For example, the processor must be able to communicate with the memory system.

4.3.3   Buses and Crossbars

A *bus* can be viewed as a set of wires that is used to connect various peripherals of the computer (Figure 4-1). Communication between resources is commonly done with a bus. Buses are usually grouped into two classes: I/O buses and memory buses. I/O buses are typically long, can have many different types of devices connected to them, and normally abide by a standard. On the other hand, memory buses are short, high speed and are usually customized to the memory system to maximize processor to memory performance (low latency and high bandwidth). Buses are very cost-effective and versatile. Once an interconnect scheme is defined by a hardware vendor, new devices such as processors and memory can be added without a lot of difficulty.

Another common means of interconnecting devices is through a crossbar. A *crossbar* is a lot like multiple independent buses that connect each of the modules on the multiprocessor (Figure 4-2). This hardware is a lot more complicated than it initially appears. This is because it must allow as many independent communications as possible while arbitrating multiple requests for the same resource, such as a memory bank. All possible nonconflicting paths can be simultaneously allowed, but it takes more hardware. In fact, the complexity grows at a very nonlinear rate. To illustrate this, suppose we have two processors and two memory banks to interconnect. In this case there are four different paths that need to be made available. If we double the resources to four processors and four memory banks, then there are SIXTEEN paths required to interconnect them all! So, crossbars can get expensive in a hurry. This is a bit frustrating because it is a lot easier to avoid interconnect bottlenecks with crossbar switches than to add devices on a single bus or two.

In order to enable high processor counts, multiple resources—typically processors—often share paths of crossbars. This typically requires hardware to arbitrate between the resources sharing the path. This arbitration inevitably takes a little time, which increases communication latency. Most, if not all, parallel applications spend most of their time getting data from the memory system instead of other processes (or threads). To take advantage of this behavior, parallel computer manufacturers have adopted a strategy of having a few processors and a memory

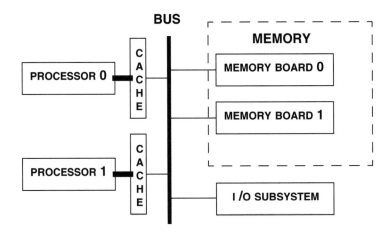

Figure 4-1   Computers with bus interconnect have few paths between peripherals.

system connected by a (fast) bus collectively share an interconnect path. This allows processors to have the opportunity of realizing low latency, high performance local memory access while keeping the number of crossbar paths relatively low.

4.3.4   Shared-memory and Coherency

Before we go any further, it's probably a good time to dig a little deeper into shared-memory functionality and put interconnects on hold for the moment. If a data item is referenced by a particular processor on a multiprocessor system, the data is copied into that processor's cache and is updated there if the processor modifies the data. If another processor references the data while a copy is still in the first processor's cache, a mechanism is needed to ensure that the second processor does not use the data from memory which is now out of date. The state that is achieved when both processors always use the latest value for the data is called *cache coherency.*

Not all shared-memory machines are cache-coherent. Those that are not typically rely on software to achieve coherence at any given time. This can be achieved with two mechanisms. The first mechanism, generally referred to as a *cache line flush*, immediately forces a cache line from the processor's cache to main memory. The second mechanism simply marks a particular cache line as being invalid but does *not* write it back to memory. This is called a *cache line purge* and basically forces the processor to explicitly load a "fresh" copy of the data from memory the next time it is accessed. An example of how these mechanisms work is illustrated in Figure 4-3.

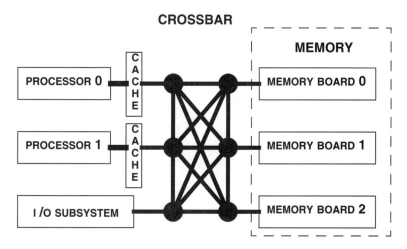

Figure 4-2 Computers with crossbar interconnect usually enjoy multiple, independent paths between peripherals.

Recall that a cache line typically contains multiple data elements. Let's suppose that x and y reside in the same cache line as shown in Figure 4-3. Assume we are processing on processor 0 and change the value of x. Later on, processor zero needs to get a "fresh" copy of y and we perform a cache line purge. Then finally we realize that it's a good time to send the new value of x back to memory so that all the other processors can see what we did to it. So, a cache line flush is performed. But, hey! That cache line was purged, so we lost the value of x, and since the cache line was marked invalid by the earlier purge, who knows what was actually flushed back to memory? Worse yet, and this is the point we were striving to make, we may have no clue that x and y were in the same cache line. This is an example of *false cache line sharing* which we'll discuss in more detail in Chapter 8.

As the previous discussion shows, performing cache coherence in software is awkward, since the application has to do purges and flushes all the time. However, performing coherence in software means that the hardware doesn't have to do it. As a result, such machines are likely to have hardware that is much less complicated and, hence, is likely to be less expensive. The Cray T3D is a good example of a shared-memory machine that doesn't perform cache coherence with hardware.

So, rather than continuously purging and flushing caches ourselves, we may be interested in a shared-memory machine which takes care of the cache coherency for us (i.e., in hardware). Roughly speaking, there are two means of accomplishing coherency: bus snooping and directory based coherency.

Let's refer to buses that connect caches to main memory as memory buses. Coherency via *bus snooping* is accomplished by having every memory bus continuously communicate what's

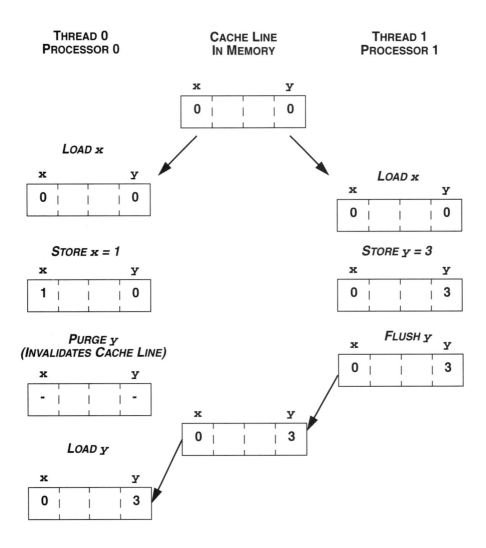

Figure 4-3 Example of false cache line sharing complicated by coherency controlled with software.

happening to it. Coherency is achieved because all the other memory buses are listening, and when another memory bus asks for a particular cache line, they immediately look in their caches to see if they have it. The memory bus whose cache had the cache line will send it to the requesting bus and send a message to the memory system indicating that the request has been resolved.

Roughly speaking, this works because moving data from one cache to another is a lot faster than pulling the cache line from main memory. Note that this approach requires that all the other memory buses be listening to all the other memory buses, that is, it requires all the memory buses to be snooping.

One important thing to note about bus snooping is that it requires a lot of bus traffic (the snooping). Clearly, adding more processors (and their caches) adds that much more snoopy traffic. As a result, the overall bus bandwidth of the machine can be overwhelmed with just a few processors. This is one reason why cache snooping is typically used on SMPs with fewer than twenty processors.

Now, let's go back to the basic issue of directory-based cache coherency. If another processor has the data you want, then you need to get it from its cache rather than main memory. This means that you need to check all of the other caches before going to memory to get the data. We want this to happen quickly, too! One way to do this is to have hardware support to maintain a set of tables which shows which cache has what data. There are, of course, a lot of large tables, which means that its size certainly approaches that of a metropolitan phone book or directory! This allows a processor to request its data from the directory, and it will find it for you whether it be in another cache or in memory. This device should have a lot of data paths because data really needs to be transferred directly from one cache to another as well as between caches and main memory. This sounds familiar, doesn't it? That's because this directory mechanism is a lot like an intelligent crossbar. It's intelligent because it has to locate data, not just move it.

The advantage of this approach, generally referred to as *directory-based coherency,* is that it is scalable. It should be fast because of all the direct paths between caches. However, we discussed why a crossbar-based system can actually degrade single processor performance above, and this certainly applies to smart crossbars as well. The advantage of using directories for coherency instead of bus snooping is scalability. Having a directory eliminates the need for all the memory buses to communicate their every move to the entire system. Furthermore, every memory bus doesn't have to be snooping either. This reduces the amount of traffic across the memory buses and, when combined with the multiple data paths in a crossbar, makes for a lot more bandwidth available to move real data. This allows directory-based SMPs to scale much better than those which use bus snooping for coherency.

The disadvantage of directory-based coherency is that it is expensive. As mentioned previously, crossbars are expensive. So, adding directory-based coherency to the crossbar only makes it that much more expensive.

4.3.5 NUMA, ccNUMA, and SCI

Multiprocessor configurations such as that discussed above result in some of the system's memory being farther away than other memory. In particular, a processor can access the memory on its node via the (fast) bus. However, if it needs data that resides on another node, then the transaction must go out onto its bus, over the crossbar and back again. Such accesses are going to take a bit longer than the local memory access. Such a system is said to be a *NonUniform*

Memory Access (NUMA) architecture. NUMA is not tied to crossbar technology; any interconnect could be used in the discussion above and still result in different memory access times. NUMA machines which have hardware-based cache coherency are simply referred to as *ccNUMA* machines.

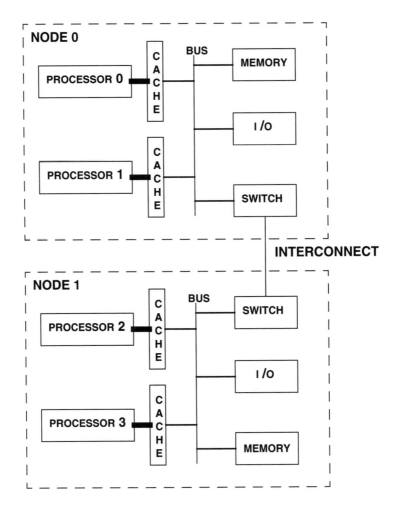

Figure 4-4   An example of a NUMA machine—two fully functional SMPs interconnected.

The Scalable Coherent Interconnect (SCI) is a set of standardized interconnect protocols defined by IEEE. SCI is basically a means of connecting multiple SMPs together into a single, large shared-memory computer. It can also be used to interconnect uniprocessors because they are a special case of SMPs. Examples of systems that use SCI (or at least a subset of the SCI protocol) to implement highly parallel ccNUMA machines are Sequent's NUMA-Q and Hewlett-Packard's Scalable Computing Architecture (SCA).

4.4 Control of Your Own Locality

Due to the inherent differences in I/O and memory latency for NUMA machines, application performance can benefit through control of thread and process allocation and placement. By defining some attributes of processes and/or threads *a priori*, the user can take advantage of her knowledge of the machine's configuration and provide information to the operating system so that it can efficiently allocate resources.

4.4.1 Why Is It Important?

Let's discuss an example before diving any deeper. Suppose we have a ccNUMA machine that has two groups of processors, memory, I/O subsystems and are interconnected with, say, SCI. Suppose there are four processors in each group so that the configuration is that shown in Figure 4-4. Now, let's assume that we start up a thread-parallel application that uses four threads. Consider two resource allocation situations.

In the first scenario, the operating system allocates all the memory for the process on node 0. Unfortunately, the operating system then schedules two of the threads (say, 0 and 1) to execute on node 0 and the other two (2 and 3) on node 1. This means that every memory access done by threads 0 and 1 will be to local memory and every memory access performed by threads 2 and 3 will have to cross the interconnect between nodes 0 and 1. Let's suppose that the additional time required to cross the interconnect takes 2x more than a local memory access. Then parallel application developers will see the following architectural characteristics.

If we assume that all 4 threads perform the same number of memory accesses, the average memory latency is then 25% slower than local memory latency:

$$((2 \text{ threads}) \times L + (2 \text{ threads}) \times (1.5 \times L)) / 4 = 1.25 \times L$$

where L represents local memory latency.

What the developers often hear from NUMA hardware vendors is that applications don't spend all their time accessing memory and that prefetching hides the additional latency anyway, hence this isn't going to be noticeable.

This is wrong! Since we're talking about a parallel application, not just an analysis of individual threads, the application finishes when the last thread finishes. So, the effective latency for the application will be the worst case situation: 1.5 times slower than local memory latency. Secondly, we've already discussed how memory systems are not keeping up with processor performance. Hence, the performance for many applications is gated by memory latency (and bandwidth). Many applications will see an increase in execution time approaching 50% unless you are lucky enough to be enjoying a lot of data reuse and/or have a huge cache.

Now compare the previous scenario to a more sophisticated operating system's approach. It will place all the memory that a thread would need to access as close to it as possible. One approach is to allocate all the memory on one node and execute all four threads on that node. Another is to allocate the memory that each thread will access on the node it will execute on. This latter scenario is non-trivial because the operating system will need some hints as to just what memory the thread plans to access. Moreover, it's not likely to be that simple because there will be data that is shared between threads

There are other issues besides memory latency that are important. Suppose you have an application that is two-way parallel and is very memory-intensive. Assume that the nodes in Figure 4-4 have a memory system that can deliver only enough bandwidth to sustain one of the two threads (or processes). Then the application is likely to execute much faster if exactly one thread executes on each node so they won't be competing for a single memory system.

Another example is best illustrated with a message-passing application. Assume that you have an application which doesn't exhibit a balanced message-passing load. That is, suppose that all the processes send about 1 MB of data in messages to each other. However, processes 0 and 2 send an additional 500 MB of data to each other. If the operating system schedules the processes so that processes 0 and 1 execute on node 0 and processes 2 and 3 execute on node 1, then 500 MB of messages will be passed across the interconnect between processes 0 and 2. Compare this to a scenario in which processes 0 and 2 are scheduled on node 0 and processes 1 and 3 are scheduled on node 1. In this second scenario, the 500 MB of messaging activity is done within the node. Therefore, it doesn't incur the additional latency and reduced bandwidth that will result from passing through the two switches and the interconnect.

There is yet another aspect of the previous example that underscores the importance of proper placement. Many hardware vendors have implemented their message-passing APIs in a way that exploits the advantages of shared-memory machines. Let's assume that the machine in Figure 4-4 is actually a cluster of two SMPs with a fast interconnect (but the computers have multiple, independent address spaces).

Since processors within SMPs share memory, there is a short cut that message-passing can take. Generally speaking, messages are passed via a third "holding" buffer, as shown in Figure 4-5. So, there are actually two copy operations involved in passing a message, one from the sending process to the intermediate buffer, and a second from the intermediate buffer to the receiving process. An advantage of cache-coherent shared-memory machines is that the holding buffer can be eliminated, as illustrated in Figure 4-6. In this case, the message can be copied directly from the sending process' address space to that of the receiving process. The result is that the operation takes only half the time it normally would have required! This type of data transfer is referred to as *process-to-process-bcopy*. For those vendors that support process-to-process-bcopy, it is typically accomplished without any intervention by the user, as it is built into the message-passing library.

Now back to our message-passing application example. If the processes are scheduled so that processes 0 and 2 are on the same node, then the 500 MB of messages can be passed

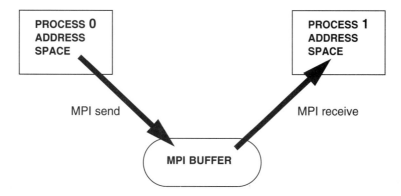

Figure 4-5   Typical MPI message-passing. Process 0 sending data to process 1 actually results in two transfers.

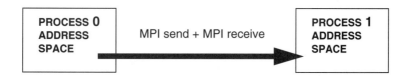

Figure 4-6   Process-to-process-bcopy exploits shared-memory machines by combining MPI sends and receives into a single data transfer from one process' address space to another.

directly from one process to the other, causing only 500 MB to actually be copied instead of almost a gigabyte (2×500 MB) of data being copied to and from the intermediate buffer.

It's worth noting that some operating systems act naively. That is, a process' memory may be allocated on a node where no thread is executing. The result is that every memory access is across the interconnect. Memory references that go across the ccNUMA interconnect are also referred to as a remote memory access.

So, by defining some attributes of processes or threads *a priori*, a user can take advantage of knowledge of the machine's configuration and provide information to the operating system so that it can efficiently allocate resources. The term *topology* is used to describe the layout of processors or nodes in a parallel architecture. It is especially useful in NUMA configurations and clusters of SMPs so that users can determine the number of processors in each node as well as how many nodes are in the overall system. Topology is also used to describe the placement of processes or threads in a multiprocessor environment. An example of how the notion of topology can be used is discussed in the next section.

4.4.2   Command Line Interfaces

Some hardware vendors have made several attempts at providing parallel applications with the tools they need to get good performance. These range from some trivial controls to some that actually came close to delivering a complete package.

The first example of such tools that we'll discuss is the mpa utility that was provided in Hewlett-Packard's SPP-UX operating system. SPP-UX executed on HP's X-Class computer systems. These systems consisted of "nodes" which had 8 to 16 processors interconnected via a crossbar to memory and other peripherals. Nodes were interconnected via HP's Coherent Toroidal Interface (CTI) ring, which is an implementation of some of the SCI protocols discussed earlier. So, this system was a true ccNUMA machine which supported up to 256 PA-RISC processors. The mpa utility (which stands for modify program attributes) is a very powerful tool for parallel applications. It has several options, among them:

- node #   Specify which node to start the first thread of a process on.
- locality   Force child processes to be created on same node as parent.
- maxth #   Specify maximum number of threads to be created per node.
- min   Specify minimum number of total threads to create.
- max   Specify maximum number of total threads that can be created.
- private   Specify type of memory that a process' data area should be allocated in.
- stacktype   Specify type of memory that a process' stack area should be allocated in.
- specific   Specify type of memory that a process' thread-specific memory should be allocated in.
- spin   Create all threads (up to maximum) so that they are spin-waiting.

Another useful utility, dplace, is available on many SGI systems. It uses memory, process, and thread placement specifications from a file (created by the user). It allows the user to:

- Identify the total number of threads to be used
- Identify the total number of memory systems to use
- Specify distribution of threads onto memory systems
- Specify text, data, and stack page sizes (similar to HP-UX's chatr capabilities)
- Place specific ranges of memory on a memory system

Recall the parallel application discussed above in which two processes passed a bulk of the total messages (500 MB between thread 0 and thread 2). Then an appropriate dplace file for this application is as follows:

```
memories 2 in topology cube
threads 4
distribute threads across memories block 1
```

This dplace file specifies that there are two memory systems and a total of 4 threads to be used by the application. It also specifies the distribution of threads to be 1 per memory system (which is a node in the context of this chapter). The effect is a round-robin type scheduling approach, that is, thread 0 is scheduled on node 0, thread 1 on node 1, thread 2 on node 0, and finally thread 3 on node 1. This is exactly the scheduling that we desire for best performance!

Note that we could have achieved the other scheduling scenario (processes 0 and 1 on node 0 with processes 2 and 3 on node 1) by changing the block specification line to:

```
distribute threads across memories block 2
```

This same utility can be used to handle the two way parallel application discussed above that is memory intensive. The following accomplishes the desired result:

```
memories 2
threads 2
distribute threads block 1
```

This forces thread 0 to be executed on node (memory) 0 and thread 1 to be executed on node 1, just as we wanted.

The drawback of both mpa and dplace are that they are command line interfaces. That is, to use either of them on an executable, they have to be invoked as:

```
mpa -node 0 ./a.out
```

or

```
dplace -place ./my_dplace_file ./a.out
```

Well, neither of these interfaces is anything close to a standard. Moreover, just as with threads before POSIX got its act together, every computer system vendor will have its own utility with a different set of options or file semantics. But even if there was a standard, it would require Independent Software Vendors (ISVs) to modify their applications to use these command line interfaces. Why is that? Because almost all parallel applications that are commercially available today are launched by a "wrapper" application. Thus, the user could launch the application with a perfectly good topology specification, but it would apply only to the wrapper application and have no effect on the parallel executable.

It should be noted that most of the functionality outlined above could be achieved through a library of procedures provided by both vendors. But, again, these procedures are very non-standard and would require application developers to extensively modify their parallel application in very non-portable ways to make use of these procedures.

4.4.3   Other Approaches

There are other approaches for the user to provide information to the operating system about their parallel applications. Among them are environmental controls, application registries, and application resource tools.

Application resource tools or managers fall into roughly two categories: ones that require a command line interface and those that are system level tools. The former has been discussed above. The latter is a powerful means of configuring virtual machines within a single system. Such virtual machines have many aliases, including subcomplex and protection domains. SPP-UX's subcomplex manager and HP-UX's Process Resource Manager (PRM) are examples of such tools. Generally speaking, this is a means of redefining the system for multiple users rather than the user providing information about her application to the operating system.

Application registries seem like a good place for parallel attributes to reside. However, a registry defines these attributes for all users of that application on that system. So, all users would have the same set of attributes applied to them unless there were multiple application registries, say, one for each user. In any case, the application provider would have to provide these registries for each operating system. Detailed utilities and instructions on how to modify these registries on a per-session basis are needed as well. Today there are no commercially available parallel applications that make thread, process, or topology controls available through registries.

One of the easiest ways to provide such information is through the user's environment. Environmental variables are used to control parallelism in most operating systems and parallel APIs. One example is MPI on HP-UX. Applications built with HP-UX's MPI provide the MPI_TOPOLOGY environment variable. It controls the application's placement of processes by enabling the user to specify the virtual machine (subcomplex), initial node, and process topology to use in the execution of the application. For example, an MPI_TOPOLOGY value of `rdbms/3:4,0,4,4` specifies that the application is to be run as follows:

- Execute on the subcomplex named `rdbms`.
- Start the initial process on node 3.
- Nodes 0, 2, and 3 will each run four processes.

Thus, processes 0, 1, 2, and 3 will execute on node 3, processes 4, 5, 6, and 7 will run on node 0, then processes 8, 9, 10, and 11 will run on node 2.

Many vendors provide environment variables to control parallelism. While this is a very convenient means of controlling parallelism, it has some drawbacks:

- The current and/or default setting is not easily identifiable by the user unless she has set it in her login environment. For example, HP-UX uses the MP_NUMBER_OF_THREADS environment variable to control the number of threads to be used by parallel applications that were implemented with compiler directives. But its default value, or even its existence, is nontrivial to identify.

- There's no protection against misspellings until after the fact. For example, in the MPI_TOPOLOGY environment variable, what if the subcomplex name was actually `rdb`? The user won't find a problem until the application begins to execute and then it may not be obvious what the problem is. Worse yet, what if the user sets the environment variable MPNUMBEROFTHREADS (forgetting the underscores)? He certainly won't get the number of threads he was asking for.

- Applications can redefine environment variables via system calls such as `putenv()`. Thus a user may set the maximum number of threads he wants to use to be one number while the application, upon execution, promptly changes that environment variable to another value.

One alternative to environment variables is the concept of limits. In general, this enables the user to set or get limitations on the system resources available to the user. Historically, this has included parameters indicating the maximum size of a process' stack, text, and data areas, as well as specifications for things like the maximum cpu time that a process can consume or the maximum number of file descriptors a process can have open.

The *limits* interface, or one like it, has also been applied to parallelism. Such use, however, is usually limited (pardon the pun) to the maximum number of threads. It does avoid the problems that environment variables have because it requires an interface to modify the parameters. It also specifies the current settings for all parameters and cannot be reset through a procedure call.

4.5 Summary

This chapter has given an overview of the computer hardware and system software issues that apply to parallel processing. Many of the topics are informative only. For example, there's not a whole lot of benefit in knowing that a machine's cache coherency is done by bus snooping or use of directories.

There is one important message though: know your environment. To make the most of the system you are executing a parallel application on, you should know the topology of your system and what the desired topology is for your applications threads and/or processes. This can make a huge difference in how fast your application runs, regardless of how well you optimized it.

The parallel controls discussed here are not covered in detail. Details of their functionality are beyond the scope of this book. However, the reader should know that such controls exist. That is, the reader now knows enough to ask the hardware vendor whether such tools exist (and if they don't, why don't they?).

References:

The following publications are excellent resources for the parallel systems and other topics discussed in this section.

1. Dagum, L. and Menon, R. *OpenMP: An Industry-Standard API for Shared Memory Programming*, IEEE Computational Science and Engineering, Vol. 5, No. 1, January/March 1998. http://www.openmp.org/.
2. Message-Passing Interface Forum. *MPI: A Message-Passing Interface Standard*, University of Tennessee, 1994.
3. Norton, S. J.; DiPasquale, M. D. *Thread Time: The MultiThreaded Programming Guide*, Prentice-Hall Professional Technical Reference, 1996.
4. Hennessy, J. L.; Patterson, D. A. *Computer Architecture, A Quantitative Approach,* Morgan Kaufmann, 1996. ISBN 1-55860-329-8.
5. Pfister, G. F. *In Search of Clusters*, Prentice Hall PTR, 1998. ISBN 0-13-899709-8.
6. Kwang, H. *Advanced Computer Architecture*, McGraw-Hill, 1993. ISBN 0-07-031622-8.

Software Techniques —
The Tools

CHAPTER   5

How the Compiler Can Help and Hinder Performance

optimization

The three most important factors in ~~selling~~ are location, location, location.

Realtor's creed

5.1 Compiler Terminology

There are several steps necessary to create computer software. The vast majority of programs start with *high-level* code written in a language such as C, C++, Java or Fortran. Processors are designed to interpret their own unique *low-level* language composed of *assembly* code instructions. To convert assembly code to a computer-understandable form, an *assembler* checks to verify that appropriate assembly language syntax is used, then translates it into a compact sequence of instructions creating *object code*. To convert a high-level language program to object code, an addition step is required. The *compiler* takes high-level language as input and produces assembly code. Once objects have been created, a *linker* puts the objects together into an *executable*, which can then be run on a computer. These steps are shown in Figure 5-1.

When computers first appeared, programmers were forced to write assembly code since there were no alternatives. This allowed programmers to write programs that were efficient for a given processor. When processors changed, the code usually had to be rewritten. Later, *high-level* languages appeared. Languages are designed for the main type of task to be accomplished. For example, Fortran was designed for scientific analysis, Cobol for business applications, and C for systems programming. The advantage of high-level languages is that they allow code developed on one type of processor to be used on other types of processors, since the code can be recompiled on other platforms. This is called *source code compatibility*. An even better feature is *object code compatibility*. This is when objects created for one version of an operating

81

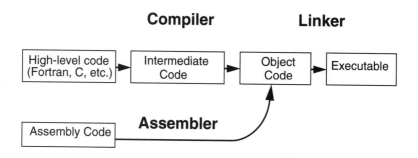

Figure 5-1   Steps to create an executable.

system or computer can be used on a different one. The pinnacle of compatibility is *binary compatibility* which is when executables created for one version of an operating system or computer can be used on a different one.

Of course, users don't have to write high-level code. They can write assembly code directly. However, assembly code takes longer to write, is harder to debug, and is less portable, so very few people write programs in assembly code anymore. Still, some programmers enjoy writing assembly code since it allows them to control the instruction sequence exactly and maximize processor performance. For relatively simple routines, code by a proficient assembly code programmer will always outperform a program written in a high-level language. One goal for any compiler is to convert a routine written in a high-level language to the most efficient assembly code possible.

Producing efficient assembly code isn't easy. The simplest thing for the compiler to do is a one-to-many translation. Each line of high-level code is converted to one or more lines of assembly code. This usually results in poorly performing assembly code since there are probably many more instructions than necessary. Compilers must apply sophisticated (and time-consuming) mathematical techniques to generate good assembly code.

Compilers are given a file or files from which to create object code. In each file there may be multiple *procedures*. In Fortran 90, procedures are called subroutines, functions or modules, while in C and C++ they are called functions or the unique main function. The compiler analyzes these by breaking them into language-independent pseudo-code called *intermediate language* code. This code is never seen by the user and is deleted once the compiler has completed the compile. This intermediate language is analyzed by breaking it into smaller pieces named *basic blocks*. Assembly code is then generated from the intermediate code.

5.1.1 Basic Blocks

A *basic block* is a region of code that contains only one entrance at the top and only one exit at the bottom. Therefore, whenever a branch is encountered, it ends the current basic block. Likewise, any location that can be branched to causes a basic block to start. For example,

```
i = 1;
j = 3;
go to location_1;
```

is contained in a single basic block, but

```
i = 1;
go to location_1;
j = 3;
```

isn't, since it has a branch in its interior. One of the most important constructs to optimize are loops. Although a loop from Fortran or C is converted to multiple basic blocks, the meat of the loop may be only a single basic block. Consider the following routine:

```
INTEGER*8 IX(N)
DO I = 1,N
   IX(I) = 0
ENDDO
```

Compilers may create a one-to-many translation as follows. Let `ri` represent hardware register `i`.

```
Pseudo-Code                   Comments
Basic Block 1:
   load addr ix(1) into r1
   r2 = n                     load n into r2
   r3 = 0                     load 0 into r3
   if (r2 <= r3) exit         if (n <= 0) exit
Basic Block 2:
   r4 = 1                     for loop counter
   r5 = 8                     increment for address of ix in bytes
   r6 = 0                     load 0 into r6
Basic Block 3:
loop:
   store r6 at r1             store 0 to the address of ix(i)
   r1 = r1 + r5               address for next ix(i)
   r3 = r3 + r4               increment loop counter
   if (r3 <= r2) go to loop   if (i <= n) loop
```

5.1.2   Higher Optimizations

Procedures consist of one or more basic blocks. As shown above, even a single loop generates multiple blocks. However, single and multiple loop structures are very common in applications, so compilers are designed to make specific optimizations for them. Compilers also make
optimizations across the multiple blocks generated by a procedure. The highest level of optimization is *interprocedural optimization*, which attempts to optimize across procedures. This can
occur during object code creation if the compiler has been given multiple routines to compile. It
can also occur during the link phase, when the executable is being created. Some, but not all,
compilers make optimizations at the following levels:

- procedure within basic blocks (we'll refer to these as general optimizations)
- procedure within single and nested loop structures
- entire procedure including all blocks and loops
- file (interprocedural analysis within a source file)
- cross file (interprocedural analysis across all procedures)

5.2 Compiler Options

Compiler writers give users many compiler options (or flags) to choose from. Users want
their code to generate correct answers and run as quickly as possible. These two goals
sometimes conflict with one another. As the complexity of the compiler optimization increases,
the chance that incorrect (buggy) code gets produced also increases. There's no standard for
compiler options, but many have optimization levels O0, O1, O2, etc. The "O" indicates
optimization while the number following it indicates the sophistication of the optimization
performed. These are usually preceded by a "-" or "+". So, using +O0 indicates a low level of
optimization. There are also optimization levels named after their functionality. Some compilers
use +Odataprefetch to indicate that prefetch instructions should be inserted to prefetch data
from memory to cache. There are no strict rules about what each level of optimization means.
One compiler may use +O0 for a one-to-many translation, +O1 for basic block optimization, +O2
for loop optimizations, +O3 for multiple loop optimizations, and +O4 for interfile optimizations,
while another may have fewer levels to choose from and may mix the optimizations in different
ways.

Using the compiler correctly to achieve good performance can be tedious. Naive users
compile at the most advanced optimization levels and are surprised when they get wrong
answers. Performance may actually be worse at higher levels of optimization than at some lower
ones. Experienced compiler users will compile code at a moderate but safe compiler optimization level, checking their answers and the amount of time the code takes to run. Many vendors
use -O for the highest "safe" level of optimization. This is a good place to start; more advanced
optimizations may be tried with answers and timing results compared at each step.

5.3 Compiler Directives and Pragmas

Many vendors allow users to place hints in the source code to help the compiler generate better assembly code. In Fortran these are called *directives*, while in C they are implemented as *pragmas*. Since each hardware vendor has his own unique set of directives/pragmas, the OpenMP model by Kuck & Associates attempts to standardize the ones used for shared-memory parallelism. This is discussed in more detail in Chapter 8.

In Fortran, directives usually start with a "C" or "!" in column one to allow the line to be recognized as a directive. This is followed by a word or words that indicate what the compiler directive is designed to accomplish. To limit the scope of the directive, some software models also require an additional directive to appear at the end of the region to which the directive applies. The following example shows how identical functionality can be achieved using three different programming models:

OpenMP directives:
```
C$OMP PARALLEL PRIVATE(J) SHARED(N)
C$OMP DO
       DO J = 1, M
          CALL INIT(A(1,J),N)
       ENDDO
C$OMP END PARALLEL
```

Hewlett-Packard directives:
```
C$DIR LOOP_PARALLEL
       DO J = 1, M
          CALL INIT(A(1,J),N)
       ENDDO
```

SGI directives:
```
C$DOACROSS LOCAL(J), SHARED(A,N)
       DO J = 1, M
          CALL INIT(A(1,J),N)
       ENDDO
```

In the C language, compiler directives are usually implemented through #pragma control lines. Thus a line of the form

```
#pragma directive-name
```

uses directive-name as the action to perform.

Directives and pragmas tell the compiler that you, the user, know more about the code than the compiler does. What if you lie to the compiler and tell it that it's safe to make an optimization when it really isn't? For example, the most common misuse of compiler directives is when a user tells a compiler that it's safe to execute a loop in parallel when it really isn't, due to a loop level dependency. In this situations, you can expect to get wrong answers some of the time, so be careful.

5.4 Metrics

In order to discuss the theoretical benefits of optimizations, some basic metrics must be defined. Most routines are constrained by the ability to move data from cache or memory to the processor.

5.4.1 In-Cache

When data is in-cache and the code is performing floating-point calculations, the goal of optimization is usually to increase the number of floating-point operations per memory operation. We use the term F to M ratio, or *F:M*, to quantify this relationship. So the loop

```
DO I = 1,M
   Z(I) = X(I) + Y(I)
ENDDO
```

has an F:M ratio of 1:3 since there is one floating-point operation for three memory operations.

5.4.2 Out-of-Cache

Quantifying the amount of data moved is very important when the data is out-of-cache. One useful metric is the number of floating-point operations per byte of data. In the above example, if the arrays used 64-bit floating-point data, then there is one floating-point operation per 24 bytes of data. If the code could use 32-bit data, then the performance of out-of-cache problems improves by a factor of two, since only half as much data is needed per floating-point operation or one floating-point operation per 12 bytes of data.

So, if the data is being loaded and stored from memory most of the time, the floating-point operations themselves don't matter much. All the time is spent performing the memory operations. The amount of data movement from memory to cache can be cumbersome to discuss. The size of the cache line varies from one processor to another and the data type also varies from one application to another. We're usually dealing with a vector containing some number of points, say, n, in any discussion of data movement.

Recall that when data is needed by the processor and it is not in cache, a cache miss occurs. When a cache miss occurs, data moves from memory to cache. Generally the processor modifies the data and puts the result back in cache. At some point later in time, a write back occurs and the data moves from cache back to memory. So for both a cache miss and a write back, data moves between memory and cache. To help quantify the data movement, we'll define a new term *memory_transfer* to be

$$memory\_transfer = n \times \text{(bytes per point)} / \text{(cache line size in bytes)}$$

Using this definition allows routines to be compared independently of data type and the processor cache line size. When n loads occur and the data is not in cache, cache misses occur and data must be loaded from memory. This causes one memory_transfer. When n stores occur and the data is already in cache, one memory_transfer occurs for the write backs. When n stores occur and the data is not in cache, there are two memory_transfers, one caused by the loads and one from the write backs.

5.5 Compiler Optimizations

The rest of this chapter discuss the actual optimizations that compilers and users can make to source code. It's a mixed bag of tools. There are some optimizations that compilers perform that are difficult or impossible for users to duplicate. For example, software pipelining is a very important optimization for RISC systems that cannot be effectively duplicated in high-level code. However, there are many other optimizations that users can make that compilers have difficulty performing. Each optimization has one or more benefits that makes it worthwhile to perform. In each section, we've placed a table with an overview of the operations and their benefits.

5.5.1 General Optimizations

There are many general or classical compiler optimizations that compilers use. Many of these result in fewer assembly code instructions or "tighter" code, which results in smaller object files. This helps decrease the chance of instruction cache conflicts. This section discusses how the compiler generates good assembly code and things you can do to help it. An overview of these optimizations is shown in Table 5-1.

Table 5-1   Optimizations That Improve Assembly Code Generation.

Technique	Reduce number of memory instructions	Reduce number of floating-point instructions	Reduce number of integer instructions	Reduce number of branch instructions	Reduce effect of memory latencies and/or memory bandwidth	Reduce effect of instruction latencies
Register allocation	✓					
C/C++ register data type	✓					
C/C++ asm macro	✓	✓				
C/C++ include file math.h	✓	✓	✓	✓		
Uniqueness of memory addresses	✓				✓	
Dead code elimination	✓	✓	✓	✓		
Constant folding and propagation	✓	✓	✓			
Common subexpression elimination	✓	✓	✓			
Strength reductions		✓	✓			
Increase fma		✓				
Fill branch delay slots			✓			

5.5.1.1   Register Allocation

Register allocation refers to the compiler assigning quantities to registers. With the exception of the C/C++ register type, programmers have little input in this and are at the mercy of the compiler to make good assignments. (This is why some programmers like to write assembly code.) Some optimizations make the compiler's job more difficult because they increase the number of registers needed. This is referred to as *increasing register pressure*. When too many registers are needed, compilers must store (or *spill*) values to memory and restore values from memory, and performance suffers greatly. Register allocation is first done at the basic block level. *Global register allocation* refers to optimizing the assignment of registers across multiple blocks. It's sometimes hard to tell if the compiler is having difficulty making register assignments. This is when it's very helpful to be able to read assembly code. You can generate assembly code from the compiler via an option (usually -S), and see if there's an inordinate number of load and store instructions. If so, the compiler is generating too many spills.

5.5.1.2   C/C++ register data type

C and C++ contain a data type named register that allows users to give hints to a compiler to encourage the compiler to keep certain values in registers. This is useful when the user knows the variable will be used many times and should not be reloaded from memory. Compilers are free to ignore the hints, though, and often do. In the example below, the values b1-b12 are used many times and should remain in registers. This assumes that the processor has enough hardware registers to make this feasible.

```
...
register double   b1, b2, b3, b4, b5, b6, b7, b8, b9, b10, b11, b12;
...
for (j = 0; j < n; j += 4)
{
   ...
  for (i = 0; i < m; i++)
  {
    c1[i] += b1 * a[i+j*lda] + b4 * a[i+(j+1)*lda]
      + b7 * a[i+(j+2)*lda] + b10 * a[i+(j+3)*lda];
    c2[i] += b2 * a[i+j*lda] + b5 * a[i+(j+1)*lda]
      + b8 * a[i+(j+2)*lda] + b11 * a[i+(j+3)*lda];
    c3[i] += b3 * a[i+j*lda] + b6 * a[i+(j+1)*lda]
      + b9 * a[i+(j+2)*lda] + b12 * a[i+(j+3)*lda];
  }
}
```

5.5.1.3   C/C++ asm macro

Some C and C++ compilers allow assembly code to be inserted directly into the instruction sequence by way of the asm macro. Of course, this makes the code non-portable, but it allows programmers to introduce the exact instruction desired into the assembly code. Note that even if a compiler supports `asm`, it may not support all assembly code instructions. Usage also varies among hardware vendors. The following example shows how an integer multiplication by two using a shift left and add (SHLADD) instruction may be accomplished using an `asm` macro:

```
#include <machine/reg.h>
#include <machine/inline.h>
void scale(n, ix, iy)
int n, *ix, *iy;
{
    int i;
    register int reg1;
    for (i = 0; i < n; i++)
    {
        /* want to perform iy[i] = (ix[i] << 1); */
        reg1 = ix[i];
        _asm("SHLADD",reg1,1,GR0,reg1);
        iy[i] = reg1;
    }
}
```

5.5.1.4   C/C++ include file math.h

Some compilers generate better (faster) code if the appropriate include files are used in the source. So this is somewhat like a compiler option. It's good practice to include `math.h` in any C routine that's generating performance intensive code. This is especially true for common math routines such as floating-point square root, `sqrt()`, and floating-point absolute value, `fabs()`. This will be discussed more in Chapter 7.

5.5.1.5   Uniqueness of memory addresses

Different languages make different assumptions on whether memory locations of different variables are unique. *Aliasing* occurs when multiple elements have the same memory location. Fortran is designed for scientific applications and assumes that different variables have different memory locations unless they are made equivalent with an EQUIVALENCE statement. For example, in

```
DO I = 1,N
   Y(I) = X(I) + Z
ENDDO
```

Fortran assumes that z and all of the values of x and y have unique memory locations. Thus z and several values of x and y could be loaded before the first location for y is stored to. The C language is more complicated. If variables are defined locally, the compiler knows they don't overlap, but globally defined variables may be aliased. So if x, y, and z are defined globally, the compiler must assume that they could overlap in the following loop:

```
for (i = 0;i < n; i++)
  y[i] = x[i] + z;
```

To see how important this can be, suppose `y[2]` and `z` are aliased and `x[1] = 1`, `x[2] = 2`, `x[3]= 3`, `z = 4`. In C the loop would proceed as

```
load x[1] = 1, load z = 4, add x[1] + z, store y[1] = 5
load x[2] = 2, load z = 4, add x[2] + z, store y[2] = z = 6
load x[3] = 3, load z = 6, add x[3] + z, store y[3] = 9
```

In Fortran, it would be perfectly legal to load z outside the loop and load two values of x before any additions and stores, such as

```
load Z = 4
load X(1) = 1, load X(2) = 2, load X(3) = 3
add Z + X(1), add Z + X(2), add Z + X(3)
store Y(1) = 5, store Y(2) = 6, store Y(3) = 7
```

So different answers are obtained. Aliasing greatly restricts compiler optimizations. Frequently, programmers know that none of the arrays overlap in memory, but, as discussed above, the C language assumes that some aliasing occurs. Therefore C compilers usually have a compiler option such as `+Onoparmsoverlap` that causes the compiler to assume none of the addresses overlap. This allows the compiler to make more aggressive optimizations. This topic will be discussed more in Chapter 7.

5.5.1.6   Dead Code Elimination

Dead code elimination is merely the removal of code that is never used. In the example below, the code in the `if` test can never be reached, so there is no point in generating object code for it or the `if` test.

```
i = 0;
if (i != 0) deadcode(i);
```

5.5.1.7   Constant Folding and Propagation

Constant folding is when expressions with multiple constants are folded together and evaluated at compile time. For example, a = 1 + 2, can be replaced by a = 3. Constant propagation is when variable references are replaced by a constant value at compile time. Using constant folding and propagation,

```
a = 1 + 2
b = a + 3
```

can be replaced by

```
a = 3
b = 6
```

5.5.1.8   Common subexpression elimination

Common subexpresssion elimination analyzes lines of code, determines where identical subexpressions are used, and creates a temporary variable to hold one instance of these values. It can then use this new variable instead of recalculating the whole subexpression each time. In the code

```
a = b + (c + d)
f = e + (c + d)
```

the expression c + d is used by both a and f. Thus c + d can be calculated first and this result used in the calculations for both a and f.

5.5.1.9   Strength reductions

Strength reduction means replacing expensive operations with cheaper ones. Compilers can improve performance significantly by doing this. Some easy ones for compilers, and users, to accomplish are

- replace integer multiplication or division by constants with shift operations
- replace 32-bit integer division by 64-bit floating point division
- replace floating-point multiplication by small constants with floating-point additions
- replace multiple floating-point divisions by one division and multiplications
- replace power function by floating-point multiplications

Replace integer multiplication or division with shift operations   Integer multiplications are expensive on most processors, so avoiding them is worthwhile. Most processors have integer shift functional units. Shifting the contents of an integer register left one bit is the same as multiplication by two. (We'll assume the sign bit is maintained.) Similarly, shifting the contents right by one bit is the same as division by two. Thus multiplication/division by powers of two can be quickly accomplished by shifting bits. This is especially useful for address calculations since these commonly use multiplication by four for 32-bit addresses and by eight for 64-bit data addresses.

Any integer multiplication by a small number can benefit by using the shift instructions. For example, multiplication of n by nine can be accomplished by shifting n to the left by three bits (multiplication by eight) and adding n. If a shift unit is unavailable or inefficient, the multiplication by a small constant could also be replaced by some number of additions.

Replace 32-bit integer division by 64-bit floating-point division   Integer division is much more expensive than floating-point division, so some processors convert 32-bit integer values to floating-point values, perform the division, and convert the result back to integer. Since the IEEE 64-bit floating-point mantissa is 52 bits wide, the answers are guaranteed to be exact.

Replace floating-point multiplication with floating-point additions   On some poorly performing processors, floating-point multiplication operations are more expensive than additions, so some compilers convert floating-point multiplications by small constants to additions. For example,

```
y = 2 * x
```

can be replaced by

```
y = x + x
```

Replace multiple floating-point divisions by division and multiplications

Division is one of the most expensive operations, so anything that reduces the number of divisions will increase performance. In the expressions

```
a = y / x
b = z / x
```

both y and z are divided by x. Some compilers have an optimization that replaces the expressions with the equivalent of

```
c = 1 / x
a = y * c
b = z * c
```

thereby removing a division at the negligible expense of a multiplication. This optimization is not completely safe since it can result in different answers from the original code. Therefore, compilers usually require the user to turn on a specific high-level compiler option to obtain this optimization.

Replace power function by floating-point multiplications   Power   calculations are very expensive and may take fifty times longer than performing a multiplication, so removing them can improve performance dramatically. Often, the exponent is a small integer constant. Calculations of this form can be replaced by a small number of multiplications. Thus

```
x = y ** 3
```

can be replaced by

```
x = y * y * y
```

5.5.1.10   Increase number of `fma` instructions

Reducing the number of instructions (especially on systems that employ pipelining extensively) is usually a good thing to do. Many processors have compound fused floating-point fused multiply and add (*fma*) instructions that operate more efficiently than individual multiplication and addition instructions. Processors that implement fma instructions usually also have a floating-point negate multiply and add (*fnma*) instruction. Thus, for three values a, b, c, an `fma` instruction performs

```
(a * b) + c
```

while an `fnma` performs

```
-(a * b) + c
```

These instructions bring up interesting issues, since the result may be more accurate than using two separate instructions. When two instructions are used, the result of the multiplication is stored to a register before being loaded for the addition. This intermediate result is limited by the precision of the operations being performed (64-bits, for example). Some rounding may occur when forming the intermediate result. When a single instruction is used, the intermediate result is not limited by the precision of the multiplication, so it may use more bits and hence be more accurate. Compilers may make use of these instructions, but usually require a compiler option to enable them.

Codes can sometimes be altered to reduce the number of floating-point instructions by maximizing the number of these compound instructions. For example, let a, b and c be complex numbers written in terms of their real and imaginary components as a = (ar, ai), b = (br, bi), c = (cr, ci). The sequence c = c + a * b is usually performed as

```
(cr,ci)+(ar,ai)*(br,bi) = (cr,ci)+((ar*br - ai*bi),(ar*bi + ai*br))
```

which uses the sequence

```
multiplication  f1 = ar*br
multiplication  f2 = ar*bi
fnma            f3 = -ai*bi + f1
fma             f4 = ai*br + f2
addition        f5 = cr + f3
addition        f6 = ci + f4
```

which uses two multiplications, a `fma`, a `fnma` and two additions. By altering the order of the instructions to

```
((cr + ar*br) - (ai*bi),(ci + ar*bi) + (ai*br))
```

the sequence can use four instructions as in

```
fma          f1 = ar*br + cr
fma          f2 = ar*bi + ci
fnma         f3 = -ai*bi + f1
fma          f4 = ai*br + f2
```

As with many optimizations, this reordering of instructions may produce slightly different results than the original code.

5.5.1.11   Fill branch delay slots

In the section on RISC processors, the creation of branch delay slots by hardware designers to increase the likelihood of hardware pipelining was discussed. Branch delay slot(s) are the instruction(s) after a branch that are always executed.

If the compiler is used with no optimization, it will probably insert a no-operation, or *nop*, into the branch delay slot. However, it's better if real work can be moved into branch delay slot, so higher levels of compiler optimizations usually attempt to do so.

5.5.2   Single Loop Optimization

Most of the optimizations discussed for loops are related to increasing the amount of data reuse. These techniques relate to reuse in space (spatial reuse) and reuse in time (temporal reuse). Loading multiple data points of a cache line into hardware registers before they are displaced from cache is cache line reuse, which is an example of spatial reuse. Using a single element of data for multiple iterations of a loop is an example of temporal reuse.

Table 5-2   Single Loop Optimizations.

Technique	Reduce number of memory instructions	Reduce number of floating-point instructions	Reduce number of integer instructions	Reduce number of branch instructions	Reduce effect of memory latencies and/or memory bandwidth	Reduce effect of instruction latencies
Induction variable optimization			✓			
Prefetching					✓	
Test promotion in loops		✓	✓	✓		
Loop peeling				✓		
Fusion	✓				✓	
Fission					✓	
Copying					✓	
Block and copy					✓	
Unrolling				✓	✓	✓
Software pipelining						✓
Loop invariant code motion	✓					
Array padding					✓	
Optimizing reductions						✓

5.5.2.1 Induction variable optimization

In the loop

```
for (i = 0; i < n; i += 2)
    ia[i] = i * k + m;
```

the variable `i` is known as the *induction variable* and `n` is the *loop stop variable*. When values in the loop are a linear function of the induction variable (a multiple of the induction variable added to a constant), the code can be simplified by replacing the expressions with a counter and replacing the multiplication by an addition. Thus this is also a strength reduction. The above code can be replaced by

```
ic = m
for (i = 0; i < n; i += 2)
{
    ia[i] = ic;
    ic = ic + k;
}
```

5.5.2.2 Prefetching

Chapter 3 discussed using prefetch operations to decrease the effective memory latency. When prefetches are under software control, they are implemented by special prefetch instructions that must be inserted into the instruction stream. Prefetch instructions can be inserted anywhere in the instruction stream, but in practice they usually occur in loop structures, since the need for prefetching in a loop is obvious.

The compiler may require a compiler option or a compiler directive/pragma to enable the inserting of prefetch instructions. One valid area for concern is what happens when the compiler prefetches off the end of an array. For example, in

```
DO I = 1,N
    X(I) = 0
ENDDO
```

suppose the prefetch instruction requests the data four elements in advance of `X(I)`. For `X(N)`, the hardware will attempt to prefetch `X(N+4)`. What if this element doesn't exist? A regular load of location `X(N+4)` can cause a program to abort if the address of `X(N+4)` is not valid. Fortunately, processors are designed to ignore prefetch instructions to illegal addresses. In fact, processors also ignore prefetch instructions to locations that have not been mapped to virtual memory, i.e., that would cause page faults. So, it's important to ensure that prefetch instructions are to locations that have been mapped to virtual memory to ensure you get a benefit from inserting them. Also, there doesn't always need to be a prefetch instruction for every original memory instruction. One prefetch per cache line is sufficient to preload the data. The following three examples show how the accesses of the `X` array affect the generation of prefetch instructions:

Example 1: Unit stride, cache line size of 128 bytes

```
REAL*8 X(N)
...
DO I = 1,N
  X(I) = 0
ENDDO
```

This requires storing the value zero to the addresses X(1) through X(N). Using compiler prefetches requires inserting at least one prefetch per cache line of X. Therefore, every 16 stores requires one prefetch instruction. Adding a prefetch instruction greatly improves out-of-cache performance, but if the data for X is already in-cache, performance may take longer by a factor of 17/16. The smaller the cache line size, the larger this effect.

Example 2: Non-unit stride, cache line size of 128 bytes

```
REAL*8 X(N)
...
DO I = 1,N,16
  X(I) = 0
ENDDO
```

In this example, only one point in each cache line is modified owing to the stride of 16 on I; therefore, a compiler should insert one prefetch instruction for each store of X. If data was already in-cache, the amount of time to execute this loop will take twice as long as the code without prefetch instructions. Lessons:

1. Unit stride code is best for prefetching (and nearly everything else related to performance).
2. Prefetching data helps performance when the data is out-of-cache, but can hurt performance when the data is already in-cache. For large problems, the data is frequently out-of-cache, so using data prefetch instructions is probably the right thing to do.

Example 3: Indirect addressing
A more difficult case to prefetch is when indirect addressing is performed, as in the loop

```
INTEGER*8 X(N), Y(N), Z(N), W(N), IA(N)
...
DO I = 1,N
  Y(I) = X(IA(I))
  Z(IA(I)) = W(I)
ENDDO
```

The elements of the array X are said to be *gathered* and the elements of Z are said to be *scattered* in the above code. Let's examine the gather in more detail and consider data prefetch instructions. The operations are

```
load IA(I)
load X(IA(I))
```

Suppose the prefetch distance is the constant M. To prefetch for X(IA(I)) requires two levels of prefetching. First, IA(I) must be prefetched. Next, a future value of IA(I) must be loaded into a hardware register; this value is used to calculate the address of the future X(IA(I)) value, and then the final prefetch for X(IA(I)) is performed. The naive way to insert prefetches for the gather would be to include

```
prefetch IA(I+2*M)   (prefetch IA(*) - twice the normal distance)
load IA(I+M)         (prepare for the final prefetch)
prefetch X(IA(I+M))  (prefetch X(IA(*)))
```

To clarify this, suppose the existence of a compiler directive C$DIR PREFETCH EXPRES-SION where EXPRESSION is the explicit element to be prefetched. The code could appear as

```
      DO I = 1,M
C$DIR PREFETCH IA(I+2*M)
C$DIR PREFETCH X(IA(I+M)
         Y(I) = X(IA(I))
      ENDDO
```

Note that the second PREFETCH directive forces IA(I+M) to be loaded into an address register. This is wrong! If IA(I+M) is not defined, then the loading from this location may cause the code to abort.

To ensure nothing illegal happens requires making two loops. The first loop includes the prefetches and the load to X(IA(I+M)) and the second cleanup loop omits them. The code could look like

```
      NEND = MAX(0,N-M)
      DO I = 1,NEND
C$DIR PREFETCH IA(I+2*M)
C$DIR PREFETCH X(IA(I+M)
         Y(I) = X(IA(I))
      ENDDO
      DO I = NEND+1,N
         Y(I) = X(IA(I))
      ENDDO
```

Note that if a processor supports prefetch instructions, and the compiler does not support a prefetch directive, one might still be able to support this functionality in C using the asm macro. For example, the C for loop

```
for (i = 0; i < n; i++)
   b[i] = a[ia[i]];
```

can be modified to insert gather prefetches using the HP C compiler and asm. On the HP PA-RISC processors, prefetch instructions are implemented by loading an address to general register 0. The above C code can be modified to insert prefetch instructions as follows:

```
#if defined(PREFETCH)
#include <machine/reg.h>
#define PREFETCH_MACRO(x) { register void *hpux_dp_target; \
   hpux_dp_target = (void*)&(x); \
   _asm("LDW", 0, 0, hpux_dp_target, R0); }
#else
#define PREFETCH_MACRO(x)
#endif

testpref(int n, double *a, long long *ia, double *b)
{
   int i, nend, ndist;
   ndist = 16;
   nend = ( n > ndist) ? n-ndist: 0 ;
   for (i = 0; i < nend ; i++)
   {
      PREFETCH_MACRO( ia[i+2*ndist] )
      PREFETCH_MACRO( a[ia[i+ndist]] )
      b[i] = a[ia[i]];
   }
   for (i = nend; i < n; i++)
      b[i] = a[ia[i]];
}
```

The above testpref() function provides the same functionality as the preceding Fortran code. All prefetch operations are in the first loop, while the second loop performs the cleanup operations. If the routine is compiled with -DPREFETCH, then the object code for the first loop contains prefetch instructions. Otherwise, these instructions are not generated.

5.5.2.3 Test promotion in loops (if-do interchange)

Branches in code can greatly reduce performance since they interfere with pipelining. In this example, the if test is not dependent on the do loop.

```
DO I = 1,N
   IF (A .GT. 0) THEN
      X(I) = X(I) + 1
   ELSE
      X(I) = 0.0
   ENDIF
ENDDO
```

Exchanging the if and do constructs results in much better code since the if test is evaluated only once instead of every time through the loop.

```
IF (A .GT. 0) THEN
   DO I = 1,N
      X(I) = X(I) + 1
   ENDDO
ELSE
   DO I = 1,N
      X(I) = 0.0
   ENDDO
ENDIF
```

Few compilers perform this optimization since it's fairly complex. If your application uses this construct, you probably should modify your source code instead of depending on the compiler to do it for you.

5.5.2.4 Loop Peeling

Many loops are written to handle boundary conditions, as in the following example:

```
DO I = 1,N
   IF (I .EQ. 1) THEN
      X(I) = 0
   ELSEIF (I .EQ. N) THEN
      X(I) = N
   ELSE
      X(I) = X(I) + Y(I)
ENDDO
```

The above example can be rewritten to eliminate the `if` tests by peeling off the edge values as

```
X(1) = 0
DO I = 2,N-1
  X(I) = X(I) + Y(I)
ENDDO
X(N) = N
```

This is another optimization that few compilers provide.

5.5.2.5   Loop Fusion

Many technical codes contain sequences of loops which may be fused to increase data reuse. Suppose the code appears as

```
for (i = 0; i < n; i++)
   temp[i] = x[i] * y[i];
for (i = 0; i < n; i++)
   z[i] = w[i] + temp[i];
```

and the only uses of the `temp` array appear in the above two loops. These loops can be fused as

```
for (i = 0; i < n; i++)
   z[i] = w[i] + x[i] * y[i];
```

This eliminates all references to `temp`. This optimization is especially important when `n` is large and there are many cache misses.

This is another difficult optimization for compilers to perform. They must look across multiple loops and check that there's not too much register pressure before performing the fusion. For example, if fusing loops causes the compiler to have to spill and restore data from memory, the fusion may be detrimental to performance.

5.5.2.6   Loop Fission

There are times when loops need to be split apart or fissioned to help performance. This is often the case when an inner loop consists of a large number of lines and the compiler has difficulty generating code without spilling and restoring data from memory. By performing loop fission, register pressure decreases, which can generate better performing code. It's not always easy to tell if data is being spilled. Some compilers generate this data, but sometimes you must look at the generated assembly code and count the number of memory operations. In general, if the loop is accessing more than six vectors or arrays, you should consider the possibility that there's too much register pressure causing data to be spilled to memory.

Even some simple loops can benefit from fusion due to cache considerations, though. Consider the loop,

```
for (i = 0; i < n; i++)
   y[i] = y[i] + x[i] + x[i+m];
```

and suppose x[i] and x[i+m] map to the same cache location in a direct mapped cache, e.g., m is a large power of two. Since cache thrashing will occur between x[i] and x[i+m], the loop should be split as

```
for (i = 0; i < n; i++)
   y[i] = y[i] + x[i];
for (i = 0; i < n; i++)
   y[i] = y[i] + x[i+m];
```

What if the cache replacement scheme is associative? Will the above fission still help? Maybe. Suppose the cache is two-way associative and a random cache line replacement scheme is used. Suppose x[0] is loaded into one side of the cache. x[m] has a 50% chance of being loaded into the other side of the cache. Even if it is, it probably won't take very long before some x[i+m] displaces x[i] in the cache due to random replacement. Of course, higher associativity and more sophisticated cache replacement strategies help get around the pathological situations, but there are many chances for poor performance when cache in involved.

5.5.2.7   Copying
The copying optimization can be thought of as performing loop fission using dynamically allocated memory. Suppose that a vector addition

```
DO I = 1,N
   Y(I) = Y(I) + X(I)
ENDDO
```

is to be performed and that X and Y are larger than the cache size. Further suppose the cache is direct mapped and X(1), Y(1) map to the same location in cache. Performance is improved by copying X to a "safe" location and then copying from this safe vector to Y. Let NC be the size of the cache in bytes. To implement this approach dynamically allocate an array XTEMP whose size is the same as the size of X and Y plus 2*NC. The starting location from XTEMP should not map to a location in the cache near X and Y. In the example below, the addresses from XTEMP are half the cache away from X and Y.

```
REAL*8 X(N), Y(N), XTEMP(N+2*NC)
NC2 = NC / 2
ISXT = MOD(%LOC(XTEMP),NC)
ISY = MOD(%LOC(Y(J)),NC)
IF (ISXT .GE. ISY) THEN
   ISTART = NC + NC2 - (ISXT-ISY)
ELSE
   ISTART = NC + NC2 + ISY-ISXT
ENDIF
ISTART = MOD(ISTART,NC)
DO I = 1,N
   XTEMP(I+ISTART) = X(I)
ENDDO
DO I = 1,N
   Y(I) = XTEMP(I+ISTART)
ENDDO
```

The original code missed cache for each load of X and twice for each store of Y. The modified code misses on a cache line basis: once for X, twice for Y, and three times for XTEMP. This removes pathologically bad cache misses.

What if the cache is associative? The discussion is similar to the one from the previous section. Associative caches help performance, but there is still the strong possibility that too many cache misses will occur.

5.5.2.8   Block and Copy

The previous example wasted a lot of space and incurred more misses than necessary. The XTEMP array could have been made much smaller by blocking, or splitting, the loops into multiple loops and then recombining the outer loops. Suppose XTEMP is dynamically allocated to be only twice the size of the data cache. As before, the location of the XTEMP array to start copying to/from can be chosen to be half a cache size away from X and Y. Let NC be the size of the cache in bytes. The code now appears as

```
REAL*8 X(*), Y(*), XTEMP(2*NC)
NC2 = NC / 2
ISXT = MOD(%LOC(XTEMP),NC)
DO J = 1,N,NC2
  ISY = MOD(%LOC(Y(J)),NC)
  IF (ISXT .GE. ISY) THEN
     ISTART = NC + NC2 - (ISXT-ISY)
  ELSE
     ISTART = NC + NC2 + ISY-ISXT
  ENDIF
  ISTART = MOD(ISTART,NC)
  DO I = J,MIN(N,J+NC2-1)
    K = I - J + 1
    XTEMP(K+ISTART) = X(I)
  ENDDO
  DO I = J,MIN(N,J+NC2-1)
    K = I - J + 1
    Y(I) = XTEMP(K+ISTART)
  ENDDO
ENDDO
```

The XTEMP array accesses half of the data cache at a time in the inner loop, which is a slight improvement over having XTEMP be the same size as X and Y. If the size of the inner loop is further reduced, the XTEMP array would not need to be written to memory as often and the number of data misses would be reduced. The optimal size for XTEMP is processor dependent, but choosing a value of around one tenth the cache size is sufficient to make the XTEMP accesses minimal, as shown in Table 5-3.

Table 5-3   Block and Copy.

Version	X load cache misses	Y store cache misses	XTEMP cache misses
original	1 per point of X	2 per point of Y	
large XTEMP	1 per cache line	2 per cache line	3 per cache line
access XTEMP using half the cache	1 per cache line	2 per cache line	2 per cache line
access XTEMP using one tenth the cache	1 per cache line	2 per cache line	0

5.5.2.9   Loop Unrolling

One of the most useful loop modifications is unrolling. This reduces the effect of branches, instruction latency, and potentially the number of cache misses. Consider the following code fragment:

```
DO I = 1,N
   Y(I) = X(I)
ENDDO
```

Without unrolling, for each iteration, the loop index must be incremented and checked to see if the loop should terminate. If there are more iterations to perform, a branch is taken to the top of the loop nest. In general, branches are expensive and interfere with pipelining, so they should be avoided. Most compilers have a compiler optimization that takes the original code and make two code sections from it: the new unrolled loop and any cleanup code necessary to finish processing. For example, if the loop is unrolled by four, it appears as

```
NEND = 4*(N/4)
DO I = 1,N,4
   Y(I)   = X(I)
   Y(I+1) = X(I+1)
   Y(I+2) = X(I+2)
   Y(I+3) = X(I+3)
ENDDO
DO I = NEND+1,N
   Y(I) = X(I)
ENDDO
```

For large N, most of the time is spent in the unrolled loop, which has one branch for every four iterations of the original loop. The compiler can also rearrange more instructions in the new loop to reduce the effect of instruction latencies.

Suppose a processor has the characteristics shown in Table 5-4.

Table 5-4   Example Instruction Latencies.

Instruction type	Clock cycles
Cost of a memory operation	1
Latency of a memory operation with data in cache	6
Number of memory operations per cycle	1

Table 5-5 shows the execution of the original loop (the branch will be ignored) and the execution of the unrolled loop where the instructions have been reordered to reduce instruction latencies.

Table 5-5 Clock Cycles in an Unrolled Loop.

Original order	Clock cycle number	Modified order	Clock cycle number
Load X(1)	1	Load X(1)	1
Store Y(1)	7	Load X(2)	2
Load X(2)	8	Load X(3)	3
Store Y(2)	14	Load X(4)	4
Load X(3)	15	Store Y(1)	7
Store Y(3)	21	Store Y(2)	8
Load X(4)	22	Store Y(3)	9
Store Y(4)	28	Store Y(4)	10

The number of clock cycles has been reduced by over half. Note, however, there is a gap in the processing pipeline. The first store still can't start until clock seven. It would be better if it could start execution at clock five.

Loading all the values of X before the values of Y reduces the possibility of cache thrashing. Another benefit of unrolling is that the amount of unrolling can decrease the number of software prefetch instructions. Ideally, the amount of unrolling should be such that only one prefetch instruction is inserted per cache line. For example, the compiler on a processor with a 64-bytes cache line that is accessing eight-byte unit stride data should unroll a loop eight-way to minimize the number of prefetch instructions. Some compilers have an option that allows users to specify the unrolling depth. Thus users can also mix their own hand unrolled code with the compiler's default unrolling depth to increase overall unrolling. This can also further reduce the possibility of cache line thrashing discussed above. However, excessive unrolling will cause data to be spilled from registers to memory, so too much unrolling will hurt performance. It can also have the undesirable effect of making the size of the object so large than more instruction cache misses occur.

5.5.2.10   Software Pipelining

Software pipelining is closely related to unrolling and is implemented by taking multiple loop iterations, breaking them apart, and reassembling them so that each new iteration contains pieces from multiple iterations from the original loop. One advantage of unrolling is that is reduces the effect of instruction latencies. Ideally, we want to avoid all stalls that occur when waiting for an instruction to finish. As shown in the previous example, the drawback of unrolling is that in each iteration of the unrolled loop, after the first instruction is initiated there may not be enough work to do until another instruction needs to use the result of the first instruction. In other words, there may be a gap in the pipeline after the first instruction is initiated, but before its result can be used.

Software pipelining also attempts to hide these instruction latencies, but instead of merging complete loop iterations, it breaks each of the original iterations into two or more pieces and reassembles them into more efficient code. For example, suppose there are five loop iterations, each of which is divided into two parts: a and b, as shown in Figure 5-2. Part a of iteration one

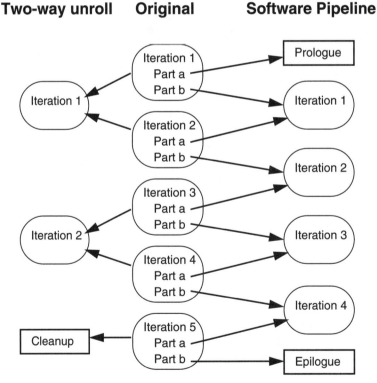

Figure 5-2   Two-way unrolling versus software pipelining.

may be moved above the loop body to comprise a prologue to the loop. Parts 1b and 2a can then be merged to form the first iteration of the new loop. The creation of new iterations continues until parts 4b and 5a are been merged to create the new iteration four. Finally, an epilogue to the loop body is created from part 5b. This approach is shown in Figure 5-2 and is contrasted with two-way unrolling.

Note that unrolling and software pipelining are independent concepts, although in practice they are usually combined. There are multiple reasons for this. First, there must be enough work to hide all instruction latencies. We've discussed that unrolling by itself is frequently not sufficient to hide all latencies. Very simple loops that use software pipelining on RISC processors may not contain enough work to hide all instruction latencies either. On both superscalar RISC and VLIW processors there should also be enough work for good instruction level parallelism. This also leads to merging the two techniques. Finally, when prefetch instructions are used, there needs to be only one prefetch instruction for every cache line. Unrolling helps minimize the number of these instructions.

The example from the previous section showed how unrolling was used to reduce the number of clock cycles from 28 to 10. Suppose the compiler unrolls the loop so that four iterations are done at a time and the loop is reordered for software pipelining as follows:

```
NEND = 4*((N-2)/4)
IF (N .GT. 2) THEN
   NEND = 0
   load X(1)
   load X(2)
   J = -3
   DO I = 1,NEND,4
     J = I
     load X(I+2)
     store Y(I)
     load X(I+3)
     store Y(I+1)
     load X(I+4)
     store Y(I+2)
     load X(I+5)
     store Y(I+3)
   ENDDO
   store Y(J+4)
   store Y(J+5)
   NEND = J+5
ENDIF
DO I = NEND+1,NEND
   load X(I)
   store Y(I)
ENDDO
```

The new loop nest has the following characteristics:.

Table 5-6   Clock Cycles in a Loop with Unrolling and
Software Pipelining.

Operation	Register number	Clock cycle number
Load X(I+2)	1	1
Store Y(I)	3	2
Load X(I+3)	2	3
Store Y(I+1)	4	4
Load X(I+4)	3	5
Store Y(I+2)	1	6
Load X(I+5)	4	7
Store Y(I+3)	2	8

While there must be a prologue of code to set up the registers and an epilogue to finish execution, the software pipelined code takes only eight cycles and the instruction latency is completely hidden.

Software pipelining is an optimization that is impossible to duplicate with high level code since the multiple assembly language instructions that a single line of high level language creates are moved around extensively. Due to the complexities involved, compilers implement software pipelining only at high optimization levels. However, a judicious choice of unrolling can help the compiler generate better software pipelined code. For example, if your compiler performs software pipelining, you can hand unroll a loop with varying amounts of unrolling to see which has the best performance. If you write efficient assembly code for loops, you will use unrolling and software pipelining.

5.5.2.11   Loop Invariant Code Motion (Hoisting and Sinking)

An expression in a loop is *loop invariant* if its value does not change from one loop iteration to the next. *Loop invariant code* motion means to move loop invariant code before or after a loop. Hoisting and sinking are terms that compiler writers use to refer to moving operations outside loops. To *hoist* a load means to move the load so that it occurs before a loop. To *sink* a store means to move a store to occur after a loop. Consider the following loop:

```
DO I = 1,N
   X(I) = X(I) * Y
ENDDO
```

The naive way to interpret this is to load `Y` and `X(I)` inside the loop. This is clearly inefficient since `Y` is loop invariant. Therefore, the load of `Y` may be performed before the loop as follows:

```
load y into register 1
DO I = 1,N
   X(I) = X(I) * register 1
ENDDO
```

Compilers usually perform simple hoist operations such as this.

Another opportunity for loop invariant code motion is

```
DO I = 1,N
   S = S + X(I)
ENDDO
```

The load for `S` may be hoisted from the loop and the store to `S` may be sunk. Hoisting and
sinking `S` removes a load and a store from the inner loop. Compilers usually perform simple
hoist/sink operations.

A slight complication of the previous loop is

```
DO I = 1,N
   Y(J) = Y(J) + X(I)
ENDDO
```

`Y(J)` should be hoisted and sunk from the loop. However, `Y` is a function of the index `J` and
some compilers have difficulty making this optimization. Changing the loop to

```
S = Y(J)
DO I = 1,N
   S = S + X(I)
ENDDO
Y(J) = S
```

usually helps the compiler hoist and sink the reference. Some compilers return information
describing the hoist and sink optimizations performed.

5.5.2.12   Array Padding

Memory and caches are composed of banks which are usually a power of two in size. Consider

```
REAL X(8,N)
DO J = 1,8
  DO I = 1,N
    X(J,I) = 0.0
    CALL SUB1(X)
    ...
  ENDDO
ENDDO
```

and suppose that the loops cannot be exchanged due to other work in the inner loop. Further suppose that the memory system has eight banks and that the data is out-of-cache. The code might be improved by increasing the leading dimension of X to nine, as discussed in Chapter 3. This requires more memory, but may perform better.

5.5.2.13   Optimizing Reductions

A *reduction* is when a vector of data is used to create a scalar by applying a function to each element of the vector. The most common type of reduction uses addition as the function and is called a *sum reduction*. We could also use multiplication or even a maximum or minimum function to form a reduction. The code

```
for (i = 0; i < n; i++)
{
   sumx += x[i];
   prod *= x[i];
}
```

creates a sum reduction and a product reduction. The first reduction above is a sum reduction since the scalar sumx is repeatedly added to, while the second is a product reduction, since multiplication is used. Compilers usually use a single register for the reduction variables. However, this constrains the rate that can be achieved to that of the floating-point add instruction latency. If the latency is four clock cycles, then one iteration of the above loop cannot take less than four cycles per iteration. If the sum reduction in the loop above is rewritten as

```
sum1 = sum2 = sum3 = sum4 = 0.0;
nend = (n >> 2) << 2;
for (i = 0; i < nend; i+=4)
{
   sum1 += x[i];
   sum2 += x[i+1];
   sum3 += x[i+2];
   sum4 += x[i+3];
}
sumx = sum1 + sum2 + sum3 + sum4;
for (i = nend; i < n; i++)
   sumx += x[i];
```

then the instruction latency is hidden. This executes much faster than the original, but may produce different results since the order of operations is different.

Some applications are very concerned about numerical accuracy even when only one sum reduction is used, so they perform sum reductions at a higher precision than the rest of the application. They convert each loaded value to a higher precision floating-point value and perform the addition at this new precision. At the conclusion of the loop, the reduction value is converted back to the original precision. This leads to more accuracy at the expense of reduced performance.

5.5.3 Nested Loop Optimizations

The next set of optimizations operates on nested loops. These can be especially tricky (and time-consuming) for a compiler to get right. Most of these optimizations operate on matrices and there are many chances for a compiler to make an optimization that slows down performance. The flip side is that many of these optimizations can significantly speed up performance. Due to the inconsistent nature of these optimizations, most compilers do not perform them by default. Users must usually turn on special compiler options to obtain them. Due to the possibility of slowing down the code, users should time code more carefully than usual to ensure that the optimizations help performance. The examples shown are all written in Fortran, which stores

Table 5-7 Nested Loop Optimizations.

Technique	Reduce number of memory instructions	Reduce number of floating-point instructions	Reduce number of integer instructions	Reduce number of branch instructions	Reduce effect of memory latencies and/or memory bandwidth	Reduce effect of instruction latencies
Loop interchange					✓	
Outer loop unrolling				✓		✓
Unroll and jam	✓					
Blocking					✓	
Block and copy					✓	

multidimensional arrays in column major order. Corresponding C examples would reverse the order of the indices. See Chapter 7 for more details on programming language issues.

5.5.3.1   Loop Interchange

One of the easiest optimizations to make for nested loops is to interchange the loops to increase the number of unit stride array references. Consider

```
DO I = 1,N
  DO J = 1,N
    X(I,J) = 0.0
  ENDDO
ENDDO
```

Interchanging the loops helps performance since it makes the array references unit stride. For large N, this helps performance due to cache line reuse (fewer cache lines misses), and virtual memory page reuse (fewer TLB misses).

5.5.3.2   Outer Loop Unrolling

In multiple loop nests, outer loop unrolling can sometimes reduce the number of load operations. Let's examine the following nested loops.

```
DO J = 1,N
  DO I = 1,N
    A(I,J) = A(I,J) + X(I) * Y(J)
  ENDDO
ENDDO
```

Suppose the compiler hoists the reference to Y(J) outside the inner loop. If the outer loop is unrolled by two, the resulting code becomes

```
DO J = 1,N,2
  DO I = 1,N
    A(I,J) = A(I,J) + X(I) * Y(J)
    A(I,J+1) = A(I,J+1) + X(I) * Y(J+1)
  ENDDO
ENDDO
```

Note that this requires half as many loads of X, since each load of X is used twice.

5.5.3.3   Unroll and Jam

Unroll and jam is a technique that refers to unrolling multiple loops and jamming them back together in ways that reduce the number of memory operations. The following is a matrix multiplication:

```
DO K = 1,N
  DO J = 1,N
    DO I = 1,N
      C(I,K) = C(I,K) + A(I,J) * B(J,K)
    ENDDO
  ENDDO
ENDDO
```

Step 1: Unroll. Suppose the two outermost loops are unrolled by two. The loops then appear as

```
DO K = 1,N,2
  DO J = 1,N,2
    DO I = 1,N
      C(I,K) = C(I,K) + A(I,J) * B(J,K)
    ENDDO
    DO I = 1,N
      C(I,K) = C(I,K) + A(I,J+1) * B(J+1,K)
    ENDDO
  ENDDO
  DO J = 1,N,2
    DO I = 1,N
      C(I,K+1) = C(I,K+1) + A(I,J) * B(J,K+1)
    ENDDO
    DO I = 1,N
      C(I,K+1) = C(I,K+1) + A(I,J+1) * B(J+1,K+1)
    ENDDO
  ENDDO
ENDDO
```

Step 2: Jam. All four DO I loops can be jammed together into a single DO I loop as follows.

```
DO K = 1,N,2
  DO J = 1,N,2
    DO I = 1,N
      C(I,K)   = C(I,K)   + A(I,J)*B(J,K)   + A(I,J+1)*B(J+1,K)
      C(I,K+1) = C(I,K+1) + A(I,J)*B(J,K+1) + A(I,J+1)*B(J+1,K+1)
    ENDDO
  ENDDO
ENDDO
```

The benefit of unroll and jam is apparent by comparing the ratio of memory to floating-point operations. Assume that the references to B are hoisted outside the innermost loop. By unrolling the outer two loops by two, the floating-point operation to memory operation ratio is increased from 2:3 to 4:3, thereby halving the number of memory operations. Some processors require a ratio of at least 2:1 for peak performance, so unroll and jam is an extremely important tool. Of course, you don't have to unroll both outer loops by only two. By increasing the unroll factors to three or four, even better memory reductions are obtained. The unroll factor on each loop need not to be the same either.

A limit to the amount of unrolling is the number of hardware registers available. For example, in the above loop nest, the number of values of the B array to hoist into registers is the product of the unrolling factors. Once the number of registers required exceeds the number of hardware registers, some B values must be reloaded in the inner loop. This defeats the whole point of the unroll and jam optimization. Thus, as the amount of unroll and jam is increased, there will be a point of maximal performance, after which performance will decrease. Table 5-8 shows the number of operations for various unrolling factors.

Table 5-8   Unroll and Jam Results.

Outer by middle unrolling factors	Loads	Stores	Floating-point operations	F:M ratio
1x1	2	1	2	0.67
2x2	4	2	8	1.33
3x3	6	3	18	2.00
3x4	7	3	24	2.40
4x4	8	4	32	2.67

This optimization is extremely important. Many of the optimizations used in Chapters 10 through 12 use unroll and jam to improve performance on linear algebra and signal processing algorithms.

5.5.3.4   Blocking

Blocking is an important optimization for decreasing the number of cache misses in nested loops. The most common blocking takes the inner loop, splits it into two loops, and then exchanges the newly created non-innermost loop with one of the original outer loops. In the code

```
REAL*8 A(N,N)
DO J = 1,N
  DO I = 1,N
    Y(I) = Y(I) + A(I,J)
  ENDDO
ENDDO
```

suppose the length of the inner loop is very long and that the amount of data in the Y array is many times the size of the data cache. Each time Y is referenced, the data must be reloaded from memory. Rewrite the code as follows:

```
NBLOCK = 1000
DO IOUTER = 1,N,BLOCK
   DO J = 1,N
      DO I = IOUTER,MIN(N,N+NBLOCK-1)
         Y(I) = Y(I) + A(I,J)
      ENDDO
   ENDDO
ENDDO
```

The resulting data accesses are illustrated in Figure 5-3.

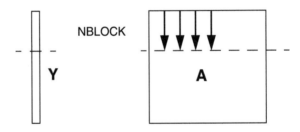

Figure 5-3   Blocking for multiple loops.

Now there are many uses of the Y array in cache before a column of A displaces it. The value of NBLOCK is a function of the cache size and page size and should be carefully chosen. If NBLOCK is too small, the prefetches on the A array are ineffectual, since the prefetched data will probably have been displaced from cache by the time the actual loads of A occur. If NBLOCK is too large, the values of Y don't get reused. For caches that are on the order of a megabyte, a blocking factor of approximately one thousand is usually sufficient to get the benefits of prefetching on A and reuse of Y.

5.5.3.5   Block and Copy

Block and copy is also important for nested loops. A routine that multiplies two square matrices is

```
SUBROUTINE MATMUL(N,LD,A,B,C)
REAL*8 A(LD,*), B(LD,*), C(LD,*)
DO L = 1,N
  DO J = 1,N
    DO I = 1,N
      C(I,J) = C(I,J) + A(I,L) * B(L,J)
    ENDDO
  ENDDO
ENDDO
END
```

Suppose the goal is to operate on blocks of data whose collective size is less than the cache size. Since the code uses eight-byte data and three arrays (A, B and C) are used, this blocking factor, NBLOCK, should be chosen such that

```
8 X 3 X NBLOCK * NBLOCK < (bytes in cache size)
```

and the code blocked as following (the cleanup steps will be ignored):

```
DO I = 1,N,NBLOCK
  DO J = 1,N,NBLOCK
    DO L = 1,N,NBLOCK
      CALL MATMUL(NBLOCK,LD,A(I,L),B(L,J),C(I,J))
    ENDDO
  ENDDO
ENDDO
```

Now the individual matrix-matrix multiplications are performed on a region that is less than the size of the cache. There can still be a large number of cache misses in the individual matrix-matrix multiplications since some of the pieces of A, B and C may map to the same location in cache. It is sometimes beneficial to copy the individual pieces of data. This is treated in more detail in Chapter 10. Suppose we define a routine, MATCOPY, to copy the individual submatrices. The blocked and copied code follows and this concept is illustrated in Figure 5-4:

```
REAL*8 TEMP(NBLOCK,NBLOCK,3)
...
DO I = 1,N,NBLOCK
  DO J = 1,N,NBLOCK
     CALL MATCOPY(NBLOCK,C(I,J),N,TEMP(1,1,3),NBLOCK)
     DO L = 1,N,NBLOCK
        CALL MATCOPY(NBLOCK,A(I,L),N,TEMP(1,1,1),NBLOCK)
        CALL MATCOPY(NBLOCK,B(L,J),N,TEMP(1,1,2),NBLOCK)
        CALL MATMUL(NBLOCK,NBLOCK,TEMP(1,1,1),
$          TEMP(1,1,2),TEMP(1,1,3))
     ENDDO
     CALL MATCOPY(NBLOCK,TEMP(1,1,3),NBLOCK,C(I,J),N)
  ENDDO
ENDDO
...

SUBROUTINE MATCOPY(N,A,LDA,B,LDB)
IMPLICIT NONE
INTEGER*4 N, LDA, LDB
INTEGER*4 I, J
REAL*8 A(LDA,*), B(LDB,*)
DO J = 1,N
  DO I = 1,N
     B(I,J) = A(I,J)
  ENDDO
ENDDO
END
```

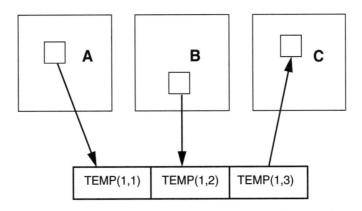

Figure 5-4   Block and copy.

5.6 Interprocedural Optimization

Interprocedural analysis looks at all routines and tries to make optimizations across routine boundaries. This may include, but is not limited to, inlining and cloning.

Table 5-9   Interprocedural Optimizations.

Technique	Reduce number of memory instructions	Reduce number of floating-point instructions	Reduce number of integer instructions	Reduce number of branch instructions	Reduce effect of memory latencies and/or memory bandwidth	Reduce effect of instruction latencies
Inlining	✓	✓	✓	✓	✓	✓
Cloning	✓	✓	✓	✓	✓	✓

5.6.1   Inlining

Many codes are written to be modular and may call routines that are only a few lines long, as in

```
...
j = 1;
for (i = 0; i < n; i++)
  j = inlineit(j);
...

int inlineit(int j)
{
  j *= 2;
  return(j);
}
```

The cost of making the function call is much higher than the cost of doing the work in the routine. Most compilers allow the user to inline routines. The only drawback is that this can cause the size of the object code to increase. Profilers (discussed in Chapter 6) can help to point out situations where inlining would be beneficial. If a routine is called many times and each call does very little work, then it is a good candidate for inlining. In the example above, the code can be rewritten as

```
...
j = 1;
for (i = 0; i < n; i++)
  j *= 2;
...
```

Another example is

```
S = DDOT( 10, X, 1, Y, 1 )
```

where DDOT is defined as

```
FUNCTION DDOT( N, X, IX, Y, IY )
REAL*8 X(0:N-1), Y(0:N-1)
S = 0.0
IF (IX .EQ. 1 .AND. IY .EQ. 1) then
  DO I = 0,N-1
    S = S + X(I) * Y(I)
  ENDDO
ELSE
  DO I = 0,N-1
    S = S + X(I*INCX) * Y(I*INCY)
  ENDDO
ENDIF
```

Inlining, constant propagation, and dead code elimination cause the pertinent code to be condensed and the useless code removed so that the final code appears as

```
S = 0.0
DO I = 0,9
  S = S + X(I) * Y(I)
ENDDO
```

5.6.2   Cloning

Cloning is closely related to inlining. Inlining takes a routine and incorporates it into a subroutine that calls it. But what if the routine is too large to profitably inline? *Cloning* takes the routine, makes a clone (copy) of it, performs interprovincial analysis on the cloned routine for each call to it, and optimizes the logic in the cloned routine. Thus there may be many clones of a routine, each generating slightly different object code.

Suppose a routine makes multiple calls to the MATMUL routine from an earlier section as

```
CALL MATMUL(2,LD,A,B,C)
CALL MATMUL(1000,LD,A,B,C)
CALL MATMUL(40,LD,A,B,C)
CALL MATMUL(N,LD,A,B,C)
```

The first call to MATMUL might inline the code completely. The second call could make a clone of MATMUL that contains only the code for the large case of N=1000. The third call could make a completely different clone of MATMUL, which is optimized for the N=40 case. Finally, the last call could call the original MATMUL routine.

5.7 Change of Algorithm

The most dramatic results in optimization are obtained by completing changing an algorithm to decrease the number of computations. These are very complex optimizations beyond the ability of compilers.

All algorithms have an *order* of complexity associated with them which measures the magnitude of the number of operations. Constant multipliers aren't important in distinguishing two algorithms of the same order. For example, to multiply two vectors x and y of length n takes n operations and hence is an order n algorithm, denoted $O(n)$. This means that the number of operations is of the form $an + b$ where a is a constant and b is some lower order function or a constant. Thus b could be something like $log\ n$ since this has lower order than n. Multiplying the same two vectors and summing their results is also an order n algorithm since it requires $2n - 1$ operations (n multiplications and $n - 1$ additions). The algorithms in this book are of $O(n^a)$ or $O(log_a n)$ or some multiple of the two where a is a constant.

Table 5-10   Change of Algorithm.

Technique	Reduce number of memory instructions	Reduce number of floating-point instructions	Reduce number of integer instructions	Reduce number of branch instructions	Reduce effect of memory latencies and/or memory bandwidth	Reduce effect of instruction latencies
Change algorithm to reduce number of operations	✓	✓	✓	✓	✓	✓
Lower computational order	✓	✓	✓	✓	✓	✓

5.7.1   Reduce the Number of Operations

Most of the time when an algorithm is changed, the order stays the same but the number of operations decreases. An example of this is the Fast Fourier Transform (FFT) discussed in Chapter 12, where a radix-4 algorithm which has $4.25n\ log_2 n$ floating-point operations is shown to be superior to a radix-2 algorithm which uses $5n \, log_2 \, n$ operations. For this algorithm change, the number of operations drops by 15%.

5.7.2   Lower the Computational Order

Lowering the order of operations for a real algorithm is usually very difficult for actual applications. A trivial example of lowering the computation order is summing up the first n integers

$$1 + 2 + 3 + 4 + ... + n$$

This is an $O(n)$ operation. By reordering as

$$(1+n) + (2 + (n-1)) + ...$$

it becomes apparent that the solution is $(n/2) \, (n+1)$ which has $O(1)$ since it contains only three operations. Thus an $O(n)$ algorithm has been replaced by an $O(1)$ algorithm.

Two famous algorithms that we'll discuss in detail are FFTs (Chapter 12) and Strassen's matrix-matrix multiplication (Chapter 10). FFT algorithms take the $O(n^2)$ 1-d Discrete Fourier Transform (DFT) algorithm and implement it as an $O(n \, log \, n)$ algorithm. Strassen's multiplication takes the $O(n^3)$ standard matrix-matrix multiplication and implements it as an algorithm whose order is $log_2 \, 7$ or approximately an $O(n^{2.8})$ algorithm.

If you can lower the order of computations, the performance gains can be nearly unbelievable. In the case of an FFT, the DFT algorithm takes $8n^2$ operations while the FFT algorithm takes $5n \, log_2 \, n$ operations. For a problem of size 1024, the number of operations is reduced from about eight million to 50 thousand operations for a reduction factor of 160x!

5.8 Summary

This chapter covered a lot of very important material. You must use a compiler to generate your application and if you care about performance (which you do or you wouldn't be reading this), you need to be able to use the compiler proficiently. More importantly, we've discussed lots of source code modifications that allow you to create applications whose performance far exceeds that of unoptimized code.

References:

1. *Parallel Programming Guide for HP-UX Systems, K-Class and V-Class Servers*, 2nd ed. Hewlett-Packard, document number B3909-90003, March 2000.
2. Dowd, K.; Severance, C.R. *High Performance Computing*, 2nd ed. Sebastopol, CA: O'Reilly & Associates, Inc., 1998, ISBN 1-56592-312-X.

3. *Origin2000 and Onyx2 Performance Tuning and Optimization Guide.* Silicon Graphics Incorporated, document number 007-3430-002, 1998.

4. Daydé, M. J.; Duff, I. S. *The RISC BLAS: A Blocked Implementation of Level 3 BLAS for RISC Processors.* ACM Transactions on Mathematical Software, Vol. 25, 316-340, 1999.

CHAPTER 6

Predicting and Measuring Performance

Measure twice, cut once.

Carpenter's motto

6.1 Introduction

Timers and profilers are tools used to measure performance and determine if optimizations help or hinder performance. They allow users to determine bottlenecks in applications to direct where optimization efforts should be expended. Once the bottlenecks are determined, they can be attacked with the optimization techniques discussed in this book. This chapter also discusses how to predict the performance of small kernels to determine if the measured results are acceptable.

A *timer* is a function, subroutine, or program that can be used to return the amount of time spent in a section of code. As in the carpenter's motto, it's important to make multiple measurements to ensure that results are consistent. A *profiler* is a tool that automatically inserts timer calls into applications. By using a profiler on an application, information is generated that summarizes timings about subroutines, functions, or even loops that were used.

Timer and profilers operate at various levels of granularity. A stop watch is a good example of a coarse timer. It can be started when a program begins and stopped when it finishes. If the program takes several minutes to run, this timer can be used to determine whether various compiler options improve performance. Some timing programs are like the stop watch in that they time only the entire program. Of course, if the program takes a tiny fraction of a second, or if a user is trying to tune part of the program that takes a small percentage of the total run time, this type of timer isn't too useful. Therefore, users can insert timers around the code they're interested in, or instruct a profiler to return this information. However, if timers are called too often, the amount of time spent executing the timers can substantially increase the run time of an application.

6.2 Timers

Before evaluating the effect of any optimization, a computer user must have a baseline measurement against which to compare all subsequent results. Computer systems have several ways to measure performance, but at the level of measuring only a few lines of code, a user needs a timer to measure performance.

Timers are usually called in one of two ways:

```
t0 = timer();
    ...
  < code segment being timed >
    ...
t1 = timer();
time = t1 - t0;
```

or

```
zero = 0.0;
t0 = timer(&zero);
    ...
  < code segment being timed >
    ...
t1 = timer(&t0);
```

In the first case, the timer can be something as basic as returning the time of day and the result of the two calls must be subtracted to return the total time. The second timer passes an argument which is subtracted inside the timer function. We will build timers that are accessed assuming the calling sequence shown in the second case.

Whenever we use a timer, we'd like it to have the following properties:

- be highly accurate
- have a low access overhead
- reset (roll over) infrequently

Many timers measure multiples of processor clock ticks and so they are integer quantities. Ideally, a timer should be accurate to the clock cycle, since this is the finest granularity possible on a computer. This is not possible to obtain on most systems. Most timers are accurate only to milliseconds, although users should use, if available, a timer that is accurate to at least microseconds.

Ideally, a timer should take no time to call; otherwise, it could distort the timing measurements. This is not possible since accessing a timer requires a call to a system routine to access a clock. The amount of time to access different system clocks varies. In Section 6.2.5, there is a routine that measures the accuracy of timers. If this code shows a highly accurate timer, then, by definition, this timer must have a low overhead since its accuracy could not be measured otherwise.

Many timers are like a car's odometer. At some point they will reset to zero, or roll over. This can also render some timers useless.

6.2.1   Roll Over

Many timers roll over too quickly. As illustrated later, some timers measure time in microseconds, so their results must be divided by a million to return seconds. Other timers measure milliseconds and hence must be divided by a thousand to return seconds.

Suppose a timer returns 32-bit integer data and measures microseconds. This timer must roll over after 2^{32} microseconds. This is only $2^{32} / 10^6 = 4295$ seconds. Therefore, this timer is incapable of measuring anything more than 1.2 hours. Timers that measure milliseconds and use 32-bit data have a longer amount of time before roll over, since 2^{32} milliseconds is 49 days. Thus there may be a trade-off between accuracy and roll over.

One solution to this problem is to return a 64-bit quantity. If a timer measures microseconds using 64-bit integer data, then the roll over time is $2^{64} / 10^6$, which is over half a million years. Another solution is to have the timer return two values: One represents seconds and one represents microseconds since the last second. Even using 32-bit integers, the roll over in this case is over a hundred years.

6.2.2   Time What?

Many timers are deplorable and should not be used due to low resolution and high overhead. Timing code should be simple, but it isn't. Different timers return the amount of time spent in different systems components and users rarely know just how accurate and expensive their timers are.

The three quantities most often returned from timers are

- user time
- system time
- CPU time (sum of user time and system time)
- elapsed time or wall clock time

The operating system is involved any time a program is run. It must arbitrate system resources such as I/O and swap processes to ensure that everyone gets access to the processors on a system. So when a job is executed, some amount of time is spent performing the work of a program (the *user time*) and some amount is spent in the operating system supporting the execution of the job (the *system time*). Most runs will have the bulk of their time spent in user time and very little in system time. *CPU time* is defined to be the sum of the user time and the system time. Many timers keep track of the user time and system time separately, while other timers just report the CPU time. Some timers return separate amounts for the parent process and its child processes. So the most general of these timers return the four quantities:

- user time of parent
- system time of parent
- user time of children
- system time of children

A very useful timer is the *wall-clock time* or the *wall time*. This time is frequently called *elapsed time*, although some documents confusingly call CPU time the elapsed time. Wall time is like using a stop watch. The stop watch is started when execution starts and stopped when execution ends. What could be simpler?

Most work done by a computer shows up as user time or system time. However, when a system is waiting for a remote device access, the time waiting is not counted against the user time or the system time. It will, of course, be a component of the wall time. On a system executing a large number of programs, the wall time for a particular program may be large, but the CPU time is small since each job competes against all other jobs for computing resources.

Parallel processing jobs represent another challenge to timers. The total time to execute is the most important time, since there are multiple processors, each accruing CPU time. So for parallel processing, you may not care what the CPU time is. However, you'll want to know how well your job is using multiple processors. The parallel efficiency of a job is found by measuring the wall time using one processor, measuring the wall time with n processors, and calculating their ratio. If this number is close to n, then you have a high degree of parallelism. Note that you must run these jobs stand-alone to ensure that the results are meaningful.

The following examples illustrate the differences between the timing quantities:

Example 1: Single processor system. The only job running on the system is your job. It executes the following code which contains an infinite loop

```
PROGRAM MAIN
N = 0
I = 0
DO WHILE (N .EQ. 0)
   I = I + 1
   IF (I .EQ. 1000) I = 0
ENDDO
END
```

Suppose you terminate the job after it runs several minutes. This job has minimal operating system requirements, so the amount of system time is small. The wall time result should be nearly the same as the CPU time result since you are not contending against other users.

Example 2: Same system and code as shown in Example 1. You and four of your colleagues start running your codes at the same time. You terminate your copy of the job after several minutes. The system time in this example is higher than in Example 1 since the operating system must distribute processor time between the five users. The system time is still small compared to the CPU and wall time. The CPU time is probably about 1/5 the wall time since the processor gets shared among the users.

Example 3: You have a two processor system all to yourself. You've written a program that consumes both processors all the time and requires few system calls. The CPU time should be about double the wall time because the program does not require much work from the O/S to distribute work among processors.

Example 4: You run the following I/O intensive program.

```
#include <fcntl.h>
#include <unistd.h>
#define FILENAME "/tmp/$$temp.test"
#define MIN(x,y) ((x)>(y)?(y):(x))

foo(n)
int n;
{
   int i, j, k;
   static int fildes[20];
   static char buffer[20][64];
   static int call_flag= 0;

   k = 0;
   for( i = 0; i < n; i += 20 )
   {
     for( j = 0; j < MIN(n-i,20); j++ )
       sprintf(buffer[j],"%s.%d",FILENAME,i+j);
     for( j = 0; j < MIN(n-i,20); j++ )
       fildes[j] = open( buffer[j], O_CREAT|O_RDWR, 0777 );
     for( j = 0; j < MIN(n-i,20); j++ )
     {
       unlink( buffer[j] );
       k++;
     }
   }
```

```
        for( j = 0; j < MIN(n-i,20); j++ )
          close( fildes[j] );
        }
        if( k!= n ) printf("**ERROR** runs(%d) != n(%d) \n",k,n);

    return(0);
    }
```

This routine performs lots of system calls and therefore spends nearly all of its time in system time and very little in user time. A timer that measures system time separately from user time is valuable here since CPU time won't distinguish between the two.

Conclusions from these examples:

1. If possible, always use a dedicated system.
2. CPU time is important for non-dedicated systems.
3. Wall time is the only timer for parallel execution.

At this point it should be obvious that the authors have a strong bias in favor of benchmarking stand-alone systems and using wall time.

6.2.3   Executable Timers

The least useful timers are those that time an entire application. These are also specific to the individual shells supported by an operating system. Below are two representative ones used on UNIX systems.

6.2.3.1   timex

Executing timex a.out causes the elapsed time (called real below), user and system (sys) time to be written as follows for a sample executable:

```
real      0.14
user      0.12
sys       0.02
```

6.2.3.2   time

Executing time a.out is more useful than using timex. It returns the user time, the system time, the wall time, and the percent of a processor used. Output such as the following is representative:

```
0.17u 0.02s 0:00.27 70.3%
```

This command may also return information on the memory space usage.

6.2.4   Code Timers

There are several timers that are commonly used. They are

- `clock` - supported by the C language
- `times` - UNIX BSD 4.3, UNIX System V r4, POSIX
- `getrusage` - UNIX BSD 4.3, UNIX System V r4
- `ETIME`, `DTIME` - Fortran language extensions
- `gettimeofday` - UNIX BSD 4.3, UNIX System V r4
- `SYSTEM_CLOCK` - supported by Fortran 90

`clock()`, `times()`, `getrusage()`, `gettimeofday()` can be assessed by most C compilers. For example they are all available from the GNU C compiler, `gcc`, used on Linux, Windows NT, and many other operating systems. Even these standard timers will vary in usage among systems, so check the documentation for your system before using them.

We'll now show you how to build your own timers that use the above system timers.

6.2.4.1   Design Your Own Timer

This section shows code examples that use calls to the above mentioned system timers to create timers that function in C as

```
double zero, t0, t1, timer;
zero = 0.0;
t0 = timer(&zero);
   ...
  < code segment being timed >
   ...
t1 = timer(&t0);
```

In Fortran, the calling sequence is

```
REAL*8 ZERO, T0, T1, TIMER
ZERO = 0.0D0
T0 = TIMER(T0)
   ...
  < code segment being timed >
   ...
T1 = TIMER(T0)
```

where `t1` contains the amount of time in seconds spent doing the work. The timers below return CPU time or wall time. Timers that return CPU time can be easily modified to return user time or system time.

6.2.4.2   clock

clock() is supported by the C language and returns the amount of CPU time measured in multiples of some fraction of a second. Check the include file <time.h> to see the usage on your system. The time includes the times of the child processes that have terminated. To get the number of seconds requires dividing by the system defined constant CLOCKS_PER_SECOND. If clock() uses 32-bit integers and CLOCKS_PER_SECOND is 10^6 or larger, this timer is not recommended since the roll over time is 1.2 hours or less.

cputime using clock

```
/*      Name: cputime.c
Description: Return CPU time = user time + system time */


# include <time.h>


static double recip = 1.0 / (double) CLOCKS_PER_SEC;


double cputime(t0)
double *t0;
{
   double time;
   static long clock_ret;
   static long base_sec = 0;
   clock_ret = clock();

   if ( base_sec == 0 )
     base_sec = clock_ret;
   time = (double) (clock_ret - base_sec) * recip - *t0;

   return(time);
}
```

6.2.4.3   times

times() returns separate values for user time and system time. It also allows users to check the user and system time for child processes. It requires dividing by the system defined constant CLK_TCK to obtain seconds. Since the user and system time are returned separately, it allows the user to gain more insight into the program than clock(). If times() uses 32-bit integers and CLK_TCK is 10^6 or larger, this timer is not recommended since the roll over time is 1.2 hours or less.

cputime using times

```
/*      Name: cputime.c
Description: Return CPU time = user time + system time */

# include <time.h>
# include <sys/times.h>

double cputime(t0)
double *t0;
{
   double time;
   static double recip;
   struct tms buffer;
   static long base_sec = 0;

   (void) times(&buffer);
   if ( base_sec == 0 )
   {
      recip = 1.0 / (double) CLK_TCK;
      base_sec = buffer.tms_utime + buffer.tms_stime;
   }
   time = ((double)(buffer.tms_utime + buffer.tms_stime -
       base_sec)) * recip - *t0;
   return(time);
}
```

6.2.4.4   getrusage

getrusage() returns the number of seconds and microseconds for user time and the number of seconds and microseconds for system time. It also returns parent and child process times in separate structures. The microsecond values must be multiplied by 10^{-6} and summed with the seconds values to obtain the time. Since the user and system time are returned separately, it allows the user to gain more insight into the program than clock(). This can be a very useful timer.

cputime using getrusage

```
/*      Name: cputime.c
Description: Return CPU time = user time + system time */

# include <sys/resource.h>

double cputime(t0)
double *t0;
{
  double time, mic, mega;
  int who;
  static long base_sec = 0;
  static long base_usec = 0;
  struct rusage buffcr;
  who  = RUSAGE_SELF;
  mega = 1.0e-6;

  getrusage (who, &buffer);
  if ( base_sec == 0 )
  {
    base_sec  = buffer.ru_utime.tv_sec + buffer.ru_stime.tv_sec;
    base_usec = buffer.ru_utime.tv_usec + buffer.ru_stime.tv_usec;
  }
  time = (double)(buffer.ru_utime.tv_sec +
      buffer.ru_stime.tv_sec - base_sec);
  mic= (double)(buffer.ru_utime.tv_usec +
      buffer.ru_stime.tv_usec - base_usec);
  time = (time + mic * mega) - *t0;
  return(tim);
}
```

6.2.4.5   ETIME, DTIME

ETIME and DTIME arc functions contained in most Fortran compilers. They take a real array of size two and return user time in the first element and system time in the second element. The function return value is the CPU time. DTIME returns the time since the last call to DTIME, while ETIME returns the total time spent in the routine so far. Like the clock() routine, the output includes the times for child processes that have terminated.

6.2.4.6   Parallel Issues

Timing parallel programs can be tricky. Note that clock(), times(), getrusage(), ETIME, and DTIME all return the user and system times for parent and all child processes. Such timers can have incredibly high overhead, especially in parallel applications. This occurs because the operating system can spend a lot of time determining which threads have child processes and which ones don't. Moreover, the data structures providing such information are often accessible by only a single thread at a time. The end result may be a timer that takes longer to execute than the rest of the program!

6.2.4.7 gettimeofday

gettimeofday() is a most useful timer. It allows a wall clock timer to be built around it. gettimeofday() returns four different values, two of which are important for timing. These two items are the number of seconds since Jan. 1, 1970, and the number of microseconds since the beginning of the last second. gettimeofday() can be used to build the general purpose walltime routine shown below.

walltime using getttimeofday

```
/* Name: walltime.c
Description: Return walltime

struct timezone is not used
struct timeval is
  struct timeval {
    unsigned long  tv_sec;      seconds since Jan. 1, 1970
    long           tv_usec;     and microseconds
  };
*/

# include <sys/time.h>
double walltime(t0)
double *t0;
{
double mic, time;
double mega = 0.000001;
struct timeval tp;
struct timezone tzp;
static long base_sec = 0;
static long base_usec = 0;

(void) gettimeofday(&tp,&tzp);
if (base_sec == 0) {
  base_sec = tp.tv_sec;
  base_usec = tp.tv_usec;
}

time = (double) (tp.tv_sec - base_sec);
mic = (double) (tp.tv_usec - base_usec);
time = (time + mic * mega) - *t0;
return(tim);
}
```

6.2.4.8   SYSTEM_CLOCK

SYSTEM_CLOCK is supported by Fortran 90 and returns three values: the current value of a system clock, the number of clocks per second, and the maximum system clock value. It allows a wall clock timer to be built around it as shown below.

walltime using SYSTEM_CLOCK

```
      REAL*8 FUNCTION WALLTIME(TIME)
C         NAME: WALLTIME.C
C DESCRIPTION: RETURN WALLTIME
C
      INTEGER COUNT, COUNT_RATE, BASE_SEC
      REAL*8  TIME, INV_COUNT_RATE
      DATA BASE_SEC/0/
      SAVE INV_COUNT_RATE
      CALL SYSTEM_CLOCK(COUNT,COUNT_RATE)
      IF (BASE_SEC .EQ. 0) THEN
        BASE_SEC = COUNT
        INV_COUNT_RATE = COUNT_RATE
        INV_COUNT_RATE = 1.0D0 / INV_COUNT_RATE
      ENDIF
      WALLTIME = (COUNT - BASE_SEC)
      WALLTIME = WALLTIME * INV_COUNT_RATE - TIME
      END
```

6.2.5   Measure the Timer Resolution

You should have a pretty good idea of how accurate a timer is before you use its results to optimize your code. For example, you don't want to try to time a section of code only to find out your timer doesn't have the necessary resolution to measure it. Therefore, we've included a C routine to allow you to determine the approximate resolution of your timers.

```
#include <stdio.h>
main()
{

  /* check timer resolution */
  double t0, t1, cputime();
  int i, j;
  double zero;

  /* bring code into the instruction cache*/
  zero = 0.0;
  t0 = timer(&zero);

  t1 = 0.0;
  j = 0;
```

```
    while (t1 == 0.0)
    {
      j++;
      zero = 0.0;
      t0 = timer(&zero);
      foo(j);
      t1 = timer(&t0);
    }
    printf (" It took %7d iterations to generate a \
        nonzero time \n",j);
    if (j == 1)
      printf (" Timer resolution less than or equal \
        to %13.7f \n",t1);
    else
      printf (" Timer resolution is %13.7f seconds\n",t1);
}

foo(n)
int n;
{
  int i, j;
  i = 0;
  for (j = 0; j < n; j++)
    i++;
  return (i);
}
```

If only one iteration is needed, the program prints an upper bound for the resolution of the timer. Otherwise, it prints the timer resolution. Be sure to run the routine a few times to ensure that results are consistent. On one RISC system, the following output was produced:

Using clock():

```
It took      682 iterations to generate a nonzero time
Timer resolution is 0.0200000 seconds
```

Using times():

```
It took      720 iterations to generate a nonzero time
Timer resolution is 0.0200000 seconds
```

Using getrusage():

```
It took     7374 iterations to generate a nonzero time
Timer resolution is      0.0002700 seconds
```

So the tested timer with the highest resolution for CPU time on this system is `getrusage()`.

6.2.6   Spin Loops

Sometimes measurements are needed for short-running kernels that take less time to run than the resolution of the most accurate timer on a system. Spin loops can be placed around the code to increase the amount of work measured. The time in the kernel is obtained by dividing the total time by the number of iterations of the spin loop. This still may not give the expected values, since the first call to a subroutine may require an inordinate amount of time due to missing the instruction cache and virtual memory page creation. Therefore, the minimum of all times may be desired. Using the minimum also helps users obtain reproducible results on non-stand-alone systems. Code using a spin loop may appear as:

```
ZERO = 0.0D0
T2 = 100000.
DO J= 1,5
   TO = TIMER(ZERO)
     CALL CODE_TO_TIME
   T1 = TIMER(TO)
   T2 = MIN(T2,T1)
ENDDO
T2 = T2 / N
PRINT *,'THE MINIMUM TIME IS',T2
```

The problem with spin loops is that sometimes sophisticated compilers can optimize them out of the code, thereby making the measurement useless. If the code to be timed is a subroutine call and interprocedural optimization is not enabled, then the code to be timed will not be removed by the compiler.

6.3 Profilers

Manually inserting calls to a timer is practical only if you're working with a small piece of code and know that the code is important for the performance of your application. Often you're given a large application to optimize without any idea where most of the time is spent. So you'd like a tool that automatically inserts timing calls, and you'd like to be able to use it on large applications to determine the critical areas to optimize. This is what profilers do. They insert calls into applications to generate timings about subroutine, functions, or even loops. The ideal profiler collects information without altering the performance of the code, but this is relatively rare. Different profilers introduce varying degrees of intrusion into the timing of a program's execution.

There are many different types of profilers used on RISC systems. Some profilers take the standard executable and use the operating system to extract timing information as the job is executed. Others require relinking the source code with special profiled libraries. Some require all source code to be recompiled and relinked to extract profile information. Compilers that require recompiling can be frustrating since sometimes you're given only object routines for the application you wish to profile. (Begging for source is an important skill to cultivate!) The granularity of profilers also varies a lot. Some profilers can perform only routine-level profiling, while others can profile down to the loop level.

When using a profiler, optimizing code becomes an iterative process:

1. Check for correct answers.
2. Profile to find the most time-consuming routines.
3. Optimize these routines using compiler options, directives/pragmas, and source code modifications.
4. Repeat steps 1-3 until the most important routines have been optimized.

Ideally, a few routines will dominate the profile with most of the time spent in a few key loops. The most difficult programs to optimize are ones that have lots of routines that each take a very small percentage of the time. Applications like this are said to have a flat profile, since a histogram showing the time spent in these routines is flat. These application are difficult to optimize since many routines have to be examined to improve performance significantly. Using profilers in conjunction with independent timers is a powerful technique. The profiler can narrow the field of routines to optimize. Timers allow these routines to be finely tuned.

The goals for profiler timers are the same as for independent timers. For example, the timing routines used by processors must be highly accurate. The user is at the mercy of the creators of the profiler for this, so be aware of this dependency.

6.3.1   Types of Profilers

Profilers are segregated into different categories based on how they collect their data. Some profilers are *sampling*-based. They use a predefined clock and every multiple of this clock tick they sample what the code is doing. Other timers are *event*-based. For example, entry into a subroutine is an event. The advantage of event-based profilers over sampling-based profilers is that sampling-based profilers might miss important events due to their using a predefined clock.

Profilers are also *trace*-based or *reductionist*. Trace-based means the compiler keeps all information it collects while reductionist means that only statistical information is kept. For example, a reductionist profiler might save only the average amount of time spent in a routine. Since a event-based or sampling-based profiler may be trace-based or reductionist, at a high level, there are four types of profilers.

6.3.2   Examples of Profilers

One profiler that has minimal overhead is the Cray hardware performance monitor that is present on some Cray vector computers. This tool is very powerful since it collects lots of data with information, including vector operations performed and Mflop/s rates. There are two reasons why it works so well. First, hardware designers realized the importance of profilers and designed special profiling registers into the processors. Second, vector computers can produce very meaningful profile information with relatively small amounts of data.

Suppose a vector computer processes a loop that consists of adding two vectors of length n. So the vectors need to be loaded, added together, and their result stored. The profiler needs to keep very little information for each vector operation: only the type of operation and its vector length. The profiler also needs to know the number of clock ticks to perform the calculations. If n is very large, the time to collect this information is small compared to the number of clock cycles it takes to actually do the calculations. The processing of the vector units can also occur simultaneously with the updating of the profile registers. Contrast this to a RISC processor where any collection of data for profiling has to compete with the normal processing and may interfere with pipelining. So profilers on vector computers have a natural advantage over other types of processors.

Most computer vendors have their own unique profilers, but there are some common ones. The Message Passing Interface (*MPI*), which will be discussed in Chapter 8, is a widely used standard for parallel programming using message passing. *XMPI* is an event-based, trace-based profiler for programs that use MPI. It is invoked by linking with a special MPI library that has been created for profiling.

The most common UNIX profilers for single processor execution are *prof* and *gprof*. At least one of these is included on most UNIX computers. These are the most common type of profiler and require code to be relinked and executed to create an output file with timing results in it. An additional routine is then called to collect these results into meaningful output. prof is a reductionist profiler that may be event-based or sampling-based. gprof is an event-based profiler and returns more information than prof.

6.3.3 gprof

To use gprof requires creating an executable that contains timing instrumentation. This can be done by relinking, but may require recompiling source. Check your Fortran and C compiler documentation to find the exact compiler options.

The LINPACK 100x100 benchmark is a good code to study for profiling. It is available from http://www.netlib.org/. This code solves a system of equations of size 100x100. The source code was compiled to use gprof (the -pg option below) on a CISC processor using the GNU version of gprof by the following:

```
fort77 -O2 -pg linpackd.f
cc -pg second.c
cc -pg *.o
a.out
gprof a.out
```

gprof produces a profile that shows the amount of time spent in each routine. For this system, gprof determined that the subroutine DAXPY was the most time-consuming routine. (This system appends an underscore to the routine names which will be ignored in this section.) Columns to note are self seconds and the number of calls. The self seconds column shows the amount of time in a routine minus the amount of time in child routines, while the number of calls is important for inlining. If the number of calls is large and the amount of time spent in each call (us/call) is small, a routine should be inlined. (Note that us/call is the number of microseconds per call while ms/call is the number of milliseconds per call.) An extract of the gprof output is

```
Each sample counts as 0.01 seconds.
     %     cumulative   self              self     total
   time    seconds     seconds   calls   us/call  us/call   name
  82.57     1.80        1.80     133874  13.45    13.45     daxpy_
  10.55     2.03        0.23     27      8518.52  8518.52   matgen_
   4.59     2.13        0.10     26      3846.15  71939.73  dgefa_
   1.38     2.16        0.03     2574    11.66    11.66     idamax_
   0.46     2.17        0.01     2574    3.89     3.89      dscal_
   0.46     2.18        0.01     26      384.62   3060.27   dgesl_
   0.00     2.18        0.00     1       0.00     0.00      dmxpy_
   0.00     2.18        0.00     1       0.00     0.00      epslon_
```

% time	the percentage of the total running time of the program used by this function.
cumulative seconds	a running sum of the number of seconds accounted for by this function and those listed above it.
self seconds	the number of seconds accounted for by this function alone. This is the major sort for this listing.
calls	the number of times this function was invoked, if this function is profiled, else blank.
self ms/call	the average number of milliseconds spent in this function per call, if this function is profiled, else blank.
total ms/call	the average number of milliseconds spent in this function and its descendents per call, if this function is profiled, else blank.
name	the name of the function. This is the minor sort for this listing. The index shows the location of the function in the gprof listing. If the index is in parenthesis it shows where it would appear in the gprof listing if it were to be printed.

gprof also produces a call graph that shows which routines call other routines. The part of the call graph relating to DAXPY is

```
index   % time    self    children   called        name
-------------------------------------------------------
                  0.10     1.77      26/26          MAIN__ [1]
[2]       85.8    0.10     1.77      26            dgefa_ [2]
                  1.73     0.00      128700/133874    daxpy_ [3]
                  0.03     0.00      2574/2574        idamax_ [6]
```

```
                        0.01    0.00      2574/2574       dscal_ [7]
     ----------------------------------------------
                        0.07    0.00      5174/133874      dgesl_ [5]
                        1.73    0.00      128700/133874    dgefa_ [2]
     [3]    82.6        1.80    0.00      133874          daxpy_ [3]
     ----------------------------------------------
                        0.01    0.07      26/26            MAIN__ [1]
     [5]     3.6        0.01    0.07      26              dgesl_ [5]
                        0.07    0.00      5174/133874      daxpy_ [3]

     ----------------------------------------------
```

```
Each entry in this table consists of several lines. The line with the
index number at the left hand margin lists the current function.
The lines above it list the functions that called this function,
and the lines below it list the functions this one called.
This line lists:
     index     A unique number given to each element of the table.
               Index numbers are sorted numerically.
               The index number is printed next to every function name so
               it is easier to look up where the function in the table.

     % time    This is the percentage of the 'total' time that was spent
               in this function and its children.  Note that due to
               different viewpoints, functions excluded by options, etc,
               these numbers will NOT add up to 100%.

     self      This is the total amount of time spent in this function.

     children  This is the total amount of time propagated into this
               function by its children.

     called    This is the number of times the function was called.
               If the function called itself recursively, the number
               only includes non-recursive calls, and is followed by
               a '+' and the number of recursive calls.

     name      The name of the current function.  The index number is
               printed after it.  If the function is a member of a
               cycle, the cycle number is printed between the
               function's name and the index number.

Index by function name

     [3] daxpy_        [8] dmxpy_        [6] idamax_
     [2] dgefa_        [7] dscal_        [4] matgen_
     [5] dgesl_        [9] epslon_
```

By studying the output, it is apparent that DAXPY is called by both DGEFA and DGESL. DAXPY was called 133874 times, with most of the calls (128700) from DGEFA. One question is ask is whether DAXPY is running as fast as it should. Also note the large number of calls to DAXPY and the small amount of time spent in each call. This makes DAXPY a good candidate for inlining.

6.3.4 CXperf

The advantage of gprof is that it is available on many different hardware platforms. It doesn't provide all of the profile information we'd like, though. The ideal profiler would provide many additional features, including

- routine and loop level analysis
- results in seconds
- Mflop/s rates
- millions of instructions per second rates
- data cache misses
- instruction cache misses
- TLB misses
- parallel information
- a Graphical User Interface(GUI)

The Hewlett-Packard profiler, CXperf, is an event-based profiler with both trace and reductionist components. It provides most of the above information (everything except the Mflop/s values). Advanced profilers like CXperf are dependent on hardware to provide support that allow them to obtain some of the information. Some HP hardware provides more profiling information than others, so CXperf may provide different types of information depending on the type of hardware used. CXperf is available for the HP C (cc), C++ (aCC), and Fortran 90 (f90) compilers. It also supports profiling routines that use MPI and compiler based parallelism.

Users move through four steps using CXperf:

- compilation
- instrumentation
- execution
- analysis

6.3.4.1 Compilation

This consists of compiling source with +pa or +pal to instrument the object code for CXperf. +pa is used for routine level analysis (like gprof), while +pal instruments for the finer loop level analysis. We'll use +pal in the following examples. Since you may not have access to all the source, CXperf contains a utility, cxoi, that allows users to take an HP-UX object file and modify it to include routine level instrumentation for use by CXperf.

Compiling and linking the previous LINPACK code with +O2 +pal produces an efficient executable that is ready for analysis by CXperf.

6.3.4.2 Instrumentation

Typing cxperf a.out starts the profiler and produces the GUI shown in Figure 6-1. Users can select the routines for analysis and whether to profile at the loop level. Various metrics

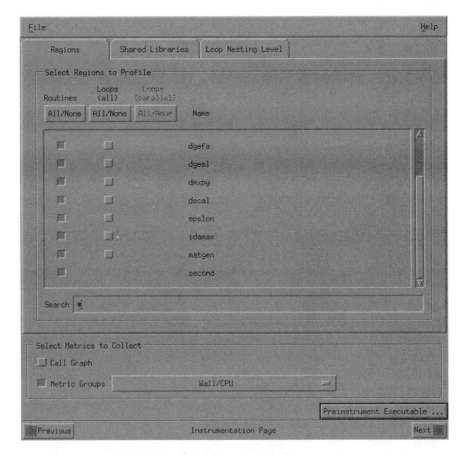

Figure 6-1   CXperf instrumentation page.

such as wall time and data cache misses can also be selected. One approach is to make multiple profiles. The first produces a routine-level profile so the user can select the few most important routines for more analysis. Then a second profile may be created using loop-level profiling on these routines. Selecting "Next" on the GUI places the user on an execution page where the routine may be initiated by selecting a start button.

6.3.4.3   Analysis

After the routine has been executed, the GUI shown in Figure 6-2 appears. It contains a histogram of the timing results showing the amount of time spent in each routine excluding children. On this processor, the routines DGEFA and DAXPY take most of the time. Users can reprofile the executable to see the individual loops in the routines that take the most time. There are many other views of the data, including a three-dimensional view for threaded, parallel results. CXperf also has the ability to combine the output from separate processes generated by MPI applica-

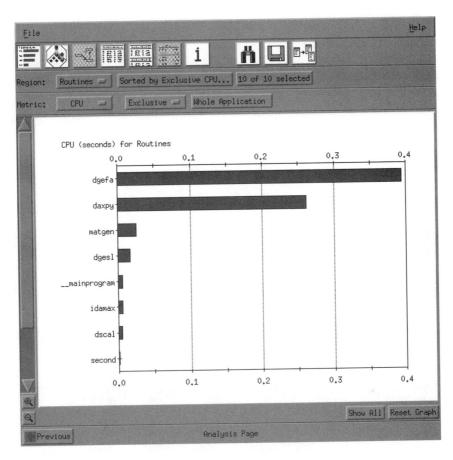

Figure 6-2   CXperf analysis page.

tions into a single file. This profiler can display the call graph as shown in Figure 6-3. Note the thickness of the arcs in the graphical call graph. These show the importance of the various processing paths. So, for example, while DAXPY is called by both DGEFA and DGESL, the call from DGEFA is much more important as shown by the thickness of the arc connecting DGEFA and DAXPY. A summary report for the whole application or for individual regions can also be created.

6.3.5   Quantify

Another profiler is the Quantify product produced by Rational software (http://www.rational.com/). The main advantage of this product is that it is available for both HP and Sun computers. The current versions are Quantify 4.5.1 for Sun and Quantify 5.0.1 for HP. It is available for the C and C++ programming languages, but not Fortran. It is similar to CXperf, but, as would be expected, it is inferior in some areas and superior in others. Like

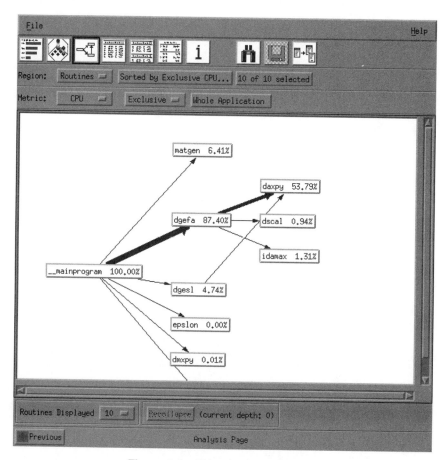

Figure 6-3 CXperf call graph.

CXperf, it is an event-based profiler with a GUI. After it is installed on a system, Quantify can be accessed by replacing "cc" with "quantify cc". Like CXperf, Quantify needs to use objects that have been modified for profiling in order to generate the maximum amount of information. If you link only with Quantify, as in

```
quantify cc -o a.out *.o
```

then Quantify creates new objects that are instrumented for profiling. When a.out is executed, it displays the normal output, some additional Quantify information, and opens a GUI for profiling.

A C version of the LINPACK 100x100 benchmark was compiled with `cc` on an HP N-Class server. It was linked with `quantify cc` and executed. The output begins with Quantify's prelude information such as

```
**** Quantify instrumented a.out (pid 1084 at Mon Nov 22 13:42:00 1999)
Quantify 5.0.1 of 23:26 Thu 09 Sep 99 HP-UX, Copyright (C) 1993-1999 Rational Software
Corp. All rights reserved.
  * For contact information type: "quantify -help"
  * Quantify licensed to Quantify Evaluation User
  * Quantify instruction counting enabled.
```

followed by the normal output from the executable. Then an epilogue gives more information.

```
Quantify: Sending data for 63 of 2982 functions
    from a.out (pid 1084)..........done.

Quantify: Resource Statistics for a.out (pid 1084)
*                                     cycles       secs
*  Total counted time:             37788604     0.189 (100.0%)
*     Time in your code:           33287204     0.166 ( 88.1%)
*     Time in system calls:         4501400     0.023 ( 11.9%)
*
*  Note: Data collected assuming a HP9000/800 with clock rate of 200 MHz.
*  Note: These times exclude Quantify overhead and possible memory effects.
*
*  Elapsed data collection time:      0.501 secs
*
*  Note: This measurement includes Quantify overhead.
*
```

It should be noted that Quantify thinks the MHz of this computer is 200 MHz, although it is actually 440 MHz. When the code is executed, the GUI shown in Figure 6-4 appears:

Figure 6-4 Quantify control panel.

Users can then request analyses similar to those of CXperf. The Function List shows the amount of time spent in the most time-consuming routines.

One nice feature of Quantify is that it automatically includes results for system library routines such as `fabs()`. Users can also select more information on individual functions. Figure 6-5 shows the Function List and the Function Details for the function `daxpy`. Although Quantify can report results in seconds and millions of instructions per second, it doesn't collect separate data on cache or TLB misses.

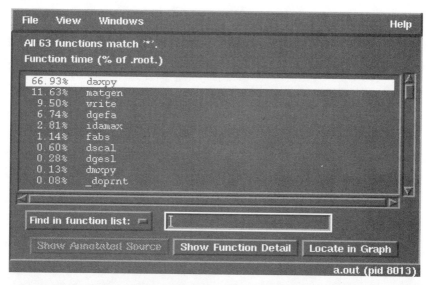

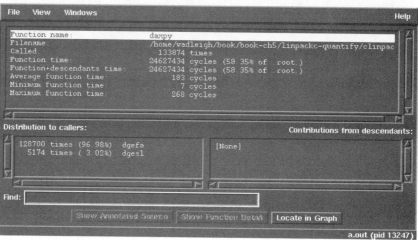

Figure 6-5   Quantify function list and function details for daxpy.

Quantify also contains a well-designed call graph that allows users to see the relationship between functions, as shown in Figure 6-6.

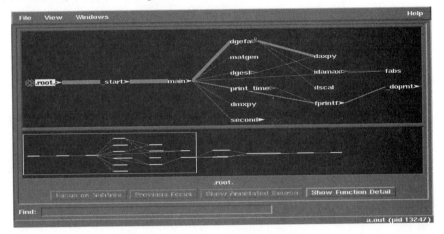

Figure 6-6   Quantify call graph.

So which profiler is best? It depends on what you want from a profiler. Table 6-1 contrasts CXperf and Quantify.

Table 6-1   CXperf and Quantify Comparison.

CXperf	Quantify	Comments
Available on HP	Available on HP, Sun	Quantify supports more hardware
Supports C, C++, Fortran 90	Supports C, C++	CXperf supports more languages
Requires compiling with +pa or +pal, or instrumenting with cxoi	Requires relinking as in quantify cc	Quantify is easier to use
Many metrics, including cache and TLB results	A few basic metrics	CXperf collects more information
Can combine performance data for each process in an MPI application	Quantify combines multi-threaded results in a single file unless the user requests multiple files	CXperf has better support for parallelism

6.3.6 DAXPY Kernel

Let's back up a little and suppose we don't have the results of a fancy profiler like CXperf or Quantify. Using gprof determined that the DAXPY subroutine was the main consumer of time in the LINPACK 100x100 benchmark. The DAXPY kernel appears as

```
      SUBROUTINE DAXPY(N,DA,DX,INCX,DY,INCY)
C
C     CONSTANT TIMES A VECTOR PLUS A VECTOR.
C     JACK DONGARRA, LINPACK, 3/11/78.
C
      DOUBLE PRECISION DX(1),DY(1),DA
      INTEGER I,INCX,INCY,IX,IY,M,MP1,N
C
      IF(N.LE.0)RETURN
      IF (DA .EQ. 0.0D0) RETURN
      IF(INCX.EQ.1.AND.INCY.EQ.1)GO TO 20
C
C     CODE FOR UNEQUAL INCREMENTS OR EQUAL INCREMENTS
C     NOT EQUAL TO 1
C
      IX = 1
      IY = 1
      IF(INCX.LT.0)IX = (-N+1)*INCX + 1
      IF(INCY.LT.0)IY = (-N+1)*INCY + 1
      DO 10 I = 1,N
        DY(IY) = DY(IY) + DA*DX(IX)
        IX = IX + INCX
        IY = IY + INCY
   10 CONTINUE
      RETURN
C
C     CODE FOR BOTH INCREMENTS EQUAL TO 1
C
   20 CONTINUE
      DO 30 I = 1,N
        DY(I) = DY(I) + DA*DX(I)
   30 CONTINUE
      RETURN
      END
```

It's helpful to determine where the time is spent in a subroutine. The call graph from gprof showed that the only routines that call DAXPY are DGEFA and DGESL, with most of the time spent in the call from DGEFA. The calling sequence for DAXPY in DGEFA is

```
CALL DAXPY(N-K,T,A(K+1,K),1,A(K+1,J),1)
```

so `INCX=INCY=1`, and therefore the `DO 30` loop is the loop to analyze. By analyzing the source code or using a loop level profiler, it can be determined that the size of N is between 1 and 99. Given the high percentage of time spent in `DAXPY`, it is worth analyzing in detail. A good technique is to create a timing driver just for `DAXPY`.

6.3.7   Timing Code - DAXPY

Although the problem size used in the LINPACK 100x100 benchmark is small, this section is going to explore `DAXPY` performance over a wide range of problem sizes. There are two types of performance to consider for kernels on modern processors: in-cache performance and out-of-cache performance. The timer below tests both cases.

```
      PROGRAM DAXPYT
C TIMER FOR DAXPY ROUTINE
      IMPLICIT NONE
      INTEGER*4 NSTART, NEND, NINCR, N, NSPIN, I, J, INCX, INCY
      REAL*8 T0, T1, TIME, WALLTIME, RATE, AMOPS, AMB, SIZE, ZERO
      PARAMETER (AMOPS = 1000000., AMB = 1048576.)
C NSTART, NEND, NINCR ARE THE BEGINNING, END, AND INCREMENT
C  FOR THE SIZES OF DAXPY TO TIME
      PARAMETER (NSTART=10000, NEND=800000, NINCR=10000)
C NSPIN IS THE SPIN LOOP VALUE
      PARAMETER (NSPIN=100)
C MAKE X TWICE THE SIZE OF NEND TO ENCOMPASS BOTH VECTORS IN
C  DAXPY CALL AND ENSURE THAT X AND Y ARE CONTIGUOUS
      REAL*8 A,X(2*NEND)
C
C INCX=INCY=1 TESTS
      INCX = 1
      INCY = INCX
      WRITE (UNIT=6,FMT='(6X,A)') ' DAXPY RESULTS'
      WRITE (UNIT=6,FMT='(6X,A,4X,A,5X,A,6X,A)')
     *'N','SIZE','TIME','RATE'
      WRITE (UNIT=6,FMT='(11X,A,4X,A,3X,A)')
     *'(MB)','(SEC)','(MFLOP/S)'
      DO N = NSTART, NEND, NINCR
C INITIALIZE THE DATA
      A = 1.0D0
      DO I = 1,2*N
        X(I) = 1.0D0
      ENDDO
C SET TIME TO A LARGE NUMBER OF SECONDS
      TIME = 1000000.
      DO J = 1,5
        ZERO = 0.0D0
        T0 = WALLTIME(ZERO)
C SPIN LOOP TO OVERCOME TIMER RESOLUTION
```

```
      DO I = 1,NSPIN
        CALL DAXPY(N, A, X, INCX, X(N+1), INCY)
      ENDDO
      T1 = WALLTIME(T0)
      TIME = MIN(TIME,T1)
    ENDDO
    TIME = TIME / NSPIN
    RATE = (2 * N / TIME) / AMOPS
    SIZE = (2 * 8 * N) / AMB
    WRITE (UNIT=6,FMT='(I8,F8.2,F10.7,F10.4)') N,SIZE,TIME,RATE
  ENDDO
  END
```

The code was run on different processors. By looking at the output, the size of the processor's cache is usually apparent. This is because once the problem size exceeds two times the cache size, the performance should be steady state, since it is likely that two points map to every location in the cache. This is easiest to observe in a direct mapped cache. Associative caches are more complex. If the cache is n-way associative, then degradations may start occurring when the problem size exceeds the size of one of the n-way portions. This is usually more pronounced in caches with a random or round-robin replacement scheme than ones that employ strategies such as least recently used (LRU), as discussed in Chapter 3.

6.3.7.1   DAXPY Performance on a HP PA-8500 Processor

The DAXPY timing code was compiled with f90 +O2 +Odataprefetch since this ensured good code generation and inclusion of software prefetch instructions according to vendor provided documentation. (Users should experiment with compiler options to get the best performance.) It was executed on a PA-8500 processor in a N-4000 series server. Note that the output contains both the loop size, N, and the number of megabytes (MB). This is calculated by taking the loop size, N, multiplication by two (for X and Y), and multiplication by eight (the number of bytes per point).

```
DAXPY RESULTS
    N        SIZE      TIME         RATE
             (MB)      (SEC)        (MFLOP/S)
   10000     0.15      0.0000456    438.8852
   20000     0.31      0.0000916    436.7766
   30000     0.46      0.0001370    437.8284
   40000     0.61      0.0001830    437.0629
   50000     0.76      0.0002286    437.3879
   60000     0.92      0.0002750    436.3636
   70000     1.07      0.0004187    334.3763
   80000     1.22      0.0006969    229.5816
   90000     1.37      0.0010175    176.9111
  100000     1.53      0.0013442    148.7885
  110000     1.68      0.0016554    132.8944
```

120000	1.83	0.0019575	122.6035
130000	1.98	0.0022495	115.5812
140000	2.14	0.0025223	111.0080
150000	2.29	0.0027905	107.5076
160000	2.44	0.0030473	105.0117
170000	2.59	0.0032966	103.1378
180000	2.75	0.0035433	101.6002
190000	2.90	0.0037828	100.4536
200000	3.05	0.0039971	100.0721

This system has consistent performance before one MB and after two MB. The processor contains a one MB, four-way associative cache with a round-robin cache line replacement scheme, so we'd expect performance to be good when the problem size is less than one MB. After two MB, each cache line has to be loaded from memory and performance is low. Between these sizes, performance is complicated and depends on how the cache lines are replaced.

6.3.7.2 DAXPY Performance on a SGI MIPS R10000 Processor

The DAXPY timing code was compiled with f90 -O3, since this ensured good code generation and inclusion of software prefetch instructions according to vendor-provided documentation. (Users should experiment with compiler options to get the best performance.) It was executed on a R10000 processor in an Origin server.

```
DAXPY RESULTS
     N       SIZE     TIME        RATE
             (MB)     (SEC)       (MFLOP/S)
   40000     0.61    0.0007735   103.4313
   80000     1.22    0.0015611   102.4898
  120000     1.83    0.0021688   110.6608
  160000     2.44    0.0029216   109.5287
  200000     3.05    0.0038347   104.3095
  240000     3.66    0.0046173   103.9566
  280000     4.27    0.0065335    85.7117
  320000     4.88    0.0091919    69.6266
  360000     5.49    0.0124616    57.7776
  400000     6.10    0.0155816    51.3425
  440000     6.71    0.0194310    45.2884
  480000     7.32    0.0226135    42.4525
  520000     7.93    0.0246022    42.2727
  560000     8.54    0.0266907    41.9621
  600000     9.16    0.0281908    42.5671
   64000     9.77    0.0304189    42.0791
```

This processor has consistent performance for problems less than four MB and for problems greater than seven MB in size. This is as expected, since this processor contains a four MB, two-way associative cache that uses an LRU replacement scheme.

6.4 Predicting Performance

Based on knowledge of the architecture, the performance of simple kernels can be predicted to a high degree. Timers and profilers can be used to determine how good the compiler is at reaching the theoretical peak. If the theoretical performance and the measured performance are close, then there is no point at attempting to optimize the code further. Conversely, if there is a large difference between the two, the kernel should be analyzed to determine the reason for the discrepancy and an attempt should be made to fix it.

6.4.1 What Am I on, and How Fast Is It?

These aren't easy questions. There's no standard way to obtain this information. You may have to contact your system administrator to be certain. There are some commands which do give some insight into the architecture, though. Two commands to try are uname and sysinfo.

Uname is a POSIX.2 routine that returns information about the processor. "uname -a" will probably return the maximum amount of information from uname. Even when it returns the processor type correctly, it will probably not tell you the processor frequency. sysinfo may produce system information which includes processor information. If you're on an SGI system, the command hinv returns very useful information which includes the processor frequency.

The previous section discussed DAXPY results on two different RISC processors. Now these processors will be examined in detail to see if the performance is acceptable. The following table gives a high level overview of the processors and systems:

Table 6-2   System Characteristics.

	Processor Speed (MHz)	Cache Size (MB)	Cache Line Size (bytes)	Latency to memory (ns)	Maximum Bandwidth (MB/s)
HP PA-8500 in N-Class	440	1	64	290	1280
SGI MIPS R10000 in Origin	250	4	128	350	700

6.4.2 HP PA-8500 Processor in the N-4000 Computer

First, we determine the theoretical peak of the DAXPY code when the data is in-cache and out-of-cache. The processor has the ability to perform two memory operations and two floating-point operations in a clock cycle. The floating-point operations include a single fused multiple-addition (fma) instruction. The processor supports software directed prefetching. The cache is four-way associative and uses a round-robin cache line replacement algorithm.

6.4.2.1 In-cache Performance

A single iteration of the DAXPY kernel consists of a load of DY, a load of DX, a fma, and a store of DY. Note that we're assuming the compiler recognizes that DA is loop invariant and hoists the load of DA outside the loop. The number of memory instructions is three times the number of floating-point instructions, so for this kernel, the memory instructions are more important than the floating-point instructions. The processor can perform two memory operations in a clock cycle, so one iteration of the loop should take 1.5 clock cycles. Again, note that there are two floating-point operations per iteration. Using the 440 MHz processor gives a theoretical rate of

$$(2 \text{ floating-point operations}) \times (440 \text{ MHz}) / (1.5 \text{ clock cycles}) = 587 \text{ Mflop/s}$$

6.4.2.2 Out-of-cache Performance

The processor has memory that is 290 ns away and can support 10 outstanding loads at a time. The processor has a cache line size of 64 bytes. A single load will therefore move data at the rate of 64 bytes / 290 ns = 220 MB/s. Thus, 10 loads can move data at a rate of 2200 MB/s. This is more than the theoretical bus maximum bandwidth of 1280 MB/s. The processor has software directed prefetching, so additional prefetch loads must be added to the instruction stream. In particular, one load must be added for each cache line of DX and each cache line of DY. Thus, every eight loads of DX and DY should have an additional prefetch load.

The HP compiler unrolls performs four-way loop unrolling and inserts one prefetch load for DX and another for DY every four iterations of the loop. Each iteration of the loop requires one load of DX, a load of DY, and a store of DY. Thus, each iteration moves 24 bytes of data to/from memory and performs two floating-point operations. Therefore, the theoretical speed is

$$(2 \text{ floating-point operations}) \times (1280 \text{ MB/s}) / (24 \text{ bytes}) = 106 \text{ Mflop/s}$$

Note that this is much slower than the in-cache case.

6.4.2.3 In-cache Performance Revisited

Since addition memory instructions had to be inserted into the instruction stream to support prefetching data from memory, the in-cache theoretical performance must slow down. Four iterations of the loop perform four loads of DX, four loads of DY, four stores of DY, a prefetch load for DX, a prefetch load for DY, and eight floating-point operations. Fourteen memory operations takes seven clock cycles; therefore, the theoretical rate is

$$(8 \text{ floating-point operations}) \times (440 \text{ MHz}) / (7 \text{ clock cycles}) = 503 \text{ Mflop/s}$$

6.4.3   SGI MIPS R10000 Processor in the Origin Computer

The first thing to determine is the theoretical peak of the DAXPY code when the data is in-cache and out-of-cache. The processor has the ability to perform one memory operation and one fma operation in a clock cycle and supports software directed prefetching. The cache is two-way associative and uses an LRU replacement algorithm.

6.4.3.1   In-cache Performance

A single iteration of the DAXPY kernel consists of a load of DY, a load of DX, a fma, and a store of DY. Note that we're assuming the compiler recognizes that DA is loop invariant and hoists the load of DA outside the loop. The number of memory instructions is three times the number of floating-point instructions, so for this kernel, the memory instructions are more important than the floating-point instructions. The processor can perform one memory operation in a clock cycle, so one iteration of the loop should take three clock cycles. Again, note that there are two floating-point operations per iteration. Using the 250 MHz processor gives a theoretical rate of

(2 floating-point operations) × (250 MHz) / (3 clock cycles) = 167 Mflop/s

6.4.3.2   Out-of-cache Performance

The processor has memory that is 350 ns away and can support four outstanding loads at a time. The processor has a cache line size of 128 bytes. A single load will therefore move data at the rate of 128 bytes / 350 ns = 366 MB/s. Thus, four loads can move data at a rate of 1463 MB/s. The theoretical peak bus maximum bandwidth is 700 MB/s, and this limits the performance. The processor has software directed prefetching, so additional prefetch loads must be added to the instruction stream. In particular, one load must be added for each cache line of DX and DY. Thus every eight loads of DX and DY should have an additional prefetch load.

The SGI compiler performs four-way loop unrolling and inserts one prefetch load for DX and another for DY every four iterations of the loop. Each iteration of the loop requires one load of DX, a load of DY, and a store of DY. Thus, each iteration moves 24 bytes of data to/from memory and performs two floating-point operations. Therefore, the theoretical speed is

(2 floating-point operations) × (700 MB/s) / (24 bytes) = 58 Mflop/s

Note that this is much slower than the in-cache case.

6.4.3.3   In-cache Performance Revisited

Since addition memory instructions had to be inserted into the instruction stream to support prefetching data from memory, the in-cache theoretical performance must slow down. Four iterations of the loop perform four loads of DX, four loads of DY, four stores of DY, a prefetch load for DX, a prefetch load for DY, and eight floating-point operations. Fourteen memory operations take 14 clock cycles, therefore the theoretical rate is

(8 floating-point operations) × (250 MHz) / (14 clock cycles) = 142 Mflop/s

6.4.3.4   Theory Versus Reality

The following table compares the theoretical performance to the measured performance:

Table 6-3   DAXPY Performance.

	Theoretical peak (Mflop/s)	Measured (Mflop/s)	Percent
PA-8500: In-cache	503	440	87
PA-8500: Out-of-cache	106	100	94
R10000: In-cache	142	111	78
R10000: Out-of-cache	58	50	86

Since the actual performance is over 75% of the theoretical performance in all cases, the compilers are doing a good job of code generation.

6.5 Summary

This chapter developed the timing tools necessary to determine the effectiveness of the optimization techniques defined in the previous chapter and showed how to predict the performance of simple kernels on high performance processors. By combining all of these tools, processor optimization can be analyzed in great detail. If your measured performance is over 80% of the theoretical peak, you should be pretty happy and move on to the next most important part of your application. If you understand the performance of more than 80% of your application, it's time to declare victory!

References:

1. *CXperf User's Guide*. Hewlett-Packard, document number B6323-96001, 1998.

2. Quantify User's Guide. Rational Software, http://www.rational.com/.

Is High Performance Computing Language Dependent?

In differentiation, not in uniformity, lies the path of progress.

Louis Brandeis

7.1 Introduction

If you were going to paint a house then you'd be more likely to get a paintbrush instead of a hammer. More generally, there are very few general-purpose tools. This was also the case with early generations of programming languages. Originally, Fortran was designed for scientific, number-crunching applications (hence the name FORmula TRANslation). The common business-oriented language (COBOL) was designed specifically for accounting applications, and the C programming language grew from system programming needs. There are many other examples, but you get the idea. Given the environments from which these languages derived, each had some underlying assumptions built into the language. Originally, this made the compiler technology for each of them simple (compared to today's descendants). Over the years, languages have grown to include functionality found in other programming languages.

There are many examples of how each language has picked up features from others. Fortran 90 provides features such as pointers, dynamic memory allocation, and select/case constructs, all of which were previously in other languages, such as C. The same is true of C, with modern compilers supplying loop optimizations and compiler directives for parallelism originally designed for Fortran.

So, are we at a point where any programming language provides the same performance for any applications? Hardly. Is there one language that gives better performance for all programs? Again, hardly. Many of today's large software applications are implemented in two, three, and sometimes four programming languages. For example, a seismic imaging application is likely to implement its graphics and user interface with C++, memory management and I/O in C, and number crunching signal processing routines in Fortran (and even assembler!). Why? Because each of these languages is well-suited to the application area mentioned. This same type of application is just as likely to be implemented entirely in a single programming language such as C. While some performance may be lost in doing so, it removes the reliance on multilingual programmers and exposure to portability issues due to using multiple languages. So, while one may not write a graphical user interface in Fortran or a simple linear algebra subroutine in C, there are many things that one can do to get good performance using any given language.

7.1.1   Assembly Code Generation

In order to detail the impact of optimizations discussed in this chapter, it is necessary to introduce the practice of examining assembly code as it is generated by the compiler. On the one hand, it isn't necessary to understand assembly language for every computer processor on the planet, but it is helpful to examine assembly generated by the compiler to see what optimizations are taking place "behind the scenes."

As discussed in Chapter 5, a compiler converts a file containing high level language (e.g., Fortran) routines into an object file containing text that is ready to be linked with other files, resulting in an executable program. Almost all compilers provide the -S option, which causes the compiler to compile the high level language into a file containing the resulting assembly instructions which can, in turn, be assembled to result in the object file mentioned above. Compiling with the -S option results in a file with the same prefix but with the .s suffix. So,

```
f90 -S myprog.f
as myprog.s
```

usually generates myprog.o just as

```
f90 -c myprog.f
```

does.   This is accomplished in an analogous way with C compilers as well. To illustrate this, let us consider the following C code, contained in a file called addabs.c:

```
#include <math.h>
double addabs( double x, double y)
{
   double temp;
   temp= fabs(x) + fabs(y);
   return( temp );
}
```

Taking this code and compiling on a Hewlett-Packard N-4000 machine with cc -S addabs.c produces the file addabs.s, which reads as follows:

```
     .LEVEL 2.0N
     .SPACE$TEXT$,SORT=8
     .SUBSPA$CODE$,QUAD=0,ALIGN=4,ACCESS=0x2c,CODE_ONLY,SORT=24
addabs
     .PROC
     .CALLINFO
     CALLER,FRAME=16,ENTRY_FR=%fr13,SAVE_RP,ARGS_SAVED,ORDERING_AWARE
     .ENTRY
     STW      %r2,-20(%r30)       ;offset 0x0
     FSTD,MA %fr12,8(%r30)        ;offset 0x4
     FSTD,MA %fr13,8(%r30)        ;offset 0x8
     LDO      48(%r30),%r30       ;offset 0xc
     .CALL    ARGW0=FR,ARGW1=FU,RTNVAL=FU         ;fpin=105;fpout=104;
     B,L      fabs,%r2            ;offset 0x10
     FCPY,DBL         %fr7,%fr12          ;offset 0x14
     FCPY,DBL         %fr4,%fr13          ;offset 0x18
     .CALL    ARGW0=FR,ARGW1=FU,RTNVAL=FU         ;fpin=105;fpout=104;
     B,L      fabs,%r2            ;offset 0x1c
     FCPY,DBL         %fr12,%fr5          ;offset 0x20
     FADD,DBL         %fr13,%fr4,%fr4 ;offset 0x24
     LDW      -84(%r30),%r2       ;offset 0x28
     LDO      -48(%r30),%r30      ;offset 0x2c
     FLDD,MB -8(%r30),%fr13       ;offset 0x30
     BVE      (%r2)    ;offset 0x34
     .EXIT
     FLDD,MB -8(%r30),%fr12       ;offset 0x38
     .PROCEND;fpin=105,107;fpout=104;
     .SPACE$TEXT$
     .SUBSPA$CODE$
     .SPACE$PRIVATE$,SORT=16
     .SUBSPA$DATA$,QUAD=1,ALIGN=64,ACCESS=0x1f,SORT=16
     .SPACE$TEXT$
     .SUBSPA$CODE$
     .EXPORT add-
abs,ENTRY,PRIV_LEV=3,ARGW0=FR,ARGW1=FU,ARGW2=FR,ARGW3=FU
     .IMPORT fabs,CODE
     .END
```

In PA-RISC assembly language, everything following a semicolon on a given line is a comment (even though the comments here are not very informative!). The intent here is not to give a short course on PA-RISC assembly, but to give one some idea of how to generate assembly code from a high level language and how to get a rough idea of what the assembly code is doing. In the example above, we can pick out the subroutine calls to fabs() by looking for the .CALL directive that precedes a B,L fabs,%register-number. Each line that begins with characters other than a period is an instruction. General (integer) registers are denoted %r#, where # is a number from 0 to 31. Similarly, floating point registers are denoted %fr#, where #

is a number from 0 to 31. Instructions that begin with F are typically floating point instructions, e.g., an instruction that starts with FLDD is a floating point load instruction which loads data into a given register. Stores are performed with FSTD instructions, copies from one floating point register to another are performed with FCPY, adds are performed with FADD, etc. As discussed in Chapter 2, most RISC processors have what is called a branch delay slot in the execution sequence, i.e., the instruction following the branch instruction is executed before the branch is actually taken.

7.2 Pointers and Aliasing

Suppose you've written a subroutine in C which is passed at least two arguments, say, aptr and bptr, which are pointers. The C programming language assumes that these pointers may not point to unique memory locations. That is, for some i and j in your subroutine, aptr[i] and bptr[j] may point to the same memory location. This is generally described as aliasing, i.e., aptr[i] aliases to bptr[j].

Aliasing doesn't only apply to pointers. A specific example is with external or global variables. Suppose xglob is an external variable and that a caller of your routine sets aptr = &xglob. Then xglob and aptr are said to be aliased.

Is aliasing unique to C? No, other language definitions are based on the assumption that pointers can be aliased. Fortran is not one of those languages, unless equivalence functionality is used. From a performance perspective, this is one area where Fortran has an advantage over C. Even though Fortran compilers support pointers, the language assumes that they are not aliased. Note that a programmer can still experience aliasing problems by violating this assumption. For example, consider the following Fortran code:

```
PROGRAM MAIN
REAL X(10)

CALL FOO( X, X, 9 )

END


SUBROUTINE FOO( A, B, N )
REAL A(*), B(*)
INTEGER N
...
```

In the subroutine FOO(), the arrays A and B are most certainly aliased!

The Fortran 90 standard defines pointers. Previous to this, pointers were not defined in Fortran standards. However, Cray Research provided a convenient implementation of pointers in Fortran (this implementation is generally referred to as "Cray pointers"). Generally speaking, if you need to use pointers in your application, then use C, C++, or hope that your Fortran compiler supports "Cray" pointers (which is usually the case).

So, what's the big deal with aliasing? Consider the following sequence of C statements:

```
double *a, *b;
...
b = a + 1;
copy( a, b, n );
```

where copy() is defined as follows:

```
void copy( a, b, n )
double *a, *b;
int n;
{
    int i;
    for( i = 0; i < n; i++)
       b[i] = a[i];
    return;
}
```

Since the compiler expects aliasing, the pseudo code generated for the loop in copy() will look something like

```
    set register %r31 = 0
    set register %r24 = n
loop:
    load x[%r31] into register %fr4
    store register %fr4 into y[%r31]
    increment %r31
    if( %r31 < %r24 ) goto loop
```

So, for example, if n is four, then we have

```
a[0] = 7
a[1] = -3
a[2] = 44
a[3] = 8
a[4] = 1000
```

before the call to copy() and afterward, due to the aliasing of a with b, we have

```
a[0] = 7
a[1] = 7
a[2] = 7
a[3] = 7
a[4] = 7
```

This situation is a classic example of a loop carried dependency caused by aliasing of a and b. Still, you ask, "Why do I care?" We're getting there.

Suppose for a moment that copy was actually a Fortran routine. The Fortran programming language assumes no aliasing of array arguments (or anything else, for that matter). So, most Fortran compilers will aggressively optimize a loop such as the one in copy(). In particular, copy() will likely be optimized using unrolling and efficient scheduling as follows:

```
    set register %r31 = 0
    set register %r24 = n
loop4:
    load a[i] into register %fr4
    load a[i+1] into register %fr5
    load a[i+2] into register %fr6
    load a[i+3] into register %fr7
    store %fr4 into b[i]
    store %fr5 into b[i+1]
    store %fr6 into b[i+2]
    store %fr7 into b[i+3]
    set %r31 = %r31 + 4
    if( %r31 < %r24 ) goto loop4
```

Of course, there's a "cleanup" loop to copy the remaining elements if n is not a multiple of four which follows the above pseudo-code.

In this case, the array a, after the copy, looks like this:

```
a[0] = 7
a[1] = 7
a[2] = -3
a[3] = 44
a[4] = 8
```

This is a lot different from what one might expect! So, if you plan to allow aliasing in your application, then you should avoid using Fortran subroutines for starters. Does this mean you should use only Fortran subroutines if you don't allow aliasing of array or pointer arguments and want optimal performance? Roughly speaking, the answer is no. But you're going to have to use a special flag or two to get the C compiler to generate optimal code.

Compiler designers have taken a serious look at C aliasing issues and most, if not all, provide compile flags that tell the compiler that you "promise none of the pointer or array arguments are aliased." That is, they do not "overlap" in terms of the memory they address.

Flags to accomplish this do not, unfortunately, have a common syntax. For example,:

HP: +Onoparmsoverlap

SGI: -OPT:alias=restrict

Sun: -xrestrict

There are a lot of subtle issues with aliasing, so let's consider several variants on the following loop:

```c
void fooreg( double *a, double *b, double *c, int n )
{
  int i;
  for( i = 0; i < n; i++ )
    c[i] += b[i] * a[i];
  return;
}
```

The following analyses will all be for the Hewlett-Packard C compiler unless specified otherwise. When compiled with `cc +O2`, the loop in `fooreg()` is unrolled, but scheduling is poor, as is demonstrated by the resulting sequence of instructions (generated by `cc +O2`):

```
$D0
        FLDD      -8(%r24),%fr7     ; Load b[i]
        FLDD      -8(%r25),%fr8     ; Load a[i]
        FLDD      -8(%r23),%fr9     ; Load c[i]
        FLDD      0(%r23),%fr6      ; Load c[i+1]
        FLDD      8(%r23),%fr5      ; Load c[i+2]
        FLDD      16(%r23),%fr4     ; Load c[i+3]
        FMPYFADD,DBL %fr7,%fr8,%fr9,%fr24    ; fr24= a[i]*b[i] + c[i]
        FSTD      %fr24,-8(%r23)    ; Store fr24 at c[i]
        FLDD      0(%r24),%fr10     ; Load b[i+1] (only after store of c[i])
        FLDD      0(%r25),%fr11     ; Load a[i+1] (only after store of c[i])
        FMPYFADD,DBL %fr10,%fr11,%fr6,%fr26  ; fr26= a[i+1]*b[i+1]+c[i+1]
        FSTD      %fr26,0(%r23)     ; Store fr26 at c[i+1]
```

```
FLDD      8(%r24),%fr22    ; Load b[i+2] (after store c[i+1])
FLDD      8(%r25),%fr23    ; Load a[i+2] (after store c[i+1])
FMPYFADD,DBL %fr22,%fr23,%fr5,%fr27   ; fr27 = a[i+2]*b[i+2]+c[i+2]
FSTD      %fr27,8(%r23)    ; Store fr27 at c[i+2]
FLDD      16(%r24),%fr25   ; Load b[i+3]
LDO       32(%r24),%r24    ; Increment address register for b
FLDD      16(%r25),%fr7    ; Load a[i+3]
LDO       32(%r25),%r25    ; Increment address register for a
FMPYFADD,DBL %fr25,%fr7,%fr4,%fr8      ; fr8= a[i+3]*b[i+3]+c[i+3]
FSTD      %fr8,16(%r23)    ; Store fr8 at c[i+3]
ADDIB,> -4,%r31,$D0        ; if more work to do goto $D0
LDO       32(%r23),%r23    ; Increment address register for c
```

The important thing to note is how the loads of a and b cannot be done until c from the previous iteration is calculated and stored.

Is this architecture dependent? Absolutely not. The same routine compiled on an SGI Origin 2000 machine results in the following assembly, which corresponds to the loop having been unrolled by a factor of two, but the scheduling suffers because the compiler is constrained on what it can do. Note that comments are preceded by "#" rather than ";" on this architecture.

```
.BB8.foreg:
    ldc1 $f3,0($4)              # load a[i]
    ldc1 $f0,0($5)              # load b[i]
    ldc1 $f2,0($6)              # load c[i]
    madd.d $f2,$f2,$f3,$f0      # f2= c[i]+a[i]*b[i]
    sdc1 $f2,0($6)             # store f2 into c[i]
    ldc1 $f0,8($4)             # load a[i+1]
    ldc1 $f1,8($5)             # load b[i+1]
    ldc1 $f3,8($6)             # load c[i+1]
    madd.d $f3,$f3,$f0,$f1      # f3= c[i+1]*a[i+1]*b[i+1]
    addiu $6,$6,16             # increment address register for c
    addiu $4,$4,16             # increment address register for a
    addiu $5,$5,16             # increment address register for b
    bne $6,$9,.BB8.foreg        # if more work to do goto .BB8.foreg
    sdc1 $f3,-8($6)            # store f3 into c[i+1]
```

Let's now consider the instructions generated with the HP C compiler, using
`cc +O2 +Onoparmsoverlap`:

```
$D0
      FLDD    -8(%r24),%fr9    ; Load b[i]
      FLDD    -8(%r25),%fr10   ; Load a[i]
      FLDD    -8(%r23),%fr11   ; Load c[i]
      FLDD    0(%r24),%fr6     ; Load b[i+1]
      FLDD    0(%r25),%fr7     ; Load a[i+2]
      FLDD    0(%r23),%fr8     ; Load c[i+1]
      FLDD    8(%r24),%fr4     ; Load b[i+2]
      FLDD    8(%r25),%fr5     ; Load a[i+2]
      FMPYFADD,DBL    %fr9,%fr10,%fr11,%fr24   ; fr24= a[i]*b[i]+c[i]
      FSTD    %fr24,-8(%r23)   ; Store c[i]= fr24
      FLDD    8(%r23),%fr22    ; Load c[i+2]
      FMPYFADD,DBL %fr6,%fr7,%fr8,%fr25       ; fr24= a[i+2]*b[i+1]+c[i+1]
      FSTD    %fr25,0(%r23)    ; Store c[i+1]
      FLDD    16(%r24),%fr23   ; Load c[i+3]
      LDO     32(%r24),%r24    ; Increment address register for c
      FMPYFADD,DBL %fr4,%fr5,%fr22,%fr28      ; fr28= a[i+2]*b[i+2]+c[i+2]
      FSTD    %fr28,8(%r23)    ; Store c[i+2]
      FLDD    16(%r25),%fr26   ; Load a[i+3]
      LDO     32(%r25),%r25    ; Increment address register for a
      FLDD    16(%r23),%fr27   ; Load b[i+3]
      FMPYFADD,DBL    %fr23,%fr26,%fr27,%fr9  ; fr9= a[i+3]*b[i+3]+c[i+3]
      FSTD    %fr9,16(%r23)    ; Store c[i+3]
      ADDIB,> -4,%r31,$D0      ; If more work to do goto $D0
      LDO     32(%r23),%r23    ; Increment address register for b
```

Observe how the load instructions are grouped at the beginning of the loop so that as many operands as possible are retrieved before the calculations are performed. In this way, the effect of instruction latency is decreased so that fewer FMPYFADD instructions are delayed.

Aliasing issues don't apply only to array arguments used in the body of the loop. The compiler is also on the alert for any of the loop control variables to be aliased as well. To illustrate this point, consider the following subroutine and recall that external or global variables can also be the "victims" of aliasing:

```
extern int globn, globi;
void fooglobstop( double *a, double *b, double *c )
{
   int i;
   for( i = 0; i < globn; i++ )
     c[i] += b[i] * a[i];
   return;
}
```

Now, not only do we have an issue with a, b, and c overlapping, but they may alias with globn as well—which could have a serious impact on what the answer is. This is true even though `globn` and the arrays are of different types! As we would expect, the compiler generates some pretty conservative code:

```
$D1
    FLDD,S  %r31(%r25),%fr4 ; Load a[i]
    FLDD,S  %r31(%r26),%fr5 ; Load b[i]
    LDO     1(%r31),%r31    ; i++
    FLDD    0(%r23),%fr6    ; Load c[i]
    FMPYFADD,DBL    %fr4,%fr5,%fr6,%fr7    ; fr7= a[i]*b[i]+c[i]
    FSTD    %fr7,0(%r23)    ; Store fr7 at c[i]
    LDW     RR'globn-$global$(%r1),%r29    ; Load globn
    CMPB,>,N %r29,%r31,$D1 ; If ( i < globn ) goto $D1
    SHLADD,L %r31,3,%r24,%r23        ; Increment address register for c
```

This is going to be brutally slow. Not only is the loop not unrolled, disabling efficient scheduling, but the value of the loop stop variable, `globn`, is loaded in every iteration!

The good news is that by compiling with +Onoparmsoverlap, the loop is unrolled and `globn` is not loaded inside the loop, so the generated instructions are analogous to that discussed above.

7.3 Complex Numbers

Fortran has a clear advantage when it comes to performing calculations with complex numbers. The next ANSI standard for C will provide complex data types, but it isn't here just yet. One of the more common methods of storing complex variables in C is through a structure similar to the following:

```
typedef struct COMPLEX
{
    float re;
    float im;
} fcomplex_t;
```

Complex arithmetic, including addition, multiplication, and division is cumbersome with C. One way to handle this situation is to define macros to perform calculations with complex numbers. For example, to multiply two complex numbers, you could use the following macro:

```
#define CMULT(r,x,y) { r.re = x.re*y.re - x.im*y.im; \
                       r.im = x.re*y.im + x.im*y.re; }
```

This simply multiplies the second and third arguments and stores the result in the first argument.

A word of caution when building one's own macros to perform such calculations—be on the lookout for floating point overflow/underflow issues. A good example is complex division. A straightforward approach to dividing a complex number `n` by a complex number `d` is as follows:

```
#define CDIV(r,n,d) {r.re = (n.re*d.re + n.im*d.im) / \
                        (d.re*d.re + d.im *d.im ); \
                        r.im = (d.re*n.im - n.re*d.im) / \
                        (d.re*d.re + d.im* d.im); }
```

However, this can unnecessarily cause overflow in the denominator. A commonly accepted algorithm for performing complex division in a more accurate manner is described below.

```
#define CDIV(r,n,d) {if( fabs(d.re) >= fabs(d.im) ) \
                        { \
                        ratio= d.im / d.re; \
                        den= d.re + ratio * d.im; \
                        c.re= (n.re + ratio * n.im) / den; \
                        c.im= (n.im - ratio * n.re) / den; \
                        } \
                        else \
                        { \
                        ratio= d.re / d.im; \
                        den= d.im + ratio * d.re; \
                        c.re= (n.re * ratio + n.im) / den;\
                        c.im= (n.im * ratio - n.re) / den; \
                        }}
```

This algorithm is actually used by many Fortran compilers to perform complex division (and fortunately it is hidden from the user). This algorithm enables complex division to be accomplished for a greater range of values (without causing floating point overflow) than the simpler form presented earlier.

7.4 Subroutine or Function Call Overhead

Many years ago the practice of "structured programming" became popular (thank goodness). One of the principle contributions of structured programming to application design was the practice of using subroutines and/or functions to replace repeated use of common operations. This makes application source code much easier to read, but it often slows things down. The reason is that calls to subroutines or functions are somewhat expensive. They cause branches to and from the *callee* (the function or subroutine being called) as well as potential instruction cache thrashing and unnecessary storing and loading of data.

One way to remove some of the performance impacts of this *call overhead* is by inlining which is described in Chapter 5. In many cases, macros can be used to replace functions or subroutines. One downside to this is that it can cause the resulting executable to be much larger. In most cases, short functions or subroutines can be replaced with macros with good performance results. A trivial example is a simple function which returns the maximum of two elements:

```
double dmax( double x, double y )
{
   if( x > y ) return( x );
   else return( y );
}
```

This function can be efficiently replaced in C or C++ by a macro such as:

```
#define dmax( x , y ) ( ( (x) > (y) ) ? (x) : (y) )
```

Programming languages have different approaches to how they call functions or subroutines. In an effort to make things a little more concise, let's expand the term *function* to describe routines which return values (traditionally called functions) as well as those that do not return values (subroutines).

Some languages pass arguments by value, while others pass them by address. C and C++ use a pass by value convention. For example, suppose the function foo() is defined as follows:

```
double foo( int n, double *x, double y );
```

Then the function foo will actually receive the value of all three arguments. Typically, this is accomplished through registers. Many RISC architectures use certain registers for arguments to function calls. When the function foo is executed on PA-RISC machines, the value of n will be in general register 26, the value of x (which is actually an address!) will be in general register 25, and the value of y will be in floating point register 7.

With a pass by address language such as Fortran, addresses are passed for each argument. To illustrate this, consider the function FOO defined in Fortran:

```
FUNCTION FOO( N, X, Y )
REAL*8 FOO
INTEGER N
REAL*8 X(*), Y
```

In this case, general register 26 contains the address where the value of N resides. General register 25 contains the address of the first element of the array X, and general register 24 contains the address of the memory location containing the value of Y. Thus, in Fortran, the value of N must be loaded from the address in general register 26, and the value of Y will have to be loaded from the address in general register 24. It's interesting to note that one doesn't have to load the address X from the address in general register 25; it's already there! A slight inconsistency, but we'll let it slide.

The subject of this is book is performance, so one should be asking why we're going down this path. Generally speaking, the pass by value convention is more efficient. The reason is

pretty simple: It eliminates the storing and loading of arguments. Consider the simple example
of integration using the rectangle method, as follows:

```
double myfunc( double x )
{
   return( x*x );
}

double rectangle_method( double *x, int n )
{
   double t;
   int i;

   t = 0.0;
   for( i = 1; i < n; i++ )
     t += (x[i] - x[i-1]) * myfunc( (x[i] + x[i-1]) * 0.5 );

   return( t );
}
```

So, we're integrating the function x^2 over n points, `x[0]` through `x[n-1]`. These same
two functions can be analogously defined in Fortran:

```
FUNCTION MYFUNC( X )
REAL*8 MYFUNC, X

MYFUNC = X * X

RETURN
END

FUNCTION RECTANGLE_METHOD( X, N )
EXTERNAL MYFUNC
REAL*8 RECTANGLE_METHOD, MYFUNC
REAL*8 T, X(*)
INTEGER I, N

T = 0.0
DO I=2, N
  T = T + ( X(I) - X(I-1) ) * MYFUNC( (X(I) + X(I-1)) * 0.5 )
END DO

RECTANGLE_METHOD = T

RETURN
END
```

Now, let's take a look at the code generated by each and compare the number of instructions. For the C example, the subroutine `myfunc()` is simply

```
BVE        (%r2)           ; return
FMPY,DBL   %fr5,%fr5,%fr4  ; return value = x * x (delay slot!)
```

The function consists of just two instructions! Note again that the instruction following a branch (the delay slot) is executed.

The sequence of instructions from the C code for the loop in `rectangle_method()` is as follows:

```
$00000006
     FLDD          8(%r3),%fr6      ; Load x[i]
     FLDD          0(%r3),%fr7      ; Load x[i-1]
     LDO           8(%r3),%r3       ; i++
     FADD,DBL      %fr6,%fr7,%fr4   ; x[i] + x[i-1]
     FSUB,DBL      %fr6,%fr7,%fr14  ; x[i] - x[i-1]
     B,L           myfunc,%r2       ; call myfunc
     FMPY,DBL      %fr4,%fr13,%fr5  ; arg (fr5) = 0.5*(x[i] +x[i-1])
     ADDIB,<       1,%r4,$00000006  ; goto $00000006 if more to do
     FMPYFADD,DBL%fr14,%fr4,%fr12,%tr12; accumulate rectangle area
```

for a total of nine instructions.

Now, let's compare the instructions generated from the Fortran version. First, we have the function MYFUNC:

```
FLDD        0(%r26),%fr5
BVE         (%r2)
FMPY,DBL    %fr5,%fr5,%fr4
```

So, Fortran has to load the argument from the address in register 26 and then calculate the return value. Not only is there an additional instruction, there is also the instruction latency impact. That is, the multiply cannot execute until the load completes.

The loop in RECTANGLE_METHOD written in Fortran results in the following instructions:

```
$0000000C
        FLDD        8(%r3),%fr5        ; Load x(i)
        FLDD        0(%r3),%fr6        ; Load x(i-1)
        LDO         -96(%r30),%r26     ; Put address for argument in r26
        LDO         8(%r3),%r3         ; i = i + 1
        FADD,DBL    %fr5,%fr6,%fr4     ; x(i) + x(i-1)
        FSUB,DBL    %fr5,%fr6,%fr14    ; x(i) - x(i-1)
        FMPY,DBL    %fr4,%fr13,%fr7    ; 0.5 * (x(i) + x(i-1) )
        B,L         myfunc,%r2         ; call myfunc
        FSTD        %fr7,-96(%r30)     ; Store function argument (fr7)
        ADDIB,<=    1,%r4,$0000000C    ; goto $0000000C if more to do
        FMPYFADD,DBL %fr14,%fr4,%fr12,%fr12; accumulate rectangle area
```

There are 11 instructions in this version of the loop. Both are caused by the store to memory required for passing the argument to MYFUNC. That is, after the value is calculated, it must then be stored to the address contained in general register 26.

This example has shown three potential performance problems that the pass by address convention can cause:

1. Additional instructions are usually required for function calls. The caller must store the arguments to memory and then the callee must load them.
2. For simple functions, the additional memory operations incur instruction latencies that delay operations being performed on the arguments.
3. Additional loads and stores cause additional memory access, risking cache misses and thrashing.

7.5 Standard Library Routines

There are several common library routines that exhibit interesting behavior depending on which compiler one uses. Most of those discussed here are often referred to as intrinsic routines. Unfortunately, there isn't a clear definition of what that means to everyone. Fortran compiler documentation describes them as built-in functions and subroutines that are available by default to every Fortran program and procedure. C compiler documentation sometimes refers to them as external routines that can be called by C or any language that the operating system supports. In this book, an *intrinsic* routine is any routine that is commonly used by many different applications to perform a fairly simple operation or, more generally, standard library routines. So, this covers everything from calculating the absolute value of a number to sorting an array. Let's consider a few of these intrinsic routines and some of the impacts they have on the computer.

7.5.1   Absolute Value and Square Root

Two commonly used operations involving a single number that are often performed in hardware are obtaining the absolute value and calculating the square root. These operations are often performed in hardware and usually have special instructions associated with them.

Fortran allows users to take the absolute value via several different intrinsics, including IIABS, JIABS, KIABS, ABS, DABS, QABS, CABS, CDABS and just plain ABS. The latter is the most commonly used because the compiler is fairly promiscuous in what data type it will allow. That is, it automatically substitutes the "right" absolute value intrinsic depending on the argument passed to it. So, if x is declared as a REAL*8 variable, then the Fortran compiler will automatically convert ABS(x) to DABS(x) for you. The downside is, of course, when you actually wanted a REAL*4 value to be returned.

C is not as forgiving as Fortran in this regard. There are (at least) three different versions of the absolute value intrinsic. To make matters worse, one of them is prototyped in the include file stdlib.h while the other two are prototyped in math.h. To get an integer value of the absolute value of something, use abs (include stdlib.h). The argument will automatically be converted to an integer and the absolute value of the result will be returned. Taking the absolute value of a floating point number should be just as straightforward. From purely a functional point of view, just use fabs(). The hitch is that fabs() is a double precision function (and expects a double precision argument). This is OK if you are doing all your arithmetic in double precision (64-bit floating point), but it might cause you a few unnecessary instructions otherwise. That is, suppose you have the following sequence of code:

```
#include <math.h>
    ...
    float x, y;
    ...
    x = fabs( y );
```

If you compile with cc -O, then the following sequence of instructions can be expected:

```
B,L            fabs,%r2      ; Perform branch to routine fabs
FCNV,SGL,DBL %fr4R,%fr5      ; Convert to double (Delay Slot!)

FCNV,DBL,SGL %fr4,%fr4L      ; Convert result from double to float
```

Note that fr5 is used to pass the first (and only, in this case) floating point register to the function call. Recall that the instruction immediately following the subroutine call branch (B,L) is executed in the delay slot and hence is actually performed before the first instruction in the function fabs(). So, the first instruction executed after the return from fabs() is the FCNV,DBL,SGL instruction (the last one in the sequence). At first glance, this looks pretty good, just three instructions. But keep in mind that we just want the absolute value of the number and it took three instructions just to call the subroutine fabs(). In addition to those are the instructions in the fabs() subroutine.

So, what's a poor user to do? It seems like there ought to be a single instruction to perform this operation; after all, it amounts to just clearing the sign bit. In fact, there is a single instruction that does exactly that on most architectures. On SPARC processors, it's FABSS() and on PA-RISC, it's FABS(). But, how does one get the compiler to generate the single instruction instead of the subroutine call? Luckily, most compilers have a handy flag that optimizes common subroutine calls such as fabs(). For Hewlett-Packard's ANSI C compiler, the flag is +Olibcalls (which roughly translates to optimize library calls). So, if we were to compile the sequence of C code above with cc -O +Olibcalls, then we'll get the following:

```
FABS,SGL      %fr4L,%fr4R; Absolute value in a single instruction!
```

Note that we got very lucky here. Not only did the compiler remove the function call to fabs(), it also eliminated the conversion to and from double. This is not always true, as we shall see with sqrt() later.

Here's a short list of flags that accomplish this with different vendors' compilers (and usually these are available only with the "premium" compilers):

```
Sun:  .       +xlibmil
HP:           +Olibcalls
```

Note that SGI C compilers inline absolute value and square root instructions by default!

Before you go off and start using these flags on your application, there are two important points that should be made. First, it is imperative that you include the appropriate include file for the subroutine you're trying to optimize (you should do this in any case). Note that math.h is included in the example above because that's where fabs() is prototyped. The second thing you must keep in mind is that the calling code must not expect to access the errno variable after the function's return. This variable, defined in errno.h, is set to a nonzero code value that more specifically identifies the particular error condition that was encountered. In many cases, the function call is replaced by an instruction or sequence of instructions, eliminating the opportunity to access error codes that might otherwise be set by a function call. So, use the flags above to improve the performance of selected library routines only when you are not performing error checking for these routines.

Another common routine that behaves similar to fabs() is sqrt(). This function is difficult to generalize because some architectures (including IA-64) implement this in software using multiple instructions. Yet other architectures implement `sqrt()` in hardware and hence as a single instruction. Suppose we have the following C code:

```
#include <math.h>
...
float x, y;
...
x = sqrt( y );
```

With Hewlett-Packard's ANSIC C compiler, if we compile with `cc -O +Olibcalls`, then we will get the following sequence of instructions:

```
FCNV,SGL,DBL  %fr4R,%fr5   ; Convert y to double
FSQRT,DBL     %fr5,%fr6    ; Calculate sqrt
FCNV,DBL,SGL  %fr6,%fr4L   ; Convert result to float
```

Well, the call to `sqrt()` was replaced by the single `FSQRT` instruction. Unfortunately, we didn't get as lucky with the conversions as we did with `fabs()`. In this case, we have to be a little more careful about data type. More precisely, if we replace `sqrt()` with `sqrtf()` (note the f suffix), then we'll get just a single instruction:

```
FSQRT,SGL     %fr5,%fr6    ; Calculate sqrtf
```

Note that the `SGL` part of the instruction causes the square root to be calculated in 32-bit precision, rather than 64-bit (double), and it removes the conversions, just as we'd hoped.

For a moment, let's go back to the absolute value topic. In particular, the integer version of absolute value, `abs()`, sometimes gets overlooked by compiler optimization. That is, `abs()` will sometimes result in a function call even with the handy flags mentioned above. Moreover, be mindful that `abs()` is usually prototyped in `stdlib.h`, not `math.h`. If you find that you need `abs()` to be done a lot faster than the system's function call, then consider redefining with a macro such as the following:

```
#define abs(x) ( (x) >= 0 ? (x) : -(x) )
```

For example, on Hewlett-Packard machines, the above macro will cause a call to `abs()` to be replace by the following sequence of instructions:

```
OR,>=   %r0,%r26,%r28   ; If x >= 0 then nullify next instruction
SUBI    0,%r28,%r28     ; x = -x
```

It's not as clean as it might be, but it replaces a function call with two instructions.

As it turns out, Fortran has a distinct advantage over C here. If one uses the "general purpose" version of the intrinsic (either `abs()` or `sqrt()`), then the `+Olibcalls` flag or their analogs is not needed. That is, the intrinsic calls are replaced with the appropriate instruction(s). It is interesting to note that, for integer absolute value, Fortran uses the same two instructions shown above!

7.5.2 Other Math Routines

Many compilers have special versions of math routines that work well with unrolled loops. One example of why this is true is that performing the same operation on two elements at a time can be faster than performing the operation twice, once for each element. To illustrate this point, consider the simple case of multiplying two complex numbers:

```
void cmult ( dcomplex_t *t, dcomplex_t *x, dcomplex_t *y )
{
   double treal, timag, xreal, ximag, yreal, yimag;

   xreal = x->re;
   ximag = x->im;
   yreal = y->re;
   yimag = y->im;
   treal = xreal * yreal - ximag * yimag;
   timag = xreal * yimag + ximag * yreal;
   t->re = treal;
   t->im = timag;
   return;
}
```

Before we proceed any further, it needs to be stressed that complex multiplication is usually inlined by Fortran compilers and, if the intrinsic mentioned earlier in this section is used, it will be inlined by C compilers. We're using this subroutine solely as an example to demonstrate the efficiency of vector intrinsics. The instructions generated for accomplishing this are roughly as follows, with the approximate clock cycle that the operation will begin on with a PA-RISC PA-8500 processor (annotated in comments):

```
FLDD              0(%r25),%fr4            ; clock 0
FLDD              0(%r24),%fr9            ; clock 0
FLDD              8(%r25),%fr6            ; clock 1
FLDD              8(%r24),%fr5            ; clock 1
FMPY,DBL          %fr4,%fr9,%fr8          ; clock 3, waiting on fr4, fr9
FMPY,DBL          %fr6,%fr9,%fr7          ; clock 4, waiting on fr5, fr6
FMPYNFADD,DBL %fr6,%fr5,%fr8,%fr10        ; clock 6; waiting on fr8
FMPYFADD,DBL  %fr4,%fr5,%fr7,%fr11        ; clock 7; waiting on fr7
FSTD              %fr10,0(%r26)           ; clock 9; waiting on fr10
BVE               (%r2)                   ; clock 9;
FSTD              %fr11,8(%r26)           ; clock 10; waiting on fr11
```

So, there's a lot of stalling going on here. It's easy to imagine that complex multiplication would be used inside a loop. If that loop were unrolled by a factor of two, then the subroutine cmult() would be called twice in each iteration of the unrolled loop. After examining the sequence of instructions above, it seems like there's some opportunity to get some additional instructions executed during some of the delays. So, let's consider using a routine to do two complex multiplications in one call:

```
void cmult2 ( dcomplex_t *t0, dcomplex_t *x0, dcomplex_t *y0,
dcomplex_t *t1, dcomplex_t *x1, dcomplex_t *y1 )
{
   double treal0, timag0, xreal0, ximag0, yreal0, yimag0,
      treal1, timag1, xreal1, ximag1, yreal1, yimag1;

   xreal0 = x0->re;
   ximag0 = x0->im;
   yreal0 = y0->re;
   yimag0 = y0->im;
   xreal1 = x1->re;
   ximag1 = x1->im;
   yreal1 = y1->re;
   yimag1 = y1->im;
   treal0 = xreal0 * yreal0 - ximag0 * yimag0;
   timag0 = xreal0 * yimag0 + ximag0 * yreal0;
   treal1 = xreal1 * yreal1 - ximag1 * yimag1;
   timag1 = xreal1 * yimag1 + ximag1 * yreal1;
   t0->re = treal0;
   t0->im = timag0;
   t1->re = treal1;
   t1->im = timag1;

   return;
}
```

The resulting assembly code is as follows (again with the approximate clock cycle when the instruction begins execution):

```
LDW          -52(%r30),%r29         ; clock 0
LDW          -56(%r30),%r31         ; clock 0
FLDD         0(%r25),%fr7           ; clock 1
FLDD         0(%r24),%fr26          ; clock 1
FLDD         8(%r25),%fr10          ; clock 2
FLDD         0(%r29),%fr4           ; clock 3, waiting on r29
FLDD         8(%r29),%fr5           ; clock 3, waiting on r29
FLDD         0(%r31),%fr24          ; clock 4
FLDD         8(%r24),%fr22          ; clock 4
FMPY,DBL     %fr7,%fr26,%fr23       ; clock 4, waiting on fr7, fr26
```

```
FMPY,DBL        %fr10,%fr26,%fr11      ; clock 5, waiting on fr10
FLDD            8(%r31),%fr6           ; clock 5
FMPY,DBL        %fr4,%fr24,%fr8        ; clock 7, waiting on fr24
FMPY,DBL        %fr5,%fr24,%fr9        ; clock 7, waiting on fr24
FMPYNFADD,DBL %fr10,%fr22,%fr23,%fr25; clock 8
FMPYFADD,DBL  %fr7,%fr22,%fr11,%fr27 ; clock 8
FMPYNFADD,DBL %fr5,%fr6,%fr8,%fr28   ; clock 10, waiting on fr8
FMPYFADD,DBL  %fr4,%fr6,%fr9,%fr29   ; clock 10, waiting on fr9
FSTD            %fr25,0(%r26)          ; clock 12, waiting on fr25
FSTD            %fr27,8(%r26)          ; clock 12, waiting on fr27
FSTD            %fr28,0(%r23)          ; clock 14, waiting on fr28
BVE             (%r2)                  ; clock 14
FSTD            %fr29,8(%r23)          ; clock 15, waiting on fr29
```

Just looking at the comments, it seems like there's a lot more waiting going on than before. However, recall that it took 10 clocks to perform a single multiply before and here we get 2 multiplications done in 15 clocks. So, that's an improvement of 25%. In addition to this performance, note that we'll be doing half as many function calls.

Other, more complicated, operations such as log, sine, cosine, exponential, etc., also benefit from performing multiple operations with a single call. This usually happens with the basic -o optimization flag with Fortran. To be safe, it is recommended to always compile and link with the flag(s) that enable optimized library calls (e.g., +Olibcalls). With C and C++, one should always use this flag and disable aliasing so that the compiler knows it can perform multiple operations at a time on arrays (e.g., +Onoparmsoverlap on HP-UX). Highly tuned, sometimes vector, versions of the math library functions sin, cos, tan, atan2, log, pow, asin, acos, atan, exp, and log10 are usually available with most compilers.

7.5.3   Sorting

One of the more common activities in many applications is sorting. So, it is no wonder that the routine qsort() is available on most systems today. This routine is a general purpose implementation of the quicksort algorithm with occasional improvements, depending on the system.

The subject of sorting algorithms has taken up volumes of literature already and there are several excellent references on the subject. This book will not be one of those. Basically, this section is intended to point out a couple of performance problems with using the qsort() library routine and how to get around them.

Let's suppose that you have an array of 64-bit floating point numbers that you want to sort in ascending order. Then you might use the following to accomplish this:

```
qsort( (void *)x, (size_t)n, sizeof( x[0] ), compare );
```

where the function compare() is defined as follows:

```
int compare( const void *x, const void *y )
{
  int retval;
  double xx, yy;
  xx = *(double *)x;
  yy = *(double *)y;
  retval = 0;
  if( xx > yy ) retval = 1;
  if( xx < yy ) retval = -1;
  return( retval );
}
```

Note that the compare routine returns a zero for elements which are identical. This is preferable to a "simpler" compare routine such as:

```
int compare( const void *x, const void *y )
{
  int retval;
  double xx, yy;
  xx = *(double *)x;
  yy = *(double *)y;
  if( xx > yy ) return(1);
  else return(-1);
}
```

This version may cause some elements to be swapped unnecessarily because two equivalent elements may result in a return value of -1, implying they are not equal and should be swapped!

It took 442 milliseconds on a single processor HP N-4000 machine to sort a randomly distributed array with 100,000 elements using the method outlined above. Moreover, sorting 1 million elements in this manner required about 4.52 seconds. An interesting side note is that this is almost linear performance, not bad for sorting which is widely recognized as being *O(n log n)*!

A serious issue with using the standard qsort() routine is that it performs a subroutine call for every comparison that is made.

7.5.4   Other Automatically Inlined Routines

In addition to the math routines mentioned above, C and C++ compilers will also inline common, simple routines such as strcpy(), alloca(), memset(), and memcpy(). Note that inlining will take place only if the function call follows the prototype definition in the appropriate header file. As a result, it's usually a good idea to always include stdlib.h along with math.h. When using routines such as strcpy(), memset(), and memcpy(), the include files string.h and strings.h contain the appropriate prototype definitions.

7.6 Odds and Ends

There are a few other differences in languages that deserve brief mention. Those covered in this section include string (or character) processing and multi-dimensional array storage format.

7.6.1 String Processing

A string is a sequence of zero or more characters. C and C++ are far better languages than Fortran to use if your application does a lot of string manipulation. There are two basic reasons for this.

C and C++ provide a full set of string manipulation routines, including those to do concatenation, comparison, case-independent comparison, copying, searching for substrings within a string, providing pointers to first and last occurrences of substrings within strings, etc. Fortran, on the other hand, has very little to offer in this area.

The way in which strings are stored in C and C++ is also different from Fortran. C and C++ strings are "null terminated," meaning that the null character (0x00) marks the end of the string. Fortran strings are not terminated with any special character. As a result, they usually have a "transparent-to-the-user" integer attached to the string which contains the number of characters in the string (but this may be accomplished differently, depending on the vendor's compiler). For every string argument in a Fortran subroutine (or function), there is an additional integer argument that is appended to the argument list. So, calling a Fortran routine which has two arguments, both of which are strings, actually results in passing four arguments (two additional integers for the string lengths). This adds more overhead to Fortran's calling convention, making it that much worse than C or C++.

7.6.2 Multi-Dimensional Array Storage

Fortran and C have a completely different way of storing multi-dimensional arrays. This is easiest to describe by using an example.

The following statement in Fortran defines an array with 2 rows and 4 columns:

```
double precision a(2,4)
```

These values are stored sequentially in memory, as illustrated in Figure 7-1.

Note that each column is stored contiguously. This method of array storage is referred to as *column-major order*, or simply *column-major*.

a(1,1)
a(2,1)
a(1,2)
a(2,2)
a(1,3)
a(2,3)
a(1,4)
a(2,4)

Figure 7-1   Memory storage of an array in column major order.

C and C++ are just the opposite of Fortran in how multi-dimensional arrays are stored. Consider the following definition of an array with 2 rows and 4 columns in C (or C++):

```
double a[2][4];
```

In these languages, the values are stored contiguously in memory, as shown in Figure 7-2.

Observe that the storage is such that each row is stored contiguously in memory, just the opposite of Fortran. This method of array storage is described as *row-major*.

a[1][1]
a[1][2]
a[1][3]
a[1][4]
a[2][1]
a[2][2]
a[2][3]
a[2][4]

Figure 7-2   Memory storage of an array in row major order.

The reason that array storage is a performance issue follows from the goal of always trying to access memory with unit stride. In order to accomplish this, nested loops will often be reversed, depending on the language you are working with. For example, suppose we want to copy one two-dimensional array to another where the dimensions of the arrays are both 100×100. In Fortran, this is most efficiently done as follows:

```
DO J= 1, M
   DO I = 1, N
      X(I,J) = Y(I,J)
   END DO
END DO
```

This causes the data in both X and Y to be accessed with unit stride in memory. Using the same loop structure in C, with the two-dimensional arrays x and y, results in the following:

```
for( j = 0; j < m; j++)
   for( i = 0; i < n; i++)
      x[i][j] = y[i][j];
```

But this will access memory with a stride of 100 (the leading dimension of x and y), destroying locality. The better way to write the loop, in C, is to switch the loops:

```
for( i = 0; i < n; i++)
  for( j = 0; j < n; j++)
    x[i][j] = y[i][j];
```

The result is that memory is accessed with unit stride, dramatically improving locality.

7.6.3   Arrays as Subroutine Arguments

There are a couple of other differences between C and Fortran that could be performance problems.

General routines for operating on multi-dimensional arrays are easier to write in Fortran. That is, it's very difficult in C or C++ to duplicate the following Fortran subroutine:

```
SUBROUTINE FOO( X, Y, M, N)
INTEGER M, N, X(N,*), Y(N,*)

DO J = 1, M
  DO I = 1, N
    X(I,J) = Y(I,J)
  END DO
END DO
```

You can write a similar routine in C if you know that the trailing dimension is actually 100:

```
void foo( int x[][100], int y[][100], int m, int n )
{
  int i, j;

  for( i = 0; i < n; i++ )
    for( j = 0; j < m; j++ )
      x[i][j] = y[i][j];

  return;
}
```

But, alas, this is not always the case. So, what one has to do is write the general purpose routine as follows:

```
void foo( int x[], int y[], int m, int n )
{
   int i, j;

   for( i = 0; i < n; i++ )
     for( j = 0; j < m; j++ )
       x[i*n + j] = y[i*n + j];

   return;
}
```

There is usually no performance impact from this, but sometimes the compiler optimization gets tangled up with the integer multiplication used in calculating the indexes.

7.6.4   Data Types

Another area of potential concern is identifying how much storage that data types actually use. In Fortran, REAL values are usually 32-bit and DOUBLE PRECISION values are usually 64-bit entities. One exception to this is found on some vector machines which actually double these values. Similarly, float values are usually 32-bit and double values are usually 64-bit in C and C++. Address and pointer sizes will vary, depending on whether you compile to use 16-, 32-, or 64-bit addressing. Fortran compilers usually support REAL*n and INTEGER*n (as well as other) data types so that you can clearly define how many bytes you want to use for your data storage. For example, REAL*8 indicates that you want to use 64-bit floating point values.

Integer data types in C and C++ can sometimes be confusing. To illustrate some of the differences, the number of bytes required for various data types is shown in Table 7-1. Note that the HP-UX 64-bit column shows storage allocated when compiling with cc +DA2.0W or cc +DD64 (for 64-bit addressing). Similarly, the IRIX 64-bit column presents storage when compiled with `cc -64`. As is usually the case, be sure to include the appropriate include files for non-typical data types such as `size_t`. The appropriate include file in this case is `stdlib.h`.

Table 7-1   Size in Bytes for Various Data Types with
Various Vendor Compilers

Data Type	Visual C++ Windows98	HP-UX C 32-bit	HP-UX C 64-bit	IRIX C 32-bit	IRIX C 64-bit
short	2	2	2	2	2
int	4	4	4	4	4
long	4	4	8	4	8
long long	N/A	8	8	4	8
long long int	N/A	8	8	8	8
size_t	4	4	8	4	8
void *	4	4	8	4	8

Now, why is this important you ask? Any time you can use less storage for your application, you should do so. For example, suppose you are frequently using a table of integers that has 250,000 entries. If you can determine that the maximum absolute value of these integers is less than 32,768 (which is 2^{16}), then defining that table as a `short` rather than an `int` will reduce the amount of storage required from around 1 MB to 500 KB and hence make it a lot more likely to reside entirely in cache.

7.6.5   Operations with Denormalized Values

In Chapter 2, we discussed the IEEE representation for floating point numbers. The smallest normalized value in this format is represented by a number which has an exponent value of one and a mantissa of zero. Smaller numbers can be represented by using denormalized values. *Denormalized* floating-point numbers are those with an exponent value of zero and a nonzero mantissa. For example, with 32-bit floating-point numbers, the smallest normalized magnitude value is $1.17549435 \times 10^{-38}$, which is 1.0×2^{-126}. Numbers with a smaller magnitude can be represented with denormalized floating-point numbers. For example, $5.87747175 \times 10^{-39}$ is represented by 0.5×2^{-127}, which has a mantissa of 0x400000 (i.e., a 1 in its leading bit) and an exponent value of zero in its IEEE 32-bit floating-point representation.

An *underflow* condition may occur when a floating-point operation attempts to produce a result that is smaller in magnitude than the smallest normalized value. On many systems, the occurrence of a denormalized operand or result, either at an intermediate stage of a computation or at the end, can generate a processor interrupt. This is done to allow the user to trap floating-point underflow conditions. Generating exceptions for such operations can reduce the speed of an application significantly. Hewlett-Packard systems with PA-RISC processors are an example of those systems that can exhibit poor performance when they encounter underflow conditions.

To illustrate the performance impact of operations involving denormalized numbers, suppose we perform a vector scaling operation on an array x and store the result in another vector y.

```
void vscale( x, y, a, n )
float *x, *y, a;
int n;
{
   int i;
   for( i = 0; i < n; i++ )
     y[i] = x[i] * a;
   return
}
```

Suppose, for simplicity, that every value of x is the smallest normalized 32-bit floating-point number, $1.17549435 \times 10^{-38}$. Moreover, assume that the scalar a has a value of 0.1 and that n is 10,000,000. The above routine, with these assumptions, executed on an HP N-4000 machine in 88.6 seconds. This amounts to less than one-eighth MFLOP/s.

There are several solutions to this problem, including:

1. Assign the value zero to data that would otherwise be denormalized.
2. Scale the entire data set upwards in magnitude so that the smallest values that occur are guaranteed to be normalized.
3. Change single-precision data storage to double-precision.
4. On systems that support it, enable flush-to-zero mode.

The first solution basically indicates that every element of the array y should be set to zero. This could be done by inserting a test to check if the value is less than the smallest normalized value and, if so, then set the value to zero. If the programmer isn't clear on where he might encounter denormalized values, then this isn't a practical solution since every operation would need to be tested. The second approach can be applied more often, but it may require a detailed understanding of the application. The third solution can sometimes be achieved without modifying the application. For example, one could compile the application with cc -Dfloat=double, which would effectively change all 32-bit floating-point data to 64-bit floating-point data. The HP Fortran has similar functionality through use of the Fortran 90 option +autodbl. Converting the single-precision storage to double-precision allowed the program to execute in 1.69 seconds—over 50 times faster!

The downside of converting data storage in this way is that it requires more memory to execute the application, sometimes causing the working set to no longer fit in cache. In order to avoid this problem, many vendors provide the capability to simply assign zero to denormalized results without raising an exception. In most situations this has no impact on the application's accuracy. After all, numbers less than $1.17549435 \times 10^{-38}$ in magnitude are very close to zero. To enable this *flush-to-zero* capability on HP systems, link with the +FPD option (or -Wl, +FPD, if you are using the compiler to perform the link operation). After doing this, the original problem executed in 1.20 seconds, an improvement of 30% over the double-precision solution.

7.7 Summary

Depending on what your application does, the choice of language can make an impact on your application's performance. However, this impact can be reduced to a minimum by using the right syntax and compiler flags. In some cases, standard library routines can be much faster, but only if the options are used correctly. On the flip side, some can be slower than what you will achieve with macros or using your own subroutines!

Generally speaking, care should be taken, when programming in C and C++, to use the correct include files whenever using standard library routines of any kind (math, string, or other operations). In particular, the two include files that you should get in the habit of using are stdlib.h and math.h.

References:

The following publications are excellent resources for language-specific issues and other topics discussed in this chapter:

1. Anderson, P. L.; Anderson, G. C. *Advanced C, Tips and Techniques,* Hayden, 1988. ISBN 0-672-48417-X.

2. Hewlett Packard, *HP C/HP-UX Programmer's Guide*, Hewlett Packard Co., 1998. Part Number 92434-90013.

3. Hewlett Packard, *HP C/HP-UX Reference Manual*, Hewlett Packard Co., 1998. Part Number 92453-90087.

4. Hewlett Packard, *HP Fortran 90 Programmer's Guide*, Hewlett Packard Co., 1998. Part Number B3909-90002.

5. Hewlett Packard, *HP Fortran 90 Programmer's Reference*, Hewlett Packard Co., 1998. Part Number B3908-90002.

6. Kernighan, B. W.; Ritchie, D. M., *The C Programming Language,* 1988. ISBN 0-13-110370-9.

7. Chapman, S. J. *Fortran 90/95 for Scientists and Engineers,* McGraw-Hill, ISBN 0-07-01938-4.

8. Metcalf, M.; Reid, J. *Fortran 90/95 Explained,* Oxford Science, 1998. ISBN 0-19-851888-9.

Parallel Processing — An Algorithmic Approach

Some people are still unaware that reality contains unparalleled beauties.

Berenice Abbott

At some point you may find that there just isn't any more performance that can be squeezed out of a single processor. The next logical progression in improving performance is to use multiple processors to do the task. This can be very simple or very difficult, depending on the work and the computer you are using. The task that you're doing may be as simple as adding two arrays together or as complex as processing car rental requests from all over the country. The former problem is easily broken into pieces of work that can be performed on multiple processors. The latter is a very complex problem, one that challenges all of today's database software vendors.

8.1 Introduction

This chapter is not a survey of parallel algorithms. Quite the contrary, it is intended to provide the reader with multiple parallel mechanisms and examples of how they can (and cannot, in some cases) be used to enable a task to be processed in parallel. Many of the basic concepts discussed in this chapter were discussed in Chapter 4, including processes, threads, etc.

To accomplish the goal of this chapter, a relatively simple problem will be examined and multiple parallel programming techniques will be applied to it. In this way, many of the concepts and techniques will be demonstrated through examples. We will also illustrate several pitfalls of parallel processing.

Consider a file which contains hundreds, perhaps thousands, of records which are delimited with a specific string of characters. The problem is that every individual record, except for its delimiter, is to be sorted. So, for example, suppose the input file is as follows:

```
DELIM:hjfjhrajnfnDELIM:qwdqsaxzfsdgfdophpjargjkjgDELIM:adqwxbncmb
```

Note that with the string DELIM: as the delimiter, there are three records in the file. We want to produce a file which has the characters within each record sorted. So, the resulting output file would be:

```
DELIM:affhhjjjnnrDELIM:aadddffggghjjjkoppqqrsswxzDELIM:abbcdmnqw
```

Unfortunately, the file doesn't contain any information about the maximum record size or the total number of records. Moreover, records can have arbitrary length.

Throughout the following case study, we shall use a file with the same form shown above. In all cases, we will use the same input file and the same computer. The input file is just over 107 MB in size and the machine we use is a Hewlett-Packard N-4000 computer. The actual sort will be an implementation of the quicksort algorithm, and record delimiters will be found using a variation of the Rabin-Karp search algorithm loosely based on the implementation by Sedgewick [1]. Unless otherwise noted, all I/O will be performed using UNIX system calls. The details of the sorting, searching, and I/O will not be examined unless they pertain to the parallel programming approach being discussed.

Let's look at how the baseline algorithm performs. There is some initial I/O required to read the data set into memory, then the records are sorted and the results written to an output file. Using /bin/time to produce the overall time on our N-4000 computer gives the following:

```
real     1:01.1
user       59.3
sys         1.7
```

So, it takes about a minute to do the task. Let's see how we can improve this with parallel processing.

8.2 Process Parallelism

One of the earliest parallel models was to simply use multiple processes, each of which executed the same program, to process multiple data sets. This paradigm is referred to as the Single Program Multiple Data (SPMD) model. One simple means of achieving this is to use the UNIX fork() and execv() system calls (or variations of them). This approach to parallel programming is generally described as the *fork/exec* model.

The fork() system call causes the creation of a new process. This new process, commonly referred to as a child process, is created as a replica of the calling process and its entire address space. The execv() system call, and all its variations, loads a program from an ordinary executable file into the current process, replacing the current program. Consider the following code segment:

```
for( i = 1; i < ncpus; i++ )
{
  pid = fork();
  switch( pid )
  {
    case 0: /* Child */
      retval = execv( "./hello", argv );
      perror("execv");
      exit(-1);
      break;
    case -1: /* Error */
      perror("fork");
      exit(-1);
      break;
    default: /* Parent */
      break;
  }
  fprintf(stderr,"MAIN: Parent started pid %d\n",pid);

}

...

for( i = 1; i < ncpus; i++ )
{
  retval = wait(&statval);
  ...
}
```

Note that the fork() system call creates two processes executing the same program with one difference. The value of pid in the parent process will be the process identification number, commonly referred to as its PID, of the newly created child process. The value of pid in this new child process will be zero. Hence, the path taken in the switch() statement following the fork will be different for the two processes. Note that the child process executes an execv() system call which, as it appears above, will execute the program ./hello and pass it the argument list in argv. The for loop creates ncpus-1 child processes in this way. It's worth noting that the perror(), exit(), and break statements will not execute unless the execv() call fails.

Once the parent process has executed the first for loop, it then executes a second for loop which waits on the children to exit. The return value from wait is actually the child's process identification number. When the parent executes the `wait()` system call, it will not return until a child process has completed, i.e., exited the machine's execution queue.

If `ncpus` has a value of three, then Figure 8-1 illustrates the sequence of events. The first `for` loop accomplishes what is roughly referred to as a *spawn* in parallel processing parlance. That is, the parent spawns multiple threads of execution. The second loop achieves synchronization of the multiple threads commonly referred to as a *join*.

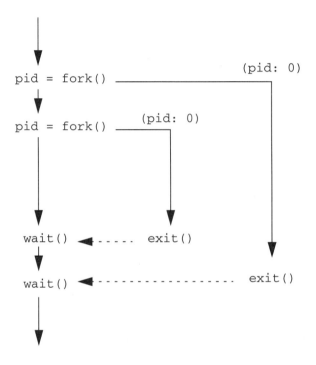

Figure 8-1   Spawning child processes with `fork()` and resuming execution with `wait()` after all child processes exit.

8.2.1   SPMD With Simple I/O

Let's get back to our problem of sorting records. It's clear that we're performing the same operation (sorting) on every single record. So, we'll create multiple processes using `fork()` as outlined above and have each process read records from the file. In order to distribute the work among N processes, we'll have each process sort records in a round-robin fashion. For example, the first process will sort records 1, N+1, 2N+1, etc.; the second process will sort records 2, N+2,

2N+2, etc.; and so on. Doing this with the fork/exec model outlined above gives the times in Table 8-1.

Table 8-1   Times for Sorting Records in Parallel with Round-robin Workload Balancing Using `fork` and `execv`.

	1 CPU	2 CPUs	4 CPUs
real	61.9	44.4	36.0
user	59.3	84.7	135.5
sys	2.2	3.4	6.2

The results are a bit discouraging. We achieved a speed up of only 1.7x on four processors. Notice that the system cpu time has almost tripled and the total user cpu time has more than doubled. Since each process has to search through the entire file, it may be causing a lot of file contention. That is, since each process is accessing the same file, there is probably a severe bottleneck in getting the data read from the file..

Table 8-2   Times for Parallel Processing Using Separate, Multiple Input Files.

	1 CPU	2 CPUs	4 CPUs
real	87.9	88.9	72.0
user	84.5	84.6	96.6
sys	2.9	4.4	4.6

The performance may benefit from breaking the file into multiple input files and processing them simultaneously yet separately. To do this, we'll have the parent process read the input file and distribute the records evenly into N separate files, where N is the number of processors to be used. Note that this requires the parent to search through the entire input file to identify the total number of records before it can begin equally distributing them. Since the quicksort algorithm is $O(\ n\ log\ n\ )$ on average, we expect that this search and distribution won't result in a lot of additional processing time. Once this is done, multiple children will be created with `fork()`, each of which will read in its own file and sort the records in it.

The resulting times, shown in Table 8-2, are also disappointing. We certainly reduced the overall system and user cpu time when compared to the "single input file" approach previously described. However, the job ran much slower; the elapsed time is twice as long as before. Looking at the breakdown of execution time in more detail, we find that it took an increasing amount of elapsed time to create the input files while the actual sorting didn't improve all that much.

Table 8-3   Breakdown of File Creation and Sorting for Parallel Processing with Multiple Files.

	1 CPU	2 CPUs	4 CPUs
file creation	26.8	27.6	39.4
sorting	87.6	88.7	71.8

Looking at the separate input file sizes we find that, for 4 processes, the input file sizes are dramatically different. The four file sizes are roughly 42 KB, 368 KB, 51 MB, and 56 MB. Hence two processes were doing over 99% of the work! Note that the number of records was distributed evenly among the processes, but the sizes of these records varies dramatically. So, two of the processes sorted some huge records while the other two sorted very small records.

8.2.2   Scheduling — File Locks

Suppose we have two processes executing with a workload consisting of six records. With the previous scheduling, the first process sorted the first half of the records and the second sorted the second half. The resulting load balance is shown in Figure 8-2.

One way to improve this situation is to have each process sort a single record at a time from the input file. The processes communicate with one another to identify which is the next record in the file to be sorted. Process #1 gets the first record and begins sorting it. Likewise, process #2 gets the second record and begins sorting it. If process #2 finished before process #1, then it gets the third record and begins sorting it. So, each process sorts the next record in the input file that hasn't been sorted yet. In this way, each process will stay busy until there is no more work to do. Given the workloads outlined in Figure 8-2, this new scheduling approach results in a better load balance, as shown in Figure 8-3.

To do this, we'll use one of the original methods of synchronization in parallel processing: *file locks*. A separate file, call it the position file, will contain the position in the file of the next record to be sorted. That is, the position file will contain a single number which is the number of bytes from the start of the input file to the next record to be sorted. Somehow we must restrict access to this position file so that only one file at a time has access to it.

An *atomic* operation is a sequence of events that are indivisible, that is, they are guaranteed to complete as if it were one instruction. Fortunately, the UNIX file system implements the open() system call as an atomic operation when used to exclusively create a file. We shall

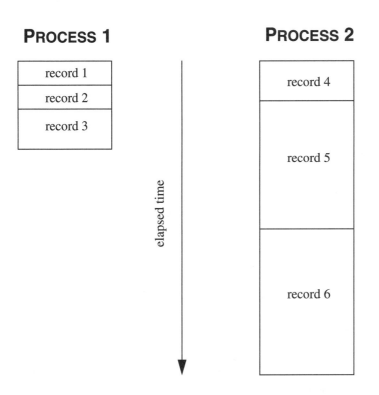

Figure 8-2   Example of poor load balancing with static scheduling.

exploit this to create a lock which prevents two or more processes from accessing the position file at the same time. This is accomplished by using the following code segment (with pseudo-code):

```
/* Loop until file can be exclusively created. */
while( (fdlck = open( lockfilename, O_CREAT|O_EXCL|O_RDWR,
    0660)) == -1 && errno == EEXIST );

  < Position of next record is read from position file. >
  < The subsequent record is identified in the input file >
  < and then the position file is updated accordingly. >

/* Release lock by closing and removing the file. */
close( fdlck );
unlink( lockfilename );
```

PROCESS 1   PROCESS 2

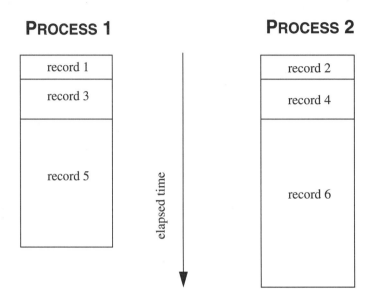

Figure 8-3 Example of improved load balancing with dynamic scheduling of workloads.

The locking mechanism is used only to get the record and update the position file with the position of the next record. The processing, i.e., sorting of the record is done outside of the lock. Otherwise we'd be defeating the whole purpose of the locking mechanism and processing would be done one record at a time (inside the lock).

The code between the acquisition of the lock and the release of the lock can be executed only by a single process. Such a segment of code is often referred to as a *critical section* or *critical region*. Note the `while` statement which iterates, or spins, until the `open()` call returns successfully. This mechanism is called a *spin lock*.

After re-architecting the algorithm to use a file locking as outlined above, the records were once again processed. The resulting times are given in Table 8-4. These are not very encouraging, as they are slower than any approach so far.

The overall parallel scaling is not too bad as we're getting just over 2x speedup with four processors. Moreover, the user cpu time is not increasing dramatically from 1 to 4 processors. However, the system time is growing exponentially. This is not a surprise really, because we're likely to be doing a tremendous number of system calls in our locking mechanism (`open`, `read`, `write`, `lseek`, `close`, `unlink`). So, our scaling is improving, but we're spending too much time in the operating system. It's probably time to take a dramatically different approach.

Table 8-4   Times For Parallel Processing Using File Locking To Achieve Dynamic Scheduling.

	1 CPU	2 CPUs	4 CPUs
real	215.8	83.1	57.2
user	58.6	59.3	60.7
sys	4.8	13.9	53.5

8.2.3   Shared-Memory Basics

When the first symmetric multiple processor (SMP) machines were built, there immediately was a demand for sharing memory between processes. After experimenting with file locks to achieve parallel synchronization, it is easy to see why! This was satisfied in different ways by two of the more successful implementations of UNIX, System V, and Berkeley Software Distributions (BSD) [2].

System V UNIX implemented a fairly aggressive set of shared-memory constructs, as well as those for semaphores, which we'll discuss later. Shared-memory could be allocated and attached to by using a few system calls:

- shmget()   Creates a memory segment and returns the shared-memory identifier associated with that memory segment.
- shmat()   Attaches the shared-memory segment associated with shared-memory identifier (provided by shmget()). It returns the virtual address of the memory segment.
- shmdt()   Detaches from the shared-memory segment attached to by shmat().

BSD UNIX implemented a simpler approach using just a couple of system calls:

- mmap()   Establishes a mapping between the process' address space and a file using the file descriptor returned by open().
- munmap()   Releases shared-memory mapping established by mmap().

The BSD mmap() maps the contents of a given file into virtual memory at a given address. This enables processes to share memory and have it initialized to the contents of a given file without having to open it, read it, or allocate memory to read the contents into.

In addition to the above functionality, mmap() provides the option to create a shared-memory segment without a file descriptor. This is useful in the presence of fork/exec models of parallelism in that a shared-memory segment can be allocated with mmap() and then all processes that are subsequently created with fork() will share that memory. Note that this is different from what happens to any memory allocated by the parent process. The child process will get a copy of the parent's address space at the time the fork() is executed, but it will be a private copy that is not shared between processes.

Let's reconsider our record sorting problem. As of now, the best performance was achieved by having all four processes read the entire file into memory and process the records in round-robin fashion (see Table 8-1). The problem with this approach is that each process has its own copy of the entire file, hence each process was using over 100 MB of memory. We could alleviate this with some clever I/O tricks. Rather than do that, let's try shared-memory using mmap() and see what the results are.

If we re-implement the round-robin algorithm using shared-memory allocated with mmap(), then we drop our overall memory use down to around 100 MB regardless of how many processes are created. However, it is not without cost. The virtual memory page sizes are usually smaller and mechanisms to manage shared-memory have a lot more overhead than typical memory segments. In addition, shared-memory brings with it some cache line sharing, i.e., thrashing problems.

False cache line sharing is a form of cache thrashing as discussed earlier. It happens when two or more processes (or threads) in a parallel application are accessing different data items in the same cache lines. As it turns out, the delimiter between records is far shorter than the 64-byte cache line size on a HP N-4000 computer. Given the nature of quicksort, it is very likely that a lot of false cache line sharing is going on. With this in mind, it is not a complete surprise to see that the shared-memory implementation of the earlier round-robin algorithm is a bit slower. The resulting times are shown in Table 8-5.

Table 8-5   Times For Parallel Processing Using mmap'd Memory with Simple Round-robin Workload Distribution.

	1 CPU	2 CPUs	4 CPUs
real	85.9	62.7	51.6
user	59.8	84.3	114.6
sys	3.9	3.3	3.7

The increase in user cpu time for two CPUs is dramatic and is likely being caused by false cache line sharing. But let's not dwell on this. We now know that the static scheduling approach, even with shared-memory, is not efficient, so let's revisit the dynamic scheduling approach.

8.2.4   Shared-Memory and Mutually Exclusive Objects

As alluded to earlier, we'd like to implement a spin lock without using the file system and associated system calls. In order to do this, we have to introduce some more advanced synchronization concepts. Since a process consists of at least one thread, these concepts are defined in the context of threads, but keep in mind that they also apply to processes.

A *mutex* is an object that allows multiple threads to synchronize access to resources that are shared by the threads. A mutex has two states: locked and unlocked. Once a mutex is locked by a particular thread, other threads that attempt to lock the mutex will block or suspend until they can lock the mutex. Note that exactly one thread can lock a mutex. Locking a mutex is often referred to as acquiring the mutex. A very similar, yet more general, locking mechanism is a *semaphore*. These are mutually exclusive objects that can be used to regulate the sharing or access of multiple resources. This is because a semaphore has a counter associated with it. If a thread needs access to a resource that is controlled by a semaphore, it acquires the semaphore by decrementing this counter. If the counter is zero, then the thread is blocked until the counter is incremented. When a thread is finished with one of the resources, it releases the semaphore, which effectively increments the counter. Note that if a semaphore has its counter initialized to one, it is referred to as a binary semaphore and is effectively the same as a mutex. Semaphores were developed by E.W. Dijkstra in 1968 and they are one of the older concepts in parallel programming.

One of the early implementations of semaphores was accomplished in System V UNIX. They are for use with UNIX processes rather than threads. There are three important interfaces to System V semaphores:

- `semget()`   Create a semaphore and return the identifier associated with it.
- `semctl()`   Interface for performing a variety of semaphore control operations.
- `semop()`   Used to atomically perform an array of semaphore operations.

One of the downfalls of System V semaphores is that they are anything but user friendly. Moreover, this interface was not available in the BSD UNIX. As a result, many early parallel programmers created their own semaphores or locks.

At the lowest level, mutually exclusive objects usually rely on synchronization primitives that are implemented in hardware. An *atomic exchange* interchanges a value in a register for a value in memory. Most systems today have special instructions that implement atomic exchanges. PA-RISC systems feature the "load and clear word" instruction, `ldcw`. Its purpose is to simply read a value from memory and set the value to be zero. More precisely, it reads the contents at a certain address and simultaneously zeros the contents of that address.

To better illustrate how this can be used to implement a spin lock, consider the following subroutine in PA-RISC assembly code:

```
__ldcws32
  .proc
  .callinfo caller
  .entry
  ldcws0(0,%arg0),%ret0
  nop
  bv   %r0(%rp)
  .exit
  nop
  .procend
  .end
```

This subroutine's prototype in C would appear as follows:

```
int __ldcws32(int *ip);
```

This function returns the contents of the integer at address `ip` and zeros that same location. Thus, we could implement a spin lock mechanism with the following routines:

```
int acquire_lock(ip)
int * volatile ip;
{
  while (1)
  {
    while ( (*ip) == 0 );
    if ( __ldcws32(ip) != 0 )
      break;
  }
  return 0;
}

int release_lock(ip)
int *ip;
{
  *ip = 1;
  return 0;
}
```

The routine `acquire_lock()` simply spins, waiting on the value at `ip` to be nonzero. Note that, as soon as the value of `*ip` changes to something other than zero, the `__ldcws32()` routine is called. If it is able to load the nonzero value, then it returns that value and control breaks out of the spin loop so that `acquire_lock()` returns. The function `release_lock()`

simply sets the value of a memory location, the lock, to one. Thus, the code sequence for a critical section would be achieved as follows:

```
acquire_lock( mylock );
/* critical section begins. */
...
/* end critical section. */
release_lock( mylock );
```

What about the `volatile` qualifier on `ip` in the definition of `acquire_lock()`? Let's first look at the instructions generated for `acquire_lock()` if we were to eliminate the volatile qualifier. In this case, if we compile with `cc -c +O2` the following assembly code results:

```
acquire_lock
    .PROC
    .CALLINFO
CALLER,FRAME=16,ENTRY_GR=%r3,SAVE_RP,ARGS_SAVED,ORDERING_AWARE
    .ENTRY
    STW %r2,-20(%r30)        ;
    STW,MA%r3,64(%r30)       ;
    COPY %r26,%r3            ;
    LDW 0(%r3),%r31          ;Load contents of ip
$D0
    CMPIB,<>,N0,%r31,loop2   ;If *ip != 0 goto loop2
loop1
    B   loop1               ;else infinite loop
    NOP
loop2
    .CALL   ARGW0=GR,RTNVAL=GR ;in=26;out=28;
    B,L __ldcws32,%r2        ;
    COPY %r3,%r26            ;
    CMPIB,=,N0,%r28,$D0      ;If( __ldcws32(ip) == 0 ) goto $D0
    LDW 0(%r3),%r31          ;
    LDW -84(%r30),%r2        ;
    COPY %r0,%r28            ;
    BVE (%r2)               ;
    .EXIT
    LDW,MB-64(%r30),%r3      ;
    .PROCEND                 ;in=26;out=28;
```

What's happened is that the optimizer sees no reason to reload `*ip` in the spin loop:

```
while( (*ip) == 0 );
```

From a compiler's perspective, this is fair. As a result, the value is loaded once and if it is zero, then we have an infinite loop.

The `volatile` qualifier is a nice addition to the C programming language to alleviate just this sort of problem. It communicates to the compiler, and hence the optimizer, that this variable may change for no obvious reason, so it needs to be reloaded every time it is accessed. If ip is declared with the `volatile` qualifier, then the infinite loop above is transformed into the following:

```
loop1
  LDW,00(%r3),%r31; Load *ip
  CMPIB,=,N0,%r31,$D1; If( *ip == 0 ) goto loop1
  nop
```

Clearly, the `volatile` qualifier is very handy for parallel programming. The alternative is to basically compile any routine that accesses shared-memory with no optimization!

Back to the record sorting problem, we're going to allocate some shared-memory to be used as a lock. It will be initialized to one so that the first process can acquire the lock. Note that this shared-memory is different from that to be used for the actual input file, so there will need to be separate calls to mmap(). The following call is used to allocate a memory segment to be used to hold the input data file:

```
buffer =(char *)mmap( NULL, (size_t) buffer_length,
  PROT_READ|PROT_WRITE, MAP_SHARED|MAP_ANONYMOUS,
  -1, (off_t) 0 );
```

Note that we're using the MAP_ANONYMOUS feature of mmap() here so there's no file descriptor needed (hence the -1 for that argument).

Now we need some additional shared-memory to contain things like the mutex and the offset to the next record to be sorted (analogous to the position file's contents used in the previous example). This is accomplished through another call to mmap(); this time we demonstrate a call using a file descriptor:

```
util_buffer = (char *)mmap( NULL, (size_t) util_buffer_length,
        PROT_READ | PROT_WRITE, MAP_SHARED, fd, (off_t) 0 );
```

Since we're using a real file descriptor, we don't use MAP_ANONYMOUS.

Using the `acquire_lock()` and `release_lock()` routines in conjunction with a mutex object located in `util_buffer` means that any processes forked off after the shared-memory is initialized will indeed share this memory and, as a result, the mutex object. With this in place, we execute the program and get the performance outlined in Table 8-6. This is indeed an

Table 8-6 Times for Parallel Processing Using Shared-Memory
Allocated with `mmap` to Achieve Dynamic Scheduling.

	1 CPU	2 CPUs	4 CPUs
real	61.3	32.1	27.6
user	59.4	59.7	101.2
sys	1.8	2.1	2.0

improvement! The scaling from 1 to 2 processors is very good, but we're not seeing much benefit using four processors instead of two. There's also a large increase in user cpu time at four processors. This is likely to be caused by false cache line sharing. Even so, the elapsed time is the
best time yet and is over two times faster than the original sequential algorithm.

8.3 Thread Parallelism

The concept of threads was introduced in Chapter 4 and now we'll go into a little more
detail by implementing our record sorting application using threads. The framework for doing so
is analogous to that of the `fork/exec` model discussed above:

```
#include <pthread.h>
...
for( i = 1; i < ncpus; i++ )
{
  retval = pthread_create( tid+i, (pthread_attr_t *) NULL,
    (void *(*)())psort_buffer,
    (void *) (pattern) );
  if( retval > 0 ) perror("pthread_create");

}
psort_buffer( pattern );

for( i = 1; i < ncpus; i++ )
{
  retval = pthread_join( tid[i], (void **) NULL );
  if( retval > 0 ) perror("pthread_create");
}
```

So, the parent thread creates additional threads, each of which execute the subroutine `psort_buffer()`. Once the additional threads are created, the parent thread also executes `psort_buffer()`. These routines can be identical because when threads other than the parent encounter the return statement in `psort_buffer()` it causes an implicit `pthread_exit()` call to be made. The latter simply terminates the thread. Use it explicitly with caution as it will terminate the main thread as well!

8.3.1 Mutually Exclusive Objects Revisited

POSIX provides an interface for operations on semaphores which is easier to use. POSIX semaphores can be used with threads and/or processes, making for a very powerful programming tool. The routines used to operate POSIX semaphores are:

- `sem_init()`   Initialize or create a semaphore.
- `sem_wait()`   Lock a semaphore; `sem_wait` will not return until it is able to lock the semaphore.
- `sem_trywait()`   Lock a semaphore if it is available; otherwise, it will return -1.
- `sem_post()`   Post the semaphore, i.e., increment the semaphore.
- `sem_destroy()`   Deallocate or destroy a semaphore.

In defining pthreads, POSIX provided a very simple mutex interface. This interface will be used to illustrate various parallel programming practices through the remainder of this chapter. The basic routines provided for pthread mutexes are:

- `pthread_mutex_init()`   Initializes a mutex with a given set of attributes.
- `pthread_mutex_lock()`   Locks a mutex object.
- `pthread_mutex_trylock()` Identical to the `pthread_mutex_lock` function except that if the mutex object cannot be acquired after one attempt, the function returns an error.
- `pthread_mutex_unlock()`   Unlocks a mutex object.
- `pthread_mutex_destroy()` Destroys or deallocates a mutex.

To implement the critical section needed to accurately communicate the location of the next record to each thread, we use the following to replace the `acquire_lock()` and `release_lock()` subroutines discussed above:

```
pthread_mutex_lock( &mutex );
{
  /* Critical section begins. */
  ...
  /* Critical section ends. */
}
pthread_mutex_unlock( &mutex );
```

Implementing the dynamic scheduling with pthreads analogously to how it was done using processes and shared-memory allocated with `mmap()` resulted in the times shown in Table 8-7.

Table 8-7   Times for Parallel Processing Using Pthreads to Achieve Dynamic Scheduling.

	1 CPU	2 CPUs	4 CPUs
real	62.0	32.1	27.3
user	59.5	59.5	59.7
sys	2.0	2.1	2.1

Note that the elapsed time improved only slightly, but the user cpu time improved dramatically. As mentioned above, this is due the additional load placed on the virtual memory system by processes sharing memory allocated with mmap.

This result was also achieved without having to use a special interface to allocate memory (such as `mmap()`), nor did it require writing the `acquire_lock()`, `release_lock()`, and `ldcw32()` routines.

8.3.2   Spawning and Joining Threads

Let's consider a different example application for the next few sections. Suppose we have a signal processing type application that reads multiple records and applies a filter to each of them. Unlike the previous example, the size of the records are known *a priori*, but they must be processed in the sequence that they arrive. Moreover, the records are actually two-dimensional, square arrays. The code for the principal loop is very simple:

```
#include <pthread.h>
typedef struct filter_struct
{
  double *buffer, *outbuffer, *filter;
  int startrow, stoprow, nrows, ncols, filter_size,
    fd, outfd, nrecords, my_tid;
} filter_t;
...
filter_t *farray;
...
```

```
for( j = 0; j < nrecords; j++ )
{
  /* Set up input, output arrays for first pass. */
  farray->buffer = inbufarray[j];
  farray->outbuffer = outbufarray[j];
  /* Set filter to use appropriate filter for first pass. */
  farray->filter = filter1;
  filter_record( farray );

  /* Use output of first pass for input to second pass. Output */
  /* will overwrite original input buffer */
  farray->buffer = outbufarray[j];
  farray->outbuffer = inbufarray[j];
  /* Set filter to use appropriate filter for second pass. */
  farray->filter = filter2;
  filter_record( farray );
}
```

We've defined `filter_record()` to accept a single argument primarily to make it easier to call with `pthread_create()`, as we'll demonstrate shortly. The structure pointer `farray` is set up so that its buffer component points to the input array for the filter to be applied and the `outbuffer` component points to the array in which the results of the filtering operation are to be stored. The structure also contains various parameters, including array dimensions, pointer to the data for the filter, etc.

The `filter_record()` function simply computes the weighted sum of all neighbors of a given point in the record. It's listed here for completeness.

```
void filter_record( filter_t *fptr )
{
  double *buffer, *outbuffer, *filter;
  int nrows, ncols;
  int i, j, fi, fj, parent_thread;
  int startrow, stoprow, irow, icol, frows, fcols;

  buffer = fptr->buffer;
  outbuffer = fptr->outbuffer;
  startrow = fptr->startrow;
  stoprow = fptr->stoprow;
  nrows = fptr->nrows;
  ncols = fptr->ncols;
  filter = fptr->filter;
  frows = fptr->filter_size;
  fcols = fptr->filter_size;
```

```
    for( i = startrow; i < stoprow; i++ )
      for( j = fcols; j < ncols-fcols; j++ )
      {
        outbuffer[ i*nrows + j ] = 0.0;
        for( fi = -frows; fi < frows; fi++ )
        {
          for( fj = -fcols; fj < fcols; fj++ )
          {
            outbuffer[ i*nrows + j ] +=
            buffer[ (i+fi)*nrows+(j+fj) ] *
            filter[fi*frows + fj];
          }
        }
      }

    return;
}
```

One further restriction on this hypothetical problem is that we need to filter the records in the order that they are stored, so our goal is to filter each record using multiple threads. The first approach is that, for a given record, we'll create multiple threads, each of which will filter a particular segment of the record. In order to do this, we define farray such that it is a bona-fide array of filter_t data. The startrow and stoprow components of each element of farray are defined such that the output buffer is divided into an equal number of rows for each thread. Once this is done, the main loop can be rewritten to use pthreads as follows:

```
for( j = 0; j < nrecords; j++ )
{
  /* Spawn threads with the appropriate farray element. */
  for( i = 1; i < ncpus; i++ )
  {
    farray[i].buffer = inbufarray[j];
    farray[i].outbuffer = outbufarray[j];
    farray[i].filter = filter1;
    retval = pthread_create( tid+i, (pthread_attr_t *) NULL,
         (void *(*)())filter_record, (void *) (farray+i) );
    if( retval != 0 ) perror("pthread_create");
  }
  /* Start parent thread to work with first element of farray. */
  farray[0].buffer = inbufarray[j];
  farray[0].outbuffer = outbufarray[j];
  farray[0].filter = filter1;
  filter_record( farray );
```

```
    /* Parent thread waits for other threads to finish. */
    for( i = 1; i < ncpus; i++ )
    {
      retval = pthread_join( tid[i], (void **) NULL );
      if( retval != 0 ) perror("pthread_join");
    }


    /* Now that first filter has been applied, do the second. */
    for( i = 1; i < ncpus; i++ )
    {
      /* Use output of first filter as input to second. */
      farray[i].buffer = outbufarray[j];
      /* Output of second filter overwrites original input. */
      farray[i].outbuffer = inbufarray[j];
      farray[i].filter = filter2;
      retval = pthread_create( tid+i, (pthread_attr_t *) NULL,
            (void *(*)())filter_record, (void *) (farray+i) );
      if( retval != 0 ) perror("pthread_create");
    }
    farray[0].buffer = outbufarray[j];
    farray[0].outbuffer = inbufarray[j];
    farray[0].filter = filter2;
    filter_record( farray );


    /* Parent waits on all threads to complete second filter. */
    for( i = 1; i < ncpus; i++ )
    {
      retval = pthread_join( tid[i], (void **) NULL );
      if( retval != 0 ) perror("pthread_join");
    }
  }
```

As it turns out, there are a large number of records: 4000 in all. Moreover, the buffers aren't very large, 63×63, and the filter is even smaller, 11×11. This makes for a lot of thread spawning and joining with not a lot of work to actually perform. The algorithm above was executed three times on 1, 2, 4, 8 and 12 processors of an HP V-Class computer. The elapsed, user cpu, and system cpu times for each of the runs are shown in Table 8-8. Given the small amount

Table 8-8 Times for Parallel Processing Using Pthreads Created and Joined for Each Record.

Threads	Real	User	System
1	60.0	60.0	0.0
	60.0	60.0	0.0
	59.6	59.6	0.0
2	37.5	66.8	1.3
	37.4	66.5	1.2
	37.5	66.6	1.3
4	19.4	66.9	3.6
	19.2	66.7	3.8
	19.1	66.7	3.6
8	17.7	74.2	6.8
	18.1	74.2	6.8
	18.2	74.2	6.8
12	17.3	77.7	10.1
	17.8	78.3	10.1
	17.2	77.7	9.9

of work to be done filtering each record, it is not a surprise to see that the scaling starts to flatten out after four threads. Beginning with four threads, things begin to get interesting. That is, there is some variation in the elapsed times. This happens because threads can be spawned on any given processor. So they may initially compete for a processor until the scheduler steps in and does some basic load balancing.

Moreover, the system cpu time begins to grow to the extent that it is a substantial amount of the overall cpu time, up to 11% using 12 threads. This is not a surprise because, using 12 processors, there will be 22 calls to `pthread_create()` and `pthread_join()` for each record, totalling a whopping 88,000 threads that have been spawned and joined. We're fortunate that the performance is this good! The HP-UX operating system, like most others, maintains a pool of threads that are waiting to be assigned to any process. Thus, the thread is not actually created with `pthread_create()`; it is assigned. Even so, there should be a more efficient way to execute this workload with less thread overhead.

8.3.3   Barriers

Things would be much nicer if the threads were already created and there was a virtual gate where they waited while each record was being read into memory. Such a mechanism is referred to as a *barrier*. More formally, a barrier is a synchronization mechanism that causes a certain number of threads to wait at a specified point in an application. Once that number of threads has arrived at the barrier, they all resume execution. Barriers are typically used to guarantee that all threads have completed a certain task before proceeding to the next task.

A barrier can be implemented with two functions: one initializes the barrier information and another basically designates at what point the threads are to block until the specified number arrive. The pthreads standard does not implement barriers, but it does provide the necessary tools to implement them, oddly enough. A typical barrier can be implemented as follows:

```c
#include <stdlib.h>
#include <pthread.h>

static int barrier_count = 0;

typedef struct barrier_structure
{
    int maximum;
    int waiting;
    pthread_mutex_t mutex;
    pthread_cond_t condition;
} barrier_t;

static barrier_t **barrier_list = NULL;

void barrierinit( int maximum, int barrierid )
{
    /* Allocate memory for this new barrier. */
    if (barrier_count == 0)
        barrier_list = (barrier_t **)malloc(sizeof(barrier_t *));
    else
        barrier_list = (barrier_t **)realloc(barrier_list,
            (barrier_count+1) * sizeof(barrier_t *));

    barrier_list[barrier_count] = malloc(sizeof(barrier_t));

    /* Initialize number of threads for this barrier to block. */
    barrier_list[barrier_count]->maximum = maximum;
    barrier_list[barrier_count]->waiting = 0;
```

```
     if ( pthread_mutex_init(
          &barrier_list[ barrier_count ]->mutex, NULL) != 0)
       perror("barrierinit_, Unable to allocate mutex");

     if ( pthread_cond_init(
          &barrier_list[barrier_count]->condition, NULL) != 0 )
       perror("barrierinit_, Unable to allocate condition");

     barrier_count++;
     return;
   }

void barrier(int barrierid)
{
   barrier_t *b = barrier_list[barrierid];

   /* Acquire the barrier's mutex. */
   pthread_mutex_lock( &b->mutex );

   /* Tally the number of threads waiting at this barrier. */
   b->waiting++;

   /* Check to see if all threads are here yet. */
   if( b->waiting >= b->maximum )
   {
     /* All threads have reached barrier, signal the others. */
     b->waiting = 0;
     pthread_cond_broadcast(&b->condition);
   }
   else
   {
     /* Wait here for the others. */
     pthread_cond_wait( &b->condition, &b->mutex );
   }

   /* Release the barrier's mutex. */
   pthread_mutex_unlock( &b->mutex );

   return;
   }
```

With these routines, we've introduced another pthread interface, *condition variables*. Condition variables are very useful synchronization mechanisms. They basically cause a thread to wait at a given point until an event occurs. So, when a thread encounters a condition variable and the event has not occurred, then the thread will wait. Subsequently, another thread will cause the event to occur and cause the condition variable to change state and thus wake up one or more threads that are waiting on the condition variable and enable them to resume processing.

Having defined the barrier mechanism, let's implement our algorithm with it and see if the performance improves. To do so, we must first initialize the barrier and start all the threads by replacing the main loop above with the following sequence:

```
/* Initialize barrier 0. */
barrierinit( ncpus, 0 );
/* Spawn additional threads. */
for( i = 1; i < ncpus; i++ )
{
  retval = pthread_create( tid+i, (pthread_attr_t *) NULL,
          (void *(*)())filter_record_par, (void *) (farray+i) );
  if( retval != 0 ) perror("pthread_create");
}
filter_record_par( farray );

/* Wait for all other threads to complete. */
for( i = 1; i < ncpus; i++ )
{
  retval = pthread_join( tid[i], (void **) NULL );
  if( retval != 0 ) perror("pthread_join");
}
```

Note first that the threads are not created for each record. Secondly, the function called by each thread is different. The function `filter_record_par()` is basically the main loop with a few important changes.

```
void filter_record_par( filter_t *fptr )
{
  int recno, nrecords;

  nrecords = fptr->nrecords;

  /* Each thread loops over the records. */
  for( recno = 0; recno < nrecords; recno++ )
  {
    /* Each thread applies first filter to its input. */
    fptr->buffer = inbufarray[recno];
    fptr->outbuffer = outbufarray[recno];
    fptr->filter = filter1;
    filter_record( fptr );
```

```
        /* Since input array will be overwritten, all threads */
        /* must complete execution before starting next filter. */
        barrier( 0 );

        fptr->buffer = outbufarray[recno];
        fptr->outbuffer = inbufarray[recno];
        fptr->filter = filter2;
        filter_record( fptr );
    }

    return;
}
```

Note that there is not a second barrier after the second filter is applied. This is possible because the input and output buffers are unique to each record. So, any given thread can start the first filter of record i+1 as soon as it has finished with the second filter of record i. The barrier between filters is necessary because a given thread may be ready to start the second filter before some other thread has finished with the first. Without a barrier, the output of the first filter may not be complete before some thread tries to use it for input to the second filter.

Table 8-9   Times for Parallel Processing Using Barriers for Synchronization.

Thread	Real	User	System
1	59.6	59.5	0.0
	59.6	59.5	0.0
	59.5	59.5	0.0
2	31.4	61.4	0.3
	31.4	61.6	0.3
	31.4	61.6	0.3
4	17.3	66.0	1.1
	17.3	66.1	1.1
	17.3	66.0	1.1
8	14.6	72.7	6.7
	17.3	72.9	12.4
	14.4	72.6	7.1
12	13.6	77.0	30.8
	12.5	77.0	27.7
	16.3	77.4	39.4

Repeating the experiment used previously (three runs on 1, 2, 4, 8, and 12 processors) resulted in the times shown in Table 8-9. Comparing these times to those in Table 8-8, we see that the performance is the same on a single thread (as we'd expect), but it is much better on multiple processors. In fact, it's as much as 27% faster when comparing the best time in Table 8-9 for 12 threads to the corresponding times in Table 8-8. This brings up an important point: we used the best time for the comparison. Even though the system was idle, there was large variation in the elapsed times on 8 and 12 processors. The system times were larger than before and they varied substantially (especially on 8 processors). The varying system times provide us with a hint as to the cause of the variation in performance.

When a thread finishes with its portion of the first filter work, it has to wait at the barrier. If the thread is blocked for several cycles, waiting on the condition variable to change state, then the operating system will transition it to a sleep state. It will remain in that state until it is ready to run again, i.e., the condition variable changes. There are at least two performance impacts when this sequence of events occurs. First, the transition of the thread's state from sleeping to ready-to-run is done by the operating system and hence takes a significant number of clock cycles, usually hundreds. Second, the thread may be restarted on a processor other than the one it had been executing on before being transitioned to the sleep state. This forces the thread to reload all of its text and data into the new processor's instruction and data caches, respectively. This, too, requires hundreds of cycles because it effectively causes multiple cache lines to be loaded from memory.

The first problem can be addressed by using spin lock mechanisms such as that described above with the use of `acquire_lock()` and `release_lock()`. However, spin locks can consume a tremendous amount of resources by repeatedly trying to acquire a semaphore. That is, by the time it takes to return from being blocked by a semaphore, it may often have been unblocked. So, spin locks can easily be abused.

On the other hand, most operating systems try to prevent the problem of threads being unnecessarily moved from one processor to another. That is, operating systems attempt to schedule the threads that have been sleeping to execute on their original processors in order to exploit the presence of any data encached during the thread's last timeslice. That is, threads have an *affinity* for their original processors. Affinity is enjoyed only if the original processor is available when the thread is ready to execute; otherwise, the thread will be moved to the first processor that becomes available (on most operating systems). So, for example, any process that runs for a short time, such as an operating system daemon, could cause a thread to be moved from one processor to another. Some operating systems provide mechanisms to increase the affinity that a thread has for a processor. This can be achieved with HP-UX by using the `mpctl()` system call. This system call is very useful as it provides a means to identify the number of processors on a system as well as the ability to change thread or process affinity.

So, let us see if improving the thread affinity in our application will help performance. To do this, we first need to get the processor numbers that the application is executing on. We do this by adding the following code sequence before the threads are created:

```
#include <sys/mpctl.h>
...
extern int cpuid[16];
...
   /* Get number of first processor in the system. */
   cpuid[0] = mpctl( MPC_GETFIRSTSPU, NULL, NULL );
   farray[0].my_tid = 0;
   for( i = 1; i < ncpus; i++ )
   {
      /* Get number of the next processor in the system. */
      cpuid[i] = mpctl( MPC_GETNEXTSPU, cpuid[i-1], NULL );
      if( cpuid[i] < 0 )
      {
         perror("mpctl(MPC_GETNEXT)");
         exit(-1);
      }
      /* Initialize the thread index in farray. */
      farray[i].my_tid = i;
   }
```

Then, in the `filter_record_par()` routine, before the loop over each record, we use `mpctl` to move the threads to unique processors by using the information in the global array `cpuid`. This is accomplished with the following code:

```
/* Move the executing thread to processor cpuid[fptr->my_tid]. */
if( mpctl( MPC_SETLWP_FORCE,
        cpuid[fptr->my_tid], MPC_SELFLWPID) < 0 )
{
   perror("mpctl(SETLWP)");
   exit(-1);
}
```

When `mpctl()` is called with the MPC_SETLWP_FORCE and MPC_SELFLWPID parameters, it asynchronously assigns the calling thread to the indicated processor number (second argument). This causes the scheduling policy to be overridden so that the thread will not execute on any other processor, even if these processors are idle and the thread is suspended, waiting on its processor to execute. As a result, this interface should be used with caution. Good results have

been obtained through use of the advisory version of the call, which is achieved by using
MPC_SETLWP in place of MPC_SETLWP_FORCE.

After implementing our program with barriers and the affinity mechanisms described
above, we then execute on the same machine in the same fashion as before. The results of these
runs are shown in Table 8-10. So, indeed, the times do not vary as much as before. Better yet,

Table 8-10   Times for Parallel Processing Using Barriers and
Improved Thread Affinity.

Threads	Real	User	System
1	60.6	60.0	0.1
	60.6	59.9	0.1
	60.8	60.2	0.1
2	31.6	61.9	0.2
	31.6	61.9	0.2
	31.6	61.9	0.2
4	17.3	66.3	0.9
	17.3	66.3	0.9
	17.3	66.3	0.9
8	14.1	73.0	5.3
	14.1	73.2	5.4
	14.1	73.0	5.3
12	12.5	76.9	17.8
	12.2	76.9	17.2
	12.5	76.9	17.9

they are uniformly as good as or better than any of the previous attempts at executing this task in
parallel. Finally, note that the system cpu times are roughly 40% less than they were without the
additional affinity effort.

8.4 Parallelism and I/O

One of the biggest challenges in parallel processing is overcoming the sequential nature of accessing data in a file. Reading and writing to a file can be, and often is, a large part of the execution time of any application. To illustrate just how easily this can come to pass, let's consider our filter subroutine from the previous section. Suppose that we are to filter records of a fixed size from a file and write them to an output file. If this file is several gigabytes in size, then it is not usually practical to allocate a single memory buffer and read the entire file into memory, filter it, and write it all out to the file. So, you might find yourself using a code sequence such as the following to perform this operation:

```
bytes_read = read( fd, inbuffer, nbytes );


farray->buffer = inbuffer;
farray->outbuffer = outbuffer;
while( bytes_read > 0 )
{
   filter_record( farray );

   retval = write( outfd, outbuffer, bytes_read );
   if( retval < bytes_read ) { perror("write"); exit(-1); }

   bytes_read = read( fd, inbuffer, nbytes );
}
```

This loop was executed on an HP N-4000 computer using a file system that is capable of I/O performance of at least 80 MB/sec. Processing 50,000 records, each of which was a two-dimensional array of double precision values, 63×63 in size, translates to reading and writing around 1.5 GB of data (each way). With `filter_record()` defined as before, this resulted in 36.7 seconds reading, 41.0 seconds filtering, and 16.2 seconds writing data. Thus, the filtering accounted for less than half of the total time and I/O for the rest! So, even if we had an infinite number of processors that we could use to filter the data, reducing that portion of the time to zero, then the best scaling we could achieve would be just under 2x. That's not very good scaling by any measure. This is an important part of understanding parallelism—scalability will only be as good as the part of your application that will execute in parallel.

A good question at this point is, "Is there any way to perform I/O in parallel?" The answer is, "Of course!"

8.4.1   POSIX Asynchronous I/O

The POSIX asynchronous I/O facility provides for an API which allows a thread to start multiple simultaneous read and/or write operations to multiple files and to wait for or obtain notification of completion of such operations. The intent is to allow a thread to overlap some other computational task with I/O operations. It provides several interfaces, including:

* `aio_read()`   Initiate an asynchronous read operation
* `aio_write()`   Initiate an asynchronous write operation
* `aio_suspend()` Wait for completion of one or more asynchronous I/O operations
* `aio_error()`   Retrieve the error status of an asynchronous I/O operation
* `aio_return()`   Obtain the return status of an asynchronous I/O operation and free any associated system resources
* `aio_cancel()`   Request cancellation of a pending asynchronous I/O operation

This API is actually defined as part of real-time extensions to POSIX, and as a result is contained in the real-time library on some systems. For example, one must link with `-lrt` on HP-UX systems.

This API can be used in our example to achieve better performance. To do this, we'll actually need two input buffers and have to modify our logic slightly to toggle between these two buffers for every iteration of the loop. That is, in any given iteration we'll want to read data into one buffer while we filter the other one and write the result to the output file. To do this, we'll need the `aio_error()` function to identify when the asynchronous read has completed and then check the status with `aio_return()`. The following code achieves the desired result:

```
#include <aio.h>
...
struct aiocb aioblk;
...
i = 0;
bytes_read = read( fd, inbuffer[i], nbytes );

/* Initialize the asynchronous I/O structure with the */
/* appropriate file descriptor, file offset, bytes to be */
/* read, and the signal (if any) to be sent upon completion. */
aioblk.aio_fildes = fd;
aioblk.aio_offset = bytes_read;
aioblk.aio_nbytes = nbytes;

/* Set up asynchronous I/O structure so that no signal is */
/* sent on completion. */
aioblk.aio_sigevent.sigev_notify  = SIGEV_NONE;
```

```
while( bytes_read > 0 )
{
   /* Point aio_read at the appropriate buffer. */
   aioblk.aio_buf = inbuffer[1-i];

   /* Initiate the asynchronous read operation. */
   retval = aio_read( &aioblk );
   if( retval != 0 ) { perror("aio_read"); exit(-1); }

   /* Meanwhile, filter the other buffer that was just read. */
   farray->buffer = inbuffer[i];
   filter_record( farray );

   /* Write out filtered result. */
   retval = write( outfd, outbuffer, bytes_read );
   if( retval < bytes_read ) { perror("write"); exit(-1); }

   /* Wait on asynchronous read to complete. */
   while( (retval = aio_error( &aioblk )) == EINPROGRESS );
   if( retval < 0 ) { perror("aio_error"); exit(-1); }

   /* Get the return value of the read operation. */
   bytes_read = aio_return( &aioblk );
   if( bytes_read < 0 ) { perror("aio_return"); exit(-1); }



   /* Set up offset for next aio_read. */
   aioblk.aio_offset += bytes_read;

   /* Toggle the buffer index. */
   i = 1 - i;
}
```

Note that the API provides for either a polling or notification model in identifying when an asynchronous I/O operation completes. In the above example, the `aio_error()` function is used to poll the status of the `aio_read()`. Also, it should be noted that the `aio_read()` function basically provides the functionality of both `lseek()` and `read()`, since the offset in the file is one of the parameters of the asynchronous I/O control structure, `aioblk`.

Implementing our test program, outlined above, with this approach reduced the effective read time from 36.7 seconds to 14.5 seconds! But ideally, we'd like to see the read time reduced to 0, that is, have it entirely overlapped by the filtering and writing tasks. As it turns out, the calls to `aio_read()` and, to a lesser degree, `aio_error()` and `aio_return()`, take more time than one might think. This is because a virtual thread must be obtained from the operating system before the `aio_read()` can return. A successful return from `aio_read()` or `aio_write()` indicates that there are sufficient system resources to execute the asynchronous

I/O operation. In some implementations, a thread is actually created and, as we have seen previously, this is not something that can be done in zero time. In any event, we did improve the performance, reducing the effective read time to less than half of what it was originally.

8.4.2   Thread Safe I/O: pread and pwrite

Another way to perform our I/O in parallel is to remove the effective thread creation that `aio_read()` and `aio_write()` perform from inside the loop. That is, we could create threads outside the loop and have some threads perform the filtering, some read data into buffers, and yet other threads write the filtered data to the output file. One problem with this is that traditional I/O interfaces such as `read()` and `write()` system calls modify the file pointer just as `lseek()` does. This is probably best illustrated by supposing that we have an application which has two threads, each of which is reading data from the same file. Let's consider a situation where one thread is to read 100 bytes, starting 150 bytes from the beginning of the file, and the other thread must read 100 bytes, starting 250 bytes from the beginning of the file. If the file descriptor for the file is shared, then so is the file pointer that is internally associated with that file descriptor. As a result, we could easily have the scenario shown in Figure 8-4. Note that thread 1, intending to read data starting 150 bytes from the beginning of the file, actually reads data starting 350 bytes from the beginning of the file! This is because the process' file system information was modified by thread 0 before thread 1 could perform the read operation. The system calls themselves are effectively single-threaded. That is, when executing a read system call for a particular file descriptor, no other thread can modify the process' information related to that file. So, it would be helpful if one had an `lseek()` and `read()` combined into a single system call. Many of today's operating systems provide exactly that in the form of the `pread()` and `pwrite()` system calls. The interface for these is very straightforward, in that the return value is defined analogously to that for `read()` and it has one additional argument which is the offset from the beginning of the file. That is,

```
retval = pread( fd, buf, nbytes, offset );
if( retval < 0 ) { perror("pread"); exit(-1); }
```

translates to the following sequence, but without a shared file pointer.

```
lseek( fd, offset, SEEK_SET );
retval = read( fd, buf, nbytes );
if( retval < 0 ) { perror("read"); exit(-1); }
```

The `pwrite()` system call is related to the `write()` system call in just the same way.

Using these thread safe I/O interfaces, users can achieve their own asynchronous I/O. With regard to our previous filtering example, there are at least two approaches. We can use either a model similar to that of `aio_read()` as discussed above, or each thread can read its own piece of the input array.

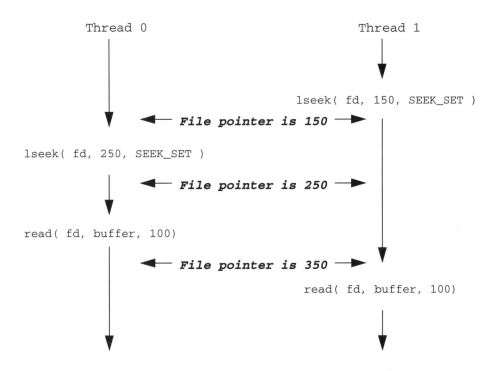

Figure 8-4   Unpredictable I/O with multiple threads using traditional system calls.

Let's consider the latter approach first. But before we do, an important feature of the filtering process needs to be examined in some detail. Consider the diagram in Figure 8-5. If the i-th row of the input buffer is the first row to be processed by thread 1 then, with a 5 × 5 filter, it requires data from the last two rows read in by thread 0 and the first three rows read in by thread 1. The resulting element in row i, column j of the output buffer, however, resides in the first row of thread 1's portion of the output buffer.

This is analogous to that illustrated in the two-filter example described in Section 8.3. That is, create threads outside the main loop as before, with each thread assigned a set of rows. Each thread then reads its piece of the input buffer into memory, applies the filter, and finally writes its rows of the output buffer to disk. Note that we'll need two barriers to get this to work correctly. The first barrier will occur after reading the data into memory. This is necessary since, when filtering the first and last few of its rows, each thread uses data from rows that are read into the input buffer by other threads (see Figure 8-5). So, the entire input buffer has to be in place before any given thread can begin filtering. Since the output buffer is not shared, each thread can write

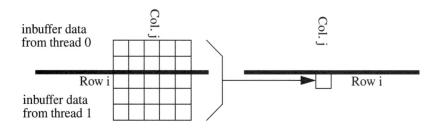

Figure 8-5 Thread sharing of input data for filtering process.

its own piece of the output buffer to disk once it has finished filtering. However, the thread must wait before reading its piece of the next input buffer, because doing so could overwrite information that is being used by other threads still filtering the previous record. As a result, we'll have to have a barrier after the output buffer is written. This sequence is illustrated in Figure 8-6. One drawback to this approach is that we now have multiple, simultaneous system calls in the read and write portions of the loop. That is, suppose we have 4 threads running. Owing to the barrier after the write, they'll all be performing pread() calls at virtually the same time, all accessing the same input file. Writing to the output file may be just as bad because all 4 threads may finish filtering at roughly the same time, and hence there could well be 4 simultaneous calls to pwrite(), all of which are accessing the same output file. Implementing this scheme is left as an exercise for the reader, but don't be surprised if the performance doesn't improve much. We'll revisit this approach in the ccNUMA section of this chapter.

Given the potential performance problems when each thread performs I/O for its portion of the input and output buffers, let us revisit the asynchronous I/O approach in the previous section. Rather than use aio_read() and aio_write(), we can create additional threads to perform the I/O. To accomplish this, we create two additional threads, one to read data into an input buffer and another to be writing data from the thread-private output buffer. In particular, we need two separate input buffers just as we did with the aio_read() example above. Each of these input buffers will have a pair of condition variables associated with them (see the earlier section on barriers). One of the condition variables will indicate whether the buffer is ready to be filtered or not. The other will be used to identify whether data can be placed into the input buffer, i.e., whether the "filtering" threads are finished with it. The former condition variable will be set by

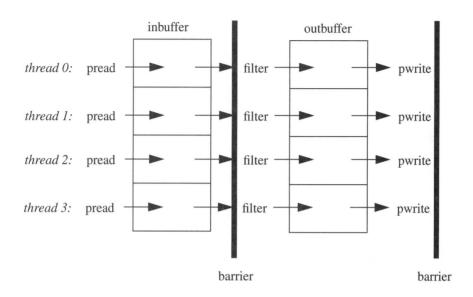

Figure 8-6   Performing I/O in parallel with `pread` and `pwrite` system calls.

the thread doing the reading and the latter will be set by the threads doing the filtering. This approach has the advantage of far fewer system calls being performed as well as the attraction of having all the I/O operations being done while other threads are performing computational tasks. The details of this approach are left as an exercise for the reader.

8.5 Memory Allocation, ccNUMA, and Performance

So far, we've avoided the issue of how and where parallel applications allocate memory. In the parallel process model, memory is allocated on the process' heap and stack as it normally is. We discussed briefly how to allocate memory that can be shared between processes using mmap. Such virtual memory is in a separate class all by itself; it's really neither heap nor stack. The same is true for shared-memory allocated with the System V protocols (shmget, shmat, etc.), and there's even a command to display information about these shared-memory segments. This command, ipcs, provides information such as the size, owner, process identification, times of creation, access, etc., for shared-memory segments and semaphores that are currently active in the system.

Processes with more than one thread enjoy other variations on how memory is allocated. How threads allocate and initialize memory can make a huge difference in the performance and success of thread-parallel applications.

8.5.1   Memory Allocation with Threads

To illustrate some of the features of thread address space, consider the following code:

```
#include <errno.h>
#include <stdlib.h>
#include <stdio.h>
#include <pthread.h>
#include <spp_prog_model.h>

int barrierinit(int x, int n), barrier(int x);

/* Create thread private data, in this case as an external. */
thread_private int x;

static pthread_mutex_t mutex;

void thread_sub(char *b)
{
  /* Automatic variables are allocated on this thread's stack. */
  int i;
  char *tb;

  /* Allocate memory on heap to be used by this thread. */
  tb = (char *)malloc( (size_t)1024 );
  if( tb == NULL ) { perror("thread malloc"); exit(-1); }

  pthread_mutex_lock( &mutex );

  i = pthread_self();
  tb[0] = 'a' + i - 1;

  fprintf(stderr,"Enter<%d>\n",pthread_self());
  fprintf(stderr,"b(x%x)=%c, ",b,b[0]);
  fprintf(stderr,"tb(x%x)=%c, ",tb,tb[0]);
  fprintf(stderr,"i(x%x)=%d, ",&i,i);
  fprintf(stderr,"x(x%x)=%d\n",&x,x);

  x = pthread_self();
  b[0] = tb[0];

  pthread_mutex_unlock( &mutex );

  barrier(0);
```

```
   pthread_mutex_lock( &mutex );

   fprintf(stderr,"Exit <%d>\n",pthread_self());
   fprintf(stderr,"b(x%x)=%c, ",b,b[0]);
   fprintf(stderr,"tb(x%x)=%c, ",tb,tb[0]);
   fprintf(stderr,"i(x%x)=%d, ",&i,i);
   fprintf(stderr,"x(x%x)=%d\n",&x,x);

   pthread_mutex_unlock( &mutex );

   return;
}

main(int argc, char **argv)
{
   /* Automatic variables are allocated on parent thread's stack. */
   int i, retval, nbytes, ncpus;
   char *buffer;
   pthread_t tid[16];

...

   nbytes = 1024;

   /* Allocate memory on the heap to be shared among all threads. */
   buffer = (char *)malloc( (size_t)nbytes );
   if( buffer == NULL ) { perror("malloc"); exit(-1); }

   /* Initialize memory with parent thread. */
   buffer[0] = 'A';
   for( i = 1; i <= ncpus; i++ )
     buffer[i] = buffer[0]+i;

   /* Initialize mutex. */
   if( pthread_mutex_init( &mutex, NULL ) != 0 )
   { perror("pthread_mutex_init"); exit(-1); }

   /* Initialize barrier. */
   barrierinit( ncpus, 0 );

   x = -1;
```

```
/* Spawn threads. */
for( i = 1; i < ncpus; i++ )
{
   buffer[i] = buffer[0]+1;
   retval = pthread_create( tid+i, (pthread_attr_t *) NULL,
        (void *(*)())thread_sub,
        (void *) (buffer) );
        if( retval > 0 ) perror("pthread_create");
}
thread_sub( buffer );


/* Wait on all threads to complete. */
for( i = 1; i < ncpus; i++ )
{
   retval = pthread_join( tid[i], (void **) NULL );
   if( retval > 0 ) perror("pthread_create");
}


printf("Good-bye world!, x= %d\n",x);


exit(0);
}
```

The qualifier `thread_private` is unique to HP's programming model and is not part of the pthread API definition. This qualifier enables the programmer to allocate thread-specific storage even before the threads themselves are created. So, each thread will have its own private copy of x (as we'll demonstrate shortly). Consider the data structures i and tb (the pointer) defined locally by `thread_sub()`. These are allocated on the stack, but the question is, what stack? When a thread is created, it has its own stack, referred to as a *thread stack*. So, memory allocated on the stack in a subroutine called by a thread is actually placed on that thread's stack. This feature is a veritable Pandora's box. Consider for a moment how stacks and heaps work. They are placed at opposite ends of the address space and "grow" toward one another. Threads share a process' address space and, as a result, the multiple thread stacks are preallocated and have a finite limit to their size. On HP systems, the default size for thread stack is 64 KB.

If we execute the above code with ncpus set to four on an HP N-4000 computer, then the following output results. The address and value for b[0], tb[0], i, and x are printed for each thread. Note that the thread id, obtained from `pthread_self()`, is printed in < >.

```
Enter<2>
b(x40022060)=A, tb(x40042010)=b, i(x68fb50e0)=2, x(x40022640)=0
Enter<1>
b(x40022060)=b, tb(x400229b0)=a, i(x68ff0a60)=1, x(x400041d0)=-1
Enter<3>
b(x40022060)=a, tb(x40062010)=c, i(x68fa40e0)=3, x(x400227c0)=0
Enter<4>
b(x40022060)=c, tb(x40082010)=d, i(x68f930e0)=4, x(x40022940)=0
Exit <4>
b(x40022060)=d, tb(x40082010)=d, i(x68f930e0)=4, x(x40022940)=4
Exit <3>
b(x40022060)=d, tb(x40062010)=c, i(x68fa40e0)=3, x(x400227c0)=3
Exit <2>
b(x40022060)=d, tb(x40042010)=b, i(x68fb50e0)=2, x(x40022640)=2
Exit <1>
b(x40022060)=d, tb(x400229b0)=a, i(x68ff0a60)=1, x(x400041d0)=1
Good-bye world!, x= 1
```

There is a lot of interesting behavior demonstrated by this program. First, note that the buffer allocated in the main program and passed into thread_sub() as b is indeed shared by all the threads. The virtual address shown for b is the same for all four threads and, as the output beginning with "Exit" illustrates, the information stored there is indeed shared. We can see this because the value of b[0] is set by the previous thread as it passes through the first critical section in thread_sub(), and that value is read by the next thread passing through the critical section. For example, when thread 2 enters the critical section, it finds the character A in b[0]. Before leaving the critical section, it stores the character b into b[0]. Subsequently, when thread 1 enters the critical section, it finds the character b in b[0]. The last thread through the critical section (thread 4) stores the character d into b[0]. Subsequently, all the other threads read d from b[0], because b is *shared* memory.

The other memory allocation done in the main program is that for x. It's interesting to note that the process' main thread (thread id of 1) initialized x to -1, and it is the only thread that shows a value of -1 upon entering thread_sub(). All the other threads (children) have x set to zero.

The memory allocated in thread_sub() (i, tb, and the data tb points to), all have unique addresses and, hence, unique values. Both i and tb are part of the thread's stack. But the memory allocated through malloc() within the threads, while being thread-specific data, is all placed on the parent process' heap. This is easily discerned by examining the address of b and comparing it to the addresses for tb, in each thread. As a result, if any given thread addresses memory outside its range for tb, then data corruption of other threads' memory will occur.

Finally, we should point out that the thread id numbers returned from pthread_self() happened to be consecutive and started with one. Generally speaking, you cannot assume that the thread id numbers of threads that are consecutively created will be consecutive and start with one.

The size of a thread's stack is the source of a large number of thread-parallel application problems. On HP-UX, if the subroutines called by a thread allocate more than 64 KB of local variables, then data corruption can (and usually will) occur. Many systems add an additional *guard page* to the end of each thread's stack. Accessing memory in this guard page will cause an error (typically a "bus error"). But modifying memory beyond this page usually results in the modification of data in another thread's stack! Moreover, unless data in the guard page is accessed, the user will likely not see an obvious error, just data corruption.

Unfortunately, a thread's stack size can't be changed external to the application (e.g., with an environment variable). The pthreads API does provide an interface to change the thread's attributes, such as stack size. The following code excerpt demonstrates how these interfaces can be used to increase a thread's stack size to 128 KB:

```
pthread_attr_t pattr;
...
/* Initialize the thread attribute object. */
retval = pthread_attr_init( &pattr );
if( retval != 0 ) { perror("pthread_attr_init"); exit(-1); }

/* Set thread stack size to 128 KB. */
tstacksize = 128 * 1024;
retval = pthread_attr_setstacksize( &pattr, tstacksize );
if( retval != 0 )
   { perror("pthread_attr_setstacksize"); exit(-1); }
/* Subsequent threads created will have stack size of 128 KB. */
...
```

8.5.2   Physical Memory Allocation for Threads

Applications that are not memory-access intensive will usually scale just as well on ccNUMA architectures as they will on uniform memory access (UMA) architectures, assuming all other architecture features are similar (i.e., processors, caches, I/O devices, etc.). Memory intensive applications can occasionally exhibit very poor scaling on ccNUMA machines. This is often caused by the way physical memory is allocated on the machine. This issue was discussed in Chapter 4 in some detail. Today's ccNUMA architectures feature several methods that can be used by application developers and users to alleviate this problem.

General speaking, there are two approaches to memory placement on ccNUMA machines: environmental controls and APIs. First, let's discuss environmental controls. Sometimes the environmental controls simply don't exist, but knowledge of the system's memory placement methodology can enable the programmer get the job done anyway. Four common schemes (there are many others) for allocating physical memory pages are

- round-robin placement,
- first-fault placement,
- fixed placement, and
- page migration

For this discussion, let us define a node as a source of physical memory with a number of processors associated with it. The association is that these processors can access this source of physical memory as fast as any other processor. For example, two SMPs that share memory via some interconnect would represent a system with two nodes (the SMPs). A node defined in this way is sometimes referred to as a *Memory Locality Domain* (MLD).

Round-robin page placement describes the practice of allocating memory pages in a round-robin fashion on each of the nodes in a system. When memory is allocated on the node associated with the first thread that accesses the page, this is referred to as *first-fault*, or *first touch*, placement. When memory is allocated from a fixed node, e.g., the initial thread of a process, this is called *fixed* placement. Finally, some systems support *page migration*. This is the ability to move pages from one node to another based on the number of memory accesses, i.e., if a thread executing on a particular node is accessing a page far more than others, then the system will move the page onto that node. The first three placement methods are static. The program will use that placement method throughout the applications execution. Page migration is a very dynamic method of memory allocation, making it very different from the others.

Not all of today's ccNUMA systems support these placement mechanisms. For example, HP-UX currently provides only first-fault placement. The default on most systems is first-fault. SGI's IRIX supports all four of the placement policies described above. These placement policies can be realized through the use of environment variables. Since first-fault is fairly common, threads should initialize and allocate memory that they will most often be accessing.

Let's consider the filtering example discussed in the section on parallel I/O. Given what we've discussed in this section, we can re-implement this algorithm so that one of the barriers is removed and it executes efficiently on ccNUMA systems with a first-fault page placement policy. The input and output buffers can be allocated (but not initialized) by the parent thread just as before. Then the algorithm would proceed as follows:

1. Spawn all threads.
2. Each thread initializes the rows it is responsible for producing in all the output buffers. The thread also initializes the same set of rows of the input buffers.
3. All threads synchronize at a barrier.
4. Using `pread()`, each thread reads the input data required to produce its portion of the output buffer. This includes the additional rows above and below the rows it initialized in the input buffer. (See Figure 8-6 above.)
5. Each thread filters the data and places the results in the output buffer.
6. Using `pwrite()`, each thread writes its rows of the output buffer to the output file.

7. All threads synchronize at a barrier.

8. If any records remain to be filtered, then go to Step 4; otherwise, return.

So, by having each thread read in all the data necessary to produce its portion of the output, the first barrier shown in Figure 8-6 has been eliminated. Note that the first I/O performed occurs in Step three, after all threads have initialized their portions of the input and output buffers. There will be some redundancy here since each thread will read in all the data it needs to perform the filtering operation and, hence, the few rows above and below the filter's portion of the input array (See Figure 8-5) will be read in two threads.

The barrier in Step three insures that all initialization has occurred as planned before the I/O operations initialize the input buffer in a different fashion. For example, suppose we have a total of 2 threads, a 5×5 filter, and each record has 200 rows. Then, without the barrier in Step three, the second thread may read in the rows 98 through 200 (note two additional rows needed for its filtering step) before the second thread finished initializing rows 99 and 100. In this case, those two rows would be first faulted by the second thread and hence placed on the node that thread is executing on.

Given the situation we just discussed, we will have some data sharing between threads. This has been the case all along; we've just not looked into the problem in detail. One improvement on the algorithm presented above would be to have each thread allocate its own subset of rows sufficient to perform its processing. That is, the parent process will not even allocate an input buffer. Instead, each thread will allocate (if the record is very big, use `malloc()` to avoid exceeding thread stack size limit) an input buffer just large enough to contain the rows it needs for the filtering process. Thus, for the example in the previous paragraph, both threads would allocate their own input buffers, each of which would be large enough to contain 102 rows.

8.6 Compiler Directives

As mentioned in Chapter 4, compiler directives make parallel programming a lot easier. Programmers don't have to explicitly create and join threads, locks and barriers are already designed and need not be invented, etc. Moreover, OpenMP [3] provides a standard way of using compiler directives to achieve parallelism. Except for I/O, most of the parallel concepts discussed in this chapter are easily managed through compiler directives.

8.6.1 Spawning and Joining Threads

The creation of threads as well as joining them is made easy for loops through the use of the `parallel for` (`parallel do` for Fortran) directive. The following loop will be executed with multiple threads:

```
#pragma omp parallel for
  for( i = 0; i < n; i++ )
    z[i] = y[i] + a * x[i];
```

More than just loops can be made to run in parallel. If you have different subroutines that you would like to run, then the parallel sections directive can be used. That is, suppose that you want two threads to execute the subroutine `foo()` and one thread to execute `bar()`. Then the following sequence of code will achieve just that:

```
#pragma omp parallel sections
{
#pragma omp section
   foo();
#pragma omp section
   foo();
#pragma omp section
   bar();
}
```

8.6.2   Scheduling Strategies with Directives

One of the real strong points of OpenMP directive specification is that it allows for various scheduling strategies. Earlier in this chapter, we demonstrated the virtue of dynamic scheduling in the presence of non-uniform workloads. Later, we used static load balancing. To handle various scheduling strategies, OpenMP provides the schedule clause. For example, to execute a loop in parallel using a dynamic scheduling approach, one would use the following directive:

```
#pragma omp parallel for schedule(dynamic)
   for( ... )
   ...
```

Other scheduling strategies provided are static and runtime. Static scheduling will cause iterations of the loop to be divided into chunks of a size specified by an optional parameter, `chunk_size`. These chunks are then assigned to the threads in a round-robin fashion. When no `chunk_size` is specified, the total number of iterations is divided into chunks that are approximately equal in size, with one chunk assigned to each thread. Runtime scheduling indicates that the parallel loop or parallel section is to be executed with a scheduling policy that is determined at runtime, based on the user's environment.

8.6.3   Synchronization Mechanisms

OpenMP provides directives and functions that implement many of the synchronization mechanisms discussed earlier in this chapter. Barriers can be implemented with a simple pragma, `omp barrier`. Similarly, critical sections can be implemented with the obviously named directive as shown below:

```
#pragma omp critical
{
    /* Code to be executed by a single thread. */
    ...
}
/* Brace effectively ends the critical section. */
```

In addition to these and other synchronization directives, the OpenMP specification defines a set of lock functions, `omp_init_lock()`, `omp_destroy_lock()`, `omp_set_lock()`, `omp_unset_lock()`, and `omp_test_lock()`. These functions are fairly straightforward in their use and the OpenMP specification provides details on their use.

8.6.4   Environmental Control

The OpenMP specification defines several useful routines for adjusting the runtime parallel environment. Two commonly used routines are `omp_set_num_threads()` and `omp_get_num_threads()`, which set the total number of threads to execute subsequent parallel code and identify total number of threads currently available to execute parallel code, respectively.

In addition to runtime functions, OpenMP provides for environmental control. These allow the application user to change the parallel behavior of the application without rebuilding it! Two very important environmental variables provided for are listed below:

- OMP_SCHEDULE   Sets the run-time scheduling policy as well as chunk size (see the discussion on parallel directives above).
- OMP_NUM_THREADS   Set the maximum number of threads to use during program execution.

8.6.5   Compilers, Directives, and Automatic Parallelism

During the late 1980's and early 1990's, there were several computer vendors trumpeting the virtues of compilers that would automatically make an application run in parallel. Bold claims were made about the sophistication of such compilers and their ability to make any application's performance to scale linearly with the number of processors. Such claims are seldom made today. Reality has proven to be more difficult.

Most of today's compilers are capable of automatically parallelizing applications. The problem is that the compiler is unable to make educated guesses on what should and should not be made to execute in parallel. To illustrate the problem, let's consider an example that is fairly representative of reality.

Suppose an application has 1,000 different loops in it. The compiler carefully creates the constructs to run every one of these in parallel. In reality, 90% of the time is spent in one loop. Moreover, the other 999 loops have a maximum iteration count of two. So, every one of them performs a spawn and join for only two iterations. As we've seen, the overhead for spawning and joining threads is nontrivial. In this case, automatic parallelization is a disaster. Loops that took only a few microseconds are now taking milliseconds because of the parallel overhead. Therefore, the 10% of the time spent outside the main loop could easily increase dramatically (as in an order of magnitude), negating any benefit the main loop may get from parallelism.

This situation is actually the rule rather than the exception. Astfalk [4] demonstrated that most applications have short loop lengths and usually do not benefit from automatic parallelization. This problem can be alleviated somewhat by runtime selection of which loops to execute in parallel. Unfortunately, this requires a test before every loop to determine if the loop length is long enough to justify parallel execution. This additional overhead may prove to be prohibitive as well.

Most programmers know where most of the time is spent in their application. Hence, it is easy for them to identify just where the parallelism would give the most benefit. If this could be the only place that parallelism is implemented, then the application is far more likely to show benefit from parallel processing.

Some compilers enable the programmer to do just this sort of thing. That is, the programmer inserts a compiler directive indicating what loop or loops are to be executed in parallel and then uses a special compiler switch to instruct the compiler to instrument only those areas for parallelism and no others. To demonstrate these concepts, consider the following subroutines that perform matrix multiplication.

In the file `matmul_dir.f` we have the following.

```
SUBROUTINE MATMUL_DIR( A, B, C, M, K, N )

DOUBLE PRECISION A(M,*), B(K,*), C(M,*)
INTEGER M, N, K
INTEGER I1, I2, I3

DO I1 = 1, M
  DO I2 = 1, N
    C(I1,I2) = 0.0
  END DO
END DO

DO I2 = 1, N
!$OMP PARALLEL DO
  DO I3 = 1, K
    DO I1 = 1, M
      C(I1,I2) = C(I1,I2) + A(I1,I3) * B(I3,I2)
    END DO
  END DO
END DO

RETURN
END
```

In another separate file, `matmul_auto.f`, we have the following subroutine which also performs a simple matrix multiplication. Note that there are no directives in this file.

```
SUBROUTINE MATMUL_AUTO( A, B, C, M, K, N )

DOUBLE PRECISION A(M,*), B(K,*), C(M,*)
INTEGER M, N, K
INTEGER I1, I2, I3

DO I1 = 1, M
  DO I2 = 1, N
    C(I1,I2) = 0.0
  END DO
END DO

DO I2 = 1, N
  DO I3 = 1, K
    DO I1 = 1, M
      C(I1,I2) = C(I1,I2) + A(I1,I3) * B(I3,I2)
    END DO
  END DO
END DO

RETURN
END
```

These two files are compiled with Hewlett-Packard's Fortran 90 compiler with two slightly different sets of options as follows:

```
f90 -c +O3 +Oparallel +Onoautopar +Oopenmp matmul_dir.f
f90 -c +O3 +Oparallel matmul_auto.f
```

Note that the file with directives is compiled with the option +Onoautopar. This option instructs the compiler to parallelize only loops which have parallel directives associated with them. In the second case, the compiler automatically parallelizes every loop that it deems fit. As a result, both the initialization loop sequence and the matrix multiplication sequence are made to execute in parallel. We have experimented with various systems and found that the directive, as placed in `matmul_dir.f`, produces the best results. Using three square matrices of dimension 500×500, the two routines exhibited startlingly different performance, as shown in Table 8-11. Comparing the fully automatic parallelism performance of `matmul_auto()` to that of the directive-based parallelism, one can see the value of using directives and having the compiler parallelize only those code segments which have directives associated with them.

Table 8-11 Performance in Mflops for Two Variations of Parallel Matrix Multiplication.

	1 CPU	2 CPUs	4 CPUs
Fully Automatic	21.9	73.2	109.5
User-Inserted Directive	122.0	449.0	703.7

One side note on the performance summarized in Table 8-11. The total size of the data in these problems is approaching six MB. Moving from 1 to 2 processors reduces the data accessed by each processor to roughly three MB. As a result, the data begins to fit efficiently into the N Class's one MB, four-way set associative cache. The performance improves dramatically, well over three times faster on two processors. Such behavior is almost always due to the overall problem's being cut up into small enough pieces so that each thread's data fits into a single processor's cache. Scaling better than the number of processors is generally referred to as *superlinear scaling*.

8.7 The Message Passing Interface (MPI)

As mentioned in Chapter 4, message-passing is a very successful parallel programming method. The MPI Standard [5] has enabled many applications to be implemented so that they can execute in parallel on shared-memory, distributed-memory, and cluster architectures with little nor no customization for any individual architecture. There are several excellent texts on writing efficient MPI applications, including Gropp et al [7] and Pacheco [8] and others [9][10].

MPI provides subroutines for many of the mechanisms we've discussed in this chapter, in addition to interprocess communication subroutines. A brief synopsis of some key MPI subroutines is given below.

- `MPI_send()`   Sends data and blocks until it is received.
- `MPI_recv()`   Receives data, blocking until it is sent.
- `MPI_isend()`   Sends data without blocking.
- `MPI_irecv()`   Receive data without blocking.

- `MPI_sendinit()`   Creates a persistent communication request for a nonblocking send operation.
- `MPI_recvinit()`   Creates a persistent communication request for a nonblocking receive operation.
- `MPI_startall()`   Starts all communications associated with persistent requests designated by its argument list.
- `MPI_waitall()`   Wait until all communications associated with persistent requests designated by its argument list.

Many parallel applications use domain-decomposition and an iterative approach to converge on the problem's solution. Such applications alternate between computation and communication phases. In the computation phase, each process updates its subset of the application's domain. For example, it may compute the new temperature at grid points inside its subdomain.

In the communication phase, data is exchanged with neighboring domains as required by the spatial dependencies of the problem. For example, in a two simulation on a rectangular and regular mesh, dependent variable vectors are exchanged with the four neighbors (north, south, east, west).

The skeleton for such an application could be represented (in C pseudo-code) as

```
main()
{
   initialize();

   while ( ! done)
   {
      compute();
      data_exchange();
   }

   gather_results();
   print_report();
   cleanup();
}
```

In the exchange phase, a process typically sends data from the same set of output buffers at every iteration. Likewise, it receives data into the same set of input buffers.

There are several ways to program this exchange. In general, the list of neighbors for a given process may not form a simple regular graph. In these cases, the most effective approach is to use MPI's persistent requests, along with the `MPI_startall()` and `MPI_waitall()` routines. For a two-dimensional simulation example, this could be done as follows:

```
MPI_request     req[8];
MPI_status      stat[8];

/* In the initialization step: */
MPI_send_init(north_out_buffer, ..., north_process, ..., &req[0]);
MPI_send_init(south_out_buffer, ..., south_process, ..., &req[1]);
MPI_send_init(east_out_buffer, ..., east_process, ..., &req[2]);
MPI_send_init(west_out_buffer, ..., west_process, ..., &req[3]);
MPI_recv_init(north_in_buffer, ..., north_process, ..., &req[4]);
MPI_recv_init(south_in_buffer, ..., south_process, ..., &req[5]);
MPI_recv_init(east_in_buffer, ..., east_process, ..., &req[6]);
MPI_recv_init(west_in_buffer, ..., west_process, ..., &req[7]);
...
while ( ! done)
{
   compute();
   /* The exchange step. */
   MPI_startall(8, req);
   MPI_waitall(8, req, stat);
}

/* In the cleanup step: */
for (i = 0; i < 8; i++)
   MPI_request_free(&req[i]);
```

Creating and destroying the eight requests outside of the main computation loop avoids this overhead in each iteration. Using MPI_startall() to initiate the exchange allows MPI to trigger all eight transfers more efficiently than if they were done via eight separate MPI_isend() and MPI_irecv() calls. Likewise, using MPI_waitall() to block until all eight transfers complete allows MPI to optimize its actions and reduce the number of redundant checks it would have to make if this was programmed using individual MPI_wait() calls, or worse, individual MPI_test() calls. Creating the four send requests before the receive requests lets MPI accelerate the sending of the data. This helps reduce the number of unnecessary status checks that MPI makes on behalf of the receive requests.

This method of programming the data exchange is quite flexible and can be very easily adapted to less regular communication patterns.

8.8 Summary

In this chapter, we have presented the basic premise of parallel programming. SPMD programming concepts were illustrated in some detail along with some of the pitfalls involved in getting good scaling without shared-memory constructs.

Two important differences in parallel process scheduling were illustrated: static work distribution and dynamic scheduling. Quite often, static scheduling enjoys the advantage of cache re-use from previous iterations, while dynamic scheduling enjoys efficient load balancing of the threads (or processes, as the case may be).

Locks and barriers are important mechanisms in parallel processing, but they should be used sparingly. They can often cause unforeseen problems, as was demonstrated in the loss of affinity when using barriers for the filtering example in Section 8.3. Unfortunately, there is not yet a portable means of increasing (or decreasing) a thread's affinity for a processor. But many systems provide tools to accomplish this, as was demonstrated with HP-UX's `mpctl()` interface.

Compiler directives can certainly make parallel programming easier. They can also remove the details from the application programmer, making it difficult to enjoy the robustness of the pthreads specification. The use of directives is almost orthogonal (but not quite) to the approach taken with explicit use of pthreads and/or processes with MPI.

Parallel I/O is, and will continue to be, an important part of parallel programming. As processor performance continues to outpace the performance of data storage access (memory, disk, etc.), we will see more and more emphasis placed on transferring data asynchronously. The recent inclusion of I/O interfaces into the MPI standard is a good example of this.

Parallel programming can be very exciting. Achieving linear (sometimes super linear) scaling on an application when executing on multiple processors is a very rewarding experience. The constructs discussed in this chapter will have hopefully whetted your appetite for parallel programming. There are many excellent resources for the parallel programmer; several are given as references at the end of this chapter.

References:

The following publications are excellent resources for the parallel programming and other topics discussed in this section.

1. Sedgewick, R. *Algorithms in C,* Addison-Wesley, 1990. ISBN 0-201-51425-7.
2. Leffler, S. J.; McKusick, M. K.; Karels, M. J.; Quarterman, J. S. The Design and Implementation of the 4.3BSD UNIX Operating System, Addison-Wesley, 1988. ISBN 0-201-06191-1.
3. Dagum, L.; Menon, R. *OpenMP: An Industry-Standard API for Shared Memory Programming*, IEEE Computational Science and Engineering, Vol. 5, No. 1, January/March 1998. http://www.openmp.org/
4. Astfalk, G. *MPP and Loop-based Parallelism: A Contradiction?*, Proceedings of the Seventh SIAM Conference on Parallel Processing, SIAM, 1995, pp 852-853.
5. Message-Passing Interface Forum. *MPI: A Message-Passing Interface Standard*, University of Tennessee, 1994.
6. Message-Passing Interface Forum. *MPI-2: Extensions to the Message-Passing Interface*, University of Tennessee, 1997. http://www.mpi-forum.org/

7. Gropp, W; Lusk, E.; Skjellum, A. *Using MPI: Portable Parallel Programming with the Message-Passing Interface,* MIT Press, 1994. ISBN 0-262-57104-8.

8. Pacheco, P. *Parallel Programming with MPI*, Morgan Kaufmann, 1996. ISBN 0-262-69184-1.

9. Hewlett-Packard Company. *HP MPI User's Guide*, 1999. Part Number B6011-96010.

10. Hewlett-Packard Company. *Exemplar Programming Guide*, 1997. Part Number B6056-96002.

11. Dowd, K. *High Performance Computing*, O'Reilly, 1993. ISBN 1-56592-312-X.

12. Norton, S. J.; DiPasquale, M. D. *Thread Time: The MultiThreaded Programming Guide*, Prentice-Hall Professional Technical Reference, 1996. ISBN 0-13-190067-6.

13. Curry, D. A. *Using C on the UNIX System*, O'Reilly and Associates, 1991. ISBN 0-937175-23-4.

14. Silicon Graphics, Incorporated. *Origin2000 and Onyx2 Performance Tuning and Optimization Guide*, 1998.

15. Hewlett-Packard Company. *Parallel Programming Guide for HP-UX Systems*, 2000. Part Number B3909-90003.

Applications —
Using the Tools

High Performance Libraries

If I have seen further it is by standing on the shoulders of giants.

Isaac Newton

9.1 Introduction

Consider again the scenario where you are a carpenter. Suppose you go to a job and find that you need a hammer, saw, sawhorses, and nails. Then you'll go back to your smelter, fire it up, add a sufficient amount of iron ore, and create a few kilograms of pure iron. Once you've done that, you'll take this iron to your forge and start beating out a hammer head, saw blade and nails. While these pieces are cooling off, you'll cut down an oak tree (or possibly hickory) and take a good size log or two to your saw mill. There you will cut a couple of small pieces for the hammer and saw handles and several long and narrow pieces, say 2×4's, for the sawhorses. After producing a suitable hammer handle and saw handle in your wood shop the hammer and saw can be assembled and subsequently the sawhorses can be built. Now, at last, you are ready to start the carpentry job.

Is this typical behavior for a carpenter? Of course not! No carpenter in his right mind will recreate his tools for every job. Similarly, no software developer in his right mind will recreate subprograms for every job. This is, of course, why there are so many software libraries around, including standard system libraries such as libc, as well as task specific third party libraries like Syncsort and CoSORT, which provide high performance libraries for sorting data.

This chapter will discuss some of the commonly used high performance libraries that are available today. The focus will be on mathematical libraries, but others will be discussed as well.

9.2 Linear Algebra Libraries and APIs

9.2.1 BLAS

The BLAS (Basic Linear Algebra Subprograms) are routines for performing basic vector and matrix operations. They are generally referred to as being divided up into three groups or levels. Level 1 BLAS are for vector operations, Level 2 BLAS are for matrix-vector operations, and Level 3 BLAS do matrix-matrix operations. The BLAS were begun in 1979 by Lawson et al [1], and continued to grow through the 1980s with the final additions, Level 3, being made in 1990 by Dongarra et al [2].

While the BLAS have been used for many years with much success, it never became a bona-fide standard. However the BLAS, are a strong and well-accepted, *ad hoc* standard. But it has some limitations in functionality. It does not provide some of the more typical routines used in many calculations, such as

```
DO I=1, N
   Z(I) = ALPHA * X(I) + Y(I)
END DO
```

Most new software development is done in languages other than Fortran. For example, far more development is being done in C and C++ than in Fortran. Given the differences in subroutine calling convention (Fortran passes arguments by address while C and C++ pass them by value), it is not straightforward to call BLAS routines from C or C++.

The combination of these issues led a group of folks, referred to as the BLAS Technical Forum, to develop a standard for the BLAS. The standard was nearly complete in 1999 and provides Fortran 77, Fortran 95, and C interfaces to all subprograms. It is largely a superset of the original (legacy) BLAS. Given that the standard is just emerging at the time of this writing, it is unclear how well-accepted it will be. The C interfaces are an improvement, but the argument lists are sometimes cumbersome and contain some Fortran-centric features that may or may not be useful with languages other than Fortran.

9.2.2 LINPACK

The linear algebra package LINPACK (LINear algebra PACKage) is a collection of Fortran subroutines for use in solving and analyzing linear equations and linear least-squares problems. It was designed for computers in use during the 1970s and early 1980s. LINPACK provides subroutines which solve linear systems whose matrices are dense, banded, symmetric, symmetric positive definite, or triangular. It is based on the Level 1 routines in the legacy BLAS.

9.2.3 EISPACK

EISPACK (EIgenvalue Software PACKage) by Smith [3], Garbow [4] and others is a collection of subroutines that compute eigenvalues and eigenvectors for several types of matrices. It, too, was developed in the late 1970s for computers of that era.

9.2.4 LAPACK

Arguably the most successful public domain library for linear algebra is LAPACK (Linear Algebra PACKage) by Anderson et al [5]. The original project was to enable the EISPACK and LINPACK libraries to execute efficiently on shared-memory vector and parallel processors. LAPACK improved the basic algorithms by redesigning them so that memory access patterns were more efficient. Moreover, the subroutines in LAPACK are written so that, wherever possible, calls to the Level 2 and Level 3 routines of the legacy BLAS subprograms are made. As will be discussed in Chapters 10 and 11, the Level 2 and Level 3 BLAS routines are much more efficient for today's computer architectures. This has also proven to be a huge benefit to users, as almost all computer vendors today provide highly tuned legacy BLAS libraries. So, LAPACK can be built with these faster libraries and provide dramatically better performance than building the entire package from scratch. Users should use LAPACK rather than LINPACK or EISPACK as it is superior to both in functionality as well as performance.

9.2.5 ScaLAPACK

The ScaLAPACK (Scalable Linear Algebra PACKage) features a subset of the LAPACK library which has been architected to execute in parallel. It is designed primarily for distributed-memory parallel computers and uses its own communication package BLACS (Basic Linear Algebra Communication Subprograms). BLACS can be built with MPI or PVM. ScaLAPACK, LAPACK, and BLAS can all be obtained from the Netlib Repository at the University of Tennessee—Knoxville and Oak Ridge National Laboratory. The URL for this repository is `http://netlib.org/`.

9.2.6 PLAPACK

Another parallel linear algebra package is PLAPACK (Parallel Linear Algebra PACKage) developed by van de Geijn [6] and Alpatov et al [7]. PLAPACK is an infrastructure for coding linear algebra algorithms at a high level of abstraction. By taking this approach to parallelization, more sophisticated algorithms can be implemented. As has been demonstrated on Cholesky, LU and QR factorization solvers, PLAPACK allows high levels of performance to be realized. See `http://www.cs.utexas.edu/users/plapack/` for more information on PLAPACK.

9.3 Signal Processing Libraries and APIs

9.3.1   FFTPACK

One of the most popular signal processing libraries is FFTPACK. This is a package of Fortran subprograms for the Fast Fourier Transform (FFT) of periodic and other symmetric sequences. This package, developed by Swarztrauber[8], is available through the netlib repository (URL provided above) and provides complex, real, sine, cosine, and quarter-wave transforms. Version 4 of this package was made available in 1985.

9.3.2   VSIPL

In an attempt to develop a standard API, several organizations began work on VSIPL (Vector/Signal/Image Processing Library). The first steps in developing this library is to provide basic FFT (Fast Fourier Transform) subroutines as well as those for vector operations and convolution. Interestingly, a lot of the functionality duplicates that in BLAS and LAPACK. For example, VSIPL provides routines for matrix multiplication, matrix decomposition (including LU, Cholesky, and QRD factorizations).

Beta versions of the VSIPL Core software were made available in the autumn of 1999. More information on VSIPL can be found at the forum's website, http://www.vsipl.org/.

9.4 Self-Tuning Libraries

9.4.1   PHiPAC

One of the first attempts at providing a library of linear algebra routines which is automatically tuned for a particular architecture was provided by Bilmes et al [9]. This package provides Portable High-Performance, ANSIC C (PHiPAC) linear algebra subprograms. Building subprograms, such as matrix multiplication, with PHiPAC first requires a "training" session. This requires the user to run a sequence of programs on the machine for which the subprogram is being built that identify an optimal set of parameters for that subprogram and machine.This training can take a while. For example, on a dedicated Hewlett-Packard N-4000 machine, it took 28 hours to build the general matrix multiplication routine dgemm(). This is a nontrivial amount of dedicated time on a 1.7 Gflop/s processor. This training needs to be done only once, but it should be done on a dedicated system; otherwise, the parameters it identifies may not be optimal. Version 1.0 of PHiPAC produces a good version of dgemm() on the Hewlett-Packard N-4000. It provides performance that is far better than the public domain Fortran reference BLAS dgemm() routine when compiled with HP's Fortran 90 compiler. It does seem to have trouble with problems that do not fit into cache, as is illustrated in Figures 9-1 and 9-2.

9.4.2 ATLAS

Another automatically tuned package is the ATLAS (Automatically Tuned Linear Algebra Software) library. Version 1.0 of ATLAS was made available by Whaley et al [10] through the netlib repository. ATLAS puts most, if not all, of its system specific information into the design of a single subroutine. Other, higher level, routines are then able to reuse the system specific routine efficiently. The end result is that the complexity of the tuning is dramatically reduced because only a single routine needs to be generated for a particular platform.

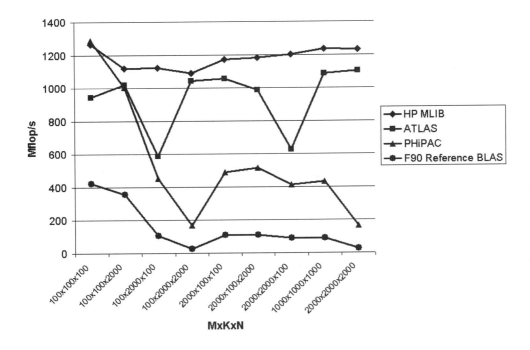

Figure 9-1   Comparison of matrix multiplication performance with various software packages.

As was the case with PHiPAC, ATLAS produced a `dgemm()` that was much better than that obtained with the public domain BLAS reference `dgemm()` routine compiled with HP's Fortran 90 compiler on a HP N-4000 machine. The results of `dgemm()` performance on various sizes of matrices with PHiPAC, ATLAS, and HP's MLIB, version 7.0, is presented in Figure 9-1. Figure 9-2 gives `dgemm()` performance when the matrices being multiplied are transposed. Note that ATLAS 1.0 automatically generates all the legacy BLAS. PHiPAC 1.0, on the other hand, has scripts to generate the dgemm() subroutine, but not very many other routines within BLAS.

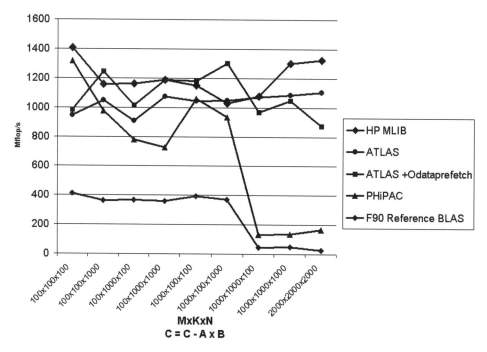

Figure 9-2   Comparison of transposed matrix multiplication performance using various software packages.

9.4.3   FFTW

The self-tuning approach to mathematical libraries used in PHiPAC and ATLAS is not isolated to linear algebra. The Fastest Fourier Transform in the West (FFTW) is a portable C package for computing multidimensional, complex, discrete Fourier transforms (DFT). The authors of FFTW, Frigo and Johnson [11], take a slightly different approach to performance tuning than PHiPAC and ATLAS do. That is, FFTW doesn't require a "training" session to define a set of parameters for the particular architecture on which it is to be built and executed. Instead, FFTW performs the optimization at runtime through an explicit call to a setup program, referred to as the "planner." The planner uses a dynamic programming algorithm to identify a near optimal set of parameters that are subsequently used by the "executor." So, calculating an FFT for a given problem size requires two subroutine calls, one to the planner and another to the executor. Note, however, that a single plan can be reused for other problems, provided they are the same size.

The performance of FFTW is quite good. At the time of its announcement, September 1997, it was faster than any other public domain FFT package available and faster than some computer vendor libraries. A performance comparison, using FFTW's timers, of FFTW 2.1.3 with FFTPACK and HP's MLIB 7.0 is given in Figure 9-3.

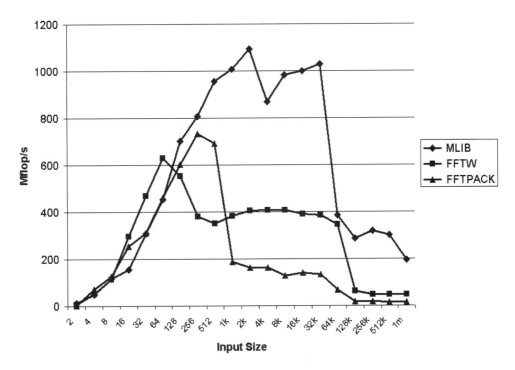

Figure 9-3 Comparison of one-dimensional, complex double precision FFT performance using various software packages.

9.4.4 Automatic Tuning Pitfalls

All of the above packages rely, to some extent, on the compiler being used to train and/or build the library. Unfortunately, compiler technology for a given processor usually matures shortly before the next processor enters the market. As a result, computer vendor libraries will sometimes perform much better than these automatically tuned packages. On the other hand, as compiler technology matures and automatic tuning research progresses, it is reasonable to expect that automatically tuned algorithms will perform even better in the future.

9.5 Commercial Libraries

Most computer hardware vendors provide high performance libraries for mathematical operations. Typically, these libraries will perform better than public domain software compiled by the user. Moreover, they are usually fully supported by the computer vendors and, as a result, they have eliminated any problems that may occur because of source errors, compiler problems, etc.

The primary reason that these libraries provide better performance is that they are developed, built, and supported by personnel who are experts on that particular computer. Many of the routines in these libraries are written by hand in assembly code, exploiting every feature of the computer's architecture.

Examples of these libraries are plentiful, including Hewlett Packard's MLIB (Mathematical software LIBrary), IBM's ESSL (Engineering and Scientific Subroutine Library), SGI's SCSL Scientific Library, and SUN's Performance Library. These libraries typically feature highly tuned BLAS, LAPACK, and signal processing packages.

Frequently, these packages provide shared-memory parallel versions as well. These tend to be very efficient, again because of the developer's expertise in the hardware platforms for which they are written.

There are also independent software vendors that provide libraries and packages for high performance computing. Examples of these are Visual Numerics' IMSL and the Numerical Algorithms Groups' Numerical Libraries; more information can be found at `http://www.vni.com/` and `http://www.nag.co.uk/`, respectively. These packages will provide all the functionality outlined above for linear algebra packages. In addition to these, they provide the latest algorithms for optimization, differential equations, interpolation, statistical correlation, probability distributions, time series and forecasting, etc. These libraries give much broader coverage of algorithms but do not necessarily provide the best performance for low-level routines such as BLAS.

9.6 Summary

In summary, there are a number of software library packages available free of charge, as well as commercially, both of which provide high performance for commonly used algorithms. Lower level routines, such as those in the BLAS, can be found that perform at or near the best possible performance on a given platform. Whenever other packages are built with these subprograms, the user can typically expect good performance. All of the packages outlined above will usually perform as well as, or better than, those you develop yourself and allow you to focus on application specific development rather than common subroutine development.

References:

The following publications are excellent resources for the libraries discussed in this section:

1. C. L. Lawson, C.L.; Hanson, R.J.; Kincaid, D.; Krogh, F.T. *Basic Linear Algebra Subprograms for FORTRAN Usage,* ACM Trans. Math. Soft., Vol. 5, pp. 308-323, 1979.

2. Dongarra, J.J.; Du Croz, J.; Duff, I.S.; Hammarling, S. *Algorithm 679: A Set of Level 3 Basic Linear Algebra Subprograms*, ACM Trans. Math. Soft., Vol. 16, pp. 18-28, 1990.

3. Smith, B.T.; Boyle, J.M.; Dongarra, J.J.; Garbow, B.S.; Ikebe, Y.; Klema, B.C.; Moler, C.B. *Matrix Eigensystem Routines—EISPACK Guide, Volume 6 of Lecture Notes in Computer Science.* Springer-Verlag, 1976. ISBN 0387075461.

4. Garbow, B.S.; Boyle, J.M.; Dongarra, J.J.; Moler, C.B. *Matrix Eigensystem Routines— EISPACK Guide Extension, Volume 51 of Lecture Notes in Computer Science.* Springer-Verlag, 1977.

5. Anderson, E.; Bai, Z.; Bischof, C.; Blackford, S.; Demmel, J.; Dongarra, J.; Du Croz, J.; Greenbaum, A.; Hammarling, S.; McKenney, A.; Sorensen, D. *LAPACK Users' Guide.* SIAM, 1999. ISBN 0-89871-447-8.

6. van de Geijn, R.A. *Using PLAPACK*. MIT Press, 1997. ISBN 0-262-72026-4.

7. Alpatov, P; Baker, G.; Edwards, C.; Gunnels, J.; Morrow, G.; Overfelt, J.; van de Geijn, R.A.; Wu, Y.J. *PLAPACK: Parallel Linear Algebra Package*, Proceedings of the SIAM Parallel Processing Conference, 1997.

8. Swarztrauber, P.N. *Vectorizing the FFTs*, Parallel Computations (G. Rodrigue, ed.). Academic Press, 1982.

9. Bilmes, J.; Asanovic, K.; Demmel, J.; Lam, D.; Chin, C.W. *PHiPAC: A Portable, High-Performance, ANSI C Coding Methodology and Its Application to Matrix Multiply*, LAPACK Working Note 111, University of Tennessee, 1996.

10. Whaley, R. C.; Dongarra, J. J. *Automatically Tuned Linear Algebra Software (ATLAS)*, Technical Report, University of Tennessee. http:/netlib.org/atlas

11. Frigo, M.; Johnson, S.G. *FFTW: An Adaptive Software Architecure for the FFT*, ICASSP Proceedings, Vol. 3, p. 1381, 1998.

12. Allan, R. J.; Hu, Y. F.; Lockey, P. *A Survey of Parallel Numerical Analysis Software*, Technical Report 99-01, CLRC Daresbury Laboratory, 1999.

13. Hewlett-Packard. *HP MLIB User's Guide (VECLIB and LAPACK)*, Hewlett-Packard Part Number B6061-96010, 1999.

## CHAPTER 10

Mathematical Kernels: The Building Blocks of High Performance

Mathematics is the gate and key to the sciences.

Roger Bacon

10.1 Building Blocks

Reuse of work saves time and money. As mentioned earlier, processors frequently have two types of caches: data and instruction. Better performance is obtained when the data in these caches is extensively reused. Reusing data is not a requirement for high performance, though. There have been many well-designed vector computers that got excellent performance on software that had very little data reuse. Once again, it comes down to money. It's very expensive to make machines that have great performance on the widest range of codes.

The same thing happens at a more abstract level; that is, the reuse of code is the cornerstone of software engineering. Why reinvent code all the time if it can be reused across many programs? So we always want

- Reuse of data
- Reuse of code

Vendors of hardware and software provide libraries containing commonly used routines. Writing code to use routines contained in these libraries also improves performance, since computer hardware and software vendors put a lot of effort into ensuring that these standard routines perform well. You can think of these routines as the nails and glue that hold together more complicated structures. In the linear algebra arena, there is a rich set of building blocks that can be used to construct high performance mathematical algorithms. These are the *Basic Linear Alge-*

bra Subprograms (BLAS). This chapter also discusses how some of these routines may be structured for parallel execution.

10.2 BLAS

The BLAS have a long history compared to most software. Over 25 years ago, the first BLAS routines were defined. They were written in Fortran and contained routines for four Fortran data types: REAL*4, REAL*8, COMPLEX*8, and COMPLEX*16. Most of the examples below use REAL*8 routines since these are the most widely used BLAS routines. The first BLAS routines became known as the Level 1 BLAS. Level 1 just refers to the routines being composed of a single loop. Later, Level 2 (two loops) and Level 3 (three loops) BLAS routines were defined. Recently, the BLAS routines have been generalized for other languages and data types by the BLAS Technical Forum to create the BLAS Standard as discussed in Chapter 9. The earlier BLAS definitions are now referred to as the Legacy BLAS. Table 10-1 shows the history of the BLAS.

Table 10-1　　BLAS Evolution.

BLAS type	Developed	Contents
Level 1 BLAS	1973-1977	vector-vector operations (one loop)
Level 2 BLAS	1984-1986	matrix-vector operations (two loops)
Level 3 BLAS	1987-1988	matrix-matrix operations (three loops)
BLAS Standard	1995-1999	multiple language functionality (Fortran 77, Fortran 95, C) mixed precision sparse operations

When the Level 1 BLAS routines were originally defined, they had good performance on vector computers, but poor performance on other types of computers since they had very little reuse of data. At the time, all high performance computers were vector computers, so it didn't matter if performance on slower CISC processors was poor. No one was too concerned because it was assumed that future high performance computers would be vector computers. Then clock periods of CISC processors started dropping toward the domain of vector computers, RISC processors appeared, and vector computers remained very expensive, so people started getting interested in making non-vector processors run well.

Having the Level 1 BLAS building blocks proved quite useful from a software design standpoint. The LINear algebra PACKage (LINPACK) was built on top of the Level 1 BLAS. This library contains routines to solve dense systems of equations. If a hardware vendor could ensure that a few key Level 1 BLAS routines performed well on her computers, then all the LIN-PACK software would run well. However, the Level 1 BLAS routines ran at rates approaching the processor's theoretical peak only on very expensive vector computers.

So why did the Level 1 BLAS run well on vector computers and not anywhere else? Vector computers have memory systems that can deliver one or more elements per clock cycle. Other processors depend on cache to achieve good performance, but this works well only if the data in cache can be reused. Level 1 BLAS routines have very little reuse of data. They usually operate on two vectors at a time. To reuse data in cache requires routines based on matrices of data. This was the rationale for the creation of the Level 2 and Level 3 BLAS.

The Level 2 BLAS contains things like matrix-vector multiplication, while the Level 3 BLAS contain matrix-matrix multiplication. If the Level 3 BLAS routines are correctly optimized, processors with caches can achieve very good performance on these kernels. When algorithms are built around the Level 3 BLAS, performance is good across all computer platforms.

The recent BLAS Standard generalizes the original Fortran routines to support Fortran 77, Fortran 95, and C. The Fortran 95 routine names are the most generic since the language allows users to call generic routines which call routines for the appropriate data type.

The following example compares the original BLAS and the BLAS Standard. One of the simplest Level 1 BLAS routines is the vector copy routine DCOPY. It appears as

```
SUBROUTINE DCOPY (N, X,INCX, Y,INCY)
REAL*8 X(*),Y(*)
IF ( N .GT. 0 ) THEN
  IF ( INCX .EQ. 1 .AND. INCY .EQ. 1 ) THEN
    DO I = 1, N
      Y(I) = X(I)
    END DO
  ELSE
    IX = 1
    IY = 1
    IF ( INCX .LT. 0 ) IX = 1 - (N-1) * INCX
    IF ( INCY .LT. 0 ) IY = 1 - (N-1) * INCY
    DO I = 1, N
      Y(IY) = X(IX)
      IX    = IX + INCX
      IY    = IY + INCY
    END DO
  END IF
END IF
RETURN
END
```

Note that when INCX or INCY are negative, the accesses of X or Y start at the end of the array and move through backwards through memory. The functionality of DCOPY is also contained in the BLAS Standard, but the name has been changed for the support of other languages. For example in Fortran 77, the routine is named F_DCOPY and is called as

```
SUBROUTINE F_DCOPY (N, X, INCY, Y, INCY)
INTEGER INCX, INCY, N
REAL*8 X(*), Y(*)
```

while in C the routine is named c_dcopy and has the calling sequence

```
void c_dcopy (int n, const ARRAY x, int incx, ARRAY y, int incy);
```

In Fortran 95 the name of the routine is COPY. The offset and stride are not needed in the Fortran 95 routine. To perform the same functionality as INCX = -1, one can pass the expression X(1:1+(N-1)*INCX) to COPY. The calling sequence for COPY is

```
SUBROUTINE COPY (X, Y)
<type>(<wp>), INTENT (IN) :: X(:)
<type>(<wp>), INTENT (OUT) :: Y(:)
```

where X and Y have SHAPE(N).

As discussed in Chapter 9, there have been attempts to automatically generate optimized Level 3 BLAS matrix-matrix multiplication routines. Since packages such as ATLAS and PhiPAC optimize only a few routines and may not optimize the data sizes you're interested in, these packages do not diminish the importance of understanding how to optimize code.

This chapter examines the vector-vector, matrix-vector, and matrix-matrix routines that comprise the BLAS. Before starting with the BLAS, we're going to examine some basic scalar arithmetic optimizations. Thus we'll have a nice progression from scalar operations through matrix building blocks.

10.3 Scalar Optimization

We've already discussed some of these optimizations in Chapter 5 in the section on strength reductions. This section also looks at some optimizations that are much too difficult for compilers to perform. There are four basic arithmetic operations: addition, subtraction, multiplication and division. These should be considered for integer, real, and complex data. (Subtraction is essentially the same as addition and will not be considered separately.) There are also logical operations such as shifting bits to the left or right which support integer operations. Integer additions and shift operations run extremely well on computers. On high performance computers, floating-point additions and multiplications also run well. This hasn't always been the case. Historically, most processors have been more efficient at performing floating-point additions than floating-point multiplications. Some processors also have special functional units for integer multiplication, but others don't. Division operations are very slow. If someone asks you to performance a floating-point division, or even worse, an integer division, just say no! Obviously there are occasions when you must perform these operations, but anything you can do to avoid them is worthwhile. Basic operations with complex arithmetic map to one or more of the corresponding floating-point operations and will also be discussed.

Scalar operations in order of increasing difficulty and inefficiency are

- Integer addition, shift operations
- Floating-point addition, complex addition
- Floating-point multiplication, complex multiplication
- Integer multiplication
- Floating-point division, complex division
- Integer division

The next sections discuss how to reduce some of these to more efficient operations.

10.3.1 Integer Operations

10.3.1.1 Multiplication by a Constant

This was discussed in Chapter 5. Multiplication of a variable by a constant can be accomplished by a combination of shifts and additions. Thus, multiplication of a variable by $2040 = 2048 - 8$ can be achieved by two left shifts and a subtract, as in

```
unsigned int i, j;
/* multiplication by 2040 */
j = (i << 11) - (i << 3);
```

10.3.1.2 Division by a Power of Two

Likewise, division by a power of two can be accomplished by a shift to the right. Thus, the division of i by eight can be accomplished by

```
unsigned int i, j;
/* division by 8 */
j = i >> 3;
```

10.3.1.3 Division of Two Variables

As discussed earlier, floating-point division is usually more efficient than integer division, and sometimes integer division can be converted to floating-point division. When the number of bits in the mantissa of a floating-point representation exceeds the number of bits in the integer representation, it is sufficient to convert the integers to floating-point, divide them, and convert the result back to integer. 32-bit integers may be converted to 64-bit IEEE floating-point numbers and division achieved as follows:

```
INTEGER*4 IA, IB, IC
REAL*8     A, B, C            .
A = IA
B = IB
C = A / B
IC = C
```

There are also IEEE formats for double-extended (64-bit mantissa) and quad-precision (113-bit mantissa) data. If floating-point division is more efficient in either of these modes than 64-bit integer division, then 64-bit integers may be converted to these floating-point precisions, the division performed and the result converted back to integer.

10.3.1.4   Division by a Constant Using Floating-Point Multiplication

When a variable is to be divided by a constant, the technique of the previous section may be employed to precalculate the inverse and replace the division by a floating-point multiplication at run time. In the following example, the variable IA is to be divided by 31.

```
INTEGER*4 IA, IB, IC
REAL*8     A, B, C
PARAMETER (IB = 31, B = 1.0D0/IB)
A = IA
C = A * B
IC = C
```

10.3.2 Floating-Point Operations

10.3.2.1   Multiplication of a Real Variable by a Constant

On some processors (not RISC processors, though), floating-point multiplication operations are more expensive than additions, so some compilers convert floating-point multiplication by small constants to additions. For example,

```
Y = 2 * X
```

can be replaced by

```
Y = X + X
```

10.3.3 Complex Operations

10.3.3.1   Multiplication of a Real Variable by a Complex Variable

When a real number is to be multiplied by a complex number, only two multiplications are needed. Some compilers promote the real number to a complex number and execute all six floating-point operations, but it should be performed as

$$s\,(x_r, x_i) = (sx_r, sx_i)$$

It's a good idea to check compiler-generated code to ensure the compiler is generating efficient code.

10.3.3.2   Multiplication of Two Complex Variables

To multiply two complex numbers requires four multiplications and two additions, as demonstrated below. Let $X = (x_r, x_i)$, $Y = (y_r, y_i)$ be two complex numbers. Their product, XY, is

$$(x_r, x_i)\,(y_r, y_i) = (x_r y_r - x_i y_i, \; x_r y_i + x_i y_r)$$

Note that if `fma` instructions are available, two `fma` and two multiplication instructions may be used.

In the past, floating-point multiplication was sometimes more expensive to perform than floating-point addition. Therefore, the following algorithm was used to replace the four multiplications and two additions by three multiplications and five additions. This technique is not profitable for scalars on today's computers since floating-point multiplication and addition usually take the same amount of time to perform. Efficient `fma` instructions also make the original code perform faster than the reduced multiplication code. This idea is important later in this chapter, so it's worth remembering. Let $X = (x_r, x_i)$, $Y = (y_r, y_i)$ be two complex numbers, and s_1, s_2, s_3 be real numbers. The complex multiplication may be performed as follows:

$$s_1 = x_r(y_r - y_i)$$
$$s_2 = y_r(x_r + x_i)$$
$$s_3 = y_i(x_r - x_i)$$
$$(x_r, x_i)\,(y_r, y_i) = (s_1 + s_3, \; s_2 - s_1)$$

10.3.3.3   Division of a Complex Variable by a Real Variable

If the denominator is a real number, the division can be achieved with only two floating-point divisions.

$$(x_r, x_i)\,/\,s = (x_r/s, \; x_i/s)$$

If you're using complex numbers extensively, it's worth checking the compiler-generated assembly code to verify that the compiler is doing a good job of code generation.

10.3.3.4   Division of Two Complex Variables

Suppose you need to divide two complex numbers. This requires a real number in the denominator. The naive way to do this is to multiply both numerator and denominator by the complex conjugate of the divisor as follows:

$$
\begin{aligned}
(x_r, x_i) / (y_r, y_i) &= [(x_r, x_i)(y_r, -y_i)] / [(y_r, y_i)(y_r, -y_i)] \\
&= (x_r y_r + x_i y_i, x_r y_i - x_i y_r) / (y_r y_r + y_i y_i)
\end{aligned}
$$

This perform two real divisions, but, as discussed in Chapter 7, it isn't numerically safe. If the components of Y are very large, calculating the denominator may lead to an overflow. So compiler writers don't implement this technique except as an unsafe optimization. If you know the data is not near the extreme value, this is a valid and efficient approach, though. What is a safe way to divide two complex numbers? One way is to ensure that none of the intermediate values overflows. This can be accomplished by finding the absolute value of each Y component and normalizing by this as the following code shows:

$$
\begin{aligned}
&if\,(\,|y_r| \geq |y_i|\,)\;then \\
&\quad s = y_i / y_r \\
&\quad d = y_r + s\,y_i \\
&\quad (x_r, x_i) / (y_r, y_i) = ((x_r + s x_i) / d, (x_i - s x_r) / d)) \\
&else \\
&\quad s = y_r / y_i \\
&\quad d = y_i + s\,y_r \\
&\quad (x_r, x_i) / (y_r, y_i) = ((s x_r + x_i) / d, (s x_i - x_r) / d)) \\
&endif
\end{aligned}
$$

This is not quite as efficient as the earlier code since it requires three floating-point divisions. This is how Fortran compiler writers implement complex division. Thus, if you are a Fortran programmer and know your data is not very large, you may want to implement the fast (but unsafe) code. If you are a C programmer, you can implement the one that is most appropriate for your data.

10.3.3.5   Division of Two COMPLEX*8 Variables

Suppose that the complex data is eight bytes long; that is, the real component uses the first four bytes and the imaginary component uses the second four bytes. An alternative to the previous techniques for COMPLEX*8 data is to convert the components to use REAL*8 quantities and use the two real division approach shown above. This is a completely safe optimization; squaring and adding the two components cannot lead to an overflow since they began as four byte data. This optimization is useful only if the cost of two REAL*8 divisions is less than the cost of three REAL*4 divisions.

```
COMPLEX*8 X, Y, Z
REAL*8    XR, XI, YR, YI, ZR, ZI, D
XR = REAL(X)
XI = AIMAG(X)
YR = REAL(Y)
YI = AIMAG(Y)
D  = YR*YR + YI*YI
ZR = (XR*YR + XI*YI)/D
ZI = (XI*YR - XR*YI)/D
Z  = CMPLX(ZR,ZI)
```

10.4 Vector Operations

Many of the optimizations discussed for loops are related to increasing the amount of data reuse. Many techniques try to increase reuse in space (*spatial reuse*) and reuse in time (*temporal reuse*). Unit stride data accesses cause multiple elements of a cache line to be used from a single cache line. This is cache line reuse and is an example of spatial reuse. Using a single element of data for multiple iterations of a loop is an example of temporal reuse.

The simplest operations employing loops are zeroing and copying vectors. These are also two of the most widely used routines since operating systems employ them extensively.

Level 1 BLAS routines are single loop codes such as DCOPY, DAXPY and DDOT. The function of the routine is usually evident from the name. For example, DCOPY stands for Double precision COPY, DAXPY stands for Double precision A times X Plus Y, while DDOT stands for Double precision DOT product. The codes shown in the examples use the unit stride version of routines for simplicity.

10.4.1 Vector Zero and Set

Two routines that set a number of bytes to a constant are bzero() and memset(). The function bzero() sets n bytes in memory to zero, while memset() sets n bytes to a user specified constant. C code to memset is shown below.

```
void memset ( char *x, int value, int n )
{
   int i;
   for( i = 0; i < n ; i++ )
     x[i] = (char)value;
   return;
}
```

The bzero() and memset() functions may be optimized to use the eight-byte integer registers found on modern computers. The hardware in many RISC computers assumes that eight-byte load and store operations occur on eight-byte boundaries. If this is not the case, executables may abort on a non-aligned memory operation. Thus, a prologue is executed until the data is eight-byte aligned. An epilogue may also be needed to cleanup the last few steps.

```
void memset ( char *x, int value, int n )
{
   int i, i1, n1, n2;
   unsigned int uvalue;
   long long int *x8ptr, value8;

   if( n < 16 )
   {
      for( i = 0; i < n ; i++ )
         x[i] = (char)value;
   }
   else
   {
      /* Move to 8 byte boundary */
      n1= 8 - (((unsigned int)x) & 0x07);
      n1= 0x07 & n1;
      for( i = 0; i < n1; i++ )
         x[i] = (char)value;
      /* x+n1 is aligned on 8 byte boundary */
      uvalue = (unsigned int) value;
      value8 = (long long int) uvalue;
      value8 = value8 << 8 | value8;
      value8 = value8 << 16 | value8;
      value8 = value8 << 32 | value8;
      x8ptr = (long long int *)(x + n1);
      /* n2 = remaining # of bytes / 8 */
      n2 = (n - n1) >> 3;
      for( i = 0 ; i < n2; i++ )
         x8ptr[i] = value8;
      /* cleanup, start at n1 + n2*8 from start of x */
      for( i = n1 + (n2 << 3); i < n; i++ )
         x[i] = (char)value;
   }
   return;
}
```

10.4.2 Vector Copy

The routines bcopy() and memcpy() routines copy n bytes of data from one memory location to another. They are very similar, with memcpy() appearing as

```
void memcpy ( char *y, char *x, int n )
{
  int i;
  for( i = 0; i < n ; i++ )
    y[i] = x[i];
  return;
}
```

These may also be optimized to use eight-byte registers, as in the memset() routine above. Another copy routine is the Level 1 BLAS routine DCOPY. The unit stride version performs

```
REAL*8 X(*), Y(*)
DO I = 1,N
  Y(I) = X(I)
ENDDO
```

There's very little that can be done to optimize this routine other than writing it in the most efficient assembly code possible.

10.4.3 Scalar Vector Accumulation

10.4.3.1   DAXPY, F_DAXPBY

The most extensively used routine by the LINPACK software is the DAXPY routine, since it is used by the routines that factor matrices. The unit stride version performs

```
REAL*8 A, X(*), Y(*)
DO I = 1,N
  Y(I) = A*X(I) + Y(I)
ENDDO
```

In the BLAS Standard, this has been generalized to the routine DAXPBY (ALPHA times X plus BETA times Y). The Fortran 77 version of this, F_DAXPBY, is

```
REAL*8 ALPHA, X(*), BETA, Y(*)
DO I = 1,N
  Y(I) = ALPHA*X(I) + BETA*Y(I)
ENDDO
```

There is not much that can be done to improve compiler generated code for DAXPY or F_DAXPBY. In the DAXPY routine, the scalar A can be checked to see if it is zero and the routine exited. F_DAXPBY can also implement special case code when ALPHA or BETA equals zero or one. The scalars should be hoisted outside the loops and the loops unrolled to reduce the effect of latencies. For large N, the code should also include prefetch instructions. Most of these optimizations should be implemented by the compiler. Note that applications written to use DAXPY may run less efficiently if the routine is replaced by a call to F_DAXPBY. This is because DAXPY requires only one multiplication and addition (or one fma instruction), while F_DAXPBY requires two multiplications and one addition (one fma and one multiplication).

10.4.3.2   ZAXPY

A COMPLEX*16 vector accumulation Level 1 BLAS routine is ZAXPY. The unit stride version appears as follows:

```
COMPLEX*16 A, X(*), Y(*)
DO I = 1,N
  Y(I) = A*X(I) + Y(I)
ENDDO
```

This requires one complex multiplication and one complex addition. These map to four real multiplications and four real additions, as demonstrated below.

```
COMPLEX*16 A, X(*), Y(*)
REAL*8 AR, AI, XR, XI, YR, YI
AR = REAL(A)
AI = AIMAG(A)
DO I = 1,N
  XR = REAL(X(I))
  XI = AIMAG(X(I))
  YR = YR + ( AR * XR - AI * XI)
  YI = YI + ( AR * XI + AI * XR)
  Y(I) = CMPLX(YR,YI)
ENDDO
```

On computers with fma instructions, this require two multiplications, two fma's, and two additions. However, if the order of operations is changed to

```
YR = ( YR + AR * XR ) - AI * XI
YI = ( YI + AR * XI ) + AI * XR
```

only four fma instructions are required.

10.4.4 Dot Product

The second most important BLAS routine used by the LINPACK software is the dot product function DDOT. It is used to solve systems of equations and the unit stride code is below.

```
DDOT = 0.0D0
DO I = 1,N
   DDOT = DDOT + X(I) * Y(I)
ENDDO
```

In the BLAS Standard for Fortran 77, the function DDOT is replaced by the subroutine F_DDOT, which performs the following:

```
DDOT = 0.0D0
DO I = 1,N
   DDOT = DDOT + X(I) * Y(I)
ENDDO
R = BETA * R + ALPHA * DDOT
```

The scalar DDOT should be hoisted and sunk from the DO loop. One potential problem with DDOT is that the same floating-point register is usually used for the reduction. This limits the speed of DDOT to that of the processor's multiply-add floating-point latency. Multiple sum reductions may be used, but this changes the order of operations and can produce slightly different answers than the original code. The number of sum reductions used should be equal to the floating-point latency multiplied by the number of multiply-add pairs that can be executed per cycle, divided by the number of load instructions that can be executed per clock cycle. So, if an fma instruction with a four cycle latency and two loads and two fused multiply-adds can be executed per clock cycle, then the four-way unrolling below is sufficient to achieve good performance.

```
DDOT1 = 0.0D0
DDOT2 = 0.0D0
DDOT3 = 0.0D0
DDOT4 = 0.0D0
NEND = 4*(N/4)
DO I = 1,NEND,4
   DDOT1 = DDOT1 + X(I) * Y(I)
   DDOT2 = DDOT2 + X(I+1) * Y(I+1)
   DDOT3 = DDOT3 + X(I+2) * Y(I+2)
   DDOT4 = DDOT4 + X(I+3) * Y(I+3)
ENDDO
DDOT = DDOT1 + DDOT2 + DDOT3 + DDOT4
DO I = NEND+1,N
   DDOT = DDOT + X(I) * Y(I)
ENDDO
R = BETA * R + ALPHA * DDOT
```

The following table compares the Level 1 BLAS routines we've discussed.

Table 10-2   Level 1 BLAS Comparison.

Routine	Performs	Memory operations per iteration	Floating-point operations per iteration	F:M ratio
DCOPY	$y_i = x_i$	2	0	0.00
DAXPY	$y_i = y_i + a\,x_i$	3	2	0.67
F_DAXPBY	$y_i = \beta\,y_i + \alpha\,x_i$	3	3	1.00
DDOT	$ddot = ddot + x_i\,y_i$	2	2	1.00
ZAXPY	$y_i = y_i + a\,x_i$	6	8	1.25

In general, DDOT and ZAXPY are more efficient than DAXPY since they contains a higher ratio of floating-point operations per memory operations than DAXPY.

10.4.5 Parallelism

The routines in this section are embarrassingly parallel. That is, they may be run on multiple processors with little or no communication necessary between the processors. Before running code in parallel, you need to determine if it is profitable to do so. If you know that the entire data fits in the data cache, then it's not worth running in parallel since the act of dividing the data across processors will take more time that just performing the calculations on a single processor. So, let's assume that you want to perform a DAXPY and N is several million in size. If the computer has M processors, then each processor can be given a range of size N/M to process. Shared-memory parallelism is easily achieved using OpenMP directives.

```
C$OMP PARALLEL SHARED (A,N,X,Y) PRIVATE(I)
C$OMP DO
        DO I = 1, N
           Y(I) = A * X(I) + Y(I)
        ENDDO
C$OMP END DO
C$OMP END PARALLEL
```

Using the compile line -WGkeep creates an output file so you can verify that the code was split up as described above. You'll see something similar to the following, where MPPID is the processor id and MPPNPR is the number of processors:

```
C!!!! PARALLEL SHARED (A,N,X,Y) PRIVATE (I)
      II3 = N1 - 1 + 1
      II4 = (II3 + MPPNPR - 1) / MPPNPR
      II1 = 1 + MPPID * II4
      II2 = MIN (N1, II1 + (II4 - 1))
C!!!! DO
      DO I1=II1,II2
         Y1(I1) = A1 * X1(I1) + Y1(I1)
      END DO
C!!!! END DO NOWAIT
C!!!! END PARALLEL
```

Vector zero, copy, and other scalar vector operations can all be parallelized in a similar fashion.

Dot products are more complicated to run in parallel since each point contributes to the reduction. Parallelism can be obtained by splitting the work up in chunks of size N/M, but each processor must maintain its own partial sum. At the conclusion of processing, each of the partial sums is sent to a single processor which sums them to obtain the final solution. This can be achieved using the attribute REDUCTION of the DO OpenMP directive, or the CRITICAL directive. The original dot product code can be modified for parallelism as follows:

```
C$OMP PARALLEL SHARED (X,Y,N,DDOT) PRIVATE(I)
C$OMP DO REDUCTION(+:DDOT)
      DO I = 1, N
         DDOT = DDOT + X(I) * Y(I)
      ENDDO
C$OMP END DO
C$OMP END PARALLEL
```

This technique should be applied to a dot product that has first been unrolled to hide the instruction latency as discussed above.

10.5 Matrix Operations

Matrix operation code consists of loop nests. Matrix copy and matrix-vector routines have two loops and include the Level 2 BLAS routines. Matrix-matrix routines have three loops and include the Level 3 BLAS routines.

10.5.1 Matrix Copy and Transpose

The need to copy matrices arises frequently, especially on cache based computers. Copying is sometimes used to move scattered data into a contiguous area of memory whose size is less than the cache size to reduce cache misses. The original Level 2 BLAS routines did not contain matrix copy routines; however, they are in the BLAS Standard. The matrix may also be transposed as part of the copy. When a matrix is transposed to create another matrix, it is said to be an *out-of-place matrix transpose*. If the transpose step replaces the original data with the transposed data, the transpose is done *in-place*.

10.5.1.1   F_DGE_COPY

The Fortran 77 routine F_DGE_COPY copies a matrix A (or its transpose) to the matrix B. When the data is not transposed, the routine performs

```
REAL*8 A(LDA,*), B(LDB,*)
DO J = 1, N
  DO I = 1, M
    B(I,J) = A(I,J)
  ENDDO
ENDDO
```

This has unit stride accesses and performs well; however, the transpose case

```
DO J = 1, N
  DO I = 1, M
    B(I,J) = A(J,I)
  ENDDO
ENDDO
```

is not so straightforward. Figure 10-1 shows the array access patterns for a matrix transpose.

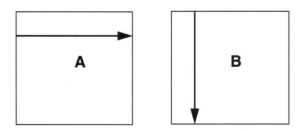

Figure 10-1   Out-of-place matrix transpose memory access patterns.

In this form, A has non-unit stride access and B has unit stride access. If the order of the loops is switched, then A has unit stride accesses and B has non-unit stride accesses. Either way, one of the accesses will not be optimal. This type of code was discussed in Chapter 5 in the section on blocking.

By unrolling the outer loop, multiple columns and rows may be accessed and data reuse will increase. Suppose the cache line size is 64 bytes and data is eight bytes long. Thus, each cache line contains eight elements, so an unrolling factor of eight would allow an entire cache line to be accessed at a time.

Suppose the length of the inner loop is very long and that the amount of data in the A and B arrays is many times the size of the data cache. Each time A is referenced, the data must be reloaded from cache. By blocking the code as shown in the following source and in Figure 10-2, there are many uses of the array A in cache before a column of B displaces it.

```
BLOCK = 1000
DO IOUTER = 1,N,BLOCK
   DO J = 1,N
      DO I = IOUTER,MIN(N,N+BLOCK-1)
         B(I,J) = A(J,I)
      ENDDO
   ENDDO
ENDDO
```

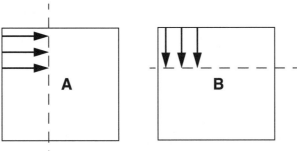

Figure 10-2 Blocking for matrix transpose.

The value of BLOCK is a function of the cache size and should be carefully chosen. If BLOCK is too small, the prefetches on the both arrays are ineffective, since the prefetched data will probably have been displaced from cache by the time the actual loads and stores occur. If BLOCK is too large, the values of A don't get reused. For caches that are on the order of a megabyte, a blocking factor of around 1000 is usually sufficient to get the benefits of prefetching and cache line reuse.

Some applications use a two-dimensional blocking when transposing data. By blocking with appropriately sized squares or rectangles, the data gets cache line reuse in both dimensions. This is demonstrated in the following code. Figure 10-3 shows a 4 × 4 block decomposition of the arrays A and B.

```
DO JOUT = 1,N,BLOCK
  DO IOUT = 1,M,BLOCK
    DO J = JOUT,MIN(JOUT+BLOCK-1,N)
      DO I = IOUT,MIN(IOUT+BLOCK-1,M)
      B(J,I) = A(I,J)
    ENDDO
    ENDDO
  ENDDO
ENDDO
```

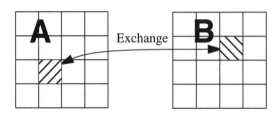

Figure 10-3   Blocking by rectangles for matrix transpose.

10.5.1.2   F_DGE_TRANS

If A exceeds the cache size, transposing A with the result overwriting the original A, may have 1.5 times better performance than transposing A to a different matrix B. Recall the definition of *memory_transfer* from Chapter 5:

memory_transfer = n × (bytes per point) / (cache line size in bytes)

where n is the number of data points. An out-of-place transpose of A to B results in three sets of memory_transfers using this definition: one memory_transfer to load A and two to store to B. The two memory_transfers for B occur because the processor must also load data from B before it can store to B. If A is transposed over itself, each point of A is loaded once and stored once, which requires two sets of memory_transfers. Table 10-3 compares the two approaches.

Table 10-3   Comparison of BLAS Standard Transpose Routines.

Routine	Operation	Instructions	Number of memory_ transfers
F_DGE_COPY	Transpose A to B	Load A, Store B	3
F_DGE_TRANS	Transpose A to A	Load A, Store A	2

There are significant problems to achieving these rates, however. To keep from using a work array in F_DGE_TRANS, values must be swapped across the main diagonal. There are a couple of ways to do this. Figure 10-4 shows one technique. It is similar to the F_DGE_COPY

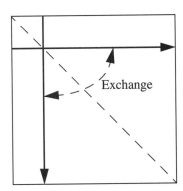

Figure 10-4   In-place matrix transpose.

code when separate input and output arrays are used. One of the array accesses will be unit stride, but the other will have stride equal to the leading dimension of one of the matrices. Code to perform this appears as

```
DO J = 1, N-1
   DO I = J+1, N
      TEMP = A(J,I)
      A(J,I) = A(I,J)
      A(I,J) = TEMP
   ENDDO
ENDDO
```

As in F_DGE_COPY, the outer loop may be unrolled to increase cache line reuse. However, the code can't be blocked as easily as F_DGE_COPY can since the data is being overwritten. Also, what if the leading dimension of the matrix of A is a large power of two? Unfortunately, this situation does occur, most notably for Fast Fourier Transforms whose lengths are large powers of two in size. There are a couple of problems with the non-unit stride memory accesses. Recall that the number of memory banks is a power of two in size. Caches are usually a power of two in size. As the data is accessed across the matrix, multiple points of a row (using Fortran column major order) may map to the same location in the cache and cause cache thrashing. Also, all points of a row may map to the same memory bank. This causes another performance problem since there is not enough time to refresh the memory banks between data accesses. It doesn't get any worse than this on a processor with cache!

One way to lessen this effect is to transpose blocks of data. This is similar to Figure 10-3 with the added complication that blocks that contain a main diagonal element have to be handled specially to ensure correct result.

Another way to decrease bank conflicts is to swap diagonals, as shown in the following code and Figure 10-5.

```
DO J = 1, N-1
  DO I = J+1, N
    TEMP = A(I-J,I)
    A(I-J,I) = A(I,I-J)
    A(I,I-J) = TEMP
  ENDDO
ENDDO
```

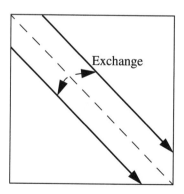

Figure 10-5   In-place matrix transpose by exchanging diagonals.

By traversing two off-diagonals that are the same distance from the main diagonal, the cache thrashing and memory bank conflicts are avoided when the leading dimension is a power of two in size. This results from the memory stride being a power of two plus one. As before, the outer loop should be unrolled to increase cache line reuse.

The obvious problem with this approach (and previous ones) is that relatively few entries from a virtual memory page are used before another page is required. This can cause a large number of TLB misses. By increasing the virtual memory page size to ensure that the entire data, or a larger part of it, is mapped into virtual memory, the number of TLB misses can be decreased.

10.5.1.3   Parallelism

There are a couple of ways to parallelize a matrix copy. One way is to split the outer loop into chunks of size N divided by the number of processors. This has the advantage of having each processor work on large contiguous chunks of code. This is called a *static allocation* of work. Another way is to have each outer loop iteration be given to a separate processor until all outer loop iterations are completed. This is the type of scheduling used to service customers waiting in a queue. It may lead to a better load balance since any imbalance of work is compensated for by the other processors. This is a *dynamic allocation* of work. The disadvantage of this approach is that there are more data transfers, with each one moving a smaller amount of data than the static allocation approach. Also, the operating system must determine who gets the next work with each iteration of the outer loop. These approaches are shown in the code extracts below, using OpenMP directives.

```
C STATIC ALLOCATION
C$OMP PARALLEL SHARED (A,B,N,M) PRIVATE(I,J)
C$OMP DO SCHEDULE(STATIC)
        DO J = 1,N
          DO I = 1,M
            B(I,J) = A(I,J)
          ENDDO
        ENDDO
C$OMP END DO
C$OMP END PARALLEL

C DYNAMIC ALLOCATION
C$OMP PARALLEL SHARED (A,B,N,M) PRIVATE(I,J)
C$OMP DO SCHEDULE(DYNAMIC)
        DO J = 1,N
          DO I = 1,M
            B(I,J) = A(I,J)
          ENDDO
        ENDDO
C$OMP END DO
C$OMP END PARALLEL
```

Which approach is best? As always, it depends on the data. For very large data sets, a dynamic allocation may be the better choice, while smaller data may be best served by static allocation.

Parallelization of a transpose is more difficult than parallelization of a regular copy. This is because, as discussed earlier, for large data one of the arrays is guaranteed to have poor cache line reuse in the original transpose code. So a dynamic allocation of work such as shown above for a matrix copy, would have multiple processors trying to access the same cache line, resulting in cache thrashing and very poor performance.

The most popular way to perform large transposes uses large blocks of data. This is similar to the blocking shown in Figure 10-3, but the blocks are chosen to be large enough so that each processor is kept busy. Then each block may use a finer level of blocking to ensure good cache line reuse.

10.5.2 Matrix-Vector Operations

The most common matrix-vector routines are the Level 2 BLAS routines DGER and DGEMV. The examples will be slightly simplified version of the BLAS routines. They will assume that vector accesses are unit stride and the scalar multipliers are set to 1.0, since this is the common case.

10.5.2.1   DGER

DGER stands for Double precision GEneral Rank-one update. The code appears as

```
DO J = 1,N
  DO I = 1,M
    A(I,J) = A(I,J) + X(I) * Y(J)
  ENDDO
ENDDO
```

The word "update" refers to the matrix A being modified or updated. Rank-one means that A is updated by a single vector at a time. For example, a rank-two update means that A gets updated by two vectors at a time.

The first thing to determine when optimizing multiple loops is which loop should be the innermost loop. It should be the one that maximizes unit stride accesses. Then an attempt should be made to minimize the number of memory operations.

For DGER, the I loop should be the innermost loop since this results in the references on A and X being unit stride. The value of Y may also be hoisted outside the innermost loop. The outer loop can then be unrolled to reduce the number of memory operations. Using four-way unrolling and ignoring the required cleanup code for non-multiples of four produces

```
DO J = 1,N,4
  Y0 = Y(J)
  Y1 = Y(J+1)
  Y2 = Y(J+2)
  Y3 = Y(J+3)
  DO I = 1,M
    A(I,J)   = A(I,J) + X(I) * Y0
    A(I,J+1) = A(I,J+1) + X(I) * Y1
    A(I,J+2) = A(I,J+2) + X(I) * Y2
    A(I,J+3) = A(I,J+3) + X(I) * Y3
  ENDDO
ENDDO
```

Therefore, four columns of A are updated with one column of X. This increases the F:M ratio from 2:3 to 8:9. Table 10-4 shows the number of operations for each approach.

Out-of-Cache   There's an additional problem for very large matrices. Suppose the size of X and each column of A exceeds the size of the cache. Each time a column of A is accessed, each cache line misses the cache. There's nothing you can do about that. However, each time X is accessed, it also misses the cache. As we demonstrated in Chapter 5, data can be blocked so that the references to X are usually in cache. The code above may be rewritten as

```
DO IOUT = 1, M, MBLOCK
  DO J = 1,N,4
    Y0 = Y(J)
    Y1 = Y(J+1)
    Y2 = Y(J+2)
    Y3 = Y(J+3)
    DO I = IOUT, MIN(IOUT+MBLOCK,M)
      A(I,J)   = A(I,J) + X(I) * Y0
      A(I,J+1) = A(I,J+1) + X(I) * Y1
      A(I,J+2) = A(I,J+2) + X(I) * Y2
      A(I,J+3) = A(I,J+3) + X(I) * Y3
    ENDDO
  ENDDO
ENDDO
```

where the value of MBLOCK is chosen to keep X cache resident most of the time, but long enough that prefetching of A and X is effective. This is shown in Figure 10-6.

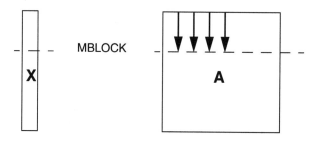

Figure 10-6   DGER blocking.

10.5.2.2   DGEMV

DGEMV stands for Double GEneral Matrix Vector multiplication. DGEMV allows the matrix to be accessed in normal form or transposed. These cases will be considered separately.

DGEMV — A Not Transposed   The code for the normal matrix-vector multiplication appears as follows:

```
DO J = 1,N
  DO I = 1,M
    Y(I) = Y(I) + A(I,J) * X(J)
  ENDDO
ENDDO
```

It is crucial to have the accesses on A be unit stride, so the I loop should be the innermost loop. As in the case of DGER, the outer loop can be unrolled to increase data reuse as follows:

```
DO J = 1,N,4
  DO I = 1,M
    Y(I) = Y(I) + A(I,J) * X(J) + A(I,J+1) * X(J+1)
$        + A(I,J+2) * X(J+2) + A(I,J+3) * X(J+3)
  ENDDO
ENDDO
```

Thus, four columns of A update one column of Y. Note, however, there is a single term Y(I) that all intermediate results sum to. Using a single reduction means that this code may be limited by the floating-point instruction latency, since four terms sum to the Y(I) term. To remove this constraint, the inner loop may be unrolled. Four-way inner loop unrolling produces

```
DO J = 1,N,4
   DO I = 1,M,4
      Y(I)   = Y(I) + A(I,J) * X(J) + A(I,J+1) * X(J+1)
$        + A(I,J+2) * X(J+2) + A(I,J+3) * X(J+3)
      Y(I+1) = Y(I+1) + A(I+1,J) * X(J) + A(I+1,J+1) * X(J+1)
$        + A(I+1,J+2) * X(J+2) + A(I+1,J+3) * X(J+3)
      Y(I+2) = Y(I+2) + A(I+2,J) * X(J) + A(I+2,J+1) * X(J+1)
$        + A(I+2,J+2) * X(J+2) + A(+2,J+3) * X(J+3)
      Y(I+3) = Y(I+3) + A(I+3,J) * X(J) + A(I+3,J+1) * X(J+1)
$        + A(I+3,J+2) * X(J+2) + A(I+3,J+3) * X(J+3)
   ENDDO
ENDDO
```

The compiler may still have difficulty interleaving the separate reductions. Some compilers attempt to perform the Y(I) calculations before starting the Y(I+1) calculations. This renders the inner loop unrolling useless. Therefore, the calculation of the individual Y values can be explicitly interleaved so that only the first multiply-addition component of each Y vector is calculated. Following that, the second multiply-addition component can be calculated. This process continues until the calculations of the inner loop are complete. This restructuring is demonstrated below.

```
DO J = 1,N,4
   DO I = 1,M,4
      Y0     = Y(I) + A(I,J) * X(J)
      Y1     = Y(I+1) + A(I+1,J) * X(J)
      Y2     = Y(I+2) + A(I+2,J) * X(J)
      Y3     = Y(I+3) + A(I+3,J) * X(J)
      Y0     = Y0 + A(I,J+1) * X(J+1)

      . . .

      Y(I)   = Y0 + A(I,J+3) * X(J+3)
      Y(I+1) = Y1 + A(I+1,J+3) * X(J+3)
      Y(I+2) = Y2 + A(I+2,J+3) * X(J+3)
      Y(I+3) = Y3 + A(I+3,J+3) * X(J+3)
   ENDDO
ENDDO
```

DGEMV — A Transposed   The code for a matrix-vector multiplication when the matrix is transposed appears as follows:

```
DO I = 1,M
   DO J = 1,N
      Y(J) = Y(J) + A(I,J) * X(I)
   ENDDO
ENDDO
```

The I loop should be the innermost loop to ensure that the accesses on A are unit stride. Outer loop unrolling also helps performance. Unrolling the outer loops by four produces the following code:

```
DO J = 1,N,4
  DO I = 1,M
    Y(J)   = Y(J)   + A(I,J)   * X(I)
    Y(J+1) = Y(J+1) + A(I,J+1) * X(I)
    Y(J+2) = Y(J+2) + A(I,J+2) * X(I)
    Y(J+3) = Y(J+3) + A(I,J+3) * X(I)
  ENDDO
ENDDO
```

As in the case of DGER, calling DGEMV with A transposed and large requires the source code to be blocked to reduce cache misses for the vector accessed in the inner loop. Table 10-4 compares the theoretical performance of the original DGER and the two DGEMV codes with the modified source.

Table 10-4   Level 2 BLAS Comparison.

Routine	Performs	Unroll factor	Memory operations per iteration	Floating-point operations per iteration	F:M ratio
DGER	$A_{ij} = A_{ij} + x_i y_j$	1	3	2	0.67
		4	9	8	0.89
DGEMV, A not transposed	$y_i = y_i + A_{ij} x_j$	1	3	2	0.67
		4	6	8	1.33
DGEMV, A transposed	$y_j = y_j + A_{ij} x_i$	1	2	2	1.00
		4	5	8	1.40

10.5.2.3   Parallelism

DGEMV with A transposed and DGER, can be parallelized with static or dynamic allocation of outer loop iterations, as discussed in the matrix copy section. When A is transposed, the code needs a reduction attribute on the elements of Y to ensure correctness of answers.

10.5.3 Matrix-Matrix Multiplication: In-cache

The cornerstone of high performance is triple-nested loops such as those found in the Level 3 BLAS matrix-matrix multiplication routine DGEMM. DGEMM stands for Double GEneral Matrix-Matrix multiplication. DGEMM computes the matrix product $C = \beta C + \alpha (A \times B)$, where A, B, and C are matrices, and α and β are scalars. The input matrices A and B may also be transposed. This section looks at each of these four possibilities. The values of α and β are assumed to be $\alpha = \beta = 1$ in the analysis below, since this is a common case.

When optimizing these loops, the first thing to determine is which loop should be the innermost loop. The innermost loop should be the one that has unit stride accesses. Then the outer loops may be modified to reduce the number of memory operations.

10.5.3.1   Neither A Nor B Is Transposed
This is the most common case and will be treated in the most detail. The loops follow:

```
DO I = 1,M
  DO J = 1,N
    DO L = 1,K
      C(I,J) = C(I,J) + A(I,L) * B(L,J)
    ENDDO
  ENDDO
ENDDO
```

The I loop should be the innermost loop since that causes the access patterns for A and C to be unit stride. Unroll and jam techniques can then be used on the outer two loops. This is called the *hoist B* matrix-matrix multiplication version of the code since the references to B may be hoisted outside of the inner loop. For example, if the outer two loops are unrolled by two and jammed together, the code appears as follows. Note that two columns of A update two columns of C.

```
DO J = 1,N,2
  DO L = 1,K,2
    B11 = B(L,J)
    B21 = B(L+1,J)
    B12 = B(L,J+1)
    B22 = B(L+1,J+1)
    DO I = 1,M
      C(I,J)   = C(I,J)   + A(I,L) * B11 + A(I,L+1) * B21
      C(I,J+1) = C(I,J+1) + A(I,L) * B12 + A(I,L+1) * B22
    ENDDO
  ENDDO
ENDDO
```

This increases the floating-point to memory operation ratio. For most processors, we want the floating-point to memory ratio to be greater than 2.0. As the amount of unrolling and jamming increases, the number of floating-point registers required also increases. For example, a 4×4 unrolling requires 16 floating-point registers for B and another four registers for C. So the number of floating-point registers available sets an upper limit on the amount of unrolling. The F:M ratio should be at least two for most processors, so this sets a lower limit for the amount of unroll and jam. Another constraint is determined by the instruction latency. The larger the latency, the more registers are required to hide it. This may require a certain amount of inner loop unrolling to increase the number of streams of instruction, which also increases the minimum number of registers required. Table 10-5 shows the effects of unroll and jam for various unrolling factors.

Table 10-5   DGEMM Data Reuse for a Hoist B Approach.

J unroll factor, (columns of C, B)	L unroll factor (columns of A)	Memory operations per iteration	Floating-point operations per iteration	F:M ratio
1	1	3	2	0.67
2	2	6	8	1.33
3	3	9	18	2.00
3	4	10	24	2.40
4	4	12	32	2.67
nb	kb	$2nb+kb$	$2(nb)(kb)$	$2(nb)(kb)/(2nb+kb)$

By studying the general formula at the bottom of the table, it is apparent that nb must be greater than or equal to two and kb must be greater than or equal to three to obtain F:M ratios greater than or equal to 2.0. (This is one reason why DGEMV performance cannot equal DGEMM performance since DGEMV has only one column to update.) Figure 10-7 shows the hoist B approach blocking.

Example: PA-8500 processor. This has 28 user accessible floating-point registers, an instruction latency of three cycles, and the ability to do two fma instructions per cycle. Thus, there must be at least six independent streams of instruction. As the table above shows, a 4×4 outer loop unrolling would result in a F:M value greater than 2.0. However, in order to have at least six streams of instruction, the inner loop must be unrolled by at least two. Therefore, 16

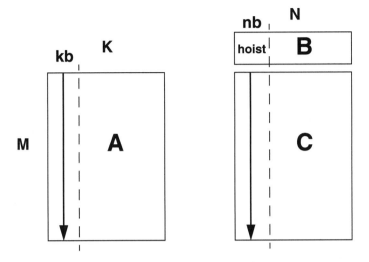

Figure 10-7 DGEMM blocking for a hoist B approach.

registers must be used for B, and eight registers must be used for C. This leaves only four registers for all of A, which is not nearly enough, due to the instruction latency.

A 3×4 outer loop unrolling also exceeds an F:M ratio of 2.0 and requires at least two-way inner loop unrolling, but uses only 12 registers for B and six for C. This leave 10 registers for A and temporary values and is much more feasible for this processor.

Middle and Outer Loops Since the I loop should be the innermost lost, the next question is whether the J or L loop should be the outermost loop. This choice influences the number of cache misses when some of the data is out of cache. If J is chosen to be the outermost loop, then L is the middle loop and all of A is accessed for some small number of columns of C. If L is the outer loop and J is the middle loop, then all of C is accessed for some small number of columns of A.

Suppose a 3×4 unrolling has been chosen. There are three columns of C and four columns of A that are being accessed in the inner loop. Each column of C must be loaded and stored, while each column of A needs only to be loaded. Suppose further than some cache misses occur and that the chance that A will not be in cache is the same as the chance that C will not be in cache. Since C must be loaded and stored, it will incur twice as many misses as A. Therefore, it is better to have J as the outermost loop (hold C fixed) and sweep through all of A for each value of J.

10.5.3.2   A Not Transposed, B Transposed

This type of matrix-matrix multiplication is very similar to the previous one.

```
DO J = 1,N
  DO L = 1,K
    DO I = 1,M
      C(I,J) = C(I,J) + A(I,L) * B(J,L)
    ENDDO
  ENDDO
ENDDO
```

Since the B values can be hoisted outside the inner loop, the optimizations that were made for the previous case can be applied here.

10.5.3.3   A Transposed, B Not Transposed

Many applications perform a matrix-multiply with the matrix A transposed as follows:

```
DO J = 1,N
  DO L = 1,K
    DO I = 1,M
      C(I,J) = C(I,J) + A(L,I) * B(L,J)
    ENDDO
  ENDDO
ENDDO
```

Having the I loop as the inner loop is a poor choice since the accesses on A will not be unit stride. However, if the L loop is the inner loop, the accesses on A and B are unit stride, and the C references may be hoisted and sunk from the inner loop.

```
DO J = 1,N
  DO I = 1,M
    DO L = 1,K
      C(I,J) = C(I,J) + A(L,I) * B(L,J)
    ENDDO
  ENDDO
ENDDO
```

This is called the *hoist/sink* C matrix-matrix multiplication approach and is superior to the hoist B approach since there are no stores in the inner loop. Performing a 2 × 2 unroll and jam produces the following code. Note that two columns of A and two columns of B update four scalar values.

```
DO J = 1,N,2
   DO I = 1,M,2
      C11 = 0.0
      C21 = 0.0
      C12 = 0.0
      C22 = 0.0
      DO L = 1,K
         C11 = C11 + A(L,I)   * B(L,J)
         C21 = C21 + A(L,I+1) * B(L,J)
         C12 = C21 + A(L,I)   * B(L,J+1)
         C22 = C22 + A(L,I+1) * B(L,J+1)
      ENDDO
      C(I,J)     = C(I,J)     + C11
      C(I+1,J)   = C(I+1,J)   + C21
      C(I,J+1)   = C(I,J+1)   + C12
      C(I+1,J+1) = C(I+1,J+1) + C22
   ENDDO
ENDDO
```

Table 10-6 shows the effects of unroll and jam for various unrolling factors.

Table 10-6   DGEMM Data Reuse for a Hoist/Sink C Approach.

J unroll factor (columns of C, B)	I unroll factor (columns of A)	Memory operations per iteration	Floating-point operations per iteration	F:M ratio
1	1	2	2	1.00
2	2	4	8	2.00
3	3	6	18	3.00
nb	mb	$nb+mb$	$2(nb)(mb)$	$2(nb)(mb)/(nb+mb)$

The hoist/sink C approach is superior to the hoist B approach in terms of the floating-point operation to memory operation ratio. It takes less unrolling for unroll and jam to achieve peak rates with the hoist/sink C approach due to the absence of store operations in the inner loop. Figure 10-8 shows the hoist/sink C approach blocking.

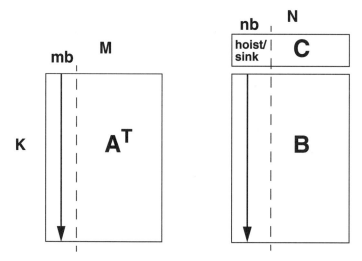

Figure 10-8   DGEMM blocking for a hoist/sink C approach.

Middle and Outer Loops   The order of the two outer loops should also be considered. Is it better to access all of A with each iteration of the outer loop or all of B? Since each of these arrays are only loaded (i.e., read), it is not apparent which is better at first. However, the accesses on C should also be considered. Note that the references to the C in the middle loop are unit stride when the I loop is the middle loop. This is especially important when the inner loop is short, so the I loop should be the inner loop.

10.5.3.4   A and B Transposed

This is the worst type of matrix multiplication to consider. Fortunately, it doesn't occur as frequently as the other types. The code appears as

```
DO J = 1,N
  DO L = 1,K
    DO I = 1,M
      C(I,J) = C(I,J) + A(L,I) * B(J,L)
    ENDDO
  ENDDO
ENDDO
```

By now you should know what to do first. Make all array references unit stride. But in this case, it can't be done. Choose J, L, or I as the inner loop and at least one of the arrays will have non-unit stride accesses. What to do?

We've seen that the hoist/sink C solution is superior to the hoist B in terms of data reuse, and since neither approach can have all accesses unit stride for this case, choosing a hoist/sink C approach is a reasonable solution for the case when both A and B are transposed. Thus, L should be chosen to be the inner loop, the accesses on A are unit stride and the accesses on B are non-unit stride. Choosing I as the middle loop makes the C accesses unit stride in the middle loop. Applying a 2×2 unroll and jam produces the following:

```
DO J = 1,N,2
  DO I = 1,M,2
    C11 = 0.0
    C21 = 0.0
    C12 = 0.0
    C22 = 0.0
    DO L = 1,K
      C11 = C11 + A(L,I) * B(J,L)
      C21 = C21 + A(L,I+1) * B(J,L)
      C12 = C21 + A(L,I) * B(J+1,L)
      C22 = C22 + A(L,I+1) * B(J+1,L)
    ENDDO
    C(I,J)     = C(I,J) + C11
    C(I+1,J)   = C(I+1,J) + C21
    C(I,J+1)   = C(I,J+1) + C12
    C(I+1,J+1) = C(I+1,J+1) + C22
  ENDDO
ENDDO
```

10.5.3.5 Hoist A Approach

Some readers might notice that we're missing one approach from our DGEMM taxonomy. We've discussed the hoist B approach, the hoist/sink C approach, but what about a *hoist A* matrix-matrix multiplication? When would this be beneficial? If A is to be hoisted, the J loop must be the inner loop. For the most common case, where neither A nor B is transposed, the code appears as

```
DO L = 1,K
  DO I = 1,M
    DO J = 1,N
      C(I,J) = C(I,J) + A(I,L) * B(L,J)
    ENDDO
  ENDDO
ENDDO
```

Note that the access patterns for C are always non-unit stride. This makes the approach unattractive for DGEMM. If both matrices C and B were transposed, it might be worth considering. However, if $C^T = C^T + AB^T$, then $C = C + B^T A$, and then the hoist/sink C approach would be better. Therefore, the hoist A approach doesn't help DGEMM performance.

10.5.4 Matrix-Matrix Multiplication: Out-of-Cache

This section examines some large matrix-matrix multiplications that arise in actual applications.

10.5.4.1   Blocking Long and Narrow Matrices for Cache

We've discussed the importance of blocking for cache for the BLAS routines DGER and DGEMV. It's even more important for DGEMM, since some applications, such as factoring a matrix, create matrix-matrix multiplications that operate on long narrow matrices. Suppose C is only a few elements wide, but hundreds of thousands in length. A single column of C will exceed the cache size of most processors. Using a hoist B matrix-matrix multiplication approach requires each cache line of C to miss cache. This is especially important since C is loaded and stored, so two misses occur for each line. However, by picking a suitable blocking factor, the misses for C can be greatly reduced, as shown in Figure 10-9.

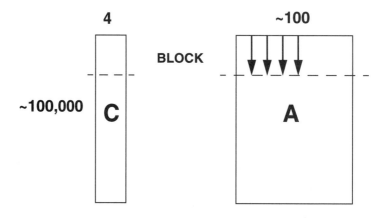

Figure 10-9   DGEMM blocking for long matrices.

10.5.4.2   Big and Stocky Matrices — Block and Copy

Block and copy is most important for nested loops. In the following examples, we'll use the BLAS Standard naming conventions since it contains matrix copy routines. The BLAS Standard routine for Fortran 77 for matrix multiplication is F_DGEMM and the matrix copy routine is F_DGE_COPY. In Chapter 5, we saw that by choosing a blocking factor BLOCK such that $8 \times 3 \times \text{BLOCK} \times \text{BLOCK}$ is less than the cache size, a matrix-matrix multiplication could be decomposed into multiple matrix-matrix multiplications, each of which fit into the data cache. For each block of C, this consists of

1. Hoist—copy a block of C to temporary storage for C
2. Loop
   a. Copy a block of A to temporary storage
   b. Copy a block of B to temporary storage
   c. Multiplication of temporary block of A and B and accumulation to temporary C
   d. Continue loop if there is more work to do
3. Sink—copy temporary C over original block of C

The data motion is shown in the following code and illustrated in Figure 10-10.

```
   ...
   REAL*8 TEMP(BLOCK,BLOCK,3)
   DO I = 1,M,BLOCK
     DO J = 1,N,BLOCK
       CALL F_DGE_COPY(BLAS_NO_TRANS, BLOCK, BLOCK, C(I,J),
  $      LDC, TEMP(1,1,3), BLOCK)
       DO L = 1,K,BLOCK
         CALL F_DGE_COPY(BLAS_NO_TRANS, BLOCK, BLOCK, A(I,L),
  $        LDA, TEMP(1,1,1), BLOCK)
         CALL F_DGE_COPY(BLAS_NO_TRANS, BLOCK, BLOCK, B(L,J),
  $        LDB, TEMP(1,1,2), BLOCK)
         IF (L .EQ. 1) THEN
           CALL F_DGEMM(BLAS_NO_TRANS, BLAS_NO_TRANS, BLOCK,
  $          BLOCK, BLOCK, ALPHA, TEMP(1,1,1), BLOCK,
  $          TEMP(1,1,2), BLOCK, BETA, TEMP(1,1,3), BLOCK)
         ELSE
           CALL F_DGEMM(BLAS_NO_TRANS, BLAS_NO_TRANS, BLOCK,
  $          BLOCK, BLOCK, ALPHA, TEMP(1,1,1), BLOCK,
  $          TEMP(1,1,2), BLOCK, 1.0D0, TEMP(1,1,3), BLOCK)
         ENDIF
       ENDDO
       CALL F_DGE_COPY(BLAS_NO_TRANS, BLOCK, BLOCK, TEMP(1,1,3),
  $      BLOCK, C(I,J), LDC)
     ENDDO
   ENDDO
   ...
```

This is really a hoist/sink C approach performed at the block level. Note that in the block inner loop, only blocks of A and B need to be copied to the TEMP array. There are also block versions of hoist B and hoist A matrix-matrix multiplication. These are inferior to the hoist/sink C approach, since each requires C to be copied to and from the TEMP array in the inner block loop.

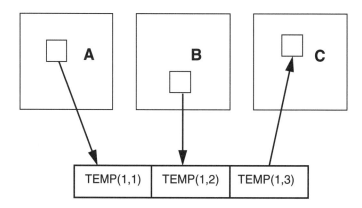

Figure 10-10   Block and copy for matrix-multiplication.

10.5.4.3   Parallelism

Matrix-matrix multiplication routines are very well-suited for parallelism which can occur at multiple levels. Using a hoist B or hoist/sink C approach, there is a natural parallelism that occurs at the outer loop level. For example, the hoist B approach shown in Figure 10-7 has *n/nb* increments of size *nb*. Each of these is independent and may be executed in parallel. All processors need to read all of A, but they need only the part of C that they update and its corresponding part of B. Likewise, the hoist/sink C approach shown in Figure 10-8 can be modified for parallelism by executing each of the *n/nb* increments in parallel.

The block and copy code shown in Figure 10-10 can also use outer loop parallelism that is very similar to the hoist/sink C code above. Each processor needs the part of C that it updates and the corresponding part of B. However, each processor does eventually need to read and use all of A. For massively parallel computers that have a very small amount of memory associated with each processor, there are techniques that limit the amount of data movement of A by having each processor receive a piece of A, operate with it, and then pass it to the next processor until all processors have accessed all of A (yet another example of pipelining). Interested readers may consult Fox [2] for more details.

10.6 BLAS and Performance

The higher level of the BLAS, the better the performance!

We have seen that increasing the complexity of the kernel by moving from vector operations such as DAXPY to matrix-matrix operations such as DGEMM improves performance, since it increases the number of flops per data point. This helps performance noticeably even on a robust memory system like those found on vector computers, but it is far more important on cache-based computers. Table 10-7 shows the ratio of floating-point to memory operations on some common BLAS routines.

Table 10-7   The BLAS and Data Reuse.

Routine	BLAS type	Optimizations	F:M ratio (upper limit)	Floating-point operations per byte
DAXPY	1	software pipelining	0.67	0.125
DDOT	1	software pipelining, multiple sum reductions	1.00	0.125
DGEMV	2	software pipelining, multiple sum reductions, blocking	2.00	0.250
DGEMM	3	software pipelining, multiple sum reductions, blocking, block and copy	> 2.00	0.750 (1 KB data cache) 28.125 (1 MB data cache)

Clearly, DGEMM is the preferred routine because it has the highest F:M ratio. Many processors require an F:M ratio of 2.0 for optimal performance. The DGEMV F:M value looks pretty good since its ratio approaches two. So at first glance, the performance of DGEMV might be expected to be close to DGEMM performance and for data that is already in-cache, the performance can be similar. It's the out-of-cache performance where DGEMM is far superior to DGEMV and the other routines. When DGEMV is performed, data is loaded from memory (far, far away) to cache. Then it is moved from cache to the functional units. For DGEMV, data from the matrix is used once and that's it. For a matrix of size $n \times n$, each point generates one fma, which, for eight byte data, results in 0.25 floating-point operations per byte. DGEMM has the opportunity to reuse data in cache much more than DGEMV.

Suppose we want to perform a square matrix multiplication of the largest size that fits in cache. In the first case, suppose the processor has a tiny one KB data cache and the A, B, C each use one-third of cache. This implies that the size of the matrix n, is $\sqrt{[(1/3) \times (1KB/8)]} = 6$ points. This is ridiculously small, but if we assume that the two matrices, A and B, are loaded into cache once (a blocked hoist/sink C approach), for the 6×6 multiplication performed, the floating-point per byte ratio is

$$2 \times 6^3 \text{ floating-point operations} / (8 \times 2 \times 6^2) \text{ bytes} = 0.75 \text{ flt.-pt. operations per byte.}$$

This has three times as much data reuse as DGEMV. Now what happens if a 1 MB cache is used? A data set of size 209 points may be performed in-cache, leading to a ratio of size 209 / 8 = 28.125 floating-point operations per byte. This is a huge improvement over the DGEMV reuse!

Figure 10-11 shows in-cache and out-of-cache performance on an HP N-Class server using the HP Math LIBrary (MLIB) versions of some of the BLAS routines we've discussed. The PA-8500 processors used in this server have a clock speed of 440 MHz and one MB data cache. Notice how well the Level 3 BLAS routine DGEMM performs both in-cache and out-of-cache and how poorly the other routines perform when the data is out-of-cache.

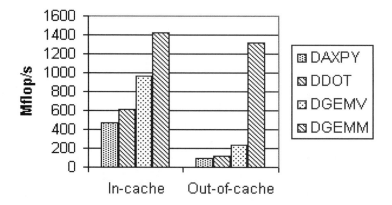

Figure 10-11 BLAS performance on HP N-Class server with PA-8500 (440 MHz) processor.

10.7 Winograd's Matrix-Matrix Multiplication

The final two sections of this chapter analyze algorithms that reduce the number of operations required for matrix-matrix multiplication. The first technique is due to Winograd [6] and reduces the number of multiplications. The second algorithm is for complex multiplication only and it reduces the number of multiplications and additions. The third algorithm was developed by Strassen [5] and actually reduces the order of the operations for a potentially huge reduction in the number of calculations!

It's easy to count the number of operations to perform matrix-matrix multiplication. The three dominant loops may appear as follows:

```
DO J = 1,N
  DO L = 1,K
    DO I = 1,M
      C(I,J) = C(I,J) + A(I,L) * B(L,J)
    ENDDO
  ENDDO
ENDDO
```

The number of number of multiplications is *kmn* with an equal number of additions. This gives a total of *2kmn* operations. For $k = m = n$, this is an $O(n^3)$ algorithm.

Winograd derived a way to reduce the number of floating-point multiplications in a matrix-matrix multiplication by half at the expense of a few more floating-point additions. This is a good technique to use on processors that don't have an efficient fma instruction. Using the code above, suppose *k* is even. The key to this algorithm is forming the product P(I,J):

```
DO J = 1,N
  DO L = 1,K/2
    DO I = 1,M
      P(I,J) = (A(I,2*L) + B(2*L-1,J)) * (A(I,2*L-1)+B(2*L,J))
    ENDDO
  ENDDO
ENDDO
```

Note that P(I,J) is composed of four terms:

```
A(I,2*L-1)*B(2*L-1,J)
A(I,2*L)*B(2*L,J)
A(I,2*L-1)*A(I,2*L)
B(2*L-1,J)*B(2*L,J)
```

The first two terms are necessary for the final matrix-matrix multiplication result, while the last two have to be dispensed with. Note that the last two values are functions of only two of the loops, though. Thus, while the calculation of P is of *O(kmn)*, the separate calculation of the A product is *O(km)* and the separate calculation of the B product is *O(kn)*. These two terms can be calculated separately and subtracted from the P term. Odd values of *k* must also be added, too. The following calculates the complete matrix-matrix multiplication:

```
DO I = 1,M
   X(I) = 0.0
ENDDO
DO L = 1,K/2
   DO I = 1,M
      X(I) = X(I) + A(I,2L-1) A(I,2L)
   ENDDO
ENDDO
DO J = 1,N
   Y(J) = 0.0
   DO L = 1,K/2
      Y(J) = Y(J) + B(2L-1,J)B(2L,J)
   ENDDO
ENDDO
IF (AND(K,1) .EQ. 0) THEN ! K IS EVEN
   DO J = 1,N
      DO I = 1,M
         C(I,J) = C(I,J) + P(I,J) - X(I) - Y(J)
      ENDDO
   ENDDO
ELSE
   DO J = 1,N
      DO I = 1,M
      C(I,J) = C(I,J) + P(I,J) - X(I) - Y(J) + A(I,K)*B(K,J)
      ENDDO
   ENDDO
ENDIF
```

Therefore, the worst case is when K is odd. The maximum number of operations is

Multiplications: $kmn/2 + k(m+n)/2 + mn$
Additions: $kmn + k(m+n)/2 + 4mn$

So the number of multiplications is reduced by approximately half and the number of additions increases slightly. This algorithm reduces the number of floating-point operations, but what about the number of instructions? If the processor has an fma instruction, the original matrix-matrix multiplication code takes kmn fma instructions. The main part of Winograd's algorithm, the calculation of the P(I,J), cannot use any fma instructions, though. Therefore, it requires $(3/2)kmn$ instructions, so this part alone exceeds the number of instructions required by the usual approach. Thus, if the processor has an efficient fma instruction, Winograd's algorithm does not help performance. However, if an fma instruction isn't available, or if it costs the same as a performing both a multiplication and an addition, then the Winograd algorithm is worth considering.

10.7.1 Winograd's Matrix-Matrix Multiplication for Complex Data

Can Winograd's algorithm improve matrix-matrix multiplication for complex data? Once again, it comes down to whether an efficient fma instruction exists. For complex data, the original matrix-matrix multiplication requires one complex multiplication and one complex addition for each index value, for a total of $2kmn$ complex operations. These map to real operations to create $4kmn$ real multiplications and $4kmn$ real additions for a total of $8kmn$ real operations. By modifying the order of operations and using fma instructions, only $4kmn$ fma instructions are required.

Consider the P term in Winograd's algorithm. It requires $kmn/2$ complex multiplications and kmn complex additions. These map to real operations to create $2kmn$ real multiplications and $3kmn$ real additions. This is a reduction in the number of operations by 5/8. However, only half of the multiplications can use fma instructions. Thus, there are kmn multiplication instructions, kmn fma instructions, and $2kmn$ add instructions, for a total of $4kmn$ instructions. So there is no advantage to using Winograd's algorithm for complex matrix-matrix multiplication if an efficient fma instruction exists on the processor. However, if there is none, this technique can reduce the number of operations to 5/8 the original code.

10.8 Complex Matrix-Matrix Multiplication with Three Real Multiplications

Earlier in this chapter, a technique to multiply two complex scalars using three real multiplications and five real additions was defined. This same approach works for matrices and is called the *3M* approach. For a general complex matrix-matrix multiplication that updates a matrix, the code appears as follows: Let $A = (A_r, A_i)$, $B = (B_r, B_i)$, $C = (C_r, C_i)$ be complex matrices decomposed into their real and imaginary components. Let $S_1, S_2, S_3, R_1, R_2, R_3$ be real matrices. Updating C by the product of A and B can be performed as follows:

$$S_1 = B_r - B_i$$
$$S_2 = A_r + A_i$$
$$S_3 = A_r - A_i$$
$$R_1 = A_r S_1$$
$$R_2 = B_r S_2$$
$$R_3 = B_i S_3$$
$$(C_r, C_i) = (C_r, C_i) + (A_r, A_i)(B_r, B_i)$$
$$= (C_r + R_1 + R_3, C_i + R_2 - R_1)$$

This contains three real multiplications and seven real additions. For square matrices, the additions use only $O(n^2)$ operations and can be ignored for very large n. By removing a real matrix-matrix multiplication, the number of operations drops to 3/4 of the usual approach.

10.8.1 When to Use the 3M Algorithm

So we know this approach should help performance for large enough matrices, but what is large enough? For a complex matrix-matrix multiplication of square matrices of size $n \times n$, we've traded a real multiplication of size $n \times n$ for three matrix additions of size $n \times n$. When the time to perform these additions is less than the time to perform the multiplication, then this algorithm can be used profitably.

Since this technique is most beneficial for large matrices, it is safe to assume that the data will exceed the size of the largest cache. Matrix multiplication and addition have very different characteristics for these large data sets. Due to optimizations such as unroll and jam, and block and copy, matrix-matrix multiplication performs excellently. The multiplication that is saved by this algorithm takes $2n^3$ floating-point operations.

However, the speed of the matrix additions is completely determined by the ability to move data between the processor and memory. These are a lot of loads and stores to support the matrix additions that must be paid for. Let's see how much data must be moved. Assume that a load of real data moves eight bytes and a store of real data moves 16 bytes (eight bytes to move the data from memory to cache and eight more to move it back to memory). The data starts as complex data of size 16 bytes, so the number of bytes per complex load is 16 and the number of bytes per complex store is 32. For each of the $n \times n$ points, the arrays and memory operations are as follows:

Table 10-8   Data Movement Required for 3M Algorithm.

Arrays	Memory operations	Bytes
A, B, C	load	$3 \times 16 = 48$
$A_r, A_i, B_r, B_i, C_r, C_i$	store and load	$6 \times (16+8) = 144$
$S_1, S_2, S_3, R_1, R_2, R_3$	store and load	$6 \times (16+8) = 144$
C	store	16
Total		352

If a processor performs matrix multiplication at a speed of y Mflop/s and can move z MB/s, then the crossover point that determines when it is profitable to use Strassen's algorithm is

$$\frac{2n^3 flop}{y\, Mflop/s} = \frac{352n^2 Bytes}{z\, MB/s}$$

or

$$n = \frac{176 \times y}{z}$$

On an HP N-Class server, a PA-8500 processor with a 440 MHz frequency can perform large matrix multiplications at about 1300 Mflop/s and move data between processor and memory at 1300 MB/s. Thus, the break-even point should be about

$n = 176 \times 1300 / 1300 = 176$

So, on an N-Class, the 3M algorithm is useful once the data exceeds 176×176. Recall that the current trend in computer architectures is that processor performance increases faster than interconnect performance, so the break-even point will not be shrinking any time soon.

What about parallelism? As processors are added, the memory bandwidth rates rarely scale as well as the number of processors, so the break-even point usually increases as the number of processors increase.

10.9 Strassen's Matrix-Matrix Multiplication

Suppose the matrices to be multiplied are of size n. In the usual matrix-matrix multiplication, there are $O(n^3)$ operations. The standard way to multiply matrices is so natural that most of us wouldn't think that the order of operations could be reduced. However, Strassen not only considered this, he actually derived a way to reduce the order! Suppose n is a power of two and each of the matrices is partitioned into four $n/2 \times n/2$ matrices as follows:

$$\begin{bmatrix} C_{11} & C_{12} \\ C_{21} & C_{22} \end{bmatrix} = \begin{bmatrix} C_{11} & C_{12} \\ C_{21} & C_{22} \end{bmatrix} + \begin{bmatrix} A_{11} & A_{12} \\ A_{21} & A_{22} \end{bmatrix} \begin{bmatrix} B_{11} & B_{12} \\ B_{21} & B_{22} \end{bmatrix}$$

Normally one would calculate C by forming the four parts

$$C_{11} = C_{11} + A_{11} B_{11} + A_{12} B_{21}$$
$$C_{21} = C_{21} + A_{21} B_{11} + A_{22} B_{21}$$
$$C_{12} = C_{12} + A_{11} B_{12} + A_{12} B_{22}$$
$$C_{22} = C_{22} + A_{21} B_{12} + A_{22} B_{22}$$

This requires eight matrix multiplications and eight matrix additions of size $n/2 \times n/2$. The matrix-matrix additions take only $O(n^2)$ operations, so we'll ignore them. If each matrix multiplication takes $2(n/2)^3$ floating-point operations, then eight of them take $2n^3$ floating-point operations, which is the same number of operations as the original algorithm.

Strassen derived a difference sequence of operations which eliminated one of the eight matrix-matrix multiplications at the expense of eleven more matrix-matrix additions. After the publication of the original algorithm, Winograd was able to remove three of these additions and his variant of Strassen's algorithm appears below.

$$S_1 = A_{21} + A_{22} \qquad M_1 = S_2 S_6 \qquad T_1 = M_1 + M_2$$
$$S_2 = S_1 - A_{11} \qquad M_2 = A_{11} B_{11} \qquad T_2 = T_1 + M_4$$
$$S_3 = A_{11} - A_{21} \qquad M_3 = A_{12} B_{21}$$
$$S_4 = A_{12} - S_2 \qquad M_4 = S_3 S_7$$
$$S_5 = B_{12} - B_{11} \qquad M_5 = S_1 S_5$$
$$S_6 = B_{22} - S_5 \qquad M_6 = S_4 B_{22}$$
$$S_7 = B_{22} - B_{12} \qquad M_7 = A_{22} S_8$$
$$S_8 = S_6 - B_{21}$$

$$C_{11} = C_{11} + M_2 + M_3$$
$$C_{12} = C_{12} + T_1 + M_5 + M_6$$
$$C_{21} = C_{21} + T_2 - M_7$$
$$C_{22} = C_{22} + T_2 + M_5$$

There are seven matrix-matrix multiplications of size $n/2 \times n/2$ that generate $(7/8) \times 2n^3$ floating-point operations. There are also 19 matrix-matrix additions of size $n/2 \times n/2$ (or 15 if the algorithm does not update preexisting C values). The true power of the algorithm becomes apparent when it is applied repeatedly. The maximum number of times this optimization can be applied is $log_2(n)$ times so the order of operations from the matrix-matrix multiplication is

$$\left(\frac{7}{8}\right)^{\log_2(n)} \times n^3$$

Therefore, the order of complexity is

$$n^{\log_2(7)} \approx n^{2.81}$$

and a large enough matrix-matrix multiplication should require many fewer operations.

Suppose we want to multiply two matrices of size 1024×1024. Since $1024 = 2^{10}$, this could use ten levels of Strassen's algorithm. First, the matrices are divided into four submatrices of size 512×512. These can be multiplied using the seven multiplications of Strassen's algorithm. These submatrices are, in turn, subdivided into four submatrices and this process continues until the lowest level, which consists of 262,144 matrices of size 2×2, is reached. How much could Strassen's algorithm speed up the operations? If each step reduced the operation count by 7/8, then the number of operations should be $(7/8)^{10} \approx 0.26$ or approximately one-fourth that of the original multiplication. But is actual performance really this good?

In practice, there exists some point where it is no longer profitable to further divide the matrices in half and perform another step of Strassen's algorithm. This is due to the large number of matrix additions that have been introduced. Strassen's algorithm is usually implemented by using it recursively until the performance of the current level matrix-matrix multiplication using a standard matrix-matrix multiplication outperforms a matrix multiplication using another Strassen step. These multiplications then use the standard matrix-matrix multiplication approach. The next section will find the break-even point when it is profitable to apply Strassen's algorithm.

Note that the algorithm is defined for square matrices that are a power of two in size. Thus, if your matrices are not square and a power of two in size, it is necessary to handle the non-power of two regions separately. This also reduces the efficiency of the algorithm. There are fast matrix multiplication algorithms like Strassen's for $n \geq 3$ and some of these algorithms reduce the order of the algorithm further. The lowest order is $n^{2.376}$ and was obtained by Coppersmith and Winograd [1]. The goal for all of these algorithms is to see how close the order can be to two. However, to date, all of the algorithms that have a lower order than the Strassen's algorithm have so much overhead that they are not useful for real-world applications.

10.9.1 When to Use Strassen's Algorithm

So we know Strassen's approach should help performance for large enough matrices, but what is large enough? For a matrix-matrix multiplication of square matrices of size $n \times n$, we've traded a multiplication of size $n/2 \times n/2$ for 15 matrix additions of size $n/2 \times n/2$. When the time to perform these additions is less than the time to perform the multiplication, then Strassen's algorithm can be used profitably.

For each element of the matrix addition, there are two loads and one store. Suppose the store uses a different array than the ones loaded and the data is eight bytes long. 32 bytes must be moved for each point (eight bytes for each load and 16 for the store). There are $(n/2)^2$ points for each matrix addition and 15 matrix additions to perform.

If a processor performs matrix multiplication at a speed of y Mflop/s and can move z MB/s, then the crossover point that determines when it is profitable to use Strassen's algorithm is

$$\frac{2(n/2)^3 flop}{y\, Mflop/s} = \frac{15 \times 32 (n/2)^2 Bytes}{z\, MB/s}$$

or

$$n = \frac{480 \times y}{z}$$

On an HP N-Class server, a PA-8500 processor with a frequency of 440 MHz can perform large matrix multiplications at about 1300 Mflop/s and move data between processor and memory at 1300 MB/s. Thus, the break-even point should be about

$n = 480 \times 1300 / 1300 = 480$

So Strassen's algorithm is not useful until the data size exceeds 480×480. As mentioned in the discussion on using the 3M approach for complex matrix-matrix multiplications, the single processor break-even point will not be shrinking in the near future and the break-even point also increases with the number of processors.

Clearly, Strassen's approach should be used only on very large matrices. Recall our calculating that it takes five iterations of Strassen's method to reduce the number of calculations to half that of the standard approach. For the N-Class, we could not hope to achieve this until the data size was at least $480 \times 2^5 = 15{,}360$. This requires three matrices whose total size is $3 \times 8 \times (15{,}360)^2 = 5.6$ GB, which is a pretty large data set! So don't expect Strassen's technique to greatly reduce the computational time significantly except for very large data!

10.9.2 Complex Matrices

These techniques can, of course, be applied to complex matrices. Actually, the crossover point to use Strassen's algorithm is even better for complex data since it has more data reuse. For 16-byte complex data, the break-even point is

$$n = \frac{240 \times y}{z}$$

so the single processor break-even point on the N-Class above is a matrix of size

$n = 240 \times 1300 / 1300 = 240$

10.9.2.1   Combining Strassen and 3M

Most processors can benefit from combining Strassen's algorithm with the 3M algorithm described earlier. As we have seen, the 3M algorithm can be improve performance for smaller size data sets than Strassen's algorithm. So when the lowest level of Strassen's algorithm is reached, the 3M approach can be used (if it helps performance) to increase the performance even further. So the steps are:

1. Apply the Strassen-Winograd algorithm until recursion no longer benefits performance.
2. Perform the lowest level complex matrix multiplications using the 3M approach.

Thus, step two gives a 3/4 reduction in the number of operations beyond that achieved by Strassen's recursive algorithm.

10.9.3   Parallelism and Strassen's Algorithm

Parallelism may be achieved by a bottom-up or top-down approach. We've seen that the lowest level of Strassen's algorithm maps to standard matrix-matrix multiplication routines that may be fairly large. If these standard routines have efficient parallel performance, then it is advisable to let the whole algorithm inherit this bottom-level parallelism. The matrix-matrix addition routines may also be optimized for parallelism to improve efficiency further. Parallelism for matrix-matrix addition is identical to the parallelism we discussed for matrix copy routines. For computers with only a few processors, this bottom-up parallelism is probably sufficient.

A coarse-grained top-down approach is also feasible, but it can be difficult to obtain a good load balance. The first level of Strassen's algorithm performs seven matrix-matrix multiplications and these may be executed independently. However, not too many users want exactly seven-way parallelism. Most users would like parallelism that leads to a good load balance on a variable number of processors. Two levels of Strassen's algorithm perform 49 matrix-matrix multiplications and the parallelism can also be structured to occur at this or other lower levels.

10.10   Summary

This chapter applied the code optimization techniques of Chapter 5 to some of the simple kernels used by many mathematical software packages and scientific programs. Some hardware and software vendors provide high performance routines that perform many of these operations. If they don't, or if you need to optimize something similar, but different from the standard routines, you can apply the techniques to improve your application's performance.

References:

1. Coopersmith, D.; Winograd, S. *Matrix Multiplication Via Arithmetic Progression.* Proceedings of the 19th Annual ACM Symposium on the Theory of Computing, 1-6, 1987.
2. Fox, G.; Johnson, M.; Lyzenga, G.; Otto, S.; Salmon, J.; Walker, D. *Solving Problems on Concurrent Processors*, Volume I. Englewood Cliffs, N.J.: Prentice-Hall, 1988, ISBN 0-13-823022-6.
3. Higham, N. Accuracy and Stability of Numerical Algorithms. Philadelphia: SIAM, 1996, ISBN 0-89871-355-2.
4. Knuth, D. *The Art of Computer Programming*, Volume II. Reading, Mass.: Addison-Wesley, 1969, ISBN 0-201-03802-1.
5. Strassen, V. *Gaussian Elimination Is Not Optimal.* Numer. Math., Vol. 13, 354-356, 1969.
6. Winograd, S. *A New Algorithm for Inner Product.* IEEE Trans. Comput., Vol. C-18, 693-694, 1968.

Faster Solutions for Systems of Equations

We share a philosophy about linear algebra: we think basis-free, we write basis-free, but when the chips are down we close the office door and compute with matrices like fury.

Irving Kaplansky

Many scientific applications spend significant amounts of time solving linear systems of equations. These may take a $n \times n$ matrix A, a vector b (also known as the right hand side vector) of size n, and solve for a vector x of unknowns. This equation is written as $Ax = b$.

Various techniques to solve systems of equations have been developed and this is one of the most researched areas of mathematics. Systems of equations are said to be *dense* if all, or nearly all, of the coefficients of A are nonzero. Systems that arise naturally in some disciplines are *sparse*, that is, most coefficients of A are zero. The *structure* of a sparse matrix refers to the location of the nonzero elements and determines which algorithms are used to optimally solve a system.

A solution of a system of equations is obtained using either *direct* or *iterative* methods. Direct methods use algorithms that return an exact solution for x after a fixed number of steps. Iterative algorithms start with a guess for the solution vector x. They perform operations which refine this to a more accurate solution for x. This process continues (iterates) until a solution with the desired accuracy is obtained. Algorithms may also be performed *in-core* or *out-of-core*. In-core methods assume that all the data (i.e., A, b and x) fits in the main memory of the computer. This is usually the case since computer memories today may be many gigabytes. All the algorithms in this book assume that the problem fits in-core. Out-of-core methods pull the data from disk to memory as the system is being solved. They can perform extremely large problems since the problem size is limited only by the amount of disk space. Algorithms have to be restructured for out-of-core accesses and some inefficiencies naturally result.

Computer vendors provide math libraries such as Hewlett-Packard's Mathematical software LIBrary (MLIB) to provide much of the functionality discussed in this chapter. Nearly all such libraries support the LAPACK math library. Some also provide sparse direct and iterative solver functionality. There are also software vendors such as the Numerical Algorithms Group (NAG) and Precision Numerics (developers of the IMSL math and statistics libraries) that provide a broad selection of routines. In general, hardware vendors provide a smaller set of functionality than software vendors, but the routines provided by hardware vendors tend to be more highly tuned for performance.

This chapter introduces some common algorithms and terminology and tries to hit some of the high spots of numerical linear algebra. Interested readers should consult Demmel [2], Dongarra [3], or Golub [5] for more in-depth analysis.

11.1 A Simple Example

Solving a small system of equations directly is very easy. At an early age, students learn how to solve two equations with two unknowns by a process known as *Gaussian elimination*. For example,

$$3y + 2z = 5$$
$$9y + 12z = 3$$

can be written as

$$\begin{bmatrix} 3 & 2 \\ 9 & 12 \end{bmatrix} \begin{bmatrix} y \\ z \end{bmatrix} = \begin{bmatrix} 5 \\ 3 \end{bmatrix}$$

Multiplying the second equation by 1/3 and subtracting it from the first equation results in

$$\begin{bmatrix} 3 & 2 \\ 0 & -2 \end{bmatrix} \begin{bmatrix} y \\ z \end{bmatrix} = \begin{bmatrix} 5 \\ 4 \end{bmatrix}$$

This is an upper triangular system (denoted U) since all of the entries below the main diagonal are 0. This is easy to solve since the second equation can be divided by -2 to obtain the value of z. The value of z can then be substituted into the first equation, which can then be solved for y.

Another way to solve the original equations is to multiply the first equation by 6 and subtract from the second equation. This results in

$$\begin{bmatrix} -9 & 0 \\ 9 & 12 \end{bmatrix} \begin{bmatrix} y \\ z \end{bmatrix} = \begin{bmatrix} -27 \\ 3 \end{bmatrix}$$

This is an example of a lower triangular (L) system since all values above the main diagonal are 0. A lower triangular system is just as easy to solve as an upper triangular system. Start with the equation with one unknown, solve it, use this value in the equation with two unknowns, and then solve for the remaining unknown. So if a system of equations can be converted into a form that can be written in terms of triangular matrices, then the solution of the original system can be easily found.

Most matrices can be written as a product of a lower triangular matrix and an upper triangular matrix. When the lower triangular matrix has all diagonal elements equal to one, the factorization is called the *LU factorization* or *LU decomposition* of the matrix. The LU factorization is unique for a given matrix and can be stored compactly. Since the LU factorization is defined to have all diagonal elements equal to one, only the non-zero off diagonal values in the lower matrix and the non-zero elements of the upper matrix need to be stored. Since this is requires no more storage than the original matrix, most numerical packages overwrite the original matrix with the LU factorization. The original matrix above can be decomposed as follows:

$$\begin{bmatrix} 3 & 2 \\ 9 & 12 \end{bmatrix} = \begin{bmatrix} 1 & 0 \\ 3 & 1 \end{bmatrix} \begin{bmatrix} 3 & 2 \\ 0 & 12 \end{bmatrix}$$

So, solving a system of equations can be performed with the following three steps:

1. Calculate the LU factorization, $A = LU$.

2. Let $y = (y_1,...,y_n) = Ux$ and solve for y. This is called *forward substitution* since y_1 is obtained first, then y_2, and so on.

3. Solve the system $Ux = y$ for $x = (x_1,...,x_n)$. This is the *backward substitution* step since x_n is calculated first, then x_{n-1}, etc.

The combination of steps two and three is called *forward-backward substitution* (FBS). The phrase "solve a system" can be confusing since it can mean to completely solve the system (including the calculation of L and U) or to just perform the forward-backward substitution after LU factorization has been performed.

11.2 LU Factorization

Code to generate a LU factorization stored in compact form (the diagonal elements of L are not stored) follows:

```
C COMPUTE LU FACTORIZATION
      DO I = 1, N-1
C
C SCALE LOWER MATRIX COLUMN
         DO J = I+1,N
            A(J,I) = A(J,I) / A(I,I)
         ENDDO
C
C RANK-ONE UPDATE OF MATRIX
         DO J = I+1, N
            DO K = I+1,N
               A(K,J) = A(K,J) - A(I,J) * A(K,I)
            ENDDO
         ENDDO
      ENDDO
```

Conceptually, this consists of the following steps:

1. Scale the ith lower matrix column by the ith diagonal
2. Perform a rank-one update on the square starting at position $(i+1, i+1)$ using the ith row and i^{th} column

This is shown in Figure 11-1.

Some questions that arise concerning the LU factorization of a system of equations are:

- Under what conditions does a solution exist?
- Will computer arithmetic introduce large errors?
- What can be done to improve performance?

11.2.1 Existence of a Unique Solution

Not all systems of equations have a unique solution. For example,

$$3y + 2z = 5$$
$$9y + 6z = 15$$

does not have a unique solution. The system as written has an unlimited number of solutions since the second equation is a multiple of the first equation. If the last element of the right-hand-side were 11 instead of 15, then the system would not have a solution at all since multiplication of the first equation by three and subtraction of the second equation results in

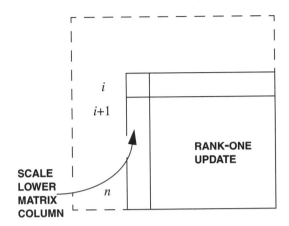

Figure 11-1 LU factorization.

$0 = 4$! We're really interested in matrices where a unique solution exists. The matrix A in these systems is called *nonsingular*. If there is not a unique solution, then A is said to be *singular*. A system is singular if and only if there is a zero on the diagonal of the upper matrix in the LU factorization. Thus, if a zero appears on the diagonal, an error condition should be generated and execution stopped.

11.2.2 Pivoting

Numerical analysts are concerned with the numerical accuracy of the solution. If computers performed operations with infinite precision, this wouldn't be an issue. The problem with the LU factorization is that each term of the lower matrix is created by dividing by a diagonal value. If a diagonal term is much smaller than the entries under it, the L values can be become unacceptably large and cause incorrect results when systems are solved. If the diagonal value starts with a value that is larger than all the entries in a column underneath it, then the division doesn't present a problem, since the results will all be less than one. So one way to improve the accuracy of a solution is to reorder the equations to put large values on the diagonal. This can be achieved using permutation matrices which interchange the rows and/or columns of a matrix.

An *identity matrix* is a matrix than contains ones on its main diagonal and zeros everywhere else. As you'd expect, multiplying a matrix by the identity matrix leaves the first matrix unchanged. A *permutation matrix* is the identity matrix with rows reordered. So multiplying a matrix by a non-identity permutation matrix results in a matrix that has the same elements as the original matrix, but whose rows are reordered. So, for example, a permutation matrix, P, could be applied to a system $Ax = b$ to obtain $PAx = Pb$. This system would, of course, have the same solution x as the original system, although the order of the operations might be different. Instead of performing an LU factorization of a matrix A, many numerical packages find a LU factorization and a permutation matrix P, such that $PA = LU$, where the steps of the LU factorization are chosen to reduce rounding errors.

This adds an additional wrinkle to the solution of a system of equations. Now the steps are

1. Decompose A so that $PA = LU$ (so $PAx = LUx = Pb$)
2. Let $y = Ux$ and solve $Ly = Pb$ for y
3. Solve $Ux = y$ for x

The most frequently used approach for the permutation is obtained by a process known as partial pivoting. At each iteration of the outer loop in the factorization, the current column in the lower matrix is searched for the element that has maximum magnitude. Once found, the elements to the right of this element are swapped with the corresponding elements in the current row. This is shown in Figure 11-2.

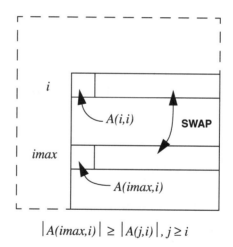

$$|A(imax,i)| \geq |A(j,i)|, j \geq i$$

Figure 11-2   Partial pivoting.

The code to perform this appears as

```
C COMPUTE LU FACTORIZATION
      DO I = 1, N-1
C
C FIND PIVOT ELEMENT
        T = 0
        IPVT(I) = I
        DO J = I,N
          IF (ABS(A(J,I)) .GT. T) THEN
            T = ABS(A(J,I))
            IPVT(I) = J
          ENDIF
        ENDDO
C SWAP REMINDER OF ROW
        DO J = I,N
          T = A(I,J)
          A(I,J) = A(IPVT(I),J)
          A(IPVT(I),J) = T
        ENDDO
        . . .
```

This is the algorithm used by the LINPACK routine DGEFA to factor a matrix. (The routine name stands for Double precision GEneral FActorization.) This is undoubtedly the most commonly used routine from the LINPACK package. It also the most time-consuming part of the LINPACK benchmarks.

11.2.3 Blocking for Performance

Ignoring the pivoting aspect for a moment, let's analyze the performance of the LU factorization. Since there are $(n-1)$ rank-one updates with vectors whose size shrinks by one each iteration, the number of calculations is

$$\sum_{i=1}^{n-1} 2i^2 \cong 2\sum_{i=1}^{n} i^2 \cong 2\left(\frac{n^3}{3}\right)$$

Since this is an $O(n^3)$ algorithm composed of rank-one updates, it should remind us of the potential of matrix-matrix multiplication. However, in LINPACK, the inner loop of the rank-one update is replaced by a call to the Level 1 BLAS DAXPY routine.

In Chapter 10, we examined DAXPY and showed that it's not a very efficient routine for computers that rely on cache to obtain good performance. After the LINPACK software was released, it was apparent that algorithms need to be based on higher BLAS routines for good performance on more types of computer platforms. We've already mentioned that the code uses a rank-one update and so could be replaced by the Level 2 BLAS routine DGER. This would help performance, but we'd really like to use a Level 3 BLAS routine to obtain the best performance. Figure 11-3 shows two consecutive iterations of the outer loop. It consists of

1. Scale column I starting at A(I+1,I) (column vector $a_{k,i}$ in Figure 11-3)
2. Rank-one update starting at A(I+1,I+1) (matrix $c_{k,j}$)
3. Scale column starting at A(I+2,I+1) (column vector $a_{k,i+1}$)
4. Rank-one update starting at A(I+2,I+2) (matrix $c_{k,j}$)

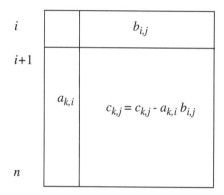 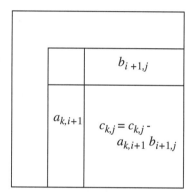

Figure 11-3   Two steps of LU factorization using rank-one updates.

Note that all of the area updated in the second update is also updated in the first update. So it should be possible to combine two iterations to perform a rank-two update or equivalently a matrix-matrix multiply $C = C - A \times B$ where A is two columns wide. As usual, unroll and jam techniques allow this to be achieved. Suppose we unroll the outer loop by two and jam the loops together. Ignoring the cleanup step, the code appears as follows:

```
      NEND = 2*((N-1)/2)
C COMPUTE LU FACTORIZATION
      DO I = 1, NEND, 2
C
C UPDATE I, I+1 LOWER MATRIX COLUMNS
C SCALE LOWER MATRIX COLUMN
         DO J = I+1,N
            A(J,I) = A(J,I) / A(I,I)
         ENDDO
```

```
C RANK-ONE UPDATE
        DO J = I+1,N
           A(J,I+1) = A(J,I+1) - A(I,I+1) * A(J,I)
        ENDDO
C SCALE LOWER MATRIX COLUMN
        DO J = I+2,N
           A(J,I+1) = A(J,I+1) / A(I+1,I+1)
        ENDDO
C
C UPDATE I, I+1 ROWS
        DO J = I+2, N
           A(I+1,J) = A(I+1,J) - A(I,J) * A(I+1,I)
        ENDDO
C
C RANK-TWO UPDATE
        DO J = I+2, N
           DO K = I+2,N
              A(K,J) = A(K,J) - A(I,J) * A(K,I) - A(I+1,J) * A(K,I+1)
           ENDDO
        ENDDO
     ENDDO
```

This is shown in Figure 11-4. The code performs the following steps:

1. LU factorization on two columns starting at A(I,I) (columns $a_{k,i}$ and $a_{k,i+1}$ in Figure 11-4)
2. update two rows starting at A(I,I+2) (this is really FBS on the rows $b_{i,j}$ and $b_{i+1,j}$)
3. rank-two update starting at A(I+2,I+2) (matrix $c_{k,j}$)

This process can continue for some arbitrary number, *nb*, of iterations to perform a rank-*nb* update (or matrix-matrix multiply). Thus, we would have LU factorization on *nb* columns, update *nb* rows, and perform a rank-*nb* update. Observe that the rank-*nb* update will be the most efficient of the components and will execute at a high percentage of DGEMM peak performance if the value of *nb* is large enough. However, if the value of *nb* is chosen too large, the amount of time in the less efficient components will exceed the time in the rank-*nb* update. So the choice of *nb* presents itself as a balancing act. *nb* should be large enough so that the rank-*nb* update is efficient, but small enough that the percent of time in the other component is small. A point of reference is that the default blocking value in many related LAPACK routines is 32 or 64.

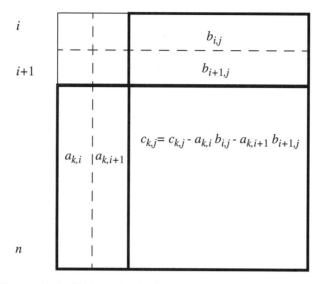

Figure 11-4   LU factorization using a rank-two update.

But what about pivoting? We still need to perform pivoting, but now it must be performed at the block level. Referring to Figure 11-4, inserting pivoting in the algorithm requires

1. LU factorization in region composed of columns of *a* with partial pivoting
2. Apply pivots obtained in step 1 to rows of regions *c*
3. Update rows of *b* (FBS)
4. Perform DGEMM in region *c*

This is the algorithm used by the routine DGETRF (Double precision GEneral TRiangular Factorization) in the LAPACK software package. Using Level 3 BLAS routines in LAPACK results in good performance across many types of computers. Obviously, not all of the work can use Level 3 BLAS, but if *nb* is chosen correctly, most of it does.

If only DGEMM is optimized (and nothing else), the LAPACK routine DGETRF achieves quite respectable performance. (Most vendors optimize DGETRF further, but we'll ignore that for now.) Table 11-1 compares performance on an HP N-4000 server using the original versions of DGEFA and DGETRF using vendor optimized BLAS routines. Two problem sizes are shown: 200

equations and unknowns (in-cache) and 1000 equations and unknowns (out-of-cache). The default block size of 64 was used.

Table 11-1 Advantage of Level 3 BLAS Building Blocks for LU Factorization.

	LU Factorization	
	LINPACK `DGEFA, DAXPY` **(Mflop/s)**	**LAPACK** `DGETRF, DGEMM` **(Mflop/s)**
200 equations (in-cache)	339	686
1000 equations (out-of-cache)	130	874

For in-cache performance, DGEMM can run three times faster than DAXPY. Not all of the time in DGETRF is spent in DGEMM, but enough is to make DGETRF run twice as fast as DGEFA. The large, out-of-cache problems are where LAPACK really excels. Due to cache line reuse, DGETRF performs over six times faster than DGEFA!

11.3 Cholesky Factorization

Real symmetric matrices arise naturally in many applications. A *symmetric* matrix is a matrix A such that $A = A^T$. A nice feature of these matrices is that only half the values need to be stored. Of course, this isn't too helpful if the LU factorization requires the full $n \times n$ elements. Another special type of matrix is a positive definite matrix. A real, symmetric matrix is *positive definite* if $x^T A x > 0$ for all vectors x that are not zero. A real, symmetric, positive definite matrix has many nice characteristics. For example, it implies that the maximum magnitude of any element in a column is less than or equal to the magnitude of the diagonal term in that column. This implies that pivoting is not required. It also implies that A can be factored as LL^T where L is a lower triangular matrix. Thus, only L needs to be stored for these types of matrices. This factorization is known as the Cholesky factorization in honor of its discoverer.

The LINPACK routine DPOFA (Double precision POsitive definite FActorization) performs a Cholesky factorization. The following code extract is similar to DPOFA:

```
DO I = 1, N
  SI = 0.0D0
  DO J = 1, I-1
    SJ = 0.0D0
    DO K = 1, J-1
      SJ = SJ + A(K,J) * A(K,I)
    ENDDO
    T = (A(J,I) - SJ) / A(J,J)
    A(J,I) = T
    SI = SI + T*T
  ENDDO
  A(I,I) = DSQRT(A(I,I) - SI)
ENDDO
```

Note that the size of the middle loop is a function of the outer loop. This reduces the number of floating-point calculations to about $(1/3)$ n^3. Thus, the Cholesky factorization requires only half the amount of storage and half the amount of calculations as LU factorization. Also, the inner loop of the DPOFA routine uses a call to DDOT. This is more efficient than the call to DAXPY used by DGEFA. The LAPACK routine DPOTRF (Double precision POsitive definite TRiangular Factorization) implements a blocked version of DPOFA that uses a call to DGEMM for the bulk of the computations.

Table 11-2 compares the performance of the LINPACK and LAPACK Cholesky factorization routines. As before, only the BLAS routines were optimized and results were obtained on an HP N-4000 server using the original versions of the LINPACK and LAPACK routines. The default block size of 64 was used.

Table 11-2   Advantage of Level 3 BLAS Building Blocks for Cholesky Factorization.

	Cholesky Factorization	
	LINPACK DPOFA, DDOT **(Mflop/s)**	**LAPACK** DPOTRF, DGEMM **(Mflop/s)**
200 equations (in-cache)	230	479
1000 equations (out-of-cache)	206	873

As expected, LAPACK substantially outperforms LINPACK. Also interesting is the comparison between the LU factorization and Cholesky factorization routines. For the in-cache case, Cholesky factorization is slower than LU factorization in units of Mflop/s. However, Cholesky factorization is faster in terms of time, and this is what really matters. Out-of-cache results are more complex. DDOT is more efficient than DAXPY for data that misses the data cache and the Cholesky factorization accesses only half as much data as LU factorization (so there is half the number of data cache misses); therefore, the LINPACK Cholesky factorization outperforms LU factorization in terms of Mflop/s. For LAPACK, Cholesky and LU factorization both use DGEMM and have nearly identical Mflop/s values, so the amount of time to perform the Cholesky factorization is half that of LU factorization.

11.4 Factorization and Parallelization

Parallelization—what a pain! One type of parallelization is easy, though. Since vendors produce parallel Level 3 BLAS routines, LAPACK built on top of these routines will inherit this parallelism. This used to be good enough. Back when vector computers were the only high performance computers, users had to worry only about small scale parallelism. Up to the early 1990s, these computers contained, at most, 16 processors. The robust memory systems of these computers were sufficient to obtain good performance using parallel Level 3 BLAS routines. Then users wanted good performance on computers built using a large number of RISC processors that were connected by lower bandwidth interconnects than those used for vector processors. Complications arise because data has to be spread among the processors performing the factorization. Look at Figure 11-1 again. Most of the time is spent in the update, but the process of scaling the lower matrix column (or its blocked analogue) must be performed before the update can occur. The information obtained from the scaling must be communicated to all processors that will perform the update. Since moving data between processors and between processors and memory is very time-consuming, performance of factorizations using Level 3 BLAS parallelism is frequently poor on non-vector computers.

Most vendors perform parallelization of the factorization at levels above the BLAS routines. As we've discussed, you usually want parallelism at the highest possible level. There are linear algebra software packages designed for high-level parallelism on distributed-memory computers. The best known ones are Scalable LAPACK (ScaLAPACK) and the Parallel Linear Algebra PACKage (PLAPACK). These libraries use MPI to achieve parallelism and are structured for the minimum amount of data traffic necessary for large-scale parallelism. By replacing LAPACK calls by their counterparts from these parallel libraries, users can obtain more efficient parallelism. Figure 11-5 shows the evolution of the numerical algebra libraries we've discussed.

11.5 Forward-Backward Substitution (FBS)

The system of equations $Ax = b$ shown at the beginning of the chapter had one right-hand-side (RHS) vector b and one solution vector x to be found. However, there could be multiple systems to solve using the matrix A. That is, we might want to solve $AX = B$ where B

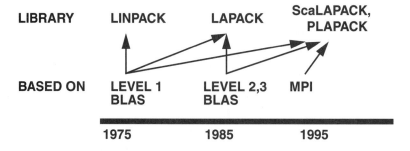

Figure 11-5   Linear algebra libraries.

consists of multiple RHS vectors. Thus, X and B may also be very large matrices. This hasn't been an issue so far since the matrix factorization is independent of the number of solution vectors.

11.5.1 Solve $Ax = b$ Where x and b Are Vectors (One RHS Vector)

As stated earlier, once an LU factorization with partial pivoting has been performed, solving a system of equations means solving $Ly=Pb$ for y, then solving $Ux=y$ for x. Numerical packages save the pivoting information from the factorization step so that it can be applied to the RHS b to reorder it as shown below.

```
C SOLVE  L*Y = PB
      DO K = 1, N-1
        T = B(IPVT(K))
        B(IPVT(K)) = B(K)
        B(K) = T
        DO I = K+1,N
          B(I) = B(I) - T * A(I,K)
        ENDDO
      ENDDO
C SOLVE  U*X = Y
      DO K = N, 1, -1
        B(K) = B(K)/A(K,K)
        T = B(K)
        DO I = 1,K-1
          B(I) = B(I) - T * A(I,K)
        ENDDO
      ENDDO
```

The FBS calculations have $O(n^2)$ data movements and calculations. Since the factorization is an $O(n^3)$ calculation, solving for a single solution vector is not as important as the factorization, but we'd still like this to run as fast as possible. The code shown above is the algorithm used by the LINPACK routine DGESL (Double precision GEneral SoLve). The inner loops are replaced by calls to the Level 1 BLAS routine DAXPY. It would be better to use a Level 2 BLAS routine for each of the steps. Since the inner loop is shrinking, this is not completely straightforward. Ignoring pivoting and using unroll and jam on the forward substitution step results in the following:

```
        NEND = 2*((N-1)/2)
C SOLVE   L*Y = B
        DO K = 1, NEND, 2
          T1 = B(K)
          B(K+1) = B(K+1) - T1 * A(K+1,K)
          T2 = B(K+1)
C 2 COLUMN MATRIX VECTOR MULTIPLY
          DO I = K+2,N
            B(I) = B(I) - T1 * A(I,K) - T2 * A(I,K+1)
          ENDDO
        ENDDO
```

This is a matrix-vector multiply where the matrix has two columns. This process can continue up to some blocking factor, *nb*, and a call to DGEMV inserted. Replacing a call to DAXPY by one to DGEMV also improves performance, as shown in the previous chapter. Blocking the backward substitution step is very similar. When the resulting blocked code includes partial pivoting, it is the same as the algorithm used by the LAPACK routine DGETRS (Double precision GEneral TRiangular Solve) using one RHS vector.

11.5.2 Solve $AX = B$ Where X and B Are Matrices (Multiple RHS Vectors)

If the number of RHS vectors is k, the solution step can actually dominant the factorization, since the solution is an $k \times O(n^2)$ algorithm. The nice thing about multiple vectors is that the result vector and solution vectors become matrices, so the DGEMV routine used when solving for one vector can be replaced by a call to DGEMM. This is another difference between the LINPACK and LAPACK software. The LINPACK solve routine DGESL makes a call to DAXPY and allows only one solution vector, whereas the similar LAPACK routine DGETRS allows multiple solution vectors and calls DGEMM, in this case.

Table 11-3 compares performance on an HP N-4000 using the original versions of DGESL and DGETRS using vendor optimized BLAS routines. Two problem sizes are shown: 200 equations and unknowns (in-cache) and 1000 equations and unknowns (out-of-cache). The default block size of 64 was used. There's not much difference in the solution rates between LINPACK and LAPACK using only one RHS vector, since DGEMM cannot be used. However, using 100 vectors allows DGEMM to be used in the LAPACK solution, and the rates are even better than the LU factorization rates!

Table 11-3   Advantage of Level 3 BLAS Building Blocks for FBS.

	Solve		
	LINPACK DGESL, DAXPY **1 RHS** **(Mflop/s)**	**LAPACK** DGETRS, DGEMV **1 RHS** **(Mflop/s)**	**LAPACK** DGETRS, DGEMM **100 RHS** **(Mflop/s)**
200 equations (in-cache)	276	276	791
1000 equations (out-of-cache)	177	187	966

(Users beware: Mixing LINPACK and LAPACK factor and solve routines will usually cause wrong answers since they use different permutation algorithms.)

11.6 Sparse Direct Systems of Equations

If you're using the popular mechanical engineering packages, such as MSC.Nastran from MSC.Software Corporation (http://www.macsch.com/) or ABAQUS from Hibbitt, Karlsson & Sorenson, Inc., (http://www.hks.com/) to design structures such as automobiles or aircraft, you're solving large sparse systems of equations. The workhorse technique for these packages is a direct solver, but frequently only the nonzero elements of the matrix and pointers to their location are stored.

11.6.1 Sparse Storage

There are many different sparse structure storage schemes. The simplest one is to have two auxiliary vectors: one to hold the number of the row that each nonzero element came from and one to hold its column number. This is called the *row and column index* sparse matrix representation. So the following matrix

$$\begin{bmatrix} 11 & 0 & 13 & 14 \\ 0 & 22 & 23 & 0 \\ 31 & 32 & 33 & 0 \\ 41 & 0 & 0 & 44 \end{bmatrix}$$

can be represented by

```
IROW =      1   3   4   2   3   1   2   3   1   4
JCOL =      1   1   1   2   2   3   3   3   4   4
A =        11  31  41  22  32  13  23  33  14  44
```

If the number of nonzero elements of an $n \times n$ matrix is represented by nz, then this storage scheme requires $3nz$ elements. If the nonzero elements and indices all use eight-byte data, then the nonzero elements require $8nz$ bytes and the indices require $16nz$ bytes. Thus, the amount of storage required for the indices is twice that used for the nonzero elements. Clearly, the storage of the JCOL values is not very efficient. Note the repetition of the column numbers. A smaller array for JCOL could be used that just stores the location of the beginning index for each column's data in the coefficient vector A. This creates the *column pointer, row index* sparse matrix representation and is demonstrated below.

```
COLPTR =    1   4   6   9  11
IROW =      1   3   4   2   3   1   2   3   1   4
A =        11  31  41  22  32  13  23  33  14  44
```

This requires $2nz+n+1$ storage elements, which is a large improvement. Note that this scheme has an equally efficient dual *row pointer, column index* sparse matrix representation that stores all column indices and a pointer to the row number.

11.6.2 Symbolic Factorization

As before, the matrix needs to be factored into the LU or LL^T form. However, the process of factorization of sparse matrices can lead to matrices that are not as sparse. So you can start with a very sparse matrix and, by factoring it, create a matrix that is too large to fit in the computer's memory. The increase in the number of nonzero elements in the matrix is referred to as *fill-in*. When we perform pivoting, we rearrange the rows or columns to minimize floating-point error. In like fashion, the matrix can be rearranged to minimize the occurrence of nonzero elements in the factored matrix. In fact, you don't even need to know any of the actual values in the matrix to perform this analysis. You need to know only where the nonzero elements of A are located. This adds a third step to the solution of the system. So before the factorization and FBS are calculated, a *symbolic factorization* is obtained which determines how the matrix will be factored.

The choice of how to symbolically factor the matrix is crucial, since it determines how large the factored matrix will be. Symbolic factorization determines the order in which the equations are eliminated, i.e., the equivalent of the permutation we discussed for dense systems. There are many reordering schemes in use. Two popular ones are Multiple Minimum Degree (MMD) [4] and METIS [7]. Difference schemes are appropriate for different types of problems. Some software packages even allow different reordering schemes to be performed and the one with the least amount of fill-in is used during the factorization phase.

Once the symbolic factorization has been performed, the numerical factorization can begin. Early algorithms performed updates based on a single column of data. These correspond to using DAXPY in the factorization routine DGEFA. Better performance is obtained by operating on multiple columns of data. This is the concept behind designing algorithms to use *supernodes*—sets of columns with identical non-zero structure. By designing algorithms to generate supernodes and using them in the matrix update, the routine DGEMM can be called to increase performance well beyond what DAXPY can achieve. Therefore, even in the case of sparse systems of equations, the low-level calculations employ dense Level 3 BLAS routines.

11.7 Iterative Techniques

Up to this point, the algorithms have used direct methods to solve a system of equations. Iterative methods start with an initial guess and refine it. These methods are, in a sense, less robust than direct methods since it is difficult to derive general approaches, to guarantee that the algorithm will converge to a solution, or to tell how many iterations are necessary to produce a good solution. Still, when conditions are favorable, an iterative solver can obtain a solution much more quickly than a direct solver. Iterative solvers don't have to perform the fill-in required by direct methods, so they have smaller storage requirements. Also, they can be embarrassingly parallel. There are many popular iterative methods, but the best known is undoubtedly the *conjugate gradient* (CG) algorithm [6]. This algorithm applies to symmetric, positive definite systems and it is guaranteed to converge to a solution after n iterations using infinite precision arithmetic. There are variants of the CG algorithm for other types of matrices. For many of these systems, these algorithms will converge to a solution, but there's no guarantee they will.

11.7.1 Conjugate Gradient Algorithm

Most of the time, the CG algorithm is applied to sparse systems. However, the first example code below solves a dense system. Let A be an $n \times n$ matrix, b a vector of length n, and suppose we want to solve $Ax = b$ for x. Let p, q, r, z be vectors of length n and α, β, ρ_0, ρ_1 and *error* be scalars. The following equations use vector and matrix notation to describe the CG algorithm:

Initialization: $x = 0.0$; $r = b$; $p = 0.0$; $\rho_0 = 1.0$; $\varepsilon = 1.0$

Do while ε (error) is large

$z = r$	preconditioner may replace this copy
$\rho_1 = \Sigma\, r^T z$	DDOT
$\beta = \rho_1 / \rho_0$	
$p = z + \beta\, p$	DAXPY
$q = Ap$	DGEMV
$\alpha = \rho_1 / \Sigma\, p^T q$	DDOT
$\rho_0 = \rho_1$	
$x = x + \alpha\, p$	DAXPY
$r = r - \alpha\, q$	DAXPY
$\varepsilon = \sqrt{rr}$	

End do

So the first question that comes to mind is, "How many iterations are required?" When the CG algorithm was derived, it was proven that the maximum number of iterations required to obtain an exact solution for a system of n equations is n. This assumes infinite precision arithmetic, though. (Recall that we wouldn't need pivoting in the direct methods if we had infinite precision arithmetic.) In practice, floating-point arithmetic can perturb the algorithm so that the incorrect answers can result. Let's suppose that the problem is well-behaved. What are the implications of taking n iterations to obtain a solution?

The most computationally significant part of the CG algorithm is the matrix-vector multiply. There are three parts which can be replaced by calls to DAXPY and two which can be replaced by calls to DDOT, but these all have only $O(n)$ operations and are insignificant compared to the matrix-vector multiply. So if it takes n matrix-vector multiplications, then about $2n^3$ operations are required. This is worse than the $n^3 / 3$ operations used by Cholesky factorization discussed above. What makes it much worse is that large matrix-matrix multiplication can run over six times faster than large matrix-vector multiplication, since blocking allows extensive cache reuse for matrix-matrix multiplication. Thus, the CG algorithm might take $(6 \times 2\, n^3) / (n^3 / 3) = 36$ times longer than a direct method if n iterations are performed, so what good is it? Clearly, it all comes down to the number of iterations required. If the number is less than, say, $n / 36$, then it might be worth trying. In practice, the number of iterations required is usually much less than n. However, the original CG may be slow to converge to a solution for a particular problem. Lots of research has been done to accelerate the rate of convergence to a good solution. The structures that accelerate iterative algorithms to reduce the number of iterations are called *preconditioners*.

In the equations that describe the CG algorithm above, the copy at the beginning of the outer loop may be replaced by a preconditioner. Preconditioners work by solving a system that is similar to A, but whose solution is easier to obtain. So with each iteration they move closer to the real solution than the unconditioned CG method. Of course, this helps only if the preconditioner is computationally inexpensive and improves convergence. There are many different preconditioners to choose from. Dongarra [3, p. 109] expresses it best: "The choice of a good preconditioner is mainly a matter of trial and error, despite our knowledge of what a good preconditioner should do."

11.7.2 Indirect Addressing

The CG description shown above is for a dense system, but most applications of iterative solvers are for sparse systems. There are many different sparse storage schemes, but they all involve either a gather operation, a scatter operation, or both.

In the section on sparse direct solvers, we discussed how the sparse structure could be manipulated to reduce fill-in and use supernodes to make locally dense operations which perform well. Since iterative algorithms are based on matrix-vector multiplication, no similar optimizations can be performed. Therefore, we have to deal with gather/scatter operations in the most computationally significant part of the algorithm. The following kernel is from the CG algorithm of the NAS Parallel Benchmarks (NPB) [1], version 2.3-serial, and is representative of the matrix-vector multiply used by CG solvers (The code can be obtained from http://www.nas.nasa.gov/Software/NPB/.)

```
DO J=1,LASTROW-FIRSTROW+1
   SUM = 0.D0
   DO K=ROWSTR(J),ROWSTR(J+1)-1
      SUM = SUM + A(K)*P(COLIDX(K))
   ENDDO
   W(J) = SUM
ENDDO
```

This code uses the row pointer, column index sparse matrix representation discussed earlier. Note that the matrix is represented by the vector A, which is multiplied by elements from the vector P. However, a gather using COLIDX must be performed for each access of P. Note that COLIDX has the same number of elements as A. If each of these uses 64-bit data, the memory bandwidth requirements is double that of just the nonzero elements contained in A. Observe that ROWSTR and the output array W are both of size N.

For good performance on memory intensive problems, data must be prefetched into memory. Although the matrix A and the vector COLIDX can be easily prefetched, the vector P is a problem. Techniques for prefetching gather/scatter operations were discussed in Chapter 5. As noted there, to prefetch a gather usually requires a compiler directive or pragma to be effective. A long loop length also helps. However, the size of the inner loop in sparse iterative solvers is the number of nonzero elements in a column (or row). This tends to be small, perhaps only a dozen or so. Thus, getting good performance from gather/scatters is made even more difficult.

At worst, performance is determined by the speed that data can be loaded from memory, which, as we discussed, is poor.

11.7.3 Parallel Performance — It's Good!

We've discussed some drawbacks of sparse solvers, but one place where they excel is parallelism. This is because, as discussed in Chapter 10, a matrix-vector multiply is easy to parallelize and a sparse matrix-vector multiply is nearly as simple. The $O(n)$ components of the system do require some amount of communication, but it is small. Further more, if there are n processors, each processor can be given $1 / n^{th}$ of the matrix to process. So if the matrix and large index vector require 100 gigabytes of data and the matrix is to be solved using 100 processors, each processor needs only one gigabyte of data!

Look at the above code fragment again. The vector P needs to be available on all processors, but this data needs only to be loaded. The array W can be divided between processors as are A and COLIDX. Figure 11-6 shows how the data structure in the above code can be divided between processors. Only the P vector needs to be shared among processors.

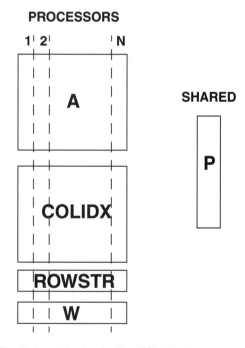

Figure 11-6   Parallel partitioning for the CG algorithm.

Since performance is determined by the ability of the computer to get data from memory, parallelism is limited by the memory bandwidth of a system. For example, suppose a computer can deliver four GB/s of memory bandwidth and each processor can request and receive one GB/s. Then the parallel performance is limited to four times the original performance no matter how many processors are actually on the system. This can render most of the processors on a system useless. For this reason and the small amount of data communication required, clusters of workstations using a low bandwidth interconnect and MPI for parallelism, can be very effective for iterative algorithms. In this case, the vector P may be replicated in the memory of each workstation. While this increases the memory requirements, the total amount of memory traffic is reduced.

11.8 Summary

You've just had a very high level view of some techniques of numerical linear algebra. Hopefully, you've gotten a flavor of how these routines can be optimized using high performance building blocks and the techniques we discussed in Chapters 5 and 10. The linear algebra routines for the BLAS, LINPACK, LAPACK and ScaLAPACK can all be found at `http://www.netlib.org/`. The routines comprising PLAPACK are located at `http://www.cs.utexas.edu/users/plapack/`. So if your computer vendor doesn't provide these, you can "roll your own" to obtain good performance.

References:

The following texts are excellent resources for linear algebra algorithms:

1. Bailey, D.; Barszcz, E.; Barton, J.; Browning, D.; Carter, R.; Dagum, L.; Fatoohi, R.; Fineberg, S.; Frederickson, P.; Lasinski, T.; Schreiber, R.; Simon, H.; Venkatakrishnan, V.; Weeratunga, S. *The NAS Parallel Benchmarks*. RNR Technical Report RNR-94-007, 1994.

2. Demmel, J. W. *Applied Numerical Linear Algebra*. Philadelphia: SIAM, 1997, ISBN 0-89871-389-7.

3. Dongarra, J. J.; Duff, I. S.; Sorensen, D. C.; van der Vorst, H. A. *Numerical Linear Algebra for High-Performance Computers*. Philadelphia: SIAM, 1998, ISBN 0-89871-428-1.

4. George, A.; Liu, J. W. H. *The Evolution of the Minimum Degree Ordering Algorithm*. SIAM Review, Vol. 31, 1-19, 1989.

5. Golub, G. H.; Van Loan, C. F. *Matrix Computations*. Baltimore: Johns Hopkins, 1993, ISBN 0-89871-414-1.

6. Hestenes, M. R; Stiefel, E. *Methods of Conjugate Gradients for Solving Linear Systems*. J. Res. Nat. Bur. Standards, Vol. 49, 409-435, 1952.

7. Karypis, G.; Kumar, V. *A Fast and High Quality Multilevel Scheme for Partitioning Irregular Graphs*. SIAM J. on Scientific Computing, Vol. 20, 359-392, 1998.

CHAPTER 1 2

High Performance Algorithms and Approaches for Signal Processing

Fourier is a mathematical poem.

Lord Kelvin

12.1 Introduction

Many signal and image processing applications generate large amounts of data which must be analyzed to find the interesting information. This is often done using convolutions and Discrete Fourier Transforms (DFTs) to filter the data. Some examples of their use are:

- To locate oil, petroleum companies set off explosions near potential deposits and then measure the amount of time it takes for the shock waves to be picked up by sensors. The sensors' signals are processed to determine where to drill.

- Astronomers working with data obtained from telescopes try to locate objects such as black holes by processing the image data to extract data in certain ranges.

- Fighter pilots need to be able to locate hostile missiles that are approaching. Data from on-board sensors are processed to highlight threats.

- Images obtained from sensors need to be processed to match the resolution of different output media, depending on whether the images are to be printed on paper or displayed on computers. Appropriate filters are applied, depending on the situation.

As we shall see, there is a close relationship between convolutions and DFTs. It's somewhat like the equivalence of matter and energy or the wave/particle duality. Convolutions can be defined in terms of DFTs, and DFTs can be defined in terms of convolutions.

Because of the rich set of algorithms related to convolutions and FFTs, there are opportunities to apply many of the techniques defined in earlier sections to improve performance. These include:

- Unroll and jam

- Replacing $O(n^2)$ algorithms by $O(n \log n)$ algorithms

- Removing non-unit stride data accesses

- Using the knowledge of the data type to reduce operations (real arithmetic vs. complex arithmetic)

- Decreasing the number of memory instructions

- Decreasing the number of floating-point instructions

- Decreasing cache misses

Once again, we're going to try to give an overview of some of the most important optimizations in a very broad field. For more detailed information, see Charles Van Loan's excellent text on Fourier Transform algorithms [9].

12.2 Convolutions and Correlations

Convolutions and correlations can be the highest performing algorithm on any architecture since the floating-point operation to memory operation ratio can be made very large. This ratio is limited only by the number of hardware registers.

Convolutions and correlations are defined as follows: Let $\{x_0,...x_{m+n-1}\}$, $\{w_0,...w_{n-1}\}$, $\{y_0,...,y_{m-1}\}$ be vectors. y is the *convolution* of x and w if

$$y_k = y_k + \sum_{i=0}^{n-1} x_{i+k} w_{n-i} \qquad k = 0, 1, ..., m-1$$

y is the *correlation* of x and w if

$$y_k = y_k + \sum_{i=0}^{n-1} x_{i+k} w_i \qquad k = 0, 1, ..., m-1$$

Since the only difference between a convolution and correlation is the direction of access for the w array, the correlation formulation will be used in the analysis below. We'll sometimes refer to x as the input vector, w as the weight vector, and y as the output vector. Note that the correlation can be formulated as a matrix-vector multiplication:

$$\begin{bmatrix} x_0 & x_1 & x_2 & \cdots & x_{n-1} \\ x_1 & x_2 & x_3 & \cdots & x_n \\ x_2 & x_3 & x_4 & \cdots & x_{n+1} \\ \cdot & \cdot & \cdot & \cdots & \cdot \\ x_{m-1} & x_m & x_{m+1} & \cdots & x_{m+n-1} \end{bmatrix} \begin{bmatrix} w_0 \\ w_1 \\ w_2 \\ \cdot \\ w_{n-1} \end{bmatrix} = \begin{bmatrix} y_0 \\ y_1 \\ y_2 \\ \cdot \\ y_{m-1} \end{bmatrix}$$

12.2.1 Code

The code to implement a correlation can be written as

```
for (i = 0; i < m; i++)
{
  y[i] = 0.;
  for (j = 0; j < n; j++)
    y[i] += x[i+j] * w[j];
}
```

There are two ways to think of the correlation. As written above, it is dot product based since the inner loop can be replaced by a call to a dot product routine. However, by swapping the loops, it becomes DAXPY based. The best choice between these two depends on the relative sizes of m and n. If n is extremely short, the DAXPY version might have better performance than the dot product version. In general, the dot production formulation is better. However, both of these ignore the true potential of the kernel.

12.2.2 Unroll and Jam

The key to improving performance is to notice the reuse of the values from the array x. All but one of the elements loaded for an iteration of i are reused on the next iteration. Therefore, the unroll and jam technique can increase the performance dramatically. Unrolling each of the loops by two produces

```
mend = (m >> 1) << 1;
nend = (n >> 1) << 1;
for (i = 0; i < mend; i += 2)
{
  y[i] = y[i+1] = 0.;
```

```
  for (j = 0; j < nend; j += 2)
  {
    y[i]   += x[i+j] * w[j];
    y[i+1] += x[i+j+1] * w[j];
    y[i]   += x[i+j+1] * w[j+1];
    y[i+1] += x[i+j+2] * w[j+1];
  }
  if (nend != n)
  {
    y[i]   += x[i+j] * w[j];
    y[i+1] += x[i+j+1] * w[j];
  }
}
if (mend != m)
{
  y[i] = 0.;
  for (j = 0; j < n; j++)
    y[i] += x[i+j] * w[j];
}
```

The original formulation contained two loads and two floating-point operations (the references to y having been hoisted and sunk). The unrolled code above has five loads and eight floating-point operations in the main loops. By increasing the amount of unrolling on both loops, the F:M ratio can be increased further. The best factors for m and n depend on the typical sizes of m and n and the number of registers available. Too much unrolling will cause registers to be spilled. Table 12-1 compares the operations using the original code and various unrolling factors on both loops.

Table 12-1   Correlation Performance.

I unroll factor	J unroll factor	Floating-point operations per iteration	Memory operations per iteration	F:M ratio
1	1	2	2	1.00
2	2	8	5	1.60
3	3	18	8	2.25
4	4	32	13	2.46
p	q	$2pq$	$p+2q-1$	$2pq/(p+2q-1)$
p	p	$2pp$	$3p-1$	$2p/3$ for p large

12.2.3 Cache Considerations

Correlations are especially cache friendly. Large problem sizes for many applications are only a few thousand points, which easily fit in most data caches. Even if the data is not in-cache to begin with, the reuse of each point is so large that performance is usually excellent.

12.2.4 Higher Dimensions

The original correlation was one-dimensional since all the data structures were vectors. Correlations can also be defined for multiple dimensions. Let y be an array of size $m_1 \times m_2$, w be of size $n_1 \times n_2$, and x be of size $(m_1 + n_1 - 1) \times (m_2 + n_2 - 1)$. A two-dimensional correlation y of x and w is defined by

$$y_{k_1, k_2} = y_{k_1, k_2} + \sum_{i_1 = 0}^{n_1 - 1} \sum_{i_2 = 0}^{n_2 - 1} x_{i_1 + k_1, i_2 + k_2} w_{i_1, i_2}$$

$$k_1 = 0, 1, ..., m_1 - 1, \ k_2 = 0, 1, ..., m_2 - 1$$

This formulation is used when filtering two-dimensional objects such as images. Two-dimensional correlations have even more data reuse than one-dimensional correlations, so they can use unroll and jam in both dimensions to achieve even better performance than one-dimensional correlations. Three-dimensional correlations can also be defined in an analogous fashion.

12.3 DFTs/FFTs

12.3.1 Definition of DFT

The Fast Fourier Transform (FFT) is the most widely used algorithm spanning almost all disciplines. Most notably, FFTs are used extensively in signal and image processing. Let $x = \{x_0, ..., x_{n-1}\}$. The *forward one-dimensional Discrete Fourier Transform (DFT)* of x is defined as

$$y_k = \sum_{j = 0}^{n - 1} x_j \omega_n^{jk} \qquad k = 0, 1, ..., n - 1$$

where ω_n is the complex vector

$$\omega_n = e^{\frac{-2\pi i}{n}} = \cos\left(\frac{2\pi}{n}\right) - i\sin\left(\frac{2\pi}{n}\right) \qquad i^2 = -1$$

The *inverse one-dimensional DFT* is created by negating the sign on the exponent and scaling, and is defined by

$$y_k = \frac{1}{n} \sum_{j=0}^{n-1} x_j \omega_n^{-jk} \qquad k = 0, 1, \dots, n-1$$

Some definitions have the scaling by $1/n$ on the forward transform, some on the inverse transform, and some scale both the forward and inverse transforms by $1/(\sqrt{n})$. Since the scaling takes only n operations, it will be ignored in the analysis below.

DFTs were implemented on early computers, but their use was restricted by the large number of computations required. To calculate a DFT of length n directly requires a matrix-vector multiplication.

$$\begin{bmatrix} \omega_n^0 & \omega_n^0 & \omega_n^0 & \dots & \omega_n^0 \\ \omega_n^0 & \omega_n^1 & \omega_n^2 & \dots & \omega_n^{n-1} \\ \omega_n^0 & \omega_n^2 & \omega_n^4 & \dots & \omega_n^{2(n-1)} \\ . & . & . & \dots & . \\ \omega_n^0 & \omega_n^{n-1} & \omega_n^{2(n-1)} & \dots & \omega_n^{(n-1)(n-1)} \end{bmatrix} \begin{bmatrix} x_0 \\ x_1 \\ x_2 \\ . \\ x_{n-1} \end{bmatrix} = \begin{bmatrix} y_0 \\ y_1 \\ y_2 \\ . \\ y_{n-1} \end{bmatrix}$$

If the input data consists of complex numbers and the calculation of the powers of ω_n are ignored, $8\,n^2$ real floating-point operations are required. Thus, a one-dimensional direct Fourier Transform (FT) is an $O(n^2)$ algorithm.

Fourier transforms are important since they allow data sequences to move from the time domain to the frequency domain and vice versa. For example, suppose you record the temperature at noon every day for ten years. This is an example of a sequence that is a linear function of time (days). The DFT of the input returns data that is a function of frequency (1/day). A filter may be applied to this output sequence to remove noise. Subsequently, an inverse DFT may be applied to return the data to the time domain.

In 1965 Cooley and Tukey [6] dramatically altered the nature of signal processing by deriving the FFT algorithm that greatly reduced the number of operations required. For an input size of 2^n, their algorithm took only $5n\ log_2\ n$ floating-point operations. (In general, FFTs will be defined as techniques to implement one-dimensional DFTs with $O(n\ log\ n)$ computations.)

The speedup by using a FFT instead of a direct FT is immense. Table 12-2 compares the number of floating-point operations required for direct FTs and FFTs for powers of 32.

Table 12-2   Direct FT Versus FFT Operations.

Length	Power of two	Direct FT floating-point operations	FFT floating-point operations	Speedup
32	5	8.192×10^3	8.000×10^2	10.24
1024	10	8.388×10^6	5.120×10^4	163.8
32,768	15	8.589×10^9	2.458×10^6	3495.
1,048,576	20	8.000×10^{12}	1.049×10^9	83886.
33,554,432	25	9.007×10^{15}	4.194×10^{10}	2147483.

The larger the size of n, the larger the reduction. FFT algorithms have spawned thousands of books and articles, a few of which are listed as references at the end of this chapter. Although FFTs caused a revolution in scientific computing, some FFT algorithm steps have unfortunate characteristics for high performance computers that include

- a separate permutation step
- temporary data storage
- non-unit stride data accesses
- short inner loop lengths
- low floating-point operation to memory operation ratio
- vectors accessed in the inner loop may be a multiple of the cache size apart (pathologically bad accesses)

12.3.2   FFTs for $n = 2^m$

The most widely use FFTs are *radix-2* algorithms. That is, they operate on an input sequence whose length is a power of two. To understand the idea behind FFTs, consider the matrix formed by the ω_n^k. The elements of the matrix are all n^{th} roots of unity since $\omega_n^{nk} = 1$. The ω_n^k matrix has interesting characteristics. The first FFT algorithm by Cooley and Tukey factored a permutation of the matrix into $log_2\, n$ sparse matrices. By permuting the input array and multiplying by these sparse matrices, the DFT was produced. Each of the sparse matrices has only two nonzero entries per row. Furthermore, each data point is naturally paired with another point so that the operations done on these two points consist of a complex multiplication, a complex addition, and a complex subtraction. To calculate the number of floating-point operations, note that there are log_2 independent matrices or steps and each step accesses all n points. For every two points in each step, there are three complex operations, or 10 floating-point operations. Therefore, the operation count for the FFT is

(10 floating-point operations / 2 points) $\times$ n points $\times$ log_2 n steps = $5n$ log_2 n operations

For $n = 4$, the matrix of $\omega_n{}^k$ is

$$
\begin{bmatrix}
\omega_4^0 & \omega_4^0 & \omega_4^0 & \omega_4^0 \\
\omega_4^0 & \omega_4^1 & \omega_4^2 & \omega_4^3 \\
\omega_4^0 & \omega_4^2 & \omega_4^4 & \omega_4^6 \\
\omega_4^0 & \omega_4^3 & \omega_4^6 & \omega_4^9
\end{bmatrix}
$$

However, by definition, ω_4 is the fourth root of one, so $\omega_4^4 = 1 = \omega_4^0$. Some of the elements in the matrix can be reduced by factoring by ω_4^4, resulting in

$$
\begin{bmatrix}
\omega_4^0 & \omega_4^0 & \omega_4^0 & \omega_4^0 \\
\omega_4^0 & \omega_4^1 & \omega_4^2 & \omega_4^3 \\
\omega_4^0 & \omega_4^2 & \omega_4^0 & \omega_4^2 \\
\omega_4^0 & \omega_4^3 & \omega_4^2 & \omega_4^1
\end{bmatrix}
$$

There are eight factorizations of this matrix or one of its permutations that are used by FFT algorithms. Three factorizations of the matrix for $n = 4$ that result in the DFT are shown below.

$$
\begin{bmatrix}
\omega_4^0 & 0 & \omega_4^0 & 0 \\
0 & \omega_4^0 & 0 & \omega_4^1 \\
\omega_4^0 & 0 & \omega_4^2 & 0 \\
0 & \omega_4^0 & 0 & \omega_4^3
\end{bmatrix}
\times
\begin{bmatrix}
\omega_4^0 & \omega_4^0 & 0 & 0 \\
\omega_4^0 & \omega_4^2 & 0 & 0 \\
0 & 0 & \omega_4^0 & \omega_4^0 \\
0 & 0 & \omega_4^0 & \omega_4^2
\end{bmatrix}
\times
\begin{bmatrix}
x_0 \\
x_2 \\
x_1 \\
x_3
\end{bmatrix}
=
\begin{bmatrix}
y_0 \\
y_1 \\
y_2 \\
y_3
\end{bmatrix}
$$

$$
\begin{bmatrix}
\omega_4^0 & \omega_4^0 & 0 & 0 \\
\omega_4^0 & \omega_4^2 & 0 & 0 \\
0 & 0 & \omega_4^0 & \omega_4^1 \\
0 & 0 & \omega_4^0 & \omega_4^3
\end{bmatrix}
\times
\begin{bmatrix}
\omega_4^0 & 0 & \omega_4^0 & 0 \\
0 & \omega_4^0 & 0 & \omega_4^0 \\
\omega_4^0 & 0 & \omega_4^2 & 0 \\
0 & \omega_4^0 & 0 & \omega_4^2
\end{bmatrix}
\times
\begin{bmatrix} x_0 \\ x_1 \\ x_2 \\ x_3 \end{bmatrix}
=
\begin{bmatrix} y_0 \\ y_2 \\ y_1 \\ y_3 \end{bmatrix}
$$

$$
\begin{bmatrix}
\omega_4^0 & \omega_4^0 & 0 & 0 \\
0 & 0 & \omega_4^0 & \omega_4^1 \\
\omega_4^0 & \omega_4^1 & 0 & 0 \\
0 & 0 & \omega_4^0 & \omega_4^3
\end{bmatrix}
\times
\begin{bmatrix}
\omega_4^0 & 0 & \omega_4^0 & 0 \\
0 & \omega_4^0 & 0 & \omega_4^0 \\
\omega_4^0 & 0 & \omega_4^0 & 0 \\
0 & \omega_4^0 & 0 & \omega_4^2
\end{bmatrix}
\times
\begin{bmatrix} x_0 \\ x_1 \\ x_2 \\ x_3 \end{bmatrix}
=
\begin{bmatrix} y_0 \\ y_1 \\ y_2 \\ y_3 \end{bmatrix}
$$

In the first set of matrices, the input array was reordered by swapping x_j with its bit-reversed position. This is found by taking the index (zero-based) of the position, writing its binary representation, reversing bits, and using this as the index to exchange with. For example, if $n = 32$, the data at location $13_{10} = 01101_2$ must be swapped with the data at location $10110_2 = 22_{10}$. The second set of matrices requires this permutation to be performed on the output array. The third set does not require a permutation of the input or output data to obtain the DFT.

The next few sections contrast the eight radix-2 sparse factorizations.

12.3.3 The FFT Algorithms

There are several components to each of the $log_2\, n$ FFT steps. These include

- input array
- work array
- array of powers of ω_n^k (hereafter referred to as the trigonometric or trig array)
- permutation requirements
- stride on the arrays
- loop length

In each step, we would like

- no work array
- trig array loads hoisted outside the inner loop
- no permutation step
- all inner loop data accesses to be unit stride
- a long inner loop length

12.3.3.1   Direct Fourier Transforms

As is often the case, we can't have everything we want. None of the eight FFT factorizations contains all the desirable characteristics listed above. We must choose the ones that have the best characteristics for a particular architecture. This chapter contains many code snippets to illustrate the characteristics of the different FFT algorithms.

For comparison, the following direct FT code is given:

```
      SUBROUTINE DIRECT(N,X,WORK,IS)
C DIRECT FOURIER TRANSFORM
C
C X IS THE ARRAY OF DATA TO BE TRANSFORMED
C N IS THE NUMBER OF DATA POINTS
C M IS THE POWER OF 2 SUCH THAT N = 2**M
C IS =  1 FOR FORWARD TRANSFORM
C IS = -1 FOR INVERSE TRANSFORM
      IMPLICIT NONE
      INTEGER N, I, J, IS
      REAL TWOPI, ANGLE, AMULT
      COMPLEX X(0:*), WORK(0:*), U
      PARAMETER (TWOPI = -2.0 * 3.14159265358979323844)
      DO I = 0,N-1
        WORK(I) = CMPLX(0.0,0.0)
        DO J = 0,N-1
          ANGLE = (IS*TWOPI*I*J)/REAL(N)
          U = CEXP(CMPLX(0.,ANGLE))
          WORK(I) = WORK(I) + U * X(J)
        ENDDO
      ENDDO
      IF (IS .EQ. 1) THEN
        AMULT = 1.0
      ELSE
        AMULT = 1.0 / N
      ENDIF
      DO I = 0,N-1
        X(I) = AMULT*WORK(I)
      ENDDO
      END
```

As shown in the sample factorizations for $n = 4$ above, some FFTs require the data to be changed to bit-reversed order at the beginning or the end of processing. Following is a routine that performs this operation:

```
        SUBROUTINE BIT_REVERSE_ORDER(N,X)
        IMPLICIT NONE
        INTEGER N, J, I, M
        COMPLEX X(*), TEMP
        J = 1
        DO I = 1,N
          IF (J .GT. I) THEN
            TEMP = X(I)
            X(I) = X(J)
            X(J) = TEMP
          ENDIF
          M = N / 2
100       IF ((M .GE. 2) .AND. (J .GT. M)) THEN
            J = J - M
            M = M / 2
            GOTO 100
          ENDIF
          J = J + M
        ENDDO
        END
```

12.3.3.2   DIT and DIF Factorizations

There are a total of eight different radix-2 sparse factorizations. These factorizations of the ω_n^k matrix fall into two groups: *decimation-in-time* (DIT) factorizations or *decimation-in-frequency* (DIF) factorizations. When Cooley and Tukey derived the first FFT, they considered the input vector x to be a function of time and the output vector y to be a function of frequency. They defined $m = n/2$ and split (decimated) the x (time component) of the DFT as

$$y_k = \sum_{j=0}^{m-1} x_{2j}\omega_n^{2jk} + \sum_{j=0}^{m-1} x_{2j+1}\omega_n^{(2j+1)k} = \sum_{j=0}^{m-1} x_{2j}\omega_m^{jk} + \omega_n^k \sum_{j=0}^{m-1} x_{2j+1}\omega_m^{jk}$$

Note that the summations use only the even or odd values of x and that ω_m^{jk} is in both terms and can be factored out. This splitting process continues for $log_2\ n$ steps to create the Cooley-Tukey FFT. For $n = 4$, this is the first FFT factorization shown in Section 12.3.2. There are three other splittings of the x vector that results in a FFT. In similar fashion, the y vector may be split to produce the four DIF factorizations. These are dual transforms to the DIT transforms and are also obtained by performing all the DIT computations in reverse order.

Since DIT factorizations split the *x* vector, they may also reorder (permute) *x*. As a result, when a permutation of *x* is required for a DIT algorithm, it is the first step of these algorithms. Therefore, when a permutation is required for a DIF algorithm, it must be the last step.

12.3.3.3   DIT Factorizations

The code for four DIT factorizations is shown below. The load of the elements of the trig array, denoted by U, is hoisted outside the inner loop in the example codes. Due to the large cost of calculating the trig array values, production codes usually precalculate these and load them from a temporary storage area. The following Fortran code uses the C preprocessor, cpp, to produce variants of the Cooley-Tukey, Pease, Stockham, or transposed Stockham FFT:

```
      SUBROUTINE DIT(N,M,X,WORK,IS)
C DECIMATION-IN-TIME APPROACHES
C
C X IS THE ARRAY OF DATA TO BE TRANSFORMED
C N IS THE NUMBER OF DATA POINTS
C M IS THE POWER OF 2 SUCH THAT N = 2**M
C IS =  1 FOR FORWARD TRANSFORM
C IS = -1 FOR INVERSE TRANSFORM

      IMPLICIT  NONE
      INTEGER   M, N, IS
      COMPLEX X(*), WORK(*)

#IF COOLEY-TUKEY || PEASE
      CALL BIT_REVERSE_ORDER(N,X)
#ENDIF
      CALL FFT_DIT_COMPUTE(IS,M,X,WORK)
      END


      SUBROUTINE FFT_DIT_COMPUTE (IS,M,X,WORK)
C
C COMPUTE PHASE
C
      IMPLICIT NONE
      INTEGER M, N, NS, L, LS, I, IS, N2
      REAL    AMULT
      COMPLEX X(*), WORK(*)
      N = 2**M
      N2 = N / 2
      IF (IS .EQ. 1) THEN
       AMULT = 1.0
      ELSEIF (IS .EQ. -1) THEN
       AMULT = 1.0 / N
      ENDIF
      DO L = 0,M-1
```

```
      LS = 2**L
      NS = N2 / LS
      CALL FFT_DIT_APPROACHES (LS,NS,X,WORK,IS)
      DO I = 1,N
       X(I) = WORK(I)
      ENDDO
     ENDDO
     DO I = 1,N
      X(I) = AMULT*X(I)
     ENDDO
     END

     SUBROUTINE FFT_DIT_APPROACHES (LS,NS,X,Y,IS)
     IMPLICIT NONE
     INTEGER M, N, NS, L, LS, I, J, IS
     REAL    PI, ANGLE
     COMPLEX U, C
#IF COOLEY-TUKEY
     COMPLEX X(LS,2,NS), Y(LS,2,NS)
#ELIF PEASE
     COMPLEX X(2,NS,LS), Y(NS,LS,2)
#ELIF STOCKHAM
     COMPLEX X(NS,2,LS), Y(NS,LS,2)
#ELIF STOCKHAM-TRANSPOSED
     COMPLEX X(LS,NS,2), Y(LS,2,NS)
#ENDIF
     PARAMETER (PI = 3.14159265358979323844)
     ANGLE = -PI*IS/LS
     DO I = 1,LS
        U = CEXP(CMPLX(0.,((I-1)*ANGLE)))
        DO J = 1,NS
#IF COOLEY-TUKEY
           C = U * X(I,2,J)
           Y(I,1,J) = X(I,1,J) + C
           Y(I,2,J) = X(I,1,J) - C
#ELIF PEASE
           C = U * X(2,J,I)
           Y(J,I,1) = X(1,J,I) + C
           Y(J,I,2) = X(1,J,I) - C
#ELIF STOCKHAM
           C = U * X(J,2,I)
           Y(J,I,1) = X(J,1,I) + C
           Y(J,I,2) = X(J,1,I) - C
#ELIF STOCKHAM-TRANSPOSED
           C = U * X(I,J,2)
           Y(I,1,J) = X(I,J,1) + C
           Y(I,2,J) = X(I,J,1) - C
#ENDIF
```

```
       ENDDO
    ENDDO
    END
```

12.3.3.4   Cooley-Tukey

The Cooley-Tukey factorization started the revolution, so it's useful to analyze in detail. As discussed earlier, it requires a permutation of the input data before any calculations are begun. The computational component of the code performs

```
COMPLEX X(LS,2,NS), Y(LS,2,NS)
...
DO I = 1,LS
   U = CEXP(CMPLX(0.,((I-1)*ANGLE)))
   DO J = 1,NS
      C = U * X(I,2,J)
      Y(I,1,J) = X(I,1,J) + C
      Y(I,2,J) = X(I,1,J) - C
   ENDDO
ENDDO
```

Note that the X and Y arrays have the same size and are accessed in the same order. Therefore, the Y array (i.e., the work array) is superfluous and can be replaced by the X array. The inner loop starts at $n/2$ and shrinks by a factor of two with each of the $log_2 n$ steps. The X accesses are not unit stride, though. To obtain this requires exchanging the loop indices, which brings the trig array accesses into the inner loop. Now the size of the inner loop starts at one and grows by a multiple of two with each of the $log_2 n$ steps. Regardless of whether the I loop or the J loop is innermost, there will be steps with a very short inner loop length. The unit stride code without a work array appears as follows:

```
COMPLEX X(LS,2,NS)
...
DO J = 1,NS
   DO I = 1,LS
      U = CEXP(CMPLX(0.,((I-1)*ANGLE)))
      C = U * X(I,2,J)
      X(I,2,J) = X(I,1,J) - C
      X(I,1,J) = X(I,1,J) + C
   ENDDO
ENDDO
```

12.3.3.5   Pease

The starting point for this algorithm is the code

```
COMPLEX X(2,NS,LS), Y(NS,LS,2)
...
DO I = 1,LS
  U = CEXP(CMPLX(0.,((I-1)*ANGLE)))
  DO J = 1,NS
    C = U * X(2,J,I)
    Y(J,I,1) = X(1,J,I) + C
    Y(J,I,2) = X(1,J,I) - C
  ENDDO
ENDDO
```

Pease noticed that this FFT has the J and I indices adjacent in X and Y. Therefore, the two loops can be combined into a single loop as

```
COMPLEX X(2,NS*LS), Y(NS*LS,2)
...
DO JI = 1,NS*LS
  I = (JI-1)/NS
  U = CEXP(CMPLX(0.,(I*ANGLE)))
  C = U * X(2,JI)
  Y(JI,1) = X(1,JI) + C
  Y(JI,2) = X(1,JI) - C
ENDDO
```

The advantage of this approach is that the loop length is always $n/2$. However, it requires a work array, the accesses of X have a stride of two elements, and if there is a temporary trig array to hold all the precomputed trig values, it will be of size $(n/2) \log_2 n$.

12.3.3.6   Stockham and Transposed Stockham

Stockham autosort algorithms [5] don't need a separate permutation step since each of the $\log_2 n$ steps performs part of the permutation.

```
COMPLEX X(NS,2,LS), Y(NS,LS,2)
...
DO I = 1,LS
  U = CEXP(CMPLX(0.,((I-1)*ANGLE)))
  DO J = 1,NS
    C = U * X(J,2,I)
    Y(J,I,1) = X(J,1,I) + C
    Y(J,I,2) = X(J,1,I) - C
  ENDDO
ENDDO
```

The Stockham code also has unit stride array accesses. The drawbacks are that there must be a work array and the inner loop length decreases with each step. The transposed Stockham algorithm is obtained by starting with

```
COMPLEX X(LS,NS,2), Y(LS,2,NS)

...

DO I = 1,LS
   U = CEXP(CMPLX(0.,((I-1)*ANGLE)))
   DO J = 1,NS
      C = U * X(I,J,2)
      Y(I,1,J) = X(I,J,1) + C
      Y(I,2,J) = X(I,J,1) - C
   ENDDO
ENDDO
```

and exchanging the I and J loops. Note that the scalar U becomes a vector which must be loaded in the inner loop.

```
COMPLEX X(LS,NS,2), Y(LS,2,NS), U(LS)

...

DO I = 1,LS
   U(I) = CEXP(CMPLX(0.,((I-1)*ANGLE)))
ENDDO
DO J = 1,NS
   DO I = 1,LS
      C = U(I) * X(I,J,2)
      Y(I,1,J) = X(I,J,1) + C
      Y(I,2,J) = X(I,J,1) - C
   ENDDO
ENDDO
```

The transposed Stockham code does not require a permutation and has unit data accesses, but must load the trig coefficients in the inner loop. The inner loop size starts small and grows with each step.

12.3.3.7 Comparing the Four DIT Transforms

Now that the four DIT algorithms have been defined and discussed, they are compared in Table 12-3 to highlight the advantages and disadvantages of each.

Table 12-3 DIT FFT Algorithms and Their Features.

	Cooley-Tukey	Pease	Stockham	Transposed Stockham
Permutation required?	✓	✓		
Work array required?		✓	✓	✓
Constant inner loop length?		✓		
Trig array loads in inner loop?	✓	✓		✓
Unit stride everywhere?	✓		✓	✓

Which of the above features are most important on modern computers? Software libraries that include FFT routines contain extensive optimizations, but we'll make some high-level observations. The DIT algorithms above were implemented in routines very similar to the examples shown. The only difference was that the calculation of the trig array was performed in a separate initialization step which was not included in the measurements. This is consistent with how vendors implement production FFT routines. So, for example, the Stockham code appeared as

```
COMPLEX X(NS,2,LS), Y(NS,LS,2), UU(*)
...
DO I = 1,LS
  U = UU(I)
  DO J = 1,NS
    C = U * X(J,2,I)
    Y(J,I,1) = X(J,1,I) + C
    Y(J,I,2) = X(J,1,I) - C
  ENDDO
ENDDO
```

This code was executed on a PA-8500 processor in an HP N-Class server for two data sizes: 64 and 1024. These used COMPLEX*8 data and both sets of data fit in the one MB data cache on this processor. Table 12-4 shows their performance.

Table 12-4   Performance for DIT FFT Algorithms.

n	Cooley-Tukey (Mflop/s)	Pease (Mflop/s)	Stockham (Mflop/s)	Transposed Stockham (Mflop/s)
64	96	119	120	112
1024	145	237	230	233

What do we learn from the results? Since all of the data fits in the data cache, the existence and size of the work array should not matter, nor should having the trig array values loaded in the inner loop or unit stride accesses. After the first call, all of this data is in-cache waiting to be accessed and no cache conflicts should occur since the data size is small. Indeed, none of these issues appears to make a difference. However, having a permutation or short inner loop length are major inhibitors of good performance. Thus, the Cooley-Tukey algorithm, which requires both a permutation and some short inner loop lengths, performs worse than the other routines. The effect of the permutation is more noticeable in the larger size problem. In the Pease algorithm, the advantage of a long loop length is offset by the disadvantage of performing a permutation. The fact that the Stockham algorithm does not require a permutation step makes it very popular. The disadvantage of requiring a work array of size n in the Pease and Stockham algorithms is usually not a big drawback. On systems with robust memory systems such as vector computers, memory bandwidth is large enough to support this extra traffic. On cache based systems, different techniques are used for problems that are in-cache and out-of-cache. For problems that are in-cache, the additional work array is an issue only for problems that are close to exceeding the size of the cache.

The Stockham does have a noticeable advantage over the Pease algorithm regarding the data requirements for the trig array. A radix-2 Stockham algorithm needs only a trig array of size $n/2$, whereas the Pease algorithm needs to use $(n/2) \, log_2 \, n$ elements. For a problem of size 1024, the Stockham routine requires 512 trig elements, while the Pease routine uses 5120 elements. Thus for large problems, the large size of the trig array limits the usefulness of the Pease algorithm. To increase the inner loop length in the Stockham algorithm, the Stockham and transposed Stockham algorithms are sometimes coupled as follows [3]:

- Perform Stockham steps until the inner loop becomes very short
- Transpose the data
- Perform transposed Stockham steps

Thus, the loop length can be kept long at the expense of doing a transpose of the data. The transpose can also be moved inside the first transposed Stockham step [10].

12.3.3.8   DIF Transforms

By performing all the DIT computations and data movements in reverse, the DIF transforms are created. The first DIF transform derived was the dual of the Cooley-Tukey transform and is called the Gentleman-Sande transform. This appears as

```
COMPLEX X(LS,2,NS), Y(LS,2,NS)
...
DO I = 1,LS
  U = CEXP(CMPLX(0.,((I-1)*ANGLE)))
  DO J = 1,NS
    Y(I,1,J) = X(I,1,J) + X(I,2,J)
    Y(I,2,J) = U * (X(I,1,J) - X(I,2,J))
  ENDDO
ENDDO
```

All the advantages/disadvantages discussed so far for the individual DIT algorithms are shared by their DIF dual algorithms. Note that the DIF algorithms have the complex multiplication occurring as the last complex floating-point operation instead of the first one. DIT algorithms are used more often than DIF algorithms, and a later optimization uses the fact that DIT algorithms have the complex multiplication occurring before the other complex operations. Later discussions often use the DIT Stockham code.

12.3.4 Radix-4 and Radix-8 FFTs

Even when the trig array memory references are hoisted outside the inner loop, the radix-2 algorithms spend significant time performing memory operations. The number of operations in the inner loop appears in Table 12-5. The floating-point operation to memory operation ratio for the radix-2 algorithm is 10:8. Since many processors are able to execute two floating-point operations for each memory operation, a ratio of at least two is desired.

The FFTs defined so far operate on data that is a power of two in size. Any power of two is a power of four multiplied by two or one. Likewise, any power of two is a power of eight multiplied by four, two or one. Therefore, a power of two Fourier transform can be performed using $n/2$ radix-4 FFT steps followed by, at most, one radix-2 step.

To improve the F:M ratio on Cray vector computers, Bailey [1,2] combined two of the log_2 steps from the Stockham algorithm to generate a radix-4 Stockham step. The previous Stockham code examples have been redefined to use two-dimensional arrays instead of three-dimensional arrays. If two consecutive steps are combined in a single routine, they appear as follows:

```
SUBROUTINE FFT_DIT_APPROACHES (LS,NS,X,Y,Z,IS)
IMPLICIT NONE
INTEGER M, N, NS, L, LS, I, J, IS
REAL    PI, ANGLE
COMPLEX U, C
COMPLEX X(4*NS,LS), Y(2*NS,2*LS), Z(NS,4*LS)
PARAMETER (PI = 3.14159265358979323844)
ANGLE  = -PI*IS/(2*LS)
DO I = 1,LS
  U = CEXP(CMPLX(0.,(2*(I-1)*ANGLE)))
  DO J = 1,2*NS
    C = U * X(J+2*NS,I)
    Y(J,I) = X(J,I) + C
    Y(J,I+LS) = X(J,I) - C
  ENDDO
ENDDO
DO I = 1,2*LS
  U = CEXP(CMPLX(0.,((I-1)*ANGLE)))
  DO J = 1,NS
    C = U * Y(J+NS,I)
    Z(J,I) - Y(J,I) + C
    Z(J,I+2*LS) = Y(J,I) - C
  ENDDO
ENDDO
END
```

By unrolling the first J loop by two and unrolling the second I loop by two and jamming the resulting loops together, the four loops can be condensed back to two loops. The stores from the first step map exactly to the loads in the second step, so these memory references can be eliminated. The inner loop of this new kernel does four times the amount of work of the inner loop of the radix-2 kernel. Thus, one would expect to need four complex multiplications and eight complex additions. However, combining the steps allows one of the complex multiplications to be eliminated. Thus, the six associated real floating-point operations are eliminated and so there are only $4.25n \: log_2 \: n$ flops required. The forward radix-4 FFT routine is shown below.

```
SUBROUTINE FFT_DIT_APPROACHESF (LS,NS,X,Y,IS)
IMPLICIT NONE
INTEGER NS, LS, I, J, IS
REAL    PI, ANGLE
COMPLEX U1, U2, U3, C0, C1, C2, C3, D0, D1, D2, D3
COMPLEX X(4*NS,LS), Y(NS,4*LS)
PARAMETER (PI = 3.14159265358979323844)
ANGLE  = -PI/(2*LS)
```

```
DO I = 1,LS
   U1 = CEXP(CMPLX(0.,((I-1)*ANGLE)))
   U2 = U1 * U1
   U3 = U1 * U2
   DO J = 1,NS
      C0 =        X(J,I)
      C1 = U1 *  X(J+NS,I)
      C2 = U2 *  X(J+2*NS,I)
      C3 = U3 *  X(J+3*NS,I)

      D0 = C0 + C2
      D1 = C0 - C2
      D2 = C1 + C3
      D3 = CMPLX(0.,-1.)*(C1-C3)

      Y(J,I)       = D0 + D2
      Y(J,I+LS)    = D1 + D3
      Y(J,I+2*LS)  = D0 - D2
      Y(J,I+3*LS)  = D1 - D3
   ENDDO
ENDDO
END
```

Table 12-5 compares the number of operations for the two approaches. For the radix-4 kernel, the F:M ratio is 34:16. This process of using higher radices can continue, but as the radix is increased the number of floating point registers required grows rapidly. A radix-8 algorithm needs more floating-point registers than are available on most RISC processors. Only IA-64 processors and some vector processors have enough registers to benefit from using a radix-8 kernel, so the radix used should be carefully chosen.

Table 12-5 Comparison of Power of Two Radices.

	Radix-2		Radix-4		Radix-8	
	Complex	Real	Complex	Real	Complex	Real
Loads	2	4	4	8	8	16
Stores	2	4	4	8	8	16
Multiplications	1	4	3	12	7	28
Additions	2	6	8	22	16	46
$n \log_2 n$		5.00		4.25		4.08
F:M ratio		1.25		2.13		2.31

Some processors use 64-bit floating-point registers that allow the left and right 32-bit components of the register to be accessed independently. For these processors, COMPLEX*8 FFTs can be implemented using 64-bit loads and stores and 32-bit floating-point calculations. This increases the F:M ratio by a factor of two.

The radix-4 Stockham DIT algorithm has many good characteristics and will be used in following sections.

12.3.5 Maximize the Number of `fma` Instructions

As previously discussed, one goal of algorithm optimization is to make the F:M ratio as large as possible. As shown in Table 12-5, the F:M ratio is greater than two for radix-4 and radix-8 algorithms, so the dominance of floating-point operations allows the memory operations to be ignored in calculations of their theoretical peak performance.

Some kernels—for example, those used in matrix-matrix multiplication—are ideal for most processors since they have an equal number of multiplication and addition operations and these can be fused to use `fma` instructions. This is not the case with any of the FFT algorithms discussed so far. So how many instructions are required and what can be done to decrease the number of instructions?

Using real arithmetic operations, the radix-4 code is as follows:

```
SUBROUTINE FFT_DIT_APPROACHESF (LS,NS,X,Y,IS)
IMPLICIT NONE
INTEGER NS, LS, I, J, IS
REAL    PI, ANGLE
REAL U1R, U1I, U2R, U2I, U3R, U3I
REAL X1R, X1I, X2R, X2I, X3R, X3I
REAL C0R, C0I, C1R, C1I, C2R, C2I, C3R, C3I
REAL D0R, D0I, D1R, D1I, D2R, D2I, D3R, D3I
REAL Y0R, Y0I, Y1R, Y1I, Y2R, Y2I, Y3R, Y3I
COMPLEX X(4*NS,LS), Y(NS,4*LS)
PARAMETER (PI = 3.14159265358979323844)
ANGLE  = -PI/(2*LS)

DO I = 1,LS
  U1R = COS((I-1)*ANGLE)
  U1I = SIN((I-1)*ANGLE)
  U2R = U1R*U1R - U1I*U1I
  U2I = 2*U1R*U1I
  U3R = U1R*U2R - U1I*U2I
  U3I = U1R*U2I + U1I*U2R
  DO J = 1,NS
    C0R =  REAL(X(J,I))
    C0I = AIMAG(X(J,I))
    X1R =  REAL(X(J+NS,I))
    X1I = AIMAG(X(J+NS,I))
```

```
      X2R =   REAL(X(J+2*NS,I))
      X2I = AIMAG(X(J+2*NS,I))
      X3R =   REAL(X(J+3*NS,I))
      X3I = AIMAG(X(J+3*NS,I))

      C1R = U1R * X1R - U1I * X1I
      C1I = U1I * X1R + U1R * X1I
      C2R = U2R * X2R - U2I * X2I
      C2I = U2I * X2R + U2R * X2I
      C3R = U3R * X3R - U3I * X3I
      C3I = U3I * X3R + U3R * X3I

      D0R = C0R + C2R
      D0I = C0I + C2I
      D1R = C0R - C2R
      D1I = C0I - C2I
      D2R = C1R + C3R
      D2I = C1I + C3I
      D3R = C1I - C3I
      D3I = C3R - C1R

      Y0R = D0R + D2R
      Y0I = D0I + D2I
      Y2R = D0R - D2R
      Y2I = D0I - D2I
      Y1R = D1R + D3R
      Y1I = D1I + D3I
      Y3R = D1R - D3R
      Y3I = D1I - D3I

      Y(J,I)       = CMPLX(Y0R, Y0I)
      Y(J,I+LS)    = CMPLX(Y1R, Y1I)
      Y(J,I+2*LS)  = CMPLX(Y2R, Y2I)
      Y(J,I+3*LS)  = CMPLX(Y3R, Y3I)
    ENDDO
  ENDDO
  END
```

As shown above, this requires 12 real multiplications and 22 real additions. On computers with fma instructions, only half of the multiplications can map naturally to fma instructions. So there are six multiplications, six fma instructions, and 16 additions for a total of 28 instructions. Note that there were only 16 memory operations, so this kernel has a very nice 28:16 F:M ratio. Thus, the floating-point instructions dominate the memory instructions. Goedecker [7] found a way to decrease the total number of floating-point instructions by increasing the number of fma instructions.

FFT algorithms perform complex multiplications of an input array (x_r, x_i) by a trig array consisting of complex *(cosine(a), sine(a))* pairs. This multiplication produces

x_r *cosine(a)* $- x_i$ *sine(a)*
x_i *cosine(a)* $+ x_r$ *sine(a)*

which is composed of a multiplication, `fnma`, multiplication, and `fma`. Note that the two multiplications cannot be combined with additions to produce `fma` instructions. Goedecker realized that by producing *(cosine(a), sine(a)/cosine(a))* pairs, i.e., *(cosine(a), tangent(a))*, more `fma` instructions could be produced. The multiplication becomes

cosine(a) $(x_r - x_i$ *tangent(a))*
cosine(a) $(x_i + x_r$ *tangent(a))*

This still consists of a multiplication, `fnma`, multiplication, and `fma`, but now the two multiplication instructions are at the conclusion of the complex multiplication and can be fused with later additions and subtractions. The *(cosine(a), tangent(a))* pairs can be precomputed to replace the *(cosine(a), sine(a))* pairs or they can be recomputed with each step as the following code shows:

```
SUBROUTINE FFT_DIT_APPROACHESF (LS,NS,X,Y,IS)
IMPLICIT NONE
INTEGER NS, LS, I, J, IS
REAL    PI, ANGLE
REAL U1R, U1I, U2R, U2I, U3R, U3I
REAL X1R, X1I, X2R, X2I, X3R, X3I
REAL C0R, C0I, C1R, C1I, C2R, C2I, C3R, C3I
REAL D0R, D0I, D1R, D1I, D2R, D2I, D3R, D3I
REAL Y0R, Y0I, Y1R, Y1I, Y2R, Y2I, Y3R, Y3I
COMPLEX X(4*NS,LS), Y(NS,4*LS)
PARAMETER (PI = 3.14159265358979323844)
ANGLE  = -PI/(2*LS)

DO I = 1,LS
   U1R = COS((I-1)*ANGLE)
   U1I = SIN((I-1)*ANGLE)
   U2R = U1R*U1R - U1I*U1I
   U2I = 2*U1R*U1I
   U3R = U1R*U2R - U1I*U2I
   U3I = U1R*U2I + U1I*U2R

   U1I  = U1I / U1R
   U2I  = U2I / U2R
```

```
  U3I  = U3I / U3R
  U3R  = U3R / U1R
  DO J = 1,NS
    C0R =  REAL(X(J,I))
    C0I = AIMAG(X(J,I))
    X1R =  REAL(X(J+NS,I))
    X1I = AIMAG(X(J+NS,I))
    X2R =  REAL(X(J+2*NS,I))
    X2I = AIMAG(X(J+2*NS,I))
    X3R =  REAL(X(J+3*NS,I))
    X3I = AIMAG(X(J+3*NS,I))

    C1R = X1R - U1I * X1I
    C1I = U1I*X1R + X1I
    C2R = X2R - U2I * X2I
    C2I = U2I*X2R + X2I
    C3R = X3R - U3I * X3I
    C3I = U3I*X3R + X3I

    D0R = C0R + U2R  * C2R
    D0I = C0I + U2R  * C2I
    D2R = C0R - U2R  * C2R
    D2I = C0I - U2R  * C2I
    D1R = C1R + U3R * C3R
    D1I = C1I + U3R * C3I
    D3R = C1I - U3R * C3I
    D3I = C1R - U3R * C3R

    Y0R = D0R + U1R * D1R
    Y0I = D0I + U1R * D1I
    Y2R = D0R - U1R * D1R
    Y2I = D0I - U1R * D1I
    Y1R = D2R + U1R * D3R
    Y1I = D2I - U1R * D3I
    Y3R = D2R - U1R * D3R
    Y3I = D2I + U1R * D3I

    Y(J,I)      = CMPLX(Y0R, Y0I)
    Y(J,I+LS)   = CMPLX(Y1R, Y1I)
    Y(J,I+2*LS) = CMPLX(Y2R, Y2I)
    Y(J,I+3*LS) = CMPLX(Y3R, Y3I)
  ENDDO
ENDDO
END
```

There's only one nagging question about the above algorithm. What happens if $\alpha = 0$? This would cause a problem since *tangent(0)* is infinity, and this would be problematic for later computations. Strangely enough, using `fma` instructions in the code gets around this. There are three trig values that could cause problems: `u1r`, `u2r`, `u3r`. However, `u1r` never takes on the value zero since the values of the angle vary from 0 to $\pi * (\text{1s-1})/(2*\text{1s})$. Fortunately, the cosine of these values is always positive. `u2r` is a problem, though. It is calculated by squaring `(u1r,u1i)`. When `u1r` = $\sqrt{2}/2$ and `u1i` = -u1r, then `u2r` should equal zero. However, the calculation of `u2r` consists of `u1r*u1r - u1i*u1i` (a multiplication and an `fnma`). Also, $\sqrt{2}/2$ cannot be exactly represented in IEEE floating-point format. As discussed earlier, the `fnma` is performed with slightly higher precision than the multiplication. Therefore, the values of `u1r*u1r` and `u1i*u1i` are, literally, a bit different. Thus, the value of `u2r` is not exactly zero. However, if these preliminary operations do not use an `fnma` instruction, undefined values will result and the algorithm will fail! Although the number of floating-point operations performed actually increases to 44, the number of instructions decreases to 22 floating-point instructions, all of which are `fma` instructions.

It's a good time to analyze the theoretical performance of some of the algorithms discussed. Suppose a processor has a floating-point functional unit that can perform one multiplication, one addition, or one `fma` per cycle. The theoretical peak for the processor is two flops per cycle. (The Hewlett-Packard PA2.0 processors can perform double these rates, so scale accordingly for them.) Using a Stockham radix-2 algorithm, the inner loop of size $n/2$ has 10 floating-point operations. If these map to two multiplications, two `fma` instructions, and four additions, the processor can achieve, at most, 10 operations in eight clocks cycles, or 1.25 floating-point operations per clock cycle. Thus, the algorithm runs at 1.25 / 2 = 62.5% of peak. Another way to view this is that it requires $(8/10) \times 5n \, log_2 \, n = 4n \, log_2 \, n$ floating-point instructions.

A radix-4 Stockham algorithm requires 34 floating-point operations for an inner loop of size $n/4$ that performs two radix-2 steps. Goedecker's algorithm allows these to be done in 22 clocks. All power of two FFTs are assumed to use $5n \, log_2 \, n$ operations, so the radix-4 kernel has a theoretical peak of

$$(4 \times 10 / 34) \times (34 \text{ floating-point ops} / 22 \text{ clocks}) = 1.82 \text{ floating-point ops/clock}$$

which is 1.82 / 2 = 91% of peak. In terms of instructions, it takes $(22/40) \times 5 = 2.75n \, log_2 \, n$ floating-point instructions to implement, which is quite an improvement.

Can we do better? Increasing the radix to higher powers of two such as radix-8 does require fewer operations that the radix-4 code. However, these higher radices are not as amenable to Goedecker's treatment and it does not improve their performance. There are other techniques [9] that have about $4n \, log_2 \, n$ floating-point operations for power of two FFTs, but they suffer from other inefficiencies such as non-unit data access patterns. The radix-4 algorithm described above is a very efficient solution for high performance FFTs, especially when the data fits in a processor's data cache.

We're always interested in knowing the theoretical minimum number of operations for an algorithm. Comparing the radix-4 and radix-2 algorithms, it becomes apparent that the number of complex additions remains the same, but there are fewer complex multiplications in the radix-4 algorithm. Similarly, a radix-8 algorithm has fewer complex multiplications than a radix-4 algorithm, but they have the same number of complex additions. So, suppose an FFT algorithm was derived that contained no complex multiplications, but the same number of complex additions as the radix-4 algorithm. This algorithm would require $2n \log_2 n$ floating-point operations which would use $2n \log_2 n$ floating-point instructions. Goedecker's algorithm requires $2.75n \log_2 n$ instructions for the radix-4 algorithm, so there are, at most, $0.75n \log_2 n$ instructions to be removed. The idea of eliminating all complex multiplications will be discussed further in Section 12.3.12 on polynomial transforms.

12.3.6 Powers of Three, Five and Composite Number FFTs

FFT algorithms can be derived for any prime number. Powers of three and five are very common and these are nearly as efficient as power of two FFTs. Radix-3 and radix-5 algorithms can also use Goedecker's algorithm to improve performance. Composite numbers that can be represented as $n = 2^k \times 3^l \times 5^m$ can be calculated by performing k radix-2 steps, followed by l radix-3 steps and m radix-5 steps. Table 12-6 shows the theoretical efficiency of these algorithms.

Table 12-6   Floating-Point Operations and Instructions.

	Radix-2		Radix-3		Radix-4		Radix-5	
	Complex	Real	Complex	Real	Complex	Real	Complex	Real
Loads and stores	4	8	6	12	8	16	10	20
Multiplications	1	4	4	12	3	12	12	32
Additions	2	6	6	16	8	22	16	40
F:M operation ratio	1.25		2.33		2.13		3.60	
Flt.-pt. operations	$5.00n \log_2 n$		$9.33n \log_3 n =$ $5.89n \log_2 n$		$4.25n \log_2 n$		$14.40n \log_5 n =$ $6.20n \log_2 n$	
Flt.-pt. instructions using fma, fnma	6		16		22		40	
F:M instruction ratio	0.75		1.33		1.37		2.00	
Flt.-pt. instructions	$3.00n \log_2 n$		$5.33n \log_3 n =$ $3.36n \log_2 n$		$2.75n \log_2 n$		$8.00n \log_5 n =$ $3.44n \log_2 n$	

12.3.7 Optimizations for Real Data

Signal and image data from sensors starts out as real numbers since sensors to collect imaginary numbers haven't been invented yet. FFTs operate on the more general complex data, so it's natural to want to make optimizations for real input. FFTs of real data have very special properties. Using the definition of DFT for a real vector x results in

$$y_k = \sum_{j=0}^{n-1} x_j \left(\cos\left(\frac{2\pi jk}{n}\right) - i\sin\left(\frac{2\pi jk}{n}\right) \right) = \sum_{j=0}^{n-1} x_j \left(\cos\left(\frac{2\pi jk}{n}\right) \right) - i \sum_{j=0}^{n-1} x_j \left(\sin\left(\frac{2\pi jk}{n}\right) \right)$$

$$k = 0, 1, ..., n-1$$

Cosine is called an *even* function because $\cos(\theta) = \cos(-\theta)$ for arbitrary angles θ. So, for example, $\cos(2\pi jk / n) = \cos(-2\pi jk / n)$. The midpoint of the DFT sequence occurs at $k = n/2$. The value at this point is $\cos(2\pi jn / 2n) = -1$ and the values of cosine are also symmetric about this point. What this means is that the values from the cosine component

$$yr_k = \sum_{j=0}^{n-1} x_j \left(\cos\left(\frac{2\pi jk}{n}\right) \right) \quad k = 0, 1, ..., n-1$$

will be symmetric about the midpoint $n/2$. Thus, $yr(n/2 + j) = yr(n/2 - j)$ for any $j < n/2$.

Sine is called an *odd* function because $\sin(\theta) = -\sin(-\theta)$. The values from the sine component on one side of the midpoint $n/2$ are also the negative of the values on the other side. Thus, if

$$yi_k = \sum_{j=0}^{n-1} x_j \left(\sin\left(\frac{2\pi jk}{n}\right) \right) \quad k = 0, 1, ..., n-1$$

$yi(n/2 + j) = -yi(n/2 - j)$. The sine component is also special since the value at $yi(0) = yi(n/2) = 0$. Since the sine component is multiplied by the imaginary number i, the FFT y_k of real data x_j has the following properties:

- y is conjugate symmetric (i.e., the values $y(n/2 + j)$ are the complex conjugate of $y(n/2 - j)$ for $j < n/2$)
- $y(0)$ and $y(n/2)$ are real values.

The first property is especially useful since only the first $n/2 + 1$ points need to be calculated. The remaining points can be obtained by taking the complex conjugate of their corresponding points. Just as the FFT of a real sequence is conjugate symmetric, the FFT of a conjugate symmetric sequence is a real sequence. Since half of the input values are ignored and half of the output samples aren't necessary, this suggests that the FFT of real data may be able to exploit this extra space to reduce the number of operations. In fact, it can.

For the next examples, let x, y and z be complex vectors of length n with real components xr, yr and zr and imaginary components xi, yi and zi. Let $conjg(x)$ indicate the complex conjugate of x.

12.3.7.1   Performing Two Real FFTs with a Complex FFT

What if two real arrays are packed into a complex word (one mapping to the real values and the other to the imaginary values) and a complex FFT is performed? Is there a way to extract the FFTs of each part from the result? Yes, there is!

Let xr_j and yr_j be two real vectors of length n and suppose you want to obtain their DFTs.

- Pack xr_j and yr_j into a complex array z_j by mapping xr_j to the real locations of z_j and yr_j to the imaginary locations of z_j, so $z_j = complex(xr_j, yr_j)$.
- Perform an in-place, length n FFT on z_j.
- Unscramble z_j as follows:
  $x_0 = complex(zr_0, 0.0)$
  $y_0 = complex(zi_0, 0.0)$
  $x_j = (1/2)\ (z_j + conjg(z_{n-j})),\ 1 \leq j \leq n/2$
  $y_j = (-i/2)\ (z_j - conjg(z_{n-j})),\ 1 \leq j \leq n/2$
- Copy to create the conjugate symmetric values:
  $x_j = conjg(x_{n-j}),\ (n/2 + 1) \leq j \leq n-1$
  $y_j = conjg(y_{n-j}),\ (n/2 + 1) \leq j \leq n-1$

This is preferable to performing one FFT at a time. Using a one-dimensional FFT takes $5n\ log_2\ n$ operations. Using the packed form takes $5n\ log_2\ n + 4n$ operations for two FFTs, so there's nearly a factor of two savings in operation count.

12.3.7.2   Performing a Real FFT with a Half-length Complex FFT

What if we wanted to perform only one real FFT and the data is a multiple of two? Can we pack it into a half-length FFT and calculate the full size DFT? Yes again! The previous section showed how to unscramble two separate length n FFTs. Note that a half length FFT has $log_2\ (n/2) = log_2\ n - 1$ steps, so if we pack the data and perform two half length FFTs, we need only one more step to finish the calculations. The following shows all the steps necessary to perform a real FFT using the half-length method:

- Pack the real vector xr_j of length n into a complex array z_j of length $n/2$, with the even values (base zero) mapping to the real locations, zr_j, and the odd values mapping to the imaginary locations, zi_j, so $z_j = complex(xr_{2j}, xr_{2j+1})$.
- Perform a length $n/2$, in-place, complex FFT treating the input as two real sequences as shown above to produce two real vectors zr_j and zi_j.

- Do one more FFT step:

$$x_0 \quad = complex(zr_0 + zi_0, 0.0)$$
$$x_{n/2} = complex(zr_0 - zi_0, 0.0)$$
$$\alpha \quad = -2\pi i / n$$
$$x_j \quad = (zr_j + e^{\alpha j}(zi_j)), \qquad 1 \le j \le n/4$$
$$x_{n/2-j} = conjg(zr_j - e^{\alpha j}(zi_j)), \quad 1 \le j \le n/4$$

- Copy for the conjugate symmetric values:

$$x_j = conjg(x_{n-j}), \ (n/2 + 1) \le j \le n-1$$

The number of operations for this approach is about $(5/2)n \, log_2 \, n + 4n$. So once again, packing the real data reduces the operation count to about one half of the original.

12.3.8 Performance

We have discussed a lot of techniques for one-dimensional FFTs, but how good is the actual performance? The above methods work well on problems that fit in data cache or execute on vector computers. This is because, in both of these cases, there is sufficient bandwidth to support the memory requirements of the algorithms. Figure 12-1 shows the results of a radix-4 FFT on an HP N-Class computer. What happens at 128 K? This is awful! Why does this occur and

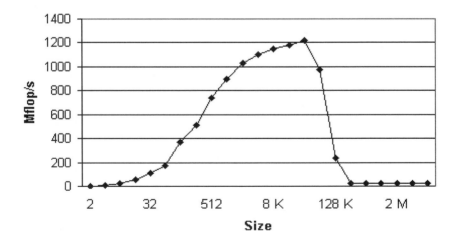

Figure 12-1   One-dimensional FFTs using COMPLEX*8 data on HP N-4000 server.

what can be done to fix it?

At this point we must take a little detour. Techniques to improve the performance of large one-dimensional FFTs rely on having good performance on smaller, simultaneous one-dimensional FFTs.

12.3.9 Simultaneous One-dimensional FFTs

Many applications generate a large number of data sets of the same length, each of which requires a DFT. There are two common cases to consider. Either each data set is stored contiguously (perform the DFT of each column) or the corresponding points of each data set are contiguous (perform the DFT of each row).

12.3.9.1   Each Data Set Is Stored Contiguously (DFT of Each Column)

We've already established techniques for one-dimensional FFTs which can be applied. One good approach is to perform just one FFT at a time (assuming each FFT fits in the data cache). Another technique uses the number of FFTs to perform as the size of the inner loop of the kernel. This keeps the vector length constant and the trig array values have increased data reuse. Using the Stockham radix-2 kernel shown earlier and assuming that there are n FFTs to perform, we create the following code sequence:

```
COMPLEX X(NS,2,LS,N), Y(NS,LS,2,N)
...
DO I = 1,LS
  U = CEXP(CMPLX(0.,((I-1)*ANGLE)))
  DO J = 1,NS
    C = U * X(J,2,I)
    DO K = 1,N
      Y(J,I,1,K) = X(J,1,I,K) + C
      Y(J,I,2,K) = X(J,1,I,K) - C
  ENDDO
ENDDO
```

Thus, if you need to perform 32 FFTs of length 32, the inner loop length can remain 32 throughout the calculations instead of shrinking with each step. This is most attractive when the problem fits into the data cache. Figure 12-2 shows how a grid may be blocked to ensure that the data being processed is less than the cache size.

To help quantify the amount of memory traffic, define *memory_transfer* as in Chapter 5 to be

memory_transfer = $n \times$ (bytes per point) / (cache line size in bytes)

where n is the number of data points.

Using this definition of memory_transfer allows algorithms to be compared independent of the FFT length, data type and the processor cache line size. When n load occurs and the data is not in-cache, the data must be loaded from memory to produce one memory_transfer. When n store occurs and the data is not in-cache, there are two memory_transfers: one to read the data from memory and one to write the new data back to memory.

block

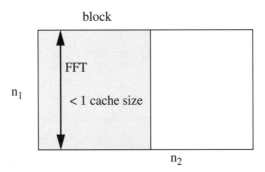

Figure 12-2   Blocking for column simultaneous FFTs.

Blocking is a very good approach since the data may miss cache to begin with, but it remains in-cache until the data is completely processed. The load and store required for the FFT calculations generate only two memory_transfers.

If the size of each FFT is larger than the data cache, then the techniques for large FFTs discussed later should be used.

12.3.9.2   Corresponding Data Points of Successive Data Sets Are Stored Contiguously (DFT of Each Row)

If the data fits in the data cache, using the number of FFTs as the inner loop length is very attractive since data accesses are unit stride. Suppose multiple FFTs can fit in the data cache. An efficient approach is to copy blocks of data into a temporary working area, perform simultaneous FFTs, and copy the data back as shown in Figure 12-3.

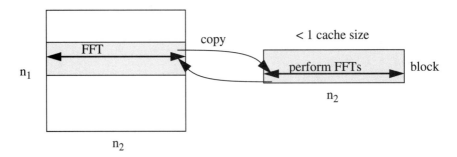

Figure 12-3   Blocking for row simultaneous FFTs.

If multiple points for a single FFT map to the same location in the data cache, a popular approach is to transpose the entire data set, perform one-dimensional FFTs of each column, and transpose the data back. This is shown in Figure 12-4.

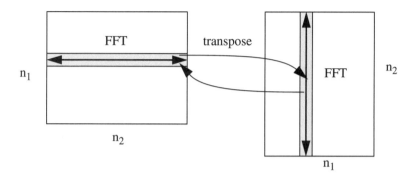

Figure 12-4   Transpose for row simultaneous DFTs.

Having to copy data for row simultaneous FFTs can be expensive. How many data memory_transfers are required? In this approach, the data must be

1. Loaded from the original grid and stored to the working area
2. Loaded and stored (the FFT performed)
3. Loaded from the working area and stored to the original grid

If the data is not in-cache to begin with, step one generates three memory_transfers (one for the load and two for the store). Step two generates two memory_transfers to support the FFT calculations. Step three generates three memory_transfers as in step one. Thus, eight memory_transfers are generated, as opposed to the corresponding column approach which generates only two memory_transfers.

One way to improve this is to choose a temporary working area that is substantially smaller than the cache size. Then there is the increased probability that some of the data will be retained in-cache between steps. For example, if the part of the original grid and the total working area don't map to the same location in the cache, then, when the FFT is performed, the data does not miss cache, which removes the two memory_transfers in step two. Likewise, the store in step one and the load in step can be eliminated, so the total number of memory_transfers may be as low as two. Due to differences in cache architectures, some experimentation may be necessary to choose the optimal blocking factor.

All of this effort to block for cache isn't necessary on vector computers. Since row simultaneous FFTs can use the number of FFTs as the inner loop length and vector computers have robust memory systems that can support the high memory bandwidth required, these FFT algorithms run well on vector computers.

12.3.10 Large One-dimensional FFTs

Look back at Figure 12-1. How can we improve the performance of large one-dimensional FFTs? Large FFTs exceed the size of the data cache. Recall that each radix-4 step accesses all of the data, thus ensuring that data points in a cache line get used at most once before the line is replaced. This is in contrast to problems that fit in data cache where cache lines never have to be reloaded after their initial load from memory. It can get even worse, though.

Most data caches have sizes that are a power of two. Since most FFTs are also a power of two, pathologically bad cache conflicts can occur. Let the size of the FFT be 2^n and suppose COMPLEX*8 data is used. This causes the input array to use $8 \times 2^n = 2^{(n+3)}$ bytes. Suppose a direct mapped cache is used and has size $2^{(n+1)}$ bytes. Using a radix-4 Stockham autosort algorithm causes the four vectors that are loaded in the first step to map to the same location in the cache for each iteration of the inner loop. A four-way or higher associative cache would help this case, but performance will still be poor since each data point is used, at most, once before its cache line is replaced.

It's now time to investigate algorithms that reuse the data points in a cache line many times before the cache line gets replaced. The most common way to reduce the number of cache misses is to treat the input vector as a matrix and operate on its individual rows and columns. To accomplish this also requires matrix transpose operations (discussed in Chapter 10) and a *twiddle multiplication*, which is just a multiplication of each point by a power of ω_n. In general, a one-dimensional DFT of a vector X of size $n = m \times k$ may be performed by

- m one-dimensional DFTs of length k (the DFT of each row)
- multiplication of every point of $X(j,h) \times \omega_n^{jh}$ (twiddle multiplication)
- k one-dimensional DFTs of length m (the DFT of each column)
- transpose $X(k,m)$ to $X(m,k)$

This is sometimes called the *twiddle factor* method or a *row/column four-step* approach. There are two other ways to interpret the above four components. If a computer is more efficient at performing DFTs of rows than columns, the *row-oriented four-step* approach may be used.

- m one-dimensional DFTs of length k (the DFT of each row)
- multiplication of every point of $X(j,h) \times \omega_n^{jh}$ (twiddle multiplication)
- transpose $X(k,m)$ to $X(m,k)$
- k one-dimensional DFTs of length m (the DFT of each row)

This approach is often used on vector processors since, as discussed earlier, they can perform row simultaneous FFTs very efficiently.

If a computer is much more efficient at performing DFTs on columns of data, the *six-step* algorithm below may be a good solution.

- transpose $X(k,m)$ to $X(m,k)$
- m one-dimensional DFTs of length k (the DFT of each column)
- transpose $X(m,k)$ to $X(k,m)$
- multiplication of every point of $X(j,h) \times \omega_n^{jh}$ (twiddle multiplication)
- k one-dimensional DFTs of length m (the DFT of each column)
- transpose $X(k,m)$ to $X(m,k)$

The six-step approach has all the FFTs operating on columns of data at the added expense of two more transpose steps than the twiddle-factor approach. Computers that depend on caches are great at operating on columns of data since an individual column usually fits in-cache. However, rows of data are more likely to exceed the cache size due to the large strides between individual points of the FFT and may have poor performance due to cache thrashing.

When n is square, a square decomposition requires only the square root of n data points for each individual FFT. For example, a size 4 M point FFT that uses eight-byte data for each point requires 32 MB of data, which is larger than most data caches. Treating this as a square of size 2 K $\times$ 2 K means each small FFT requires only 32 KB of data, which easily fits into data cache on most computers. If the problem size is so large that the small FFTs still don't fit in-cache, the four- or six-step algorithms can be applied recursively until the individual FFTs can fit in-cache. Therefore, the number of cache misses is greatly reduced.

The six-step approach is also well-suited to parallelism. The most complicated part is the parallelism of the transposes which was discussed in Chapter 10. The individual FFTs can be performed in parallel, as can each column of the twiddle multiplication.

Figure 12-5 compares the twiddle, six-step, and a soon-to-be-discussed seven-step method. All of the small simultaneous FFTs in these approaches use the Stockham autosort algorithm. A blocked transpose is used for the transpose steps.

The twiddle approach is clearly better than the six-step approach. As usual, the goal for large problems is to minimize the number of cache misses. How many memory_transfers are generated and what can be done to improve them?

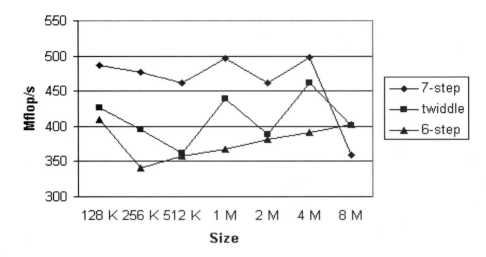

Figure 12-5 Large one-dimensional FFTs using
`COMPLEX*8` data on HP N-4000 server.

12.3.10.1   Number of Memory_transfers Using the Six-Step and Twiddle Approaches

The six-step approach takes an input array X of size $n = k \times m$, a work array Y of size n, and an array of roots of unity (twiddle factors) U of size n and performs:

1. Transpose $X(k, m)$ to $Y(m, k)$
2. k simultaneous FFTs of length m using Y
3. Transpose $Y(m, k)$ to $X(k, m)$
4. Twiddle factor multiplication $U(k, m) \times X(k, m) = Y(k, m)$
5. m simultaneous FFTs of length k using Y
6. Transpose $Y(k, m)$ to $X(m, k)$

Although the individual FFTs may fit in-cache, many cache misses may occur in the other steps. The six-step approach may be modified to a seven-step approach which has better cache characteristics and requires less memory [11].

Let X be the input array of length $n = k \times m$, and let Y be a work array of size n. Let U be an array of size n that contains the twiddle factors. Using the earlier definition of memory_transfer, a transpose or copy of X to Y causes three memory_transfers: one for the load of X and two for the store of Y. This definition implies that the entire six-step approach causes 17 memory_transfers.

The twiddle method has fewer memory_transfers than the four-step method. Steps four through six of the six-step method are the same as steps two through four of the twiddle method. It's hard to analyze step one of the twiddle method. For large powers of two, we're guaranteed that multiple points in the DFT map to the same cache line; therefore, the data for an FFT should be copied to a contiguous work array, the FFT performed and the data copied back as shown in Figure 12-3. This may take as many as eight memory_transfers (identical to the six-step approach). If the work space can be chosen to be small enough, then all memory_transfers except those associated with the work space may vanish. This leaves only the three memory_transfers associated with X. Therefore, the twiddle approach takes somewhere between 12 and 17 memory_transfers.

Back to the six-step approach. If the work space is ignored, the total number of memory_transfers for the row FFTs is three since it's guaranteed that the load of X will have been knocked out-of-cache before the FFT of X can be stored. Thus, the twiddle method might generate only 12 memory_transfers.

The goal is to decrease the number of memory_transfers. If the transpose can be done in-place, the Y array is eliminated, and the number of memory_transfers decreases. If $n = k^2$, then this is feasible. Table 12-7 shows the number of memory_transfers for both approaches.

Table 12-7   Six-step Approaches.

Step	With workspace		Without workspace	
	Data movement	Memory_transfers	Data movement	Memory_transfers
1. Transpose	$X_{i,j} \rightarrow Y_{j,i}$	3	$X_{i,j} \rightarrow X_{j,i}$	2
2. m FFTs of length k	$Y_{j,i} \rightarrow Y_{j,i}$	2	$X_{j,i} \rightarrow X_{j,i}$	2
3. Transpose	$Y_{j,i} \rightarrow X_{i,j}$	3	$X_{j,i} \rightarrow X_{i,j}$	2
4. Twiddle Multiplication	$U_{i,j} \times X_{i,j} \rightarrow Y_{i,j}$	4	$U_{i,j} \times X_{i,j} \rightarrow X_{i,j}$	3
5. k FFTs of length m	$Y_{i,j} \rightarrow Y_{i,j}$	2	$X_{i,j} \rightarrow X_{i,j}$	2
6. Transpose	$Y_{i,j} \rightarrow X_{j,i}$	3	$X_{i,j} \rightarrow X_{j,i}$	2
Total		17		13

This is substantially better than the first approach since it generates 13 memory_transfers instead of 17. It also reduces the memory space requirements by a third. The general case of the product of powers of two, three and five is explored by Wadleigh [11], but we'll just analyze powers of two. Note that $n = 2^{2k+p}$ where p is zero or one and k is an integer.

Case 1, $p = 0$ ($n = 2^{2k}$)   Treat the data as a square array of size $s \times s$ where $s = 2^k$. To transpose the array X requires only swapping diagonals across the main diagonal, as in shown in Chapter 10.

This transpose may be blocked for good cache line reuse and does not require a work array. The six-step approach can be performed as shown in Table 12-7 with $X_{i,j}$ being overwritten in each step.

Case 2, $p = 1$ ($n = 2 \times 2^{2k}$)   The data may be decomposed as $n = s \times t \times t$ where $s = 2$ and $t = 2^k$. Thus, the problem is composed of two squares of size $t \times t$. In the previous section, we were able to transpose the data in-place by exchanging a diagonal below the main diagonal with its corresponding diagonal above the main diagonal. For non-square matrices, there is no main diagonal and this approach is not possible. For example, if the matrix is of size $2t \times t$, it's not clear which element $(t+2, 1)$ should be swapped. It certainly isn't element $(1, t+2)$ since this location isn't even defined. Note that the first and third steps don't need to be complete transposes, though. In the first step, treat each of the squares separately and swap points across their main diagonals. Perform the second step simultaneous FFTs on this array. For the third step, repeat the swapping operations of the first step. At the conclusion of the third step, the data is back in proper order for the remaining steps. The fourth and fifth steps may proceed as before. The sixth step is a problem since it must be a complete transpose. To accomplish this, break the transform into two parts. Let $r_1 = t$, and $r_2 = t$. The goal is to transpose $X(s \times r_1 , r_2)$ to $X(r_2 , s \times r_1)$. Treat the data as three-dimensional arrays. The data $X(s \times r_1 , r_2) = X(r_1 , s , r_2)$ must be transposed to $X(r_2 , s, r_1) = X(r_2 , s \times r_1)$. The transpose may be achieved by:

transpose $X((r_1 , s), r_2)$ to $X((s , r_1), r_2)$
transpose $X((s , r_1), r_2)$ to $X(r_2, (s , r_1))$

The first transpose operates on a column of data at a time and the second transpose is the same operation as the partial transposes of steps one and three. The first transpose is problematic since it is difficult to perform in-place. However, using a work array Y of size $s \times r_1$ allows this transpose to be implemented by

transpose $X((r_1 , s), r_2)$ to $Y(s, r_1)$
copy $Y(s, r_1)$ to $X((s , r_1), r_2)$

This work area is small and fits into the cache. Since it will stay in the cache for each column of X, the work array Y can be ignored in terms of cache memory_transfers. The two transposes above completes the transform. The number of steps has increased from six to seven, but the number of memory_transfers is the same in the square six-step approach and the seven-step approach.

Refinements   The fourth through sixth steps should be considered together. Since a work array Y of size $s \times t$ is used in step six, these steps can be simplified by operating on a column of data at a time. The output from the twiddle multiplication is stored to the work area of size $s \times t$. The FFT of size $s \times t$ is performed on this data. The first part of the complete transpose is performed and the result is stored in X. In step four, a column of the arrays U and X is loaded and the results are stored to the small column array Y. This results in two memory_transfers: one for X and one for U. Since Y remains in-cache as the columns are processed from X and U, it does not contribute any additional memory_transfers. Step five does not introduce any memory_transfers since Y is in-cache. Step six assumes that Y is in-cache and the column of X being processed is still in-cache from step four. Therefore, the one memory_transfers in step six is caused by storing X to memory. Thus, an FFT of length n can be performed with only 11 memory_transfers, as shown in Table 12-8.

Table 12-8   Seven-step Approach.

Step	Data movement	Memory_ transfers
1. Transpose within squares	$X_{i,j} \rightarrow X_{j',i'}$	2
2. $s \times t$ FFTs of length t	$X_{j',i'} \rightarrow X_{j',i'}$	2
3. Transpose within squares	$X_{j',i'} \rightarrow X_{i,j}$	2
4. Twiddle multiplication	$U_{i,j} \times X_{i,j} \rightarrow Y_i$	2
5. t FFTs of length $s \times t$	$Y_i \rightarrow Y_i$	0
6. Transpose within columns	$Y_i \rightarrow X_{j',i'}$	1
7. Transpose within squares	$X_{j',i'} \rightarrow X_{i,j}$	2
Total		11

The advantage of the seven-step approach is shown in Figure 12-5. Note that once the problem size reaches 8 M points, more cache misses start occurring. A larger data cache would move this degradation so that it occurs at a larger point. All of the approaches will have a similar degradation in performance at some point. These techniques can be applied recursively to minimize this.

12.3.11 Two-dimensional FFTs

Let x be a two-dimensional array of size (n_1, n_2). The forward two-dimensional DFT of x is defined as

$$y_{k_1, k_2} = \sum_{j_1 = 0}^{n_1 - 1} \sum_{j_2 = 0}^{n_2 - 1} x_{j_1, j_2} \omega_{n_1}^{j_1 k_1} \omega_{n_2}^{j_2 k_2}$$

$$k_1 = 0, 1, ..., n_1 - 1, \quad k_2 = 0, 1, ..., n_2 - 1$$

This is just a one-dimensional DFT of each column followed by a one-dimensional DFT of each row, that is, n_2 simultaneous one-dimensional DFTs of length n_1, followed by n_1 simultaneous DFTs of length n_2. The inverse two-dimensional DFT is defined by negating the sign on the exponents and scaling appropriately. The techniques to use for simultaneous one-dimensional FFTs have already been discussed. Let $ops1d(n)$ be the number of operations for a one-dimensional FFT. The number of operations for a two-dimensional FFT on a rectangle of size $n_1 \times n_2$ is then

$$n_1 \times ops1d(n_2) + n_2 \times ops1d(n_1)$$

Thus, when n_1 and n_2 are powers of two and both equal to n, there are $10n^2 \, log_2 \, n$ operations.

12.3.12 Why Polynomial Transforms Don't Work Well

It's logical to wonder if two-dimensional FFTs allow a reduction in operations beyond that achieved by mapping to one-dimensional FFTs. Nussbaumer [8] showed how the rows of the two-dimensional input matrix can be modified so they can be treated as polynomials. He defined a polynomial transform operating on these rows which is basically a DFT with all nontrivial complex multiplications removed. These can be defined for arbitrary powers of two, but for simplicity we'll analyze the case for square matrices. Calculating a two-dimensional FFT of size $n \times n$ where n is a power of two requires

- multiplication of every point of $X(j,k)$ by ω_n^{-k}
- polynomial transform
- n one-dimensional DFTs of length n (the DFT of each row)
- multiplication of every point of $X(j,k)$ by ω_n^{k}
- permutation of the output from $X(j(2k+1),k)$ to $X(j,k)$

The polynomial transform requires a complex addition and subtraction for each point, but no multiplication. It produces $2n^2 \, log_2 \, n$ floating-point operations. The two complex multiplications produce $2 \times 6n^2$ real operations and the FFTs require $5n^2 \, log_2 \, n$ floating-point operations. Therefore, the number of operations is $7n^2 \, log_2 \, n + 12n^2$ floating-point operations. At what point is it advantageous to use this approach? Mapping to one-dimensional FFTs takes $10n^2 \, log_2$ n operations, so for problems where $n > 16$, the polynomial approach should require fewer floating-point operations and hence perform better. Or should it?

We've gone to great pains to optimize one-dimensional FFTs. What happens if we look at the number of instructions required instead of the number of floating-point operations? Using fma instructions in the complex multiplications generates $2 \times 4n^2$ instructions. The one-dimensional FFTs generate $2.75n^2 \, log_2 \, n$ instructions using a radix-4 kernel with Goedecker's optimization, while the polynomial transform generates $2n^2 \, log_2 \, n$ instructions. Now we must check when the polynomial transform approach has the same number of instructions as the one-dimensional DFT approach, i.e., when

$$4.75n^2 \, log_2 \, n + 8n^2 = 5.5n^2 \, log_2 \, n$$

The break-even point now occurs when $n = 1625$. This requires over 21 MB using eight-byte data and will exceed the size of most data caches. Also, the permutation required in the last step wreaks havoc with good cache management schemes, so this approach is not a good one for cache based computers.

12.3.13 Three-dimensional FFTs

Let x be a three-dimensional array of size (n_1, n_2, n_3). The forward three-dimensional DFT of x is defined as

$$y_{k_1, k_2, k_3} = \sum_{j_1 = 0}^{n_1 - 1} \sum_{j_2 = 0}^{n_2 - 1} \sum_{j_3 = 0}^{n_3 - 1} x_{j_1, j_2, j_3} \omega_{n_1}^{j_1 k_1} \omega_{n_2}^{j_2 k_2} \omega_{n_3}^{j_3 k_3}$$

$$k_1 = 0, 1, ..., n_1 - 1, \quad k_2 = 0, 1, ..., n_2 - 1, \quad k_3 = 0, 1, ..., n_3 - 1$$

This is just one-dimensional DFTs of each column followed by one-dimensional DFTs of each row, followed by one-dimensional DFTs of each row going back into the plane. The inverse three-dimensional DFT is defined by negating the sign on the exponents and scaling appropriately. For a box of size $n_1 \times n_2 \times n_3$, the number of operations for a three-dimensional FFT is

$$n_1 \, n_2 \times ops1d(n_3) + n_1 \, n_3 \times ops1d(n_2) + n_2 \, n_3 \times ops1d(n_3)$$

Thus, when n_1, n_2, n_3 are powers of two and all equal to n, there are $15n^3 \, log_2 \, n$ operations.

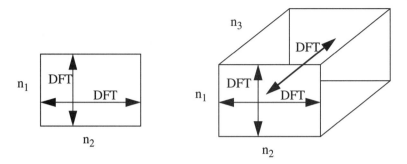

Figure 12-6   Two-dimensional and three-dimensional structures for DFTs.

The previously defined techniques for simultaneous FFTs can be applied. The real question is when to copy data to a work array whose size is smaller than cache. Cases to consider include:

- In-cache. Everything works great. There's no need to copy anything anywhere.
- Two-dimensional planes fit in-cache, but the total problem exceeds cache. This is quite common in practice. The problem can be viewed as n_3 two-dimensional FFTs of size $n_1 \times n_2$ followed by $n_1 n_2$ simultaneous FFTs of size n_3. Use the previous techniques to perform the component FFTs.
- All one-dimensional FFTs out-of-cache. What does this mean? On a computer with a 1 MB cache, this requires a problem of size 1 MB × 1 MB × 1 MB or one GB problem. This is big! You won't encounter problems of this size often. However, back when data caches were very small, some applications used the following approach:

1. $n_2 n_3$ FFTs of size n_1
2. transpose $n_1 \times n_2 \times n_3$ to $n_2 \times n_3 \times n_1$
3. $n_1 n_3$ FFTs of size n_2
4. transpose $n_2 \times n_3 \times n_1$ to $n_3 \times n_1 \times n_2$
5. $n_1 n_2$ FFTs of size n_3
6. transpose $n_3 \times n_1 \times n_2$ to $n_1 \times n_2 \times n_3$

12.4 The Relationship Between Convolutions and FFTs

Convolutions and correlations are intimately connected with DFTs. Convolutions can be used to calculate DFTs and DFTs can be used to calculate convolutions.

12.4.1 Using DFTs to Calculate Convolutions

If a convolution is small, then the techniques shown in Section 12.2 are adequate. However, what if the length of the data is many million of points? Performing a convolution is a $O(n^2)$ operation, so it can be quite time-consuming. FFTs can reduce this to an $O(n \log n)$ algorithm, though! Convolutions can be defined by DFTs as follows. Let $\{x_0,...x_{m+n-1}\}$, $\{w_0,...w_{n-1}\}$, $\{y_0,....,y_{m-1}\}$ be vectors. Extend w to have length $m+n-1$ by padding with zeros. The convolution, y, of x and w is

$$y = \text{last } m \text{ elements of (inverse DFT \{ forward DFT } (x) \times \text{ forward DFT } (w) \text{ \})}$$

where the DFTs are of length $m+n-1$ and only the first m elements of the inverse DFT are retained for y.

Thus, three DFTs and a pointwise multiplication perform the convolution. Similarly, the correlation of x and w can be calculated by accessing the w array backwards as follows:

$$y = \text{last } m \text{ elements of (inverse DFT}$$
$$\text{\{ forward DFT } (x) \times \text{ forward DFT } (\{w_{n-1}, w_{n-2},...,w_0\}) \text{ \})}$$

Due to this relationship, large convolutions and correlations are frequently performed using Fourier transforms. However, this technique is not without cost.

12.4.1.1 When Is It Better to Use DFTs?

The DFTs used in the above formula have length $m+n-1$. In practice, the length of weight vector, w, is usually much shorter than the length of x, so w must be extended with many zeros to make it the same length as x. Likewise, the inverse DFT calculates many more elements than are necessary and all but m results are discarded.

It is easier to calculate some DFT lengths (notably ones that are a power of two) than others. This means that all the arrays will probably need to be padded to the next greater power of two before the DFT is calculated.

So when is it advisable to use FFTs to evaluate convolutions? Suppose x has length $m+n-1$, w has length n, and y has length m. To calculate the convolutions using a direct approach takes $2mn$ floating-point operations. Suppose the size of x is just one element past a power of two, so all the vectors must be extended with zeros to have $2m+2n-3$ elements. The FFT approach requires three FFTs and a complex vector-vector multiplication for a total of $15 (2m+2n-3) \log_2 (2m+2n-3) + 8 (2m+2n-3)$ floating-point operations. (We're being pretty simplistic here; for example, we can reduce the number of operations by using real-to-complex FFTs. However, convolutions run closer to peak than FFTs, so we'll ignore both for now.) A common size for m is 1024. The break-even point where it is advantageous to use the FFT approach for this size problem is $n = 214$. This is larger than the weight vector used in most applications. However, if the size of the weight is large, say, $m = 500$, the direct approach takes

1,024,000 floating-point operations while the FFT approach takes only 552,921 floating-point operations, so the FFT approach looks very attractive.

Convolutions are also used to filter two-dimensional objects such as images. Assume the weight array, w, is an $m \times m$ grid and the input array is of size $n \times n$. The direct approach takes $2m^2n^2$ operations. If m is a power of two plus one, the worst case padding for the FFT approach takes $3 \times 10 \, (2m+2n-3)^2 \, log_2 \, (2m+2n-3) + 8 \, (2m+2n-3)^2$ operations. A common size for n is 1024. When $m < 27$, the direct approach is probably faster for this problem size, but larger values of m may benefit by using the DFT approach.

12.4.1.2   New FFT Possibilities

A neat thing about the above relationship is that the forward and inverse FFT algorithms can be chosen such that the permutations which occur in some FFT algorithms don't have to be performed. This is one time that the Stockham transforms may not be the best choice to evaluate the DFT. Recall that decimation-in-frequency (DIF) transforms such as Gentleman-Sande perform the permutation at the conclusion of the calculations, while decimation-in-time (DIT) transforms such as Cooley-Tukey perform the permutations at the beginning (see Table 12-3). The pointwise multiplication that occurs between the forward and inverse FFTs doesn't care if the data is permuted or not. The convolution may be obtained by performing a DIF forward FFT omitting the permutation on x and w, doing a vector multiplication and then the dual DIT inverse FFT on the product, but not performing its permutation. If work space is at a premium, convolutions can be performed using a Gentleman-Sande FFT for the first two DFTs and a Cooley-Tukey FFT for the last DFT with all FFTs omitting the permutation step. Similarly, if it is more important to have a constant inner loop length, the DIF-Pease and Pease transforms can be used without their permutation steps.

12.4.2 Using Convolutions to Calculate DFTs

One of the problems of FFTs is that they are usually defined only for sizes that are small primes and their products. What if you want to take the DFT of a vector of length 509? This is a prime number, but you probably don't want to derive an FFT for this special case (at least we don't want to). You could pad the length of the data with three zeros and do a length 512 FFT. In fact, this technique is often used, and it does get close to the right answer, but it doesn't really give you the result of performing a length 509 DFT.

FFTs can be defined in terms of convolutions though. The best known way is by using Bluestein's chirp z-transform [3]. A DFT may be calculated as follows. Let x be the input vector and have size n.

- Perform a vector multiplication $y(j) = x(j) \, \omega_n^{(j*j)/2}$
- Append n zeros to y so that it has $2n$ elements
- Perform a convolution of $y(j)$ and $\omega_n^{-(j*j)/2}$ to create a vector $z(k)$ of length n
- Perform a vector multiplication $w(k) = z(k) \, \omega_n^{(k*k)/2}$

Thus, the DFT is defined in terms of a complex convolution and two complex vector multiplications. Performing the convolution and three vector multiplications directly would take $(8)(2n)(n) + (3)(8n) = 16n^2 + 24n$ floating-point operations. However, we know we can use FFTs to calculate the convolution by bumping the problem size up to the next power of two and performing radix-2 FFTs. So we can calculate an arbitrary length FFT by mapping it to a convolution, which is, in turn, mapped to three FFTs. The worst case for the FFTs occurs when the length $2n$ convolution is two more than power of two. This takes $(3)(5)(4n-4) \times log_2(4n-4) + 8(2n+4n-4)$ floating-point operations. However, the break-even point for this case is only 26, so using three FFTs is the best approach for even fairly small problems.

12.5 Summary

FFTs and convolutions give rise to fascinating algorithms which are interconnected at a deep mathematical level. Using the techniques developed in previous chapters allowed us to optimize some of these algorithms until they execute close to the peak processor performance. We also explored algorithmic optimizations that reduce the order of the calculations so the run time required is a tiny fraction of the original time.

References:

1. Bailey, D. H. *A High-Performance Fast Fourier Algorithm for the Cray-2*. J. Supercomputing, Vol. 1, 43-60, 1987.

2. Bailey, D. H. *A High-Performance FFT Algorithm for Vector Supercomputers*. International. J. of Supercomputing Applications, Vol. 2, 82-87, 1988.

3. Bluestein, L.I. *A Linear Filtering Approach to the Computation of the Discrete Fourier Transform*. IEEE Trans. Audio and Electroacoustics AU-18, 451-455, 1970.

4. Brigham, E. O. *The Fast Fourier Transform*. Englewood Cliffs, N.J.: Prentice-Hall, 1973, ISBN 0-13-307496-X.

5. Cochrane, W. R.; Cooley, J. W.; Favin, J. W.; Helms, D. L.; Kaenel, R.A.; Lang, W.W.; Maling, G.C. ; Nelson, D.E.; Rader, C.M. ; Welch, P.D. *What Is the Fast Fourier Transform?*. IEEE Trans. Audio and Electoacoustics, AU-15, 45-55, 1967.

6. Cooley, J. W.; Tukey, J. W. *An Algorithm for the Machine Calculation of Complex Fourier Series*. Math. Comp., Vol. 19, 297-301, 1965.

7. Goedecker, S. *Fast Radix 2, 3, 4, and 5 Kernels for Fast Fourier Transformations on Computers with Overlapping Multiply-add Instructions*. SIAM J. Sci. Comput., Vol. 18, 1605-1611, 1997.

8. Nussbaumer, H.J. *Fast Fourier Transform and Convolution Algorithms*. New York: Springer-Verlag, 1982, ISBN 0-387-10159-4.

9. Van Loan, C. *Computational Frameworks for the Fast Fourier Transform*. Philadelphia: SIAM, 1992, ISBN 0-89871-285-8.

10. Wadleigh, K. R.; Gostin, G.B.; Liu, J. *High-Performance FFT Algorithms for the Convex C4/XA Supercomputer*. J. Supercomputing, Vol. 9, 163-178, 1995.

11. Wadleigh, K. R. *High Performance FFT Algorithms for Cache-Coherent Multiprocessors*. Int. J. of High Performance Computing Applications, Vol. 2, 163-171, 1999.

Index

DATE DE RETOUR - Brault

0 9 AOUT 2001

Bibliofiche 297B